Praise for *Outrages*

"A heartbreaking, eye-opening book . . . *Outrages* is revelatory in the way it brings together sometimes unbearably painful personal narratives with political and literary history . . . [a] remarkable book."

— *HARPER'S BAZAAR*

"A remarkable and moving work."

— LARRY KRAMER, author of
Faggots and *The Normal Heart*

"With precision and sensitivity, Naomi Wolf traces how the state came to police the private sphere; she brings into the light the lives of those whose resistance to this brutality was a beacon for the future. *Outrages* is a remarkable, revelatory book."

— ERICA WAGNER, author of
Chief Engineer: The Man Who Built the Brooklyn Bridge

"*Outrages* is a fascinating history book with a cast of characters and an epic sweep that make it read like a novel Charles Dickens could have written, if he had ever written one about queers."

— *NEW YORK JOURNAL OF BOOKS*

"In *Outrages*, Naomi Wolf reveals a largely forgotten history of how science, law, and culture have intersected to suppress and silence sexual expression. As expanding acceptance threatens to erase a history of LGBTQ marginalization and struggle—and as we descend into authoritarian rule across so many countries—this is an important, powerful tale."

— SHAHID BUTTAR,
marriage equality activist and attorney

"[A] long-overdue literary investigation into censorship and the life of a tormented trailblazer, a prescient father of the modern gay rights movement."

— *OPRAH MAGAZINE*

"[This] remarkable book is a tour de force of research and insight into Symonds' life and work and the related evolution of public and state attitudes toward homosexuality. [Wolf's] is an essential contribution not only to queer history but also to studies of nineteenth-century culture. It is not to be missed."

— *BOOKLIST*, starred review

"Wolf provides engrossing accounts of Whitman and Symonds, yet her story is even more compelling in its wider portrait of the societies and institutions in America as well as England that served to shape the fears and prejudices that have lingered into our modern age. An absorbing and thoughtfully researched must-read for anyone interested in the history of censorship and issues relating to gay male sexuality."

— *KIRKUS REVIEWS*

"This ambitious literary, biographical, and historical treatise from Wolf (*The Beauty Myth*) examines both 19th-century Britain's persecution of gay men and the work and life of the relatively obscure gay writer John Addington Symonds (1840–1893) . . . a fascinating look at this period and these writers."

— *PUBLISHERS WEEKLY*

OUTRAGES

ALSO BY NAOMI WOLF

The Beauty Myth:
How Images of Beauty Are Used against Women

Fire with Fire:
The New Female Power and
How It Will Change the Twenty-First Century

Promiscuities:
The Secret Struggle for Womanhood

Misconceptions:
Truth, Lies and the Unexpected on
the Journey to Motherhood

The Treehouse:
Eccentric Wisdom from My Father on
How to Live, Love and See

The End of America:
Letter of Warning to a Young Patriot

Give Me Liberty:
A Handbook for American Revolutionaries

Vagina:
A New Biography

OUTRAGES

Sex, Censorship, and the Criminalization of Love

Naomi Wolf

Chelsea Green Publishing
White River Junction, Vermont
London, UK

Front cover image from akg-images of *The Sleepers and the One who Watcheth*
by Simeon Solomon (watercolor, Leamington Spa Art Gallery and Museum).

Copy Editor: Zoe Gullen
Proofreader: Nancy Ringer
Indexer: Shana Milkie
Designer: Melissa Jacobson

Printed in Canada.
First printing September 2020.
10 9 8 7 6 5 4 3 2 1   20 21 22 23 24

Our Commitment to Green Publishing
Chelsea Green sees publishing as a tool for cultural change and ecological stewardship. We
strive to align our book manufacturing practices with our editorial mission and to reduce the
impact of our business enterprise in the environment. We print our books and catalogs on
chlorine-free recycled paper, using vegetable-based inks whenever possible. This book may
cost slightly more because it was printed on paper that contains recycled fiber, and we hope
you'll agree that it's worth it. *Outrages* was printed on paper supplied by Marquis that is made
of recycled materials and other controlled sources.

ISBN 978-1-64502-016-5 (paperback) | ISBN 978-1-64502-017-2 (ebook)

Library of Congress Cataloging-in-Publication Data is available upon request.
Library of Congress Control Number: 2020944487

Chelsea Green Publishing
85 North Main Street, Suite 120
White River Junction, Vermont USA

Somerset House
London, UK

www.chelseagreen.com

MIX
Paper from
responsible sources
FSC® C103567

For Dr. Stefano-Maria Evangelista
αγαπητό δάσκαλο μου
My esteemed teacher

"Come, I am determined to unbare this broad breast of mine—I have long enough stifled and choked; [. . .] I will raise, with it, immortal reverberations . . . I will give an example to lovers . . ."

—WALT WHITMAN, "Calamus,"
Leaves of Grass, 1860

"N'importe [no matter]. I will go on writing, because I am sure that I love, in my way, and love finds a voice of some sort."

—JOHN ADDINGTON SYMONDS, 1892

Contents

Introduction

You must apply for a reader's card to gain access to the rare manuscripts section of the Morgan Library and Museum in Manhattan, which is called the Sherman Fairchild Reading Room. At the top level of the imposing stone Beaux Arts building on Madison Avenue, the former private home of banker J. Pierpont Morgan, the rare books reading room is hushed.

You place your possessions in a wood-paneled locker and lock it. You make sure you have secured in the locker any object that might possibly create a mark. You wash your hands at a little sink with a steel basin, so you don't inadvertently smear the grime of modern Manhattan onto the precious, perhaps ancient, pages you will soon touch.

The rare manuscripts room has diffuse lamps, and opaque skylights overhead. Its lighting is indirect so that manuscripts will not fade. The dim lighting and the extreme care that the librarians take with every page laid in front of readers create an atmosphere of secular sanctity. That mood is intensified by the fact that readers around you are seated in front of wooden pedestals, which support open books and manuscripts; the deep indentation at the center of each pedestal, in which books are nestled and opened, protects the spines from cracking.

When the librarian brings you a book or manuscript that you have requested, she opens it carefully. She teaches you to lay across the pages a chain of heavy beads, like a necklace, encased in an ivory or a deep red fabric sleeve. This chain keeps the book partly open, while still protecting pages from creasing.

Ms. Maria Molestina, one of the librarians at the Reading Room, and her colleagues are all highly trained in "codicology," the study and care of books as physical objects. For books that are too fragile to turn by hand, Ms. Molestina or another librarian will bring you a slip of heavy paper with a sharply angled edge, which you may slide between brittle pages to open them with surgical precision.

I was at the Morgan Library and Museum looking for a young man, now long dead—a nineteen-year-old student at Balliol College, Oxford. In 1859, John Addington Symonds was deeply in love with a fellow adolescent whom, I knew, he had identified carefully only as "W." I was looking for the only handwritten manuscript of the unpublished love letter Symonds had written, which at once celebrated this teenage love and mourned its apparent renunciation.

The love letter took the form of a long poetic manuscript, written entirely in quatrains. Phyllis Grosskurth, who in 1964 had written a biography of Symonds titled *The Woeful Victorian*, had in passing described this love poem, as had others who knew about Symonds's now largely forgotten work. The poem's name is "In Memoriam Arcadie."

What had young Symonds meant by the title? In Greek mythology, "Arkady" is the rugged mountainous home of the god Pan, where human beings lived in harmony with the natural order. Pan was also the deity of unbridled sexual impulse, a mischief-maker, and a musician.

"In Memoriam" is Latin for "in the memory of," a phrase used in elegies—that is, in verses written to say goodbye forever to lost loved ones. This nineteen-year-old, in other words, was signaling in his title that he was writing an elegy for a lost love, and a lost paradise.

But like much of Symonds's most important writing, the love letter/poem had not been formally published during his lifetime. In fact, this work had never been published at all. And Symonds had made as sure as he could that a researcher would have to track this manuscript down in person and then supplicate a trusted custodian of the text in order to have a look at it. He had continually buried his true meanings, even while leaving clues for their discovery.

Symonds's undergraduate college was Balliol College, at the University of Oxford; his graduate college, at the same university, Magdalen. A hundred and fifty-five years later, I was a graduate student too, at New College, just a few streets away from both. My thesis adviser was Dr. Stefano-Maria Evangelista, who had written an influential book about Victorian homosexuality and the idea of the Greeks, called *British Aestheticism and Ancient Greece: Hellenism, Reception, Gods in Exile.*

One day, in the comfortable top-floor study at Trinity College where we met weekly so he could review my work, Dr. Evangelista handed me two immense volumes bound in a deep-olive-green fabric. There was a third volume waiting on his bookshelf, to be taken up when I was finished with the first two. The books contained the letters of someone of whom I had never heard—John Addington Symonds. "You should read these," my professor had said.

This began a journey of five years of study, during which I grew increasingly fascinated with this elusive, tormented, world-changing character.

The more I got to know John Addington Symonds through his letters, and the more I read about the men and women around him, the more present he seemed: in spite of the lapse of time between our lives, in Oxford especially, he often seemed to be just down the street; at times, when I was reading his letters in the Bodleian, the main research library at the University of Oxford, or the New College Library, his prescient voice seemed just a carrel away.

Every day, as I walked over the cobblestones leading out of New College, passed under the arched Bridge of Sighs, and went out along Broad Street, I saw Balliol's neo-Gothic doorway on my right. I could glance in at the smooth lawns of the courtyard and at the gabled rooms where this love affair, between lovers who were just grown out of boyhood, had been carried out—and then, it seemed, been cut painfully short.

In life, Symonds composed volumes and volumes—biographies, travel essays, books of verse, art criticism, translations, and textbooks. His letters alone, as I mentioned, constitute three massive tomes. He was, if anything, persistent in expressing himself. Nonetheless, he also insisted on silences. Symonds became the centerpiece of my 2015 doctoral thesis—but even after that was completed and handed in, I kept learning more about him from the astonishing clues that he had left behind for archivists and scholars. Those discoveries led me to write this book.

Though little known today outside the academic disciplines of Victorian studies and queer studies, Symonds should have a far more prominent place in history. He can truly be identified as one of the fathers of the modern gay rights movement. He can even be called an originator of what we now understand as the modern identity of male homosexuality in the West. His insistence regarding how to think about love—and his demand that male-male love and attraction be recognized as innate, natural, and healthy, rather than as acquired "neuroses," degeneracies, or diseases—helped craft our modern understanding of what it means to be a man who loves and desires other men.

Symonds would, until the very end of his life, use code to express his messages about love between men: he employed metaphors, misdirections, visual emblems, embargoed manuscripts, and lockboxes both rhetorical and real. He would spend his life creating and then hiding those true meanings, leaving signals for us, the men and women of the future, to decipher.

He tried to address the issue of men loving men in a wide range of genres: translating biographies and sonnets of homosexual artists such as Michelangelo Buonarroti and Benvenuto Cellini; composing a textbook of the lives of classical Greek poets; offering thinly veiled satire to a college journal; producing unpublished manifestos that scarcely saw the light of day; and publishing collections of love poems, using feminine pronouns to mask the true gender of the Beloved. He tried to address the central issue of his life and work by publicly collecting art by a disgraced artist, and by publishing reviews to defend homosexual writers who were under attack.

He died relatively young. But by working assiduously for slightly more than three decades, he scattered deliberately into the future a set of seeds for a more progressive world than the one in which he lived—seeds of the world we now see around us, if we live in the West. Symonds tried to express his belief that sexual love between men was innate and natural before there were concepts, let alone language, to support this idea. He was one of the people who invented the language. He spoke in every way he could as doing so became more and more illegal.

This book will follow John Addington Symonds's life as an essayist, poet, advocate, husband, father, and lover. Symonds's personal story offers a lens through which we may see a greater cultural and political struggle.

But the personal biography is also a story of state intervention in our personal lives and in our words—and a cautionary tale about what happens to us when that is permitted to be.

In his quest for freedom and equality for men who loved men, Symonds had help from an unlikely source. *Leaves of Grass*—a volume of poems published in 1855 by the American poet Walt Whitman—would be the catalyst of a lifetime for Symonds. This collection, in an utterly original voice, robustly celebrates the self and its euphoric relationship to the natural world and to other men and women. It sent transformational ripples through British and American subcultures. It would affect groups of London bohemians, Boston Transcendentalists, artists, writers, feminists, Socialists, Utopians, reformers, and revolutionaries, who would in turn create new ways of seeing human sexuality, social equality, and love itself, and who would use that vision in turn to build new institutions.

There would eventually be seven to ten authorized editions of the book, depending, as scholars point out, on what you count as an edition. There would be the real *Leaves of Grass*; the forged *Leaves of Grass*; the pirated *Leaves of Grass*; the bowdlerized, legal *Leaves of Grass*; and the smuggled, uncensored, illegal *Leaves of Grass*. There would be the *Leaves of Grass* that was read in private groups of workingmen in northern Britain, who felt it spoke especially to them, and the *Leaves of Grass* that early feminists read in London, New York City, and Philadelphia, who believed that it spoke uniquely to them as well.

After reading *Leaves of Grass* as a young man, Symonds would spend the rest of his life trying to respond to the book's provocative themes.

Physically fragile, status-conscious, fearful of social rejection, Symonds recognized a temperamental opposite in Whitman. The older poet was fearless, physically robust, all-embracing, stubborn in his convictions, unashamedly prophetic, and perfectly ready to upset everybody. Symonds never met Whitman in person, but the two maintained an epistolary friendship across the Atlantic, at a time when letters were transported on six-week journeys by ships under sail. The Englishman's sometimes overbearing literary courtship of Whitman would span more than two decades.

Comforted and provoked by this friendship, Symonds gradually became less and less guarded. At the very end of his life, he finally stopped trying to express his feelings in veiled ways and burst out at last into straightforward advocacy. His foundational essay, *A Problem in Modern Ethics*, circulated secretly before his death, declared outright that love between men was natural, and that it was good. At the end of his life, he collaborated on the sexological treatise *Sexual Inversion*, which would introduce the concept of homosexuality as an identity on a natural spectrum of sexual identities, as we understand it today. That argument bears with it an implicit claim for equal treatment of men who love men. *A Problem in Modern Ethics* could well have been the first gay rights manifesto in English.

Given the significance in LGBTQ+ history of John Addington Symonds's story, I asked many members of that community to read this book in manuscript. Based on their responses, I wish to share some notes.

Language about sexuality and gender is always evolving. I did my best, when describing the past, to use language that was accurate for the time, while still being alert to present-day usage.

My research found a deep connection between the origins of the feminist movement in the West, the modern (re-)invention of Western homophobia, and the start of the Western gay rights movement; this emboldened me to a degree to undertake this task.

Nonetheless I had a sense of humility, not being identified as a member of the LGBTQ+ community, in undertaking to tell this story. I was advised by my LGBTQ+ readers of the importance of the author's transparency.

So I am sharing that while I do not identify as a member of this community, I am aware of the responsibilities of an ally. This research material came my way; I was moved to do my utmost to shine a light on it.

By the time of Symonds's death, in 1893, a new generation of men such as Oscar Wilde were less indirectly signaling in their work what we would call gay themes and were no longer so willing to inhabit what we today call "the closet." Many commentators describe the movement for gay rights as originating with Wilde and the trials of 1895 that brought down the playwright, sentencing him to two years' hard labor in prison.

But a generation before Wilde, a small group of "sexual dissidents," influenced by Symonds and his loving friend and sometime adversary Walt Whitman, struggled at great personal risk and in the face of extraordinary oppression to advocate for these freedoms.[1]

PART I

A Gentle Angel

CHAPTER 1

"In Memoriam Arcadie"

M s. Maria Molestina brought out the copy of "In Memoriam Arcadie" from the dark stacks.

The notebook—for that was what it was—gave off the scent of another time, an era when people read and wrote by gaslight while warming themselves before coal fires. The notebook had originally been a series of ordinary foolscap pages—the sort of paper a Victorian schoolboy would keep handy for essays. The pages were thick, almost furry. They were sewn together awkwardly, perhaps by the teenage Symonds himself.

It is a love poem to a young man identified only as "W." In a painstaking cursive hand, the teenager spelled out, in quatrain after quatrain, on page after page, his feelings. He drew scenes of two boys together in many settings. The couple stood reverently side by side in a medieval church, listening to the chords of an organ. They lay together on the grass and gazed at birds circling in autumn skies. Symonds wrote about warm first kisses, about embraces, and about the boys' longing for more.

Years after Symonds's death, the notebook was saved from a bonfire by his literary executor, the critic and man-about-town Edmund Gosse.[1] On the opening page of the notebook, Gosse wrote, "This 'In Memoriam Arcadie' is the earliest surviving work of John Addington Symonds. It was begun in 1859, when the author was an undergraduate at Balliol, but chiefly written at Clifton in the vacations. W. was a fellow-student at Oxford, named Wright. No part of 'In Mem. Arcadie' has ever, to my knowledge, been printed."

Those were the days when April dawn
Wakened my heart to think of him,
When evening grey with shadows dim
Oerspread the tree embowered lawn [. . .]

Young Symonds had clearly been influenced by another love poem written by one young man for another. The two poems share the same ABBA rhyme scheme. Ten years before, the poet Alfred, Lord Tennyson, had written a poem in honor of his lost beloved friend Arthur Henry Hallam. Tennyson's poem was similarly titled: "In Memoriam A. H. H." Hallam and Tennyson had been students together at Cambridge University. Tennyson's biographer Christopher Ricks described the deep friendship between the two young men as being one of the formative experiences of Tennyson's life.[2]

Hallam had died suddenly at age twenty-two, of a cerebral hemorrhage, during a journey to Vienna with his father. His father had returned from a meeting to find the young man dead on the sofa.

Tennyson had grieved:

My Arthur, whom I shall not see
Till all my widow'd race be run;
Dear as the mother to the son,
More than my brothers are to me.[3]

Symonds similarly described remembered landscapes "Where we had talked; & his dear voice / Still clung to every fluttering leaf . . ."

But reading Symonds's lyrics in the notebook isn't a straightforward process. A page has been glued in after the first one, but it is left unpaginated. The verse on the pasted-in, unnumbered page reads:

These were the times when day by day
I sought with loving steps the shrine
Where rang his youthful voice divine,
To watch the light around him play:

The more banal scenes were paginated—that is, given page numbers—but a scene of love and attachment between the young men was left without a page number.

The page numbers pick up again with a scene of shame and regret: on the following page, which is the third page, but which is misleadingly given the number "2," the idyll of the two boys is interrupted by a nightmarish intervention. The author first describes a tender closeness: the boys are like "two acorns on one stem." But a taboo touch of the "two acorns on one stem" turns the former emotional and physical closeness of the boys into horror, and a life sentence of separation and loneliness:

> *But as I touched them, [. . .]*
> *One fell, & from his heart a worm*
> *Writhed on the grassy beads of dew.*
>
> *The other stayed, & he will grow*
> *Great with decay, & all alone*
> *Will blossom, all forsaken own*
> *The autumn rain and summer glow.*

Anyone who has ever been a heartbroken teenager, or comforted one, can hear in these words the universal rebellion of a young person against the first experience of pain and loss in love. But there was an extra layer of grief here, and a sense of needless separation.

On the upper right corner of each page with openly homoerotic content, there is almost always a green penciled "X." So Symonds left a poem that can be read as a palimpsest, or understood best in code. If you read only the paginated page sequences *without* the green Xs, nothing can be identified as untoward in the vaguely defined friendship between the boys. However, if you include in your reading the pages *with* the green Xs, you have the more complete history of a sexual and romantic affair between the youths.

Page 6, marked with a green X, is one example: it seems that at some point it had been cut out of the notebook. It then had apparently been folded into quarters—carried in a pocket, in preparation to be mailed to someone for safekeeping? Or handed to someone? Or set aside to be burned?

And then, as if Symonds had rethought this banishing of the page that had once been part of the complete poem, he, or someone else, had unfolded it and reattached it to what appears to be a cut-off edge. The reattached page reads:

> *I saw a vision of deep eyes*
> *In morning sleep when dreams are true—*
> *Wide humid eyes of hazy blue,*
> *Like seas that kiss the horizon skies.*
>
> *And, as I gazed, I felt the rain*
> *Of soft warm curls about my cheek,*

And heard a whisper low & meek—
"I love, & canst thou love again?"

A gentle youth beside me bent;
His cool moist lips to mine were pressed
That throbbed & burned with love's unrest—
When lo! The powers of sleep were spent [. . .]

But I can never rest again:—
The flocks of morning dreams are true;
And till I find these eyes of blue
And golden curls I walk in pain.

Such mutilations and reassessments occur throughout. The notebook—carefully created, then cut apart, then cut up; then pasted together, made somewhat whole, paginated and, upon reflection, unpaginated—is an object that vividly illustrates the conflict within Symonds. The very text models a loving, expressive, compartmentalized, "closeted" heart.

A verse is inscribed opposite the title page, in Symonds's slightly altered hand. Its title is "Set Apology." The handwriting here seems older, firmer, more self-conscious; the ink is different, darker. Preceding the poem is a note, also in ink: "These verses date from October 1859." Then, in pencil, the words: "to about Oct 1861."

What follows in tortured syntax is a preamble to the manuscript as a whole, one that basically disavows it. The preamble claims that all that is to follow should be read as fiction—as the passing imaginings of a "childish brain." Don't imagine, Reader, it warns, that these are passages about sexual passion; these feelings are no more passionate than a child's happiness to see his mother's eyes. Reader, it states, there was never actually a real couple to mourn.

To offer set Apology for this—
[. . .]
Were to defeat my object: as the fruit
Falls from the tree unripe, so fell these lines—
Smote by the frost a dry and sickly shoot—[. . .]

Scorn not its Sadness; let no doubt arise
That such weak veins throbbed more tumultuously

Than a child's throb to see its mother's eyes,
Or that in such a passion as here shown
Is more than memory mourning all alone.

These convolutions express so much. The "apology" that now precedes the poem is "set," as in British schoolboy locution—a school text that has been assigned, something you *must* do. So don't, Reader, misconstrue this erotic love poem about one real boy's adoration of another real boy—"such a passion as here shown"—as having anything to do with genuine human and erotic feelings. It is merely "memory mourning all alone."

Why would the young author write about his passionate love in quatrain after quatrain for fifty-something pages—then one day go back to declare that the whole pamphlet of heartfelt outpourings should be read as a lie, or as mere phantasm?

Symonds was nineteen, then twenty, when he wrote "In Memoriam Arcadie." In 1859, the young Symonds was free in his own love poem to imitate not only Tennyson's rhyme scheme but also his unmuted, passionate voice.

Sodomy itself, of course, had been outlawed by the British state by statute since 1533. Men received the death penalty for sodomy into the nineteenth century. Professor H. G. Cocks, associate professor at the University of Nottingham and author of the landmark study *Nameless Offences: Homosexual Desire in the 19th Century*, cites the government record: "[T]here were 56 executions for sodomy in England and Wales between 1806 and 1835. The last one was in November 1835 but the capital penalty remained on the statute book until 1861. The source for all this is the Judicial Statistics of the Parliamentary Papers, the official statistical record of the British government at the time, which can be seen at House of Commons papers [. . .] the figures for such sentences were small compared with the prosecution of all other 'unnatural offences,' although [. . .] these figures were dwarfed by 20th century prosecutions, thousands of which took place *after* the decriminalisation of male homosexuality in 1967."[4] H. G. Cocks's study of the *Judicial Statistics of the Parliamentary Papers*, and his cross-referencing of court trials against newspaper accounts, found that "[b]etween 1806 and 1861, 404 men received a death sentence for sodomy, of whom fifty-six were executed."[5] The executions all took place, he found, as noted, before 1835.

But though reports of death sentences recorded in trials appeared in regional and London newspaper crime tables after 1835, men were no longer executed for sodomy in England and Wales by the time Symonds was born.

Prof. Cocks explains the nuanced effect of death sentences still being on the books after 1835: "[N]o one was executed [for sodomy] after 1835 [. . .] However, it is also true that people were formally sentenced to death between 1835 and 1861 in all sorts of courts (rural assizes and in London and other cities), even though they might not have been executed[.]"[6]

Professor Paul Johnson's view is that the death sentence being on the books still had an impact on men who loved men: he describes a parliamentary debate in 1841, "six years," he notes, "after the last execution for buggery in 1835":

> Parliament's abhorrence of buggery during the 19th century is plainly illustrated by its attitude towards punishing offenders with death. When a bill was introduced into the House of Commons in 1841, that proposed to abolish death as a punishment for those convicted under English law of buggery, rape or unlawful carnal knowledge of a girl under the age of ten years, replacing it with transportation beyond the seas or imprisonment, MPs were uneasy at making this change on the basis that, for example, "there could be no doubt that the more atrocious cases of the kind were as deserving of death as any crime."
>
> Although the House of Commons ultimately accepted the removal of the punishment of death for buggery, the House of Lords did not concur. The Earl of Wicklow argued, for example, that "the people of this country would never confirm" that "sodomy and rape were not crimes of so heinous a character as to deserve death." The Earl of Winchilsea, who was strongly against any change in the law regarding buggery, "implored their Lordships not to withdraw the punishment of death from a crime so utterly abhorrent to the feelings of human nature" and proposed an amendment designed to omit the reference to buggery in the bill, allowing the punishment of death to continue for that offence. The Marquess of Normanby stated that if Parliament "commuted the punishment to transportation for life, that would necessarily imply communion of the offenders with other prisoners, which would be highly improper", and the amendment was agreed. As a consequence, Parliament

abolished the punishment of death for rape and unlawful carnal knowledge of a girl under the age of ten years, but retained that punishment for buggery.

What this demonstrates is that some parliamentarians were fervent in their desire to retain the capital sentence for buggery, and this view won the day until 1861. As a consequence, the courts continued to hand down capital sentences for buggery and, at the discretion of judges (discretion bestowed by a general statute), commute those sentences to lesser punishments. This was not a free pardon, and it was not letting people off.

The important point is that those people convicted right up to 1861 would have had no reason not to fear that they were going to be hanged. As the work of [Prof.] Cocks shows, this fear would have been compounded by the significant number of executions up to 1835.[7]

Graham Robb found that of 78 men sentenced to death for sodomy from 1810–1835, 46 were executed. "A further 32 were sentenced to death but reprieved. The remaining 713 who were convicted of sodomy or a related offence received a milder sentence—pillory (until 1816) or imprisonment."[8]

While scholars disagree on the nature of the emotional impact on men who loved men of this situation, Prof. Cocks, Prof. Charles Upchurch, and Graham Robb found a record of sentencing for both sodomy and other same-sex sex acts that is far more severe than is commonly understood. "It certainly is true that more consenting acts were prosecuted in the 19th century than ever before in England and Wales," explains Prof Cocks.[9]

Nonetheless, paradoxically, what we would today see as romantic love between men in general—including physical intimacy of all kinds—was still often within the bounds of social acceptability.

Contemporary letters show that in the 1850s, when Symonds "went up" to Oxford, British men used endearments with one another; they expressed the desire to embrace and kiss one another; and they walked—as confirmed in journals and newspapers, cartoons and novels, and even photographs—intimately, arm in arm, in the streets. There is an entire genre of photographs from this period in which a man sits on another man's lap as they embrace.

It was socially normative in the 1850s for a man to sleep every night in the same bed with another man. Men routinely bathed naked together in public bodies of water such as the Serpentine in Hyde Park and in "Parson's Pleasure," a bend of the River Cherwell in Oxford.[10] (This acceptance of physical closeness between men existed, as we will see, in the United States in this period, as well.)

There were many kinds of spaces, both public and private, for men to share the kinds of physical intimacy that the young poet's journal of first love, in verse, describes. But by 1862 this world had begun to change. The state was still arresting men and boys for sodomy and for lesser sexual offenses, though the death penalty had been abolished the year Symonds turned twenty-one. And other laws had recently been passed that turned speech about male-male love, and about other forms of sexuality, into crimes.

So by that year, a piece of writing such as "In Memoriam Arcadie" could get an author sentenced to imprisonment for a speech crime. Though the poem itself hadn't changed, its status was changing.

Turning the booklet on its side, and holding it up to the skylight, you notice that some pages have been cut out and then not repasted back in at all. Indeed, six pages are simply gone.

What created the gaps in sequence, and the jagged edges left along the notebook's spine?

I showed these edges to Ms. Molestina and asked her what I was looking at.

"Those pages," she said, "have been cut out of the notebook with a knife."

CHAPTER 2

"A Gentle Angel Enter'd"

Symonds was an unlikely revolutionary. He was born into a family that aspired to lives of convention and respectability, and his father in particular—whose name was also John Addington Symonds—was an intent social climber who sought and secured an eminent role in the British establishment.

The elder John Addington Symonds was born in Oxford into an accomplished, exacting family. Symonds's grandfather had been a Dissenter —a critic of the Church of England. John Addington Symonds the elder, the poet's father, was educated at the Magdalen College School and went on to attain a medical degree from the University of Edinburgh. He also trained as an assistant to his own father, a physician, in an era when a career in medicine lacked social status and was thought to require no great skill.

The elder Symonds married Harriet Sykes, who was also from an established bourgeois family. In 1831 the couple made the move to Bristol, a beautiful and thriving city, so that Symonds Sr. could take a position at the local general hospital. Soon he was lecturing on forensic medicine at the Bristol Medical School. The couple had five children. John Addington Symonds the younger was born in 1840; he was the only boy. As the child grew, he was closest to his older sister Charlotte.

Symonds's mother died when he was four. The son's secret journal recorded only impressionistic memories of her: he recalled her blond hair flying on one occasion when he rode with her in a carriage and the horse startled. He wrote of feeling guilty that he experienced little or no sense of loss. The thought of a mother, or a mother's death, had been only hazy to him as a child.

His father held his position teaching forensic medicine until the year after his wife's death. But he was now a single parent to five small children. Symonds's father relied on his own unmarried sisters—two stern aunts—to help him raise the children and manage the household and its retinue of

DR. SYMONDS — J.A. SYMONDS.
AND MRS GREEN

JAS, his sister Charlotte Symonds Green, and
the imperious Dr. Symonds, 1867.

servants. His son recalled that time as gloomy, and his aunts as very religious and strict.

When the boy was ten, the family moved to Clifton Hill House, a gracious, if ostentatious, Palladian home near Bristol. His father bought the house in part, no doubt, to demonstrate his status and financial success. Symonds later described this house and its rolling green vistas, overlooking the Bath hills, the city of Clifton, and the River Avon, as fostering his sense of the beautiful.

In spite of the protective setting of his new home, Symonds's childhood was tormented. His father was often busy and distant and yet communicated to the child rigid moral standards that put tremendous pressure on him, and his aunts were more demanding than nurturing.

The child suffered from fragile physical health. He was also afflicted with terrible anxiety, as well as with bouts of a sense of detachment from his immediate reality, which were almost like seizures.

He was troubled by terrible nightmares; he imagined that there were corpses under his bed. And he was prone to sleepwalking. One night he walked outdoors in his sleep to the edge of a cistern full of rainwater; there, as he later described the experience, a gentle angel—a radiant being with wavy blond hair and blue eyes—awakened him and led him back to safety.

Symonds was sent to Harrow School for his secondary education at age eleven. This public school (the British term for private school) for boys, founded in 1572 by a charter given by Queen Elizabeth, was one of the three or four most selective schools in England.[1] Symonds's classmates were sons of the aristocracy and gentry. It was no easy place for the boy to be. He badly missed his sister Charlotte and his other siblings, his father, and the shelter of Clifton Hill House.

He was ill-equipped to deal with the public school experience. According to descriptions in many contemporary biographies and letters, Harrow and other such institutions fostered a competitive, coercive culture that was often vicious. Sports were extremely important, but Symonds could not participate. He was seen as being too weak, with low resistance. Symonds also suffered miserably under the public school "fag" system, by which younger boys were forced in general to serve older ones. Older boys were often cruel to their younger "fags" at this time. Obedience to the older boys' demands often included sexual submission.

Symonds struggled with feelings for boys—especially for some who sang in the church choir. He noted in his secret journal that this sense of attraction solely to boys and men had been with him since early childhood. In his later, equally secretive advocacy, he insisted that these memories served as evidence that such feelings were innate and not the result of "morbid" influences or "degenerate" life experiences.

At the same time, Symonds reacted against the boy-to-boy relationships that he observed at school: he objected to what he saw as the crude, animalistic sexuality mixed with emotional abuse in these relationships.

Harrow's headmaster, Dr. Charles John Vaughan, oversaw the studies and the moral lives of the students. Dr. Vaughan was an Anglican priest whose father and brother were also vicars. His influence and reputation were at a zenith; he had taken on the school when it was in disarray—with slack academics, few students, and little discipline—and had boosted the student body to over two hundred pupils. He had brought Harrow to the top rank of public schools and built its reputation for high academic standards. In a fairly savage educational context, Vaughan was known for his sensitive treatment of students. His strong bond with them, and theirs with him, was part of his impressive reputation. Contemporary etchings present him as a vigorous, youthful-looking man, with straight dark hair parted on the side, a gentleman's conventional muttonchop sideburns, intelligent eyes, and a mild expression.

Symonds struggled at Harrow. He tried to reconcile his deep desire for love and intimacy with the abusive sexual norms of his peers. He had no models for the type of romantic relationship for which he longed. Yet unbeknownst to him, a book was being published across the ocean that would change this. It would eventually open up an altogether new life for Symonds.

The book was Walt Whitman's *Leaves of Grass*.

The origins and early experiences of the two men couldn't be more different.

Whitman described himself as a "rough." This is a self-dramatizing term, but he was indeed born to a family that had to work very hard for its sustenance. He was born in 1819, twenty-one years earlier than Symonds, on Long Island, New York, to Walter Whitman, a not particularly well-to-do carpenter, and his wife, the former Louisa Van Velsor, a strong-willed and intelligent woman whose ancestors had been Dutch settlers. Both of Walt Whitman's parents descended from some of the first non-native families to settle on Long Island. Walt Whitman was one of four brothers; he had two sisters as well.

Walter Whitman Sr. would build a house, his family would live in it briefly, and he would sell it, and they would move on. In 1823, Walter Whitman moved his family to the borough of Brooklyn, which was in the midst of a building boom. The family moved often, within Brooklyn, then back to Long Island, and again back to Brooklyn.

In 1830, the eleven-year-old Walt left school to work as an office boy and then became a printer's apprentice for the *Long Island Patriot*. Two years later, he was working as a printer at Worthington's printing house, eventually becoming a compositor for the *Long Island Star*, and later still, he became a printer in Manhattan.

It was a compelling time for a young writer to learn the printing trade. Before the nineteenth century, books were rare artisanal objects, affordable to only a few. Type was set by hand, and each book was sewn and bound by manual labor. By the 1830s, however, mechanization was making the mass production of books possible. These publications, cheaper and greater in number, became accessible to masses of newly literate readers. Whitman would have understood that the printing industry was placing books into the hands of a wider range of classes, genders, and races than ever before. More books, more readers—a potentially transformational combination, which might threaten the established power structure and social order.

Whitman continued to move from job to job; according to his employers and colleagues, he rarely distinguished himself in any of these positions. In 1836, back on Long Island, he took a position as a schoolteacher. Yet he disliked the cold winters and the isolation of the one-room schoolhouses.

Today, it is not easy to look at the Long Island locations where Walt Whitman lived or visited—Dix Hills, Whitestone—and imagine a wilderness sublime enough to nurture a great romantic voice and great visionary. The Island is of course overbuilt. The Long Island Railroad bisects the peninsula, and a crowded highway cleaves it as well; strip malls and housing developments obscure the horizons.

But when you are out on Long Island Sound, or when you catch a breeze from the Atlantic and look up at the freshly washed light of the sky, you can still feel a bit of what Whitman might have felt 190 years ago. In the 1830s, Long Island was in many areas a true wilderness, ringed with empty white beaches and flat, bird-dense meadows. In others, it was only thinly settled.

Long Island Sound had been a conduit point for men and women traveling by canoe or other watercraft for thousands of years before Henry Hudson arrived in 1609 at what is now Canarsie. When Whitman lived on Long Island, settlements of long-established Native American tribes were still present, though their formerly extensive tribal lands had been whittled down by British officials during colonial times. These groups—Shinnecock, Massapequa, Setauket, and others—made their living as whalers and as fishermen. By the time Whitman was a teenager, many Long Island Native Americans lived on reservations, most of them in poverty. They spoke languages related to Algonquin and worshipped divine spirits while acknowledging evil ones within the natural world. Whitman was acquainted with some members of these tribes.

As an adolescent and young man amid Long Island's multiethnic and multicultural settlements, Whitman was exposed at least from time to time to a non-European perspective. He heard place names that descended from Algonquin: Sewanhacky, Wamponomon, and Paumanake. Whitman included Algonquin and Lenni Lenape place names[2]—as in "Starting from Paumanok"—and in Mannahatta, in various editions of *Leaves of Grass*.[3] A sense of the divine aspects of the natural world, along with these non-European place names, would radiate through the descriptions of a mostly wild peninsula and animate *Leaves of Grass*.

These invocations and echoes conveyed to European and British readers, in closed, heated rooms, a sense of radically different values, unmediated landscapes, and as-yet-unimagined possibilities.

Whitman left Long Island in 1841 to work at newspapers in Brooklyn and in New York City; he dabbled in politics. He was named editor of the *Aurora*, the *Tatler*, and the *Statesman*—all scrappy newspapers competing for readers in the city and its boroughs. In 1846, he finally landed a permanent position as an editor of the *Brooklyn Daily Eagle*.[4] But as he churned out reams of conventional journalism and followed City Hall, he also paid attention to New York's weekly literary reviews, which summarized dispatches from England, and republished British literary news.

In the 1840s, Whitman was also writing fiction; one of his first published stories features a tender love between two men.

The 1841 short story, which appeared in the New York broadsheet *A New World*, was titled "A Child's Champion." In the story, John Lankton, a cynical, dissipated older man trained in medicine, encounters a ragged youth, Charles, in an inn. A drunken sailor has forced Charles to drink liquor against his will, an image suggestive of oral violation: "Charles stood, his cheek flushed and his heart throbbing, wiping the trickling drops from his face with a handkerchief." The sailor is about to beat the youth for resisting.

Lankton fends off the sailor, rescues the younger man, and invites Charles to share his bed for the night. There, holding Charles, Lankton experiences feelings of "unsullied affection": "He [Lankton] folded his arms around [Charles] and, while he slept, the boy's cheek rested on his bosom."[5] Whitman describes the men's affection as romantic, and also as physical.

An angel enters the room to bless the men sleeping in each other's arms:

> With one of the brightest and earliest rays of the warm sun a gentle angel entered his apartment, and hovering over the sleepers on invisible wings, looked down with a pleasant smile and blessed them. Then noiselessly taking a stand by the bed, the angel bent over the boy's face, and whispered strange words into his ear: thus it came that he had beautiful visions. No sound was heard but the slight breathing of those who slumbered there in each other's arms; and the angel paused a moment, and smiled another and a doubly sweet smile as he drank in the scene with his large soft eyes. Bending over again to the boy's lips, he touched them with a kiss, as the languid wind touches a flower.

As the historian Jonathan Ned Katz points out, this short story lacks the kind of language that we now associate with modern ideas about either homoeroticism or homophobia. There is no statement of what would be, in modern terms, a "sexual identity," nor does the story involve any sense of the lovers defying a social taboo. What is important in the story is not, particularly, the gender of the lovers; instead, Whitman insists upon the redemptive nature of love. Charles's purity of heart draws Lankton away from nihilism.

Lankton goes on to marry a woman. Whitman matter-of-factly narrates this event, as if this kind of love triangle were common enough in the 1840s in New York. Lankton's attachment to the younger man remains intact nonetheless: "the close knit love of the boy and him grew not slack with time."[6]

The story demonstrates the freedom of expression that Walt Whitman and others could take for granted on the topic of men who loved men in early-to-mid-nineteenth-century America. Whitman was free to write in this relaxed way because of broad inconsistencies in the laws relating to love and sex between men.

In the United States in 1841, many states had no laws against many kinds of physical and sexual intimacy between men. Jonathan Ned Katz, in *Love Stories: Sex between Men before Homosexuality*, writes that although some legal documents and newspaper accounts of this period mention the act of sodomy and refer to individuals as "sodomites," nonetheless, many forms of physical affection and sexual intimacy between men were completely unlegislated.[7] Indeed, Katz's conclusions, accepted now by many queer studies historians but little known outside of that discipline, are worth quoting: "Intense 'love' relations between men were approved of in the nineteenth century [. . .] these stories [to follow in his book] reveal gender nonconformity being newly linked with erotic deviance [. . .] These tales show how the early nineteenth century's narrow construction of 'sodomy' was challenged at century's end by a broad, new sexual crime, sometimes called 'gross indecency.' That law, and others like it, first made oral-genital contact a crime [. . .]"

For most of the nineteenth century, in America, on the state level, the acts that were criminalized, were criminalized inconsistently. And there was no federal statute against sodomy at all.[8]

Fellatio and male-male mutual masturbation were not crimes at all, either, in some states in America in the 1840s, though these acts were not openly discussed. Sodomy was indeed a serious crime in most states, but prosecutions for sodomy itself in America in the first half of the nineteenth century were inconsistent and, as in Britain, relatively few.

Going back to earlier American history, we see the same uneven patch-work of prohibitions. Vicious punishments, including capital punishment, for sodomy existed during the colonial era: Virginia wrote such a prohibition against sodomy in 1610 (it was repealed eight years later). Plymouth Colony, settled by religious separatists, outlawed sodomy based on the passage against it in Leviticus and made sodomy a capital crime. George Painter, in his essay "The Sensibilities of Our Forefathers: The History of Sodomy Laws in the United States," points out that the British colonies in America received English common law, including the Elizabethan statute that established "buggery" as a secular crime.

"Three of the original 13 colonies [. . .] were not settled by the English and, of the ten that were, only in Maryland and, possibly, Virginia were English laws presumed to be in force from the beginning of colonization without local enactment. Death was the penalty of choice by statute and, in some cases, by usage."[9] In these colonies, prosecution for sodomy could result in a sentence of death.[10]

But at the other extreme, many acts of intimacy between men were not even regulated in early American history. And punishment was erratic in the colonial period; in Massachusetts, for instance, men accused of sodomy were sent back to England for trial. Other colonies were far more lenient. In New Hampshire, apparently nothing at all happened to offenders. There were only three known prosecutions for sodomy in the colonial period in New York and New Jersey, for instance, as these regions followed Dutch law, and Pennsylvania's mild Quaker traditions set a maximum of six months in jail as punishment for the act. Delaware, when first settled, had no statute against sodomy at all. North and South Carolina had no prohibitions against sodomy for almost fifty years after their founding. And Georgia had no law outlawing sodomy for the whole of the eighteenth century.[11]

By 1841, in America, however, many laws had become more stream-lined: twelve states now had statutes against sodomy, though these varied in severity. But still, as we saw, there was no federal law against it. The legal offense of "sodomy" was still narrowly defined in Whitman's young adulthood: it referred only to anal intercourse and to bestiality.

In 1841, fellatio was not a federal crime in America—and it was not "sodomy"—so many men were free to engage in it.[12] In addition, "cunnilingus, tribadism, interfemoral intercourse, and mutual masturbation were found not to be included in the act," writes Painter, confirming Jonathan Ned Katz's point. At this moment in time, there were many ways for

American men to be intimate with men that were not prohibited by law, either in its theory or in its practice.

Try to imagine the world of 1841 being one that precedes many labels we have today. There have of course always been people whom we today would identify as exclusively homosexual, who are attracted only to other men, or only to other women, and know that about themselves from the earliest age. In his 1948 *Sexual Behavior in the Human Male* and his 1953 *Sexual Behavior in the Human Female*, the sexologist Alfred Kinsey found that in his samples, 37 percent of males and 13 percent of females had at least some overt homosexual experience to orgasm, 10 percent of males were more or less exclusively homosexual, between 2 and 6 percent of women were exclusively attracted to other women, and 4 percent of males and 1 to 3 percent of females had been exclusively homosexual after the onset of adolescence and up to the time of Kinsey's interview.[13] In the nineteenth century, however, while surely people who felt this way constituted the same part of the population, sex acts between men and between women were not understood in terms of a particular "sexual identity." Only later, with the rise of sexology, would the concept of sexual identity come to be defined and eventually accepted. Before sexology, since our contemporary understanding of a sexual identity did not exist, of course a movement to demand social equality for people with this sexual identity could not yet exist. "Homosexuality," let alone bisexual, lesbian, transgender, or genderqueer identities, were not yet categories recognized in the ways that they are today.

As in Britain, a wide range of physical affection was socially acceptable as well as legal for all men in nineteenth-century America. Same-sex intimacy was completely legal for nineteenth-century women in America and in Britain, as there were no laws at all against it.

The Whitman scholar Dr. David Reynolds points out that "showing passion and affection [between men] was a more common part of the daily experience than it is today."[14] Katz notes that in America and Britain, romantic love between men was viewed with admiration; while it was not assumed to include eroticism, at the same time, these intimacies did unfold in a context that permitted many kinds of eroticism. In April 1837, for instance, the then-legislator twenty-eight-year-old Abraham Lincoln, in Springfield, Illinois, encountered twenty-four-year-old Joshua Fry Speed. Speed offered to share his double bed with Lincoln. For over three years the two men slept together, and Speed remembered years afterward that "no two men were ever more intimate." Speed told Lincoln's eventual biographer,

William Herndon, that Lincoln "disclosed his whole heart to me"; and Herndon concluded that Lincoln "loved this man more than anyone dead or living," not excluding, as Katz points out, Lincoln's wife.[15] The late writer Larry Kramer faced a backlash when, in his novel *The American People*, volume 1, he wrote about same-sex desires of prominent Americans, including President Lincoln. But Kramer wasn't being inflammatory—merely factual. The record is clear: "From our present standpoint," writes Katz, "we can see that these intimate friendships often left evidence of extremely intense, complex desires, including, sometimes, what we today recognize as erotic feelings and acts. Evidence survives of a surprising variety of physical and sometimes sensual modes of relating among male friends in the nineteenth century."[16] What these men lacked, he points out, is the language that we have today: his evidence of stories of male-male love "show us men struggling for affirmative words to name and characterize those intimacies."[17]

It was understood that intense, physically expressed love between two men could arise, though such love was not sanctioned in the way that marriage between a woman and a man was. Scholars today fiercely debate whether the many kinds of same-sex love that appear in the nineteenth-century historical record should be categorized as "gay" or "not gay." But one conclusion is clear, and Columbia University professor of history George Chauncey, author of *Gay New York: Gender, Urban Culture, and the Making of the Gay Male World, 1890–1940,* makes this point: the labels we have today do not suffice to describe the richness of relationships between men or between women in the past.[18] Chauncey found in the late nineteenth century a malleability of sexual identities and a broad acceptance of what we would call "homosexual" activities among American working-class men—men whom today we would call "heterosexual" or "heteronormative."[19]

It is well documented that nineteenth-century America was replete with many kinds of intimacy that we would identify today as exclusively "homosexual," between men who never desired women and between women who never desired men; records also confirm many physical, sexual relationships between men whom we identify today as primarily "heterosexual" and who saw themselves as being primarily attracted to women, just as records confirm that married women or women who would eventually marry had passionate physical attachments to other women. Scholars, such as recent biographers and critics of Emily Dickinson, have filled out these pictures, showing that passionate same-sex attachments were often, socially, not even remarkable.[20]

"Susie, forgive me Darling, for every word I say—my heart is full of you, none other than you is in my thoughts, yet when I seek to say to you something not for the world, words fail me. If you were here—" wrote Emily Dickinson to Susan Gilbert.[21]

Before sexology, there was desire, there was love, there were of course couples; all of these lacked the language that we use today.

From where did Whitman's bold assertions concerning the broad range of human sexuality, and his glimpses of a promised world based on social equality, spring? One clue is a trip the poet took in 1848 to a city in the Deep South with an unusual history.

In 1848, Whitman either quit, or was fired from, the *Daily Eagle*. The publisher of the *New Orleans Daily Crescent* invited Whitman, who was not yet forty, to edit that newspaper instead. Whitman accepted and made the arduous trip south, in the company of his younger brother Jeff, who was fifteen years old.

The two went by flatboat down the Mississippi to New Orleans—a dangerous, exotic trip on what was then the central "highway" of the United States. The brothers stayed for four months, until the publisher decided that he no longer needed Whitman as an editor.

New Orleans was at that time hardly an American city at all. It had been founded by French colonists in 1718, then taken over by Spanish colonial administrators in 1763; by 1802, the city was again administered by the French. Many North American visitors to New Orleans in the 1840s described how "other" it was—how French, Spanish, and African customs persevered, just under the surface of the city and state administration.

The colonial origins of the city extended to its legal structure. New Orleans based its laws on a version of France's Napoleonic Code.[22] French criminal law since the fourteenth century had punished sodomy by burning, although this sentence was in practice rare. But during the Enlightenment, French philosophers felt that although they strongly disapproved of sodomy, the state had no right to intrude on private decisions about sexuality. A 1791 law completely decriminalized homosexual relations in private between two consenting male adults.[23] A legal code continuing this tradition was introduced in France by Napoleon Bonaparte in 1804, and it was so successful that it was widely copied throughout Europe. The Napoleonic Code created a haven in France for generations of British men who loved men.

The Napoleonic Code legalized the Enlightenment's laissez-faire attitude, at least in France and its territories, and this code influenced the law that governed early-nineteenth-century Louisiana.[24]

To this day in New Orleans you can still feel some of the influences that likely affected Whitman. To one side of the central Spanish colonial square, with its sugar-white cathedral now surrounded by street musicians, stands a narrow independent bookstore. If you ask the proprietor, he will, without missing a beat, reach to the top of a crowded bookcase and hand you down a hardcover book.

Brothels, Depravity, and Abandoned Women: Illegal Sex in Antebellum New Orleans, by the sociologist Judith Kelleher Schafer, answers these questions. Schafer read the *New Orleans Daily Picayune,* a rival paper to Whitman's, as well as the city's court records, from the dates 1848 through 1862. Both sources made casual note of same-sex couples living together as families and raising children. Well-known local personalities, the documents confirmed, included men who routinely dressed as women and women who dressed as men (though the latter were treated more severely). Press commentary often described these individuals in tones of affection and amusement—not of sober moral outrage. And "[t]here is not one case on the docket of the First District Court of New Orleans, the criminal court, of a prosecution for homosexual sex or even for 'crime against nature,' or sodomy," she found. "Nor did newspapers ever report that one of the city's recorders ruled on such activity."[25]

That relative tolerance extended to the demimonde. Diverse sexual choices and living arrangements seem to have been taken for granted then in New Orleans among sex workers of all kinds, and sex work, including what may have been same-sex sex work, was thinly regulated by police.

The ethnic makeup of early-to-mid-nineteenth-century New Orleans was also different from that of other United States cities. The institution of slavery, savage of course everywhere, was uniquely notorious in certain ways in New Orleans: in the public marketplace, for instance, young women were categorized by skin tone as "quadroon" or "octoroon" (terms referring to one-quarter or one-eighth of African descent), costed out, and sold as sex slaves. At the same time, paradoxically, free black citizens formed a powerful community in New Orleans; they ran businesses and held property, and many were pillars of the city's civic life.

Elsewhere in America, the rape of female slaves was as widespread as their enslavement, and yet consensual interracial relationships were against the law. But in New Orleans, which also countenanced the continual rape of enslaved women by their owners, consensual personal, business, and even romantic relationships among free black citizens and Irish, German, and Jewish ones were common, and complex.[26] Common law consensual marriages between Caucasian and African American citizens were accepted in New Orleans, at least among the city's working poor. The historian Elizabeth Fussell calls nineteenth-century New Orleans strikingly racially interconnected for the period: a "cultural gumbo."[27]

So for a few months, Walt Whitman lived in the one place in America—perhaps one of the few places in the world at that time—where it was possible to touch certain threads of the future, even though they were interwoven with the brutal world of 1848, where human beings were for sale in the public arena.

Did witnessing these anomalies change Whitman? It wasn't just Whitman's treatment of same-sex love that would be transformational to readers. It was also the way in which he invoked radical inclusion and equality of other kinds. In a manuscript so tattered that archivists believe it spent time on the Rome Brothers' Brooklyn printing-house floor—in notes that were a "proto-version" of sections of *Leaves of Grass*—Whitman explored these preoccupations:

> *And I know that the spirit of God is the eldest brother of my own,*
> *And that all the men ever born are also my brothers . . . . and the*
> *   women my sisters and lovers, [. . .]*[28]

> *I go with the slaves of the earth equally with the masters*
> *And I will stand between the masters and the slaves,*
> *Entering into both so that both will understand me alike.*[29]

Whitman would create, in *Leaves of Grass*, an imagined world in which people of all races and genders and sexualities were free and equal and might love one another freely—a shocking, exhilarating, but strangely realistic glimpse of the future that galvanized its readers.

Upon his return to Manhattan, Whitman was no better established professionally than he had been before he left. He remained as itinerant as ever.

He produced a radical newspaper of his own, which he called the *Freeman*. From 1849 to 1854, he lived in a succession of inexpensive boardinghouses, filled with motley characters; he sold books in a bookstore and placed articles as a freelance journalist. Whitman spent a good deal of time in the underground bars frequented by other ill-paid journalists. He spent his days wandering around Manhattan; he visited friends, many of them workingmen, at the dockyards of what was then a great shipping island. Some of the laborers whom he met around the city became his lovers.

He never married. These friendships with men of all backgrounds were the emotional center of his life.

His prose style as a journalist remained extremely conventional—similar to the voices of his contemporaries. Like them, he covered corrupt politicians and engaging social trends; he also wrote, when requested, routine prose-for-hire, such as a reverie on the fact that it was Christmas Day.

But still, something entirely original was taking shape in his poetry: a fresh voice was emerging, and a new world invoked. In his notebooks he wrote:

> *I am the poet of the body*
> *And I am the poet of the soul.*[30]

CHAPTER 3

1855: *Leaves of Grass*

On May 15, 1855, Whitman took out a copyright for his finalized collection of poetry, *Leaves of Grass*. In the first week of July, the Rome Brothers in Brooklyn formally printed 795 copies.

In producing the first edition, Whitman drew on what he had learned as a journeyman printer. He and the Rome Brothers printers set the type by hand; due to errors they made, this print run itself was unique. Whitman did not wish to waste a single volume, so he corrected them as he went along. Some volumes in this printing differ slightly from one another.

He had the front cover bound in moss-green fabric; he stamped the title in embossed gold letters. The lettering was unusual: Whitman designed every letter with curling shoots, as if tree branches were emerging from it. The letters look alive. Something alchemical, perhaps because of Whitman's unusual hands-on involvement, seemed to happen to this volume. For decades thereafter, readers would react to this edition of *Leaves of Grass* as if they were touching, and making a connection with, the body of the poet himself.

The result was a slender volume, containing a ten-page preface; it was only ninety-five pages in total. Whitman later expressed his hope that this light, eccentrically designed volume would be taken outside and read in a natural setting. This wish was in itself a departure from the behavior expected then of most readers.

Today we think of reading as a private, solitary activity: you have a book and an electric light. But in 1855, reading was most often a communal, semi-public activity. Books and lighting were both

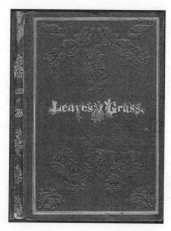

A first edition (1855) of *Leaves of Grass*.

costly, and homes were lit by gas lamps, oil lanterns, or candles. For all but the wealthy, evening reading took place aloud, from a shared book, with family members seated around a shared light source, at what was called the "family table." Even when people brought their own books to the shared lantern or gas lamp, others could monitor their reading. Men of the nineteenth-century household were supposed to control the reading of the women, servants, and minors who lived with them.

Whitman's invitation in *Leaves of Grass*, in an edition published in 1856 by Fowler and Wells, another printing firm in Brooklyn, by contrast, draws the reader into a far more daring reading experience.

I CELEBRATE myself,
And what I assume you shall assume,
For every atom belonging to me, as good belongs to you.

I loafe and invite my soul,
I lean and loafe at my ease, observing a spear of summer grass.

Houses and rooms are full of perfumes—the shelves are crowded
*   with perfumes,*
I breathe the fragrance myself, and know it and like it,
The distillation would intoxicate me also, but I shall not let it.[1]

There are many reasons why this little volume would create such shock and disruption. One has to do with its challenge to established ways of thinking about religion.

During the mid-nineteenth century, longstanding religious truths were challenged. In 1835, David Friedrich Strauss published *The Life of Jesus*, and dozens of similar books followed—encouraging believers to search for the historical, rather than to accept the theological, figure of Jesus. Whitman's audiences had been exposed to books that shook deep-rooted certainties about the Gospel narratives—and about God Himself.[2]

Other books and news articles were assailing people's sense of the origins of human beings. Archaeologists were sifting ancient sites and finding prehistoric artifacts, remains of mammoths, and even dinosaur bones; these discoveries led some readers to question the biblical account of Creation, and the age of the world that had been extrapolated from it. A formerly eternal-seeming rural landscape was being torn apart by railroad tracks, coal mines, and telegraph poles.

What would replace traditional versions of the divine, and the relationship of human beings to God, as so many religious beliefs became subject to doubt?

Leaves of Grass had one kind of answer. In its verse, the tension between an increasingly questioned God and questing human beings—between the divine and the everyday—is magnificently released into the universe. For Whitman, the natural, the human, and the heavenly worlds are all one world, and they are all ablaze with the light of the divine. In Whitman's presentation, nature is both sacred and carnal. For American and British readers who had been raised in faiths and denominations that burdened them with sexual shame, Whitman's book provided a vision of a prelapsarian paradise on this earth. In that world, there is never

> *any more heaven and hell than there is now.*
> *Urge and urge and urge,*
> *Always the procreant urge of the world.*[3]

Indeed, Nature herself—or himself—is a lover. In one of his most often-quoted passages, Whitman uses sensual metaphors for the natural world and speaks as if he is making love to it: "I will go to the bank by the wood and become undisguised and naked," he writes. "I am mad for it to be in contact with me." The language of the lover is homoerotic: "loveroot [. . .] crotch and vine" and "Trickling sap of maple, fibre of manly wheat, it shall be you" and "Winds whose soft-tickling genitals rub against me it shall be you."[4]

In another passage often quoted by contemporary readers, an idyllic outdoor love scene between two men seems to be one of fellatio:

> *You settled your head athwart my hips and gently turned over upon me,*
> *And parted the shirt from my bosom-bone, and plunged your tongue to*
>   *my barestript heart*
> *And reached till you felt my beard, and reached till you held my feet.*
> *Swiftly arose and spread around me the peace and joy and knowledge . . .*
> *And I know that the hand of God is the elderhand of my own.*[5]

Even in that context, the atmosphere is one of reverence. Likewise, Whitman condemns those who condemn any kind of love:

Through me forbidden voices
Voices of sexes and lusts . . . voices veiled, and I remove the veil.
Voices indecent by me clarified and transfigured . . .
I do not press my finger across my mouth . . .
Copulation is no more rank to me than death is.[6]

The narrator greets his lovers in settings that could be understood as domestic and heterosexual—the "soft bed"—and also in public spaces clearly understood by nineteenth-century readers as being exclusively male. Those described as loving the narrator, who cry "Ahoy!" to him on the docks by the "rocks of the river," are male workers who are loading and unloading ships at anchor in the Hudson or the East River.

Whitman speaks to his readers—whomever they are, of whatever gender—as if they too are his lovers—"lovers of me," he calls them: "I have embraced you, and henceforth possess you to myself."[7] Whitman's Utopian voice allowed American—and then British—readers to imagine standing, like the author, "with his arm round the neck of a man or a woman."

Which was it? It perhaps did not matter.

Whitman goes on to claim, with startling sexual imagery, that his embrace can even strengthen democracy: "On women fit for conception I start bigger and nimbler babes, / This day I am jetting the stuff of far more arrogant republics."[8]

He declares that all of the religious gatekeepers' measures of sin and redemption were of less value than a spurt of his own ejaculate:

Magnifying [. . .] come I
Outbidding at the start the old cautious hucksters.
The most they offer for mankind and eternity less than a spirt [sic] of my
own seminal wet.[9]

For many readers, Whitman's all-embracing eroticism at times seemed overly exuberant: "Span of youth! Ever-pushed elasticity! Manhood-balanced floral and full!" But overall, his was a vision that readers, from 1855 up to today, experienced as liberating and prophetic.

As Kenneth Price and Ed Folsom, who produced a scholarly edition of Whitman's archives, put it, "*Leaves of Grass* was not a book that set out to shock the reader so much as to merge with the reader, and to make him or her more aware of the body each reader inhabited [. . .] to convince us that the body and soul were conjoined and inseparable."

It wasn't just the language of *Leaves of Grass* that sparked such a response. Plenty of readers also fell in love with the poet himself. Whitman was certainly complicit in this seduction. He made choices throughout his career that would lead people not just to love his writing but also to wish to touch, confess to, and even make love to the poet himself.

One provocation was the author's image on the frontispiece of *Leaves of Grass.* Whitman commissioned this lithograph, based on a daguerreotype

1855 *Leaves of Grass* frontispiece: Walt Whitman, aged thirty-five; a new image of a poet— perhaps a new image of a man. Based on a daguerreotype by his friend Gabriel Harrison.

by the New York photographer Gabriel Harrison. At a time when photography itself was fairly new, the image soon became iconic on both sides of the Atlantic.

Whitman poses with his right hip thrust out provocatively, his right hand resting on it. The poet wears a white workman's blouse, open, showing his strong, sunburned chest; he wears a laborer's felt hat with a floppy brim. The lithograph reveals most of the poet's body, at a time when male writers were represented from the starched collar or neckerchief up. In the United States, Ralph Waldo Emerson, Henry David Thoreau, and Mark Twain appeared in this manner, as did Charles Dickens and Wilkie Collins in Britain. Whitman's stance reveals that he is comfortable with himself and his own erotic nature, just exactly as he is—echoing the message of the book. This was a new model of a poet—perhaps a new model of a man.[10]

Transcendentalism, the idealistic American philosophy popularized since the 1830s by Ralph Waldo Emerson and Henry David Thoreau, also maintained a Romantic view of the relationship between human beings, nature, and the divine. *Leaves of Grass* attracted readers in this progressive egalitarian community. In Boston's Transcendentalist circles, both male and female readers were passing the volume hand to hand. Emerson wrote an encouraging letter to the poet: "I give you joy of your free and brave thought [. . .] I have great joy in it. I find incomparable things said incomparably well, as they must be. I find the courage of treatment, which so delights us, and which large perception only can inspire." He concluded, "I greet you at the beginning of a great career."[11]

The 1855 edition of *Leaves of Grass* was received by some in Britain and America as a visionary if rough text, fresh from the future; others dismissed it as a screed.

It's unlikely that Symonds was aware of the book then, given the overall lack of attention the 1855 edition received from British critics. Before 1860, fewer than ten mentions of the book appeared in the British press.

But if the book was under-noticed, there was nothing yet illegal about printing it, selling it, or reading it.

That was soon to change.

PART II

1857: Outrages

CHAPTER 4

Inventing the Modern Crime
of Obscenity

The year that Symonds turned seventeen, 1857, was one of sweeping change. That year, social foment led to what was in effect the invention of modern ideas of "the obscene." Many essential ideas that undergird our assumptions about Western society—from the notion that the state has a role to play in deciding what is said or read, to the idea of modern civil divorce and its triggers, to the availability of hard labor as a punishment for crimes such as male-male sex acts—were codified and systematized.

Let's start with the state and speech. Before 1857, it was not that easy to get arrested by the state for speech in Britain. There were offenses you could commit by speaking, but these were mostly ecclesiastical: notably, blasphemy and heresy. A person could also be censored by the state for committing treason or printing "common libel." This was what happened to the printer and essayist Samuel Richardson in 1723, when he printed a Jacobite pamphlet that was critical of the government. Five years later, the anti-papist commentator Edmund Curll, author of the satire *The Nun in Her Smock*, was convicted of "disturbing the King's peace."[1] These are early examples in Britain of a speech crime being considered a civil offense.

Still, such cases were rare. And Curll's conviction was not that strong a precedent. Then, in 1748, John Cleland was prosecuted because his highly explicit novel *Fanny Hill: Memoirs of a Woman of Pleasure* was deemed to be "corrupting the King's subjects."[2] But Cleland's sentence too was a slap on the wrist. The distribution of *Fanny Hill* was indeed eventually suspended, but not before its publisher had earned himself ten thousand pounds.

But that relative state tolerance for free speech would change. With the coming of the French Revolution, many radicals in Britain were inspired by the uprising across the Channel; activists such as Thomas Paine and Richard Price called for universal freedoms and for government by the people. So elites' fears of domestic populism and of radical groups led to innovations in systematically crushing dissent. In one state crackdown, for instance, British dissidents were labeled "Jacobins" and identified with terrorists, and press hysteria led to vigilante groups engaging in violence against them. In 1792, after having lost the American colonies, King George III issued a "Royal Proclamation against Seditious Writings." A year later, William Pitt sent spies to infiltrate British activist groups in his "reign of terror." In 1794, the government suspended habeas corpus law—and arrested activists who sought to flee. Then the "Gagging Acts" were passed, which made it a crime to hold public meetings.[3] Powerful tests of modern state controls of speech were essayed and proven out.

In spite of these persecutions, some of the ideals of the French Revolution did successfully take root across the Channel. These influences could be seen in the work of radical newsletter distributors such as Richard Carlile, who promoted American-style independence and self-government. Soon thereafter, two forms of subversiveness—political dissidence and obscenity—became linked in the eyes of the state.

And indeed there was a rationale for the state to link them: many of the pamphleteers on Holywell Street, the center of pornography distribution in Victorian London, were in fact also publishing and distributing radical political tracts. "Dissent and disorder had to be eradicated at home and abroad," writes Lynda Nead in *Victorian Babylon: People, Streets, and Images in Nineteenth-Century London.* "The submission of the radical traders of Holywell Street was called for [. . .]" by a nation seeking new "Imperial technologies" to impose order on both "deviance" and dissent.[4]

By the 1830s, there were additional good reasons for elites to find new tools to manage British speech and dissent. In 1836, huge numbers of British working men, uniting in the Chartist

Holywell Street, a main site of British pornography distribution, mid-nineteenth century.

movement, joined forces to petition Parliament for greater representation and for more rights for working people in general, including wider voting rights. In 1839, 1842, and 1848, the movement's leaders presented petitions to Parliament—and they were rejected. The third petition, its supporters asserted, contained six million names.[5]

New laws also established publicly funded education; it became clear that in the future, children of all classes would be literate enough to demand rights of their own, including, perhaps, claims to more of the wealth. By the 1850s, newly literate middle-class women clamored for property, educational, marriage, divorce, and voting rights, joining the general pressure for a more egalitarian British civil society.

Pressure from below led British political elites in the middle of the nineteenth century to look to the law in search of better ways to control domestic populations. The invention of new forms of sodomy law and obscenity law would give the state effective new tools to do so.

A drive to restrict speech also came from "voluntary associations" or "voluntary societies." These were formed in the first decade of the nineteenth century initially as ill-funded, marginal groups whose mission was to clean up "vice," such as salacious printed material and prostitution. The activist William Wilberforce, best known today for fighting to abolish slavery in Britain, was a founder of one of the most influential of these groups, the Society for the Suppression of Vice.

In the first half of the nineteenth century, such societies were made up of people who could easily be disregarded; the members were not affluent, and they were mostly female and elderly. These societies, when they were noticed at all, were gently mocked. By midcentury, though, the groups started to gain the backing of aristocrats and of other members of the elite. Powerful patrons bestowed funding that allowed the societies to purchase and destroy pornography and other illicit books and images, to bring criminal charges against distributors, and to pay lawyers' fees.

By the 1850s, the voluntary societies had a new cause to bring before the public: the influx of mass-produced pornography. Pornography flooded in from France, arriving at main distribution points in London in many forms: in lithographs, booklets of illustrations, and pamphlets that told sexually explicit stories. All of Holywell Street in London was devoted to this profitable trade.[6]

In the early 1850s, public opinion, at least as reflected in news accounts, saw the pornography-selling districts as funny, or at worst, as being a minor nuisance. When the voluntary societies initially sought to bring the wide availability of pornography to the attention of Parliament, the statesmen dismissed the groups' concerns, insisting that "indecency" was inevitably subjective: one man's Venus de Milo was another man's smut. Parliamentary debates reflected the MPs' general view—that more serious matters faced the nation.

But by 1857, the same shops that sold pornography were described, in opinion pieces, in news articles, and even in parliamentary debate, in very different ways. Now the material sold there was "filth" that could "poison" and "infect" the community, and could especially endanger the susceptible young. As public opinion and parliamentary discussion shifted to support the mission of the voluntary societies, these societies became bolder.

France, the source of alarming revolutionary influences, experienced its own backlash against freedom of speech. In the spring of 1857, the great French novelist Gustave Flaubert was prosecuted in Paris. His offense was having published sections of the novel *Madame Bovary* in serialized form in *La Revue de Paris*. To avoid prosecution, the magazine's editor, Léon Laurent-Pichat, had sought to excise several passages.

Nonetheless, Flaubert, alongside two codefendants—Laurent-Pichat and the magazine's printer, Auguste-Alexis Pillet—all faced arrest. The charge was "outrage to public and religious morals and to morality" and "offending public mores."

The government's attorney, Ernest Pinard, stressed that the crime in question was not the writing of the novel but rather its publication.[7] According to the set of concepts introduced in the trial, the printer of a book was supposed to be a guarantor of its moral purity. Attorney Pinard argued, "There is no crime without publicity, and all those who have contributed to the publicity must be equally charged." Flaubert's counsel, for his part, made the case that Flaubert was in fact promoting virtue by exposing vice. Flaubert himself sought refuge by comparing his "obscene" text with the racy classics.

While one might expect that other creators and producers of literature would have objected aloud to the prosecution of Flaubert and his publisher and printer, the trial truly intimidated Flaubert's peers. Not one author, journalist, publisher, or printer openly protested the terms that the prosecution set out. This trial established the precedent that those who wrote, edited, and printed text had an obligation to maintain "public order" and that the state, in turn, had the responsibility of managing the producers of texts.

This definition of the responsibility of the author, editor, and printer was confirmed in the verdict. On February 7, Judge Eugène Dubarle ruled against the magazine series "Madame Bovary." "Printers must read," he wrote. "[W]hen they have not read something or had it read to them, it is at their risks and perils that the Printers are not machines; they have a privilege, they swear an oath, they are in a special situation, they are responsible. Once again, they are advance sentinels; if they let an offense get by, it's as if they let pass the enemy."[8]

This metaphor revealed the attitude of the French state toward the press at that moment: the printer and publisher were now expected to protect the public safety—to serve the state. The author, editor, and printer were now all cast as patriot-warriors, defending social stability against attacks of ideas that might weaken or sicken the country.

The men involved in producing the magazine series "Madame Bovary" were chastised for contributing to the exposition of "theories" involving "realism." In other words, they were accused of creating and distributing an un-idealized portrayal of a marriage in crisis and descriptions of an adulterous wife. These stark depictions of a damaged marriage, the court found, were contrary to "the good habits, the institutions, which are the base of society."[9]

All the men were acquitted—but the trial left its mark. Followers of the Flaubert trial experienced the first presentation of a notion that is so familiar to us that we take it for granted: that words—mere air or mere marks on a page—can damage a secular *thing* of some kind that holds us all together. The trial established for the modern state that there was such a secular *thing* as "public mores" or "public order," and that books could threaten this new thing. The idea, codified in modern form in France in 1857, was further developed and adapted in England and ultimately reached the United States. It has endured in similar phrasing as a legal concept to this day. It has been exported around the world, and now into cyberspace.

It's not, according to this formulation, that the private act of writing inflicts "damages"; the damage is done when "bad" or problematic words go public. As the historian Christine Haynes points out, modern censorship—that is, censorship by the state rather than the church—is about suppressing *public* speech and affecting *public* sentiment.[10]

The French government wasted no time in using this new power to suppress speech critical of—the French government.[11] Shortly after the Flaubert trial, it suspended publication of *La Revue de Paris* for a month because the magazine had run articles that criticized the government. Soon after that, the state accused the magazine of supporting "sedition"—a word derived from Old French and meaning "speech intended to encourage people to disobey a government."[12] The magazine, already weakened by the Flaubert trial, finally ceased publication altogether.

Observers saw that state censorship—starting with the easy targets, sexual speech and imagery—was an effective weapon against political dissent in general. Was outrage against a novel about adultery really just a pretext for a novel way to persecute critics of the government? Was Emma's unruly lust the problem—or did a theatrical display of a government being upset about it propose, for that same government, a new kind of solution?

The same year, the poet Charles Baudelaire was also tried in France. Baudelaire was charged with "offending public decency" with the publication of his volume of poetry *Les Fleurs du Mal*. Six of the poems were banned and the poet was convicted and fined, along with his editors.[13] Baudelaire's trial, like the Madame Bovary trial earlier, was widely reported in Britain.

After this second famous trial, Flaubert began to censor himself prior to publication. He had been afraid that his next book, *The Temptation of St. Anthony*, would trigger another courtroom battle. Now he yielded to pressure to delete "obscene" passages in *Madame Bovary* before the manuscript was published in book form, marking scenes for deletion with a wavy line. But when it came time to set the manuscript in print, Flaubert rethought this approach and bravely instructed his book publisher, Michael Levy, to restore "everything that is crossed out in a wavy line."[14]

These French trials introduced several fresh and useful concepts to British elites and to British secular government: that there was a commons of secular (as opposed to religious) consciousness, that its well-being depended on public moral health, and that this moral health could be threatened by words and ideas, codified vaguely as "immoral literature." The core themes of modern censorship had been invented and proven effective; and they now made their way across the English Channel.

These themes, and the tools for control that they represented, reached an England being shaken in ever more extreme ways. In 1857 the Indian Rebellion took place. Sepoys—military enlistees—under the control of the British East India Company rose up against a range of what they saw as injustices; leaders of the rebels, and British women and children as well, died violently, and revolts broke out in many districts, threatening the very basis of British power in India. As the British at home read about these bloody uprisings in the crown jewel of the British Empire, they learned that British might wasn't unassailable.

In that vulnerable moment in 1857, the Society for the Suppression of Vice initiated the prosecutions of sixty-four cases. And in response, Lord John Campbell, the Lord Chief Justice of Britain, asked that a new bill against pornographic material be passed. Without such a law, he noted, prosecution for obscene publication was difficult. Lord Campbell declared that pornography was more toxic than "prussic acid, strychnine or arsenic."[15]

A number of peers opposed Lord Campbell, arguing that pornography was disgusting, yet it would be problematic to give police power to seize and destroy such material or to enter bookstores without warrants. The question "What is obscenity?" was once again pointed out in Parliament by these opponents as being a vexed and unanswerable one.

Debate over the bill was heated. It passed only after the Lord Chief Justice assured Parliament that the law was "intended to apply exclusively to works written for the single purpose of corrupting the morals of youth and of a nature calculated to shock the common feelings of decency in any well-regulated mind."[16] This phrasing would haunt five generations of British writers. Legal culpability now shifted away from the actual content created by the author to the far more nebulous issue of the intentions of the author and distributor. Lord Campbell had criminalized the interior of the author's mind in the act of literary imagination.

Also, what exactly *are* the "common feelings of decency in any well-regulated mind"?

The Obscene Publications Act of 1857 was a watershed piece of legislation. The bill gave magistrates powers to confiscate material deemed obscene, but it failed, just as opposing peers had feared, actually clearly to define "obscenity."[17] Decisions as to what crossed the line were left to the cool or the fervid imaginations of magistrates.[18] Because of this legislation, the professions of writer, editor, publisher, and bookseller had become tangibly more dangerous by the time John Addington Symonds came to professional maturity.

It was certainly a changed climate in Britain when the updated 1860 edition of *Leaves of Grass*—a version even more explicit than the first— crossed the Atlantic.

CHAPTER 5

The War against "Filth"

We've seen that by 1857, it was common to refer to mass-produced pornography as "filth" that could "infect" others. This metaphor about ideas is in use today. It is fascinating to peel back some reasons as to why this metaphor came to be so commonplace.

Not long before 1857, and for the first time in British history, cities had effectively handled outbreaks of infectious disease. The success of these major public-health measures introduced a lasting conceptual framework based on ideas of filth and infection. According to this notion, one person's moral filth is infectious to others, even to complete strangers. Even if a person has no direct connection to the purveyor of the threatening material, he or she is at risk of infection. An innovative public-health war against actual filth empowered the voluntary societies to make a new kind of case for war against "moral filth."

Victorian England's urban settings were, from our point of view, unimaginably disgusting. For example, consider human feces. Today we scarcely notice it because it is whisked away, behind closed doors, by modern plumbing. But in Symonds's London, human excrement was inescapable.

In the 1830s and 1840s, cesspits—holes, basically—were dug into the basements of the homes of the wealthy and poor alike. The inhabitants of a house defecated directly into these cesspits, and the fumes rose up into the rest of the home. Kitchens and pantries were often situated near these pools of human feces, which created many opportunities for a family's food and water supplies to become contaminated. When cesspits were full—and some did overflow—"nightsoil men" retrieved the raw feces and took it away through the streets in open wheelbarrows. Channels of raw sewage ran down the middle of some city streets: sewers used to be open, and thus human feces flowed through densely populated areas. Sewage and other filth flowed into the Thames, where people swam, washed clothing, and traveled by boat.

Other delivery systems for dirt and bacteria were the voluminous floor-length gowns, undergirded with masses of petticoats and sometimes adorned with trains, that middle-class and wealthy women wore by the 1850s. Their fashionable flounces swept the muddy roadways and followed the wearer from house to house.

Sections of every city in Britain stank, but London stank especially. Whole neighborhoods were filled with smelly fogs, which the townspeople called "miasmas" or "bad air." Stench was especially brutal where the residences of the very poor were intermingled with slaughterhouses and tanneries. The problem of how to dispose of immense quantities of feces and other filth was constantly vexing city planners and municipal officials. How a city with a booming population was to deal with what was euphemistically called "drains" was a distressing theme in letters to newspaper editors and in opinion pieces.

Not surprisingly, infectious disease epidemics were rampant. The most feared diseases, cholera and typhus, had no effective cures, let alone treatments.

The first case of cholera killed a British victim in 1831. Typhus, cholera, and tuberculosis swept repeatedly through British cities, killing tens of thousands in sequential epidemics in the 1830s and 1840s.

The way these diseases progressed was terrifying. A healthy young person would have no symptoms at all on Wednesday, appearing bright-eyed and

"Monster Soup": cartoon depicting the hazards of Thames water as seen under a microscope, circa 1828.

well; by Saturday, a cholera infection could cause her to be yellow-skinned and delusional. By that time, her body would emit streams of diarrhea so diluted that observers compared it to rice water; her intestines were lique-fying. By Sunday she would be dead.

Entire neighborhoods were carried away by these epidemics. A disease could claim a whole family in a short span of time, until only strangers were left to care for the last family member who fell ill. Desperate for an explanation, people came to believe that these diseases originated in the smells that surrounded them.

By the 1830s, microscopes had become effective enough to reveal microorganisms in drops of water. But epidemiology was in its infancy; no one realized that the diseases were being spread by infected water and through mosquito bites.

Then, in 1839, Charles Blomfield, the bishop of London, recommended to the House of Lords that an inquiry be made into the sanitation of the poor. The result: Edwin Chadwick's *Report on the Sanitary Condition of the Labouring Population of Great Britain* of 1842.[1] Across the realm, newspapers featured insights from this four-hundred-page tome. The report firmed up two ideas in the public mind: first, that there was a direct connection between unsanitary living conditions and disease; and second, that this unsanitary living on the part of some people cost everyone public money. The effects of poor living conditions—drunkenness and immorality—had economic consequences. In other words, this report established the idea (in civic rather than in religious terms) that uncleanness was not just a personal physical issue, but also a public and moral one. Since filth generated public costs and consequences, the state had a role to play in its management. Thus a framework for a "moral economy" in civil society was put into place.

The motto of this new mid-Victorian idea could be summarized as "one [diseased] member of a society threatens all."[2] We have for so long held this idea—that someone else's filth can affect us, and that the state is responsible for cleaning it up on our behalf—that we scarcely question it. But it is part of recent modernity; it is an idea that was invented less than two hundred years ago.

In the aftermath of this sensational report, Parliament passed the Nuisances Removal and Diseases Prevention Act of 1846, which was also known as the Cholera Bill. The new law allowed municipal inspectors to enter a person's home and demand information about how that person's household disposed of human waste. The bill also forced homeowners to connect their formerly private and isolated, if disgusting, cesspools to a brand-new utility: the public municipal sewer. The sewer system was a network, of course, that connected everybody. It created a commons of filth.[3] Susan Sontag's 1978 essay "Illness as Metaphor" is grounded, as are many modern ideas about psychic and physical contamination, on this mid-Victorian understanding of infection: "Any disease that is treated as a mystery and acutely enough feared will be felt to be morally, if not literally, contagious."[4]

From the 1840s through the 1860s, various cities' ongoing fights against waves of deaths from cholera, typhus, and other contagious diseases contributed to proliferation of the "contagion theme" in civil debate.[5] These public health battles boosted the rationale for aggressive, even intrusive, state intervention in spaces that used to be considered completely personal. It was the British who had expressed their traditional love of privacy by invoking, for people of any class, that "a man's home is his castle." But if the "home" was unwholesome and endangered others, it could now be—indeed, *should* be—breached by state experts.

In 1849, a wave of disease claimed fifty-three thousand British lives. Many of the victims sickened and died within twelve hours.[6] This trauma prepared people to accept intrusions they might otherwise have resisted. Thus the laws against actual physical filth became ever more aggressive. (Additional Nuisance Removal Acts would follow in 1855, 1863, and 1866.)[7]

John Snow, a British physician, was not convinced by the "miasma" theory of infection. Through careful epidemiological study, in 1854 he located a pump in Soho with contaminated water. People who drew their water from this pump, he saw, disproportionately fell ill and died. The London council found Snow's argument persuasive enough to conduct an experiment: the pump's handle was removed. Death rates in the neighborhood plummeted.

After this revelation of the waterborne origin of cholera, London further overhauled its recently constructed sewer system. The city now separated channels for sewage from channels for drinking water; though this seems hard for us to believe, it was the first time in Britain that sources of drinking water and human waste were separated by the municipality. The city routed sewage away from communities and started to sink pipes underground. A massive public works program began to enclose eighty-two miles of sewers; this eliminated much of the danger and the "stink." Civil engineers engaged with this overhaul, such as engineer Sir Joseph Bazalgette, became heroes.

This transformation in the handling of human waste was a massive feat of engineering. It naturally became a hugely popular public-health success.

Metropolitan Board of Works's chief engineer Joseph Bazalgette (*top right*) at London's Abbey Mills pumping station sewer construction, 1862.

The intensity of disease epidemics died down. This vast underground network of pipes that now carried drinking water into houses and human waste out of houses connected everyone in a newly intimate way.

After the new discoveries about transmission of typhoid and cholera, municipal and state campaigns to sterilize or isolate infectious agents escalated. Vaccination offers a parallel example: the Vaccination Act of 1853, which made it compulsory to vaccinate infants for smallpox, was followed by that of 1867, which added cumulative fines for parents' noncompliance and extended the age of children to be vaccinated.[8] By 1885 a vaccination officer had the power to press charges, and new justifications as well to continually intrude upon and monitor what had been, previously, citizens' private lives.

The metaphor of contagion has proven durable: phrases invoking contagion were used during the Communist and Nazi eras to justify imprisoning Jews, union leaders, editors, activists, and homosexuals. The same metaphors surfaced during the AIDS scares of the 1980s in Britain and the United States. In that decade, a great deal of energy was devoted to public discussion in the United States in order to reassure a phobic public that AIDS could not be caught through the air or through casual contact; there was an irrational resistance to the science of actual HIV transmission. Indeed, fairly recent homophobic law invokes these ideas virtually intact: Britain's Section 28 of the Local Government Act, passed in 1988, took aim squarely at both "lifestyles" and words considered capable of "infecting" the commons: it forbade local authorities from "intentionally promot[ing]" homosexuality, or from teaching the acceptance of homosexual "pretended family relationship[s]."[9] It also prevented councils from spending money on educational materials that were seen as promoting a homosexual lifestyle.

The contagion metaphor descended to us in many forms.

Surely this reflexive use of it dates back to the Victorian period, when the notion of "social infection" was invented to explain how "filth" affects everyone.

The reflex of using a "social contagion" trope is prevalent in the way that modern commentators, religious activists, and men and women on the street express homophobia. Its legacy is also often apparent when censorship is being justified.

How exactly does what I read on my computer, in my private home, affect others? How do we describe the way it matters to others what someone says in a lecture on a college-campus speaker's stage? Could we not just as reasonably maintain the Enlightenment notion that these are just words, ideas, to be considered by reasoning minds, and not actually fearsome germs that may invade the commons and infect new hosts? The Victorian fight against cholera and typhus and the success of the London sewer system also foreordained how we now talk about the Internet. Like the early sewer system, that "network" is seen as connecting us all, whether we are clean or unclean. The discussion of censorship today invokes the illogical premise that if you "scrub" speech that some may find offensive or hateful from public view, you can maintain social health. Indeed, in 2018 Twitter started to put users who had spoken in ways that Twitter found objectionable into "quarantine."

Once ideas were characterized as "filth" or as infectious agents, the state was able to secure a role, and thus power, in cleaning up the commons. Over time it would seek, increasingly aggressively, to define the "commons"—and to decide what and who was "clean." The cholera battle and Snow's and Bazalgette's victory against it handed a trope to the British judiciary as well. The idea that the invasion of private spaces was "for the good of all" almost immediately expanded to include other kinds of scrutiny of personal actions and bodily functions and fluids—a policing of the body and consensual relationships, as we'll see in chapter 15, that had not previously been considered a function of the modern state. Public moral health could be threatened by immoral words and behaviors.

Sentencing followed the state's arrogation of the right to police the body and intrude on personal privacy.

CHAPTER 6

Sodomy as Part of the 1857 Reform of Divorce Law

The circumstances of the re-invention of modern homophobia were so unique that one could say that it was influenced by something largely unrelated to what men did together in bed. There is a case to be made that one influence on modern homophobia, among many, is the perpetuation of the sexual double standard between men and women that was codified in a set of decisions crafted to protect the privilege of straight men to commit adultery and other much more serious sexual misdeeds, without the inconvenience of facing too much social opprobrium or of being divorced by their wives—the decisions that resulted in the 1857 Matrimonial Causes Act.

Before 1857, modern civil divorce, readily available to the masses, didn't exist in Britain. Obtaining a divorce through the Church of England was the primary option available: "The ecclesiastical courts had jurisdiction over divorce cases and issued two kinds of decrees," writes Professor Mary Lyndon Shanley in "'One Must Ride Behind': Married Women's Rights and the Divorce Act of 1857."[1] These were called *a mensa et thoro* (divorce from bed and board) and *a vinculo matrimonii* (divorce from the bonds of marriage). Parliament was the only institution that could grant the second form of divorce, which did permit subsequent remarriage. As Professor Stuart Anderson points out, decrees *a mensa* were "effectively legal separations and [. . .] only the Parliamentary decree enabled remarriage."[2]

Ecclesiastical divorce proceedings were hard to get, slow-moving, and costly. One could get a divorce, as noted, via "a private act of parliament." But, as Professor Shanley showed, "[o]btaining a parliamentary divorce was legally complex and extraordinarily expensive."[3] As a result of these hurdles, there were very few divorces in Britain every year.

The situation was worsened by what many women of the time saw as an onerous double standard for women seeking divorce. "Aggravating a married woman's plight was the fact that it was extremely difficult for her to extricate herself from the bonds of matrimony."[4] It was almost impossible for a woman to leave even a severely abusive husband. In order to do so, she had to prove to the ecclesiastical court that her husband's physical abuse was severe enough to harm her health or even threaten her life.

At midcentury, though, there was pressure for reform. The first generation of women to receive publicly funded education, many of those in the broadening middle classes, were now young adults. For the first time in recorded Western history women were formally organizing on behalf of their own gender.

The very first of these feminist groups had started to meet in London. One of the leaders who emerged from this foment was the extraordinary Barbara Smith Bodichon. She was the daughter of a radical MP, Benjamin Smith, and a milliner, Anne Longden. Longden had been seduced by Smith when she was just seventeen. The couple had lived together openly but had never married, which was a scandal at the time. (This unusual family nurtured strong-willed women: it also produced Bodichon's cousin, the radical nurse-activist Florence Nightingale.) Barbara Smith's mother had died from tuberculosis during Smith's childhood.

Bodichon grew up experiencing both the social privilege of having an independent income and the social alienation of being the child of an unmarried union.

By the 1850s, she was rich in friendships with remarkable women of the time. Among her closest friends was the already-legendary novelist George Eliot. The writer Christina Rossetti was an acquaintance.

Etchings and paintings of Bodichon show a fair-haired woman with pale skin and a Roman profile. In one painting, by her friend Mary Osborne, Bodichon sits up very straight, at work at her easel—yet dressed in a sumptuous jade-green satin gown, trimmed at the neck and bosom with what looks like fox or mink. She holds up her chin proudly; her gaze is distant and self-possessed.

In 1854, Bodichon published an essay, *A Brief Summary in Plain Language of the Most Important Laws Concerning Women, Together with a Few Observations Thereon*. One of the first arguments to identify and attack the sexual exploitation of women by men, it was widely discussed.[5] Bodichon argued that women should be in possession of their own sexual bodies. The legal reality, though, as she pointed out, was very different: "A woman's body," she complained, "belongs to her husband [. . .] she is in his custody, and he can enforce his right by a writ of habeas corpus. What was her personal property before marriage, such as money in hand, money at the bank, jewels, household goods, clothes, etc., becomes absolutely her husband's, and he may a sign or dispose of them at his pleasure whether he and his wife live together or not."[6]

The same year that Bodichon published her *Brief Summary*, the conservative poet Coventry Patmore wrote his popular poem "The Angel in the House," which sketched out an extreme ideal of mid-Victorian feminine submissiveness. "Her disposition is devout," he hymned piously; "Her countenance angelical." In 1854, Caroline Norton, a writer who had suffered under ecclesiastical divorce law, circulated *English Laws for Women in the 19th Century*, a powerfully written essay that attacked laws regarding married women's property rights.

Norton also lobbied Queen Victoria, publishing *A Letter to the Queen on Lord Chancellor Cranworth's Marriage and Divorce Bill* in 1855. Norton "denounced the obliteration under the common law of a woman's legal personality upon marriage, which made it impossible for a wife to hold property in her own name. She also condemned a proposed divorce law that would have lent statutory sanction to the sexual double standard by making it possible for husbands to divorce their wives, but not wives their husbands."[7] After this letter appeared, "the issues of married women's rights to control their own property and of the sexual double standard and divorce became inextricably intertwined as Parliament debated and amended the bill that would become the Divorce Act of 1857."[8]

A group of Bodichon's female friends and colleagues formed an activist group to write commentary and mobilize petitions, calling themselves the Langham Place group; mockers referred to them as the "Ladies of Langham." Bodichon spoke to the House of Commons committee that sought to address inequalities in the laws affecting married women and their property; in the 1850s Barbara Leigh Smith and the Langham Place group petitioned Parliament to end the double standard in how men's and women's property was treated. When that request looked as if it would fail, they sought the insertion of provisions that benefited women in the Divorce Act of 1857. The group aggressively lobbied Parliament to pass laws to give married women rights over their own incomes—and over their own bodies—joining what would be an epic fight for these basic rights.[9] (The formal suffrage movement as started by Bodichon and Emily Davies gained momentum almost a decade later, when—via John Stuart

Mill—they presented a petition signed by 1,500 women and men to Parliament in 1866.[10]) As the right to property was connected to the right to
vote, this petition argued that women with property should also be entitled
to vote. These early feminists sought educational, economic, suffrage, and
sexual rights and worked out a model for future feminist activism. Women
lobbied Parliament assertively starting from the 1850s and extending into
a second generation, with peaks of activism leading up to 1870 related to
the 1870 Married Women's Property Act, and again into the 1880s and
1890s, to pass laws to give married women increasing rights over their own
incomes—and over their bodies.[11] The 1880s also witnessed, as we will see,
intense organized activism to protect young girls from being trafficked
sexually.[12]

Dozens of petitions addressing inequalities affecting women poured
into Parliament, often with thousands of signatures.[13] An 1856 petition
seeking to reform property law garnered as many as 3,000 signatures from
London and 26,000 from the entire country.[14]

Women "denounced the sexual double standard implicit in the differing
grounds of divorce for men and women, and they deplored the inability of
married women—including wives who were separated but not divorced from
their husbands—to hold property in their own names."[15] The sexual double
standard was galling to many women: "The action for criminal conversion,"
for instance, in which an adulterer is accused, could only be initiated by
men and not by women.[16] "In addition to providing a monetary award, a
successful action for criminal conversion was a prerequisite for entering a
suit for a parliamentary divorce, the only way to end a marriage other than
by ecclesiastical annulment."[17] Another inequity was that, under common
law, fathers had unassailable rights in gaining custody of children.[18]

Emboldened by this spectacle, other small cells of female activists
started to publish feminist tracts too and to pass them from hand to hand—
just as *Leaves of Grass* was now being passed from reader to reader. The
fight over woman's role—as agent of her own destiny or as domesticated,
other-defined "Angel in the House"—was dramatically underway. Though
now largely erased from accounts of the Victorian era studied in schools
and colleges, these "first-wave" feminist battles over the status and role of
women were as pronounced and passionate, and as widely covered in the
press, if not more so, as any of the feminist battles in more recent Western
history. "The Woman Question" became one of the most pressing debates
of the decade, and it did not abate for the rest of the century.

Central to this fierce debate was the institution of marriage and the question of how to end it if a marriage was insupportable. Dozens of novels and poems elucidated the double standard in marriage and divorce. Bestsellers, read voraciously by women, dramatized the injustices of what women were starting to call the "slave market" of middle-class marriage and the "slavery" of forced prostitution. Women's fiction also depicted working-class, poor, and rural women being treated as sexual playthings by affluent men. Elizabeth Gaskell's *Ruth* (1853) and George Eliot's *The Mill on the Floss* (1860) sympathetically portrayed naive young women from the provinces, "ruined" by older, wealthy men and then cast aside. Eliot may have been influenced by the thinking of her friend Barbara Bodichon.

Reform of divorce law had been under discussion for some time: a Royal Commission for Divorce had been convened in 1850. "England had no provision for civil divorce other than the extraordinary procedure of a private act of parliament," Prof. Mary Shanley points out, adding that for all practical purposes, then, divorce with permission to remarry was available only to wealthy men; only four women had ever managed to secure a parliamentary divorce. The commission recommended that Parliament create a civil court to grant divorce *a vinculo*.[19] But the commissioners also advised that only a wife's adultery, not a husband's, be cause for this kind of divorce.

In 1854, Lord Cranworth, the Lord Chancellor, presented a divorce bill, which went nowhere. He again submitted a bill in 1856. This time around, the tenor of the debate was very different—in part due to the impact of Caroline Norton's *A Letter to the Queen*.[20] Some who had championed married women's property rights joined forces with Norton in attacking the provisions of Cranworth's bill, which, in line with the commission's recommendations, treated men and women differently in specifying grounds for divorce.[21]

In 1857, women nationwide intensely followed feminist agitation. At the same time that the petition regarding married women's property was being presented to Parliament, "[t]he House of Lords was debating a bill to create a civil Divorce Court." Prof. Shanley notes that while before this time, the issues of married women's property and the divorce bill issues were seen as separate, from this moment on, the issues were "inseparably linked."[22]

Now parliamentarians turned their attention to the clamoring women around Barbara Bodichon, who continued to call for reforms to property, marriage, and voting laws. "The conjunction of [. . .] various interests helped convince Parliament to pass many of the measures sought by feminists. The reforms dealing with marriage law, however, invariably fell short of the principle of spousal equality, which lay at the heart of feminists' proposals."[23] Newspapers reported daily on the progress of the divorce bill in Westminster. Women stated clearly that the bill should do away with the sexual double standard in divorce, whereby women lost their property, their children, and their places in society when they left even a very bad husband. They also wanted to end the double standard concerning adultery.

The debate record of 1856 and 1857 shows that parliamentarians, all of them of course male, decided almost immediately that a man could divorce his wife if she had committed adultery. "[M]ost members of Parliament were very far from thinking that a husband's adultery was as serious as a wife's [. . .] [N]either the Lords nor the Commons accepted Lord Lynd-hurst's proposal to equalize the grounds for divorce."[24] Also, as Shanley notes, "Members of Parliament seemed reluctant to curtail the sexual adventures of members of their own class."[25]

Then—there was an awkward pause. The legislators seemed to realize that if they responded to feminist pressure with equal language for wives, then they—and indeed all of the men of Britain—would be stuck with a law granting wives the same right: to divorce a husband simply on the grounds of his adultery. In records of the discussion, the MPs circled around and around this issue, stalling and uncomfortable.

Finally, several parliamentarians stepped in: they proposed, instead, a few rare situations in which a wife might indeed divorce her husband. If the husband was extremely cruel, for instance, and if he abandoned his wife altogether, well then, she might divorce him. These minor concessions seemed to present a promising solution.

William Ewart Gladstone, the Liverpool-born member of Parliament who helped found the Liberal Party, was a force in the House. He now jumped into the fray, hoping, no doubt, to craft a policy that would be popular among men—who voted—and also be tolerable to the women who were watching so closely. He had added dozens of changes to the bill. Now he contributed to the debate his recommendation that a woman might divorce her husband in the event of rape (of another woman; marital rape was legal). The members agreed to Gladstone's proposal.

Still the debate continued, anxiously, as the parliamentarians wrestled to find circumstances that would seem somewhat fair to the ladies yet still have minimal effects on the gentlemen. Though men had the absolute right to divorce adulterous wives, they did not wish to grant wives the right to divorce them in turn for mere male heterosexual adultery.

Finally, the MPs resolved the matter. They wrote into the bill that female adultery was grounds for divorce, and male adultery wasn't. They left the sexual double standard unchanged. The parliamentarians got what they knew many heterosexual male constituents wanted.

But that inequitable resolution sounded, of course, too nakedly unjust. So they wrote in the exceptions. Male adultery provided grounds for a wife's divorce, they added, but they then created a thicket of tricky caveats and certain extreme permissible circumstances: if her husband had committed adultery with a relative of the wife's, or if he had done so right in the marital home, or if he was bigamously married to another wife at the same time and then had the energy to betray both wives with a third partner; they included Gladstone's suggestion, granting divorce to a wife who could prove that her husband had raped another woman; a woman would receive a divorce if she was able to prove that her husband was adulterous, but with such an extreme level of cruelty to herself that the cruelty alone would have otherwise entitled her to a divorce, or if she was able to prove that her husband had not only committed adultery but also that he had deserted her for over two years . . . and so on. As if all of these conditions were not enough to safeguard the privileges of male heterosexual adultery, another MP, Mr. Wigham, proposed finally that the words "being proved by conviction" be added to the entirety of conditions in the bill: in other words, it was up to the wronged wife to provide definitive proof that any such situation existed in her marriage.[26]

So, finally: if the adulterous husband didn't bring his mistress home, if he didn't assault his mistress, if his adulterous lover wasn't an actual blood relative of his wife's, if he carried on his affair but didn't abandon his wife, if he abandoned her for just a year and a half while carrying on his affair, if he didn't commit himself to a bigamous second marriage, and so on—whew— under the conditions of most ordinary adultery on a husband's part, then that husband would be just fine.

"The majority in the Parliaments of 1856 and 1857 [. . .] would go no further than to allow women to divorce their husbands for such egregious offenses as incest, bigamy, or gross physical cruelty—a reflection of their ardent desire to change the traditional law of marriage, and the traditional status of married women, as little as possible [. . .] [T]he Divorce Act sanctioned and perpetuated a patriarchal understanding of the marriage bond."[27]

Thus the shape of the first British civil divorce bill applicable to the masses became clear: a man could divorce his adulterous wife, plain and simple, but a heterosexual man could be divorced by his wife only if he committed various arcane, very strenuous, or rare sexual and emotional misdeeds.

To keep these husband-friendly carve-outs from seeming too obviously absurd, one presumably heterosexual parliamentarian came up with two additional circumstances under which a woman had the right to leave her husband: if he had sex with an animal—"bestiality" was added to Gladstone's clause concerning marital rape—or if he had sodomitical sex (which had been grounds for divorce before the reform as well, but which was a stipulation that had been part of a divorce process affecting far fewer people in the past).[28]

So the bill now coined the tripartite phrase: a woman could divorce a man guilty of "rape or sodomy or bestiality."[29]

The average adulterous heterosexual man who wished to stay married but also wished to continue to have sex with women outside of marriage—but who did not have any interest in having sex with animals or sodomitical sex, perhaps with other men—was quite safe now to continue his heterosexually adulterous ways.

The Matrimonial Causes Act of 1857 stated:

> [I]t shall be lawful for any Wife to present a Petition to the said Court, praying that her Marriage may be dissolved, on the Ground that since the Celebration thereof her Husband has been guilty of incestuous Adultery, or of Bigamy with Adultery, or of Rape, or of Sodomy or Bestiality, or of Adultery coupled with such Cruelty as without Adultery would have entitled her to a Divorce *Mens et Thoro*, or of Adultery coupled with Desertion, without reasonable Excuse, for Two Years or upwards . . .[30]

At this breakthrough, most members of Parliament engaged in the discussion seemed to pause and breathe a collective sigh of relief.

Edward Sugden, First Baron St. Leonards, was a member of the House of Lords who demurred. Sugden was an unusual member of the House of Lords; like Barbara Bodichon, he had risen from origins outside the Establishment. His father had been a tradesman. As an adolescent, Sugden had struggled to secure an education. His political opponents had used this modest family background to mock him. Nonetheless, as a brilliant barrister who specialized in property law, he had risen rapidly in his profession. An etching portrays him as energetic-looking, with curling brown hair, large, expressive hands clasped on his knee, and a quizzical, half-smiling expression.

Lord St. Leonards offered a dissent and sought to cut from the bill the words "rape or sodomy or bestiality." Including them, St. Leonards warned, would create a precedent that would prove "unworkable."[31] It was not too hard for a few present at this turning point to foresee the morass of impossible-to-prove accusations, and the numberless broken lives that lay ahead with the adoption of this wording.

But Lord St. Leonards did not prevail. The bill, with the tripartite coinage of the "worst things ever" a man could do, was passed.

British women recognized this patently unjust tangle of conditions from the outset for what it was and vociferously criticized the conditions. But it was too late: the Matrimonial Causes Act of 1857 was now the law of the land.

Shanley describes how Caroline Norton had foreseen this equivocation: "Why did men balk so at the suggestion that Parliament should enact a uniform divorce law holding men and women to the same standard of conduct? In part because 'men fear to curb the license of their own pleasures,' Norton asserted."[32]

So sodomy between two men now mattered in a new way because it mattered legally to heterosexual men in a law that affected the masses. That is to say, since the prosecution of male-male sodomy could now be used to distract attention from heterosexual men's adultery, the sodomy of men with other consenting men now mattered to heterosexual men who themselves had no personal involvement with the "sodomites" in question. And recasting that consensual sodomy between adults as "the worst thing" imaginable that a man might do sexually, along with the crimes of rape and bestiality—as a terrible social threat, an outrageous spectacle of degradation—now had proven value to those whose own private lives benefited from this distraction.

Since sodomy was now a category of inquiry in a civil divorce law that would affect thousands, the state was even more interested in the act and had an even stronger incentive to demonize it.

But now, because of the way the divorce bill had made use of men's relations with other men—I would argue, as a distraction—sodomy changed its valence.

This redefinition—giving the majority of heterosexual men a reason to care about other men's sodomy, even if it was consensual—is at the very center of the modern revision of homophobia. This redefinition is indeed part of the DNA of modern homophobia and helps explain some of its deeply irrational essence. Like the earlier "filth," now "sodomy" was defined by the leaders of the state as having a direct effect on the commons—women and children; heterosexual marriage; the very stability of society.

This recasting of sodomy was a new way to let the state indicate that sodomy was among the worst things a man could do.[33] The Matrimonial Causes Act construed sodomy as directly undermining the patriarchal family; the act of sodomy was now worse than anything that faithless, violent or cruel heterosexual men might choose to do to women. The law placed sodomy in a legal category in a way that affected the masses, alongside sexual violence, and also alongside the most unnatural act the human imagination could conjure: sexual species transgression.

And so the phrase "rape or sodomy or bestiality" was codified into a law that affected the many, and not the few.

We tend to be encouraged to think that sodomy was always proscribed in such terms—and that these have been consistent in the West. We are asked to believe that the human condition has always included the aversive emotionality and heightened, emotional language of modern homophobia.

But this is not the case.

The language describing sodomy from the eighteenth century to 1857 in Britain had ranged from gossipy to amused to heated to religiously censorious to legalistic. But in some public platforms, it ramped up into a phobic emotionality that was almost hysterical. Following the passage of the Matrimonial Causes Act, newspaper opinion pieces, court records, and pamphlets erupted anew with language in relation to sodomy and to sodomites. Civil society in many areas, but notably in the popular press, tried to find ways to say "the thing that is beyond the pale," "the thing so bad it cannot even be identified": "vicious," "heinous," "morbid," "unspeakable."

It is worth casting back to understand how laws against sodomy, opinions about sodomites, and language describing them have differed at various times. Certainly the Roman Catholic Church has a constant violent history of condemning male-male intimacy, and specifically sodomy. One source is certain translations of the Hebrew Bible that employed highly charged words. In the King James Version, Leviticus 18:22, for instance, is translated as "Thou shalt not lie with mankind as with womankind: it is abomination." To this day, homophobes cite this passage in denouncing, presumably with God's imprimatur, the act of men sleeping with men. But the reality of even that quotation is not that black and white.

The word "abomination" and even the word "sodomite" have had mutable meanings.[34] Sodomy law in Britain goes back to two medieval strictures, called *Fleta* and *Britton*. Alok Gupta, in *This Alien Legacy: The Origin of "Sodomy" Laws in British Colonialism*, argues that *Fleta* called for "[a]postate Christians, sorcerers, and the like," as well as sodomites, to be drawn and quartered. The Hon. Michael Kirby, a retired justice of the High Court of Australia, points out in "The Sodomy Offense: England's Least Lovely Export?" that in the Middle Ages, "sodomy" did not only denote anal sex between men; it could also indicate any sex act deemed "irregular." "Sodomy" in the Middle Ages could refer to any nonprocreative sex act, such as masturbation.[35]

And the term could include even more practices in which people whom we would today call heterosexuals engaged. According to Gupta, with *Fleta*, "sodomy" was what you committed if you had sexual contact with a Jew or a Jewess, or with a Saracen, or if you were a man having sex with another man. In any such case, the appropriate punishment was to be buried alive. *Britton*, for its part, also called for death for sodomites, along with the burning of heretics and of "renegades." Gupta makes the point that this "grab-bag of offenses" was not meant to single out men who had sex with men in particular, but rather to target various "enemies within" in what had become a "persecuting society." In such a setting, anyone who might pose the threat of pollution—witches, heretics, sorcerers, Turks, people engaged in various types of nonreproductive sex—had to be controlled: "It was a way of segregating the Christian, European self from alien entities that menaced it with infection."[36]

Some historians argue that levels of prosecution and social acceptance of men who slept with men varied at different times and places across Europe in the Middle Ages.[37] The late Yale medievalist John Boswell makes this case in his important book *Christianity, Social Tolerance, and Homosexuality: Gay People in Western Europe from the Beginning of the Christian Era to the Fourteenth Century*. He argues that in the early medieval period, there was often an "absence of the negative attitudes" to homosexuality "ubiquitous in the Modern West."[38] Other historians take issue with this reading and warn against minimizing the church's centuries of crimes against gay men. This serious debate about the cultural history of homophobia in the West does at least reveal that both homophobia, as we understand the notion today, and also a quiet or implicit social acceptance of male-male love have taken many forms in the past.

The streamlining of British laws under Henry VIII led to a 1533 statute, the Buggery Act, criminalizing "sodomy" as a state concern rather than solely as the purview of the church. It spelled out the "detestable and abominable Vice of Buggery committed with mankind or beast," and it was punishable by execution. After 1533, British men convicted of sodomy were hanged.

From the Renaissance until the late eighteenth century, courts in Europe were restrictive in specifying the acts to which the term "sodomy" actually referred. Nonetheless, there were extraordinary flare-ups of violent hysteria: in 1730, for instance, more than 250 Dutch men were accused of the crime, and 24 were put to death. But in general, during these centuries, prosecutions for sodomy, a difficult crime to prove prior to the invention of medical forensics, were infrequent. Many European countries did not treat the act as a crime at all. In France it had been a capital offense, but as we saw, in 1791, it was totally decriminalized.

In *Nameless Offences*, H. G. Cocks found 8,000 committals in the nineteenth century, and looked at 105 petitions for mercy written by those accused of same-sex offenses before 1870: "A large proportion relate to ordinary offenders and even illiterate laborers who had been condemned to death."[39]

He identifies about eight terms for same-sex offenses and uses a methodology that cross-references court records with newspaper accounts. Dr. Charles Upchurch, in *Before Wilde: Sex between Men in Britain's Age of Reform*, finds comparable high figures using a similar methodology; analyzing newspaper accounts and court records, he found 471 trials between 1820 and 1870 reported in the *Morning Post*, while the *Times* reported on "321 cases heard in the criminal courts or police courts" in the same period.[40] His conclusion is that newspapers such as the *Times* (the newspapers that Symonds's family read) were filled with stories of same-sex offense and extortion trials.

A 1781 British case established the precedent that, in order for sodomy to be proven to have occurred, a prosecutor had to establish that semen had been emitted into another man's body. So from 1781 to 1828, male-male sex did not necessarily result in a capital sentence in Britain—as long as a man charged could assert that he had withdrawn his penis from the body of his lover prior to ejaculation.[41] Prof. Cocks sees the "larger story" of legal persecution of men for sodomy in the nineteenth century as "the gradual assumption by the state of the routine business of policing sexual behaviour. This can be seen in the increasingly pervasive laws against homoerotic behaviour in the 19th century. The story there is the development of laws (from the early 18th century onwards) which criminalise *all* forms of homoerotic behaviour between men, and not only sodomy."[42]

As Prof. Cocks puts it:

> The state of English law on same-sex acts (between men) was as follows: by the early 18th century at the latest, all homoerotic acts, suggestions or invitations to such were regarded by the courts as illegal under the 1533 law of Henry VIII (even though that law outlawed sodomy alone and did not specify any particular sexual acts). After 1698 all forms of homoeroticism that fell short of anal penetration were regarded in law as "attempts" to commit the felony (sodomy), even in cases where no such attempt to penetrate someone had actually been made. As the common law developed in the 18th and early 19th century, it became clear that all same-sex acts or invitations to them were illegal, including oral sex. So there were essentially two homoerotic offences: sodomy and "attempts" to commit it. There were also invitations, incitements and conspiracies to commit the offence [. . .] [V]agrancy laws could also be used against soliciting, "importuning" etc. The other "unnatural offence" was bestiality (maybe 25% of the total in the first half of the century, mostly occurring in rural areas).[43]

In 1827 an arrest for sodomy involved a nineteen-year-old, James Farthing. But the charge went nowhere: "his Majesty postponed the case of Farthing and respited the rest 'during his royal pleasure.'"[44] The Crown itself announced that it was looking away when presented with such evidence.

As I noted earlier, microscopes were not readily available until the end of this period—and even then, they were costly and cumbersome. An exhibit of microscopes at the Museo Galileo in Florence, Italy, reveals that the average size of microscopes in the early nineteenth century was several feet high.[45] They were massive toys collected by aristocrats for their private museums of curiosities; these instruments were very difficult for ordinary prosecutors to secure.[46] Their cost and bulk made it hard for most prosecutors to use them to prove the location of emission on the accused's body, or indeed whether ejaculation had taken place at all.

There are no mentions of sodomy at all given in a search of Hansard (the British parliamentary record) for the years 1818 to 1828. (Scholars on this subject point out that parliamentarians avoided using the term "sodomy," so this search would not yield the full record of parliamentary discussions of bills or laws about same-sex offenses.) But by 1828 the Offences Against the Person Act updated the 1533 law against "buggery." There are no further mentions of "sodomy" convictions in a search of Hansard until 1830.

Most current historians report, as I mentioned, that 1835 was the last year in which men were killed for sodomy in Britain: "the last two Englishmen who were hanged for sodomy were executed in 1835. James Pratt and John Smith died in front of Newgate Prison in London on 27 November of that year."[47]

But in spite of severe laws remaining on the books, men found ways to be together.

That relative privacy did not last. The decision maintaining that the crime of sodomy depended upon proof that a man had ejaculated into another man's body had been overturned in 1832.[48] The case was *Rex v. Reekspear*, and an act of Parliament concluded that Robert Reekspear's conviction for sodomy must stand, even though Reekspear had in fact not ejaculated inside his male partner's body.

So after 1832, in Britain, men could be sentenced to prison if proved to have engaged in any penetration at all "per anum," whether or not there was an ejaculation in the body of the other man.[49]

From 1828 to 1857, prosecutions escalated. A review of the British Library regional British newspapers database from those thirty years for mentions of "sodomy" yields only forty-five results. But Charles Upchurch, as we saw, found that there were hundreds of arrests and committals for same-sex offenses in the nineteenth century, as do H. G. Cocks and Graham Robb.

In 1850, the *Morning Chronicle* crime tables showed ten convictions for sodomy over the course of an entire decade.[50]

The systematizing of the news media and the police forces during the 1850s heralded a change. London newspapers began to publish an annual national crime table in 1853. The Metropolitan Police had been created in 1829, and a funded police force, whose arrests are reported in news outlets, needs to show results.[51] As the human rights lawyer Baroness Helena Kennedy points out, when police forces are created, they need crimes to prosecute because the new municipal expenditure must be accounted for.[52]

New mobilizations of police officers out on the beat, and the way the state began to count and publicize arrests, criminalized public spaces in new ways.

Parliamentarians and policemen complained that juries had been too reluctant to issue severe sentences.[53] Two years later, the Penal Servitude Act of 1857 formalized the option of hard labor as a sentence.[54]

This act was another dubious social invention in a year of several major social inventions.[55] In lieu of transportation or forced exile (to Australia,[56] typically, or to hard labor in penal staging areas in Gibraltar or Bermuda), the law now gave judges the option of assigning hard labor in a domestic prison, in some ways a cheaper option for the state.[57]

What is penal servitude? A brutal, terrifying regimen. Prisoners were set to walking on treadmills that went nowhere, or condemned to turning vast useless cranks, or made to pick oakum—to unravel fibers of ropes used in shipping—until their hands bled. They were used as unpaid laborers to hew stones out of quarries and to drag vessels into docks. Prisoners worked ten hours a day at these tasks. Physical anguish was intensified by deliberately inflicted psychological suffering. Prisoners were condemned to continual silence. Though they could exercise in the yard for an hour a day, they were forbidden even to whisper to one another. Isolation, as we now know, causes permanent psychological damage.

Hard labor also involved punishments of personal humiliation. The revolting prison diet led to constant diarrhea. Defecation had to take place in public, and their illnesses weakened the prisoners. The regimen devastated the digestive tract, a condition that lasted long after release from hard labor. Many former prisoners remained lifelong invalids.

In 1857, John Williams was sentenced to a year for sodomy. Courts censored how the crime of sodomy was noted in their records. For instance, twenty-eight-year-old John Thomas Burns was sentenced for two years for "the attempt" at "B———y."[58] The word "buggery," a colloquial term for sodomy, was often bowdlerized thus in official documents—and increasingly so as time went on, as the word itself became too taboo to even to spell out. Working-class boys and men were being sent to prison for experiences that many upper-class boys had as an open secret.

The year 1857 inaugurated, according to the Proceedings of the Old Bailey database, the first arrests of consenting adult male couples, though Cocks, Robb, and Upchurch found, by looking at national and London newspapers as well as court records around the country, as noted, many committals. The following is a characteristic Proceedings of the Old Bailey record of two men in Britain arrested as a couple: "On Wednesday, the 11th Day of March, at 11 O'Clock am [. . .] Ridgley Thomas and Good Christopher, Sodomy."[59] Contrary to presumptions that those arrested were violent or child abusers, H. G. Cocks found that almost half of the offenses reported in the press, 1800–1900, were explicitly consensual or nonviolent, and involved consenting acts, soliciting, or "meeting together."[60]

Charles Upchurch found an explosion of crimes of blackmail for sodomy in the middle of the nineteenth century: "Between 1811 and 1860, there were 864 trials for attempted sodomy in the London criminal courts, compared with only 116 cases of sodomy."[61] (He found that "although sodomy still carried the death penalty, and in practice was punished with a ten-year sentence after the mid-1830s, the two-year sentence for attempted sodomy was more often applied."[62]) Dr. Cocks found peaks of committals for "sodomy and related misdemeanors" in about 1833, 1845, 1861, and 1891. He notes that these are a tiny fraction of the population: "however, it has to be borne in mind that sodomy was one of the few capital crimes to survive Peel's reform of the death penalty, and that other 'unnatural crimes' were regarded as some of the most serious which could be committed."[63]

Sodomy convictions in the earlier part of the nineteenth century mostly ensnared workingmen—laborers, sailors, artisans—according to the Old Bailey Proceedings archive searches, and show that arrests began to creep up the social scale. But Upchurch's research shows that punishment did not entirely spare men of the middle classes. Prof. Cocks, in contrast, found that most of those prosecuted for same-sex offenses were poor. As Prof. Cocks put it, "For most of the century these cases emerged from everyday life—from domestic or workplace situations, or from the streets where only the incautious or the unlucky were really ever arrested. These were crimes of proximity." Their books describe men from all walks of life being targeted with arrest and even with entrapment throughout the century. The authorities, these authors found, targeted clerks, merchant seamen, small landowners, and shop owners as well as laborers.[64]

By 1857, this criminalization of everything men could do together that was intimate, reported in national newspapers that he and his friends and family read, must have been terrifying to the seventeen-year-old Symonds.

In the years 1857 through 1885, some of those convicted on charges of sodomy had to receive sentences of up to fifteen years of hard labor.

Paradoxically, now that execution wasn't the required sentence, judges seemed, at least at the Old Bailey, more willing to convict. Graham Robb explains: "The unofficial abolition of the death penalty coincided with an increase in the number of death sentences, as if judges and juries now felt free to issue their grisly warnings."[65]

In Britain, for four decades following 1857, public attention was successfully directed away from a surprisingly widespread feminist confrontation with heterosexual male sexual privilege and toward these sexual "outsiders," deemed horrifying in new ways by society's gatekeepers, who had rebranded sodomy between men as "the worst possible thing" and thus reoriented British society; this slowed the initially successful effort by angry women to start policing the sexuality of heterosexual men. The task of policing the sexuality of homosexual men was presented, and in many quarters accepted, as the real emergency.

In this way, male-male consensual sodomy was defined in the middle of the nineteenth century in Britain as worse than the rape of women by men; worse than men's purchase of barely pubescent girls for sexual violation; worse than men's seduction, impregnation, and abandonment of lower-status women and girls; worse than a husband's brutal beating of his wife; worse than a husband's theft of his wife's money; worse than a man's transmission of venereal disease to infect his wife and their unborn children; worse than a husband's false claim that his wife was insane in order to incarcerate her in an asylum—and certainly worse than heterosexual male adultery.

All of these feminist issues had been at the forefront of women's campaigns in the 1850s. But with a newly prominent sexual scapegoat, presented to British society in newly lurid terms, and in the shadow of the whipped-up anti-sodomy hysteria that followed, feminist arguments about the perfidy of heterosexual men, and the "wrongs of woman," had a much harder time gaining traction in the public arena.

And not only was heterosexual male sexual privilege protected and feminist struggle intensified; the criminology of modern homophobia was consolidated, along with the social terminology that grew up around it.

It's commonly believed that the defining moment of prosecution of gay men for same-sex sexual offenses in the nineteenth century occurred in 1895, when the author Oscar Wilde was sentenced to two years at hard labor for gross indecency.[66] But some scholars, such as H. G. Cocks, argue that little was changed by that trial.

Cocks, in *Nameless Offences: Homosexual Desire in the 19th Century*, and other scholars of queer history, such as Randolph Trumbach, author of *Sex and the Gender Revolution*, volume 1: *Heterosexuality and the Third Gender in Enlightenment London*; Jeffery Weeks, author of *Coming Out: Homosexual Politics in Britain from the Nineteenth Century to the Present*; Sean Brady, in *Masculinity and Male Homosexuality in Britain, 1861–1913*; Graham Robb, in *Strangers: Homosexual Love in the Nineteenth Century*; Charles Upchurch, in *Before Wilde: Sex between Men in Britain's Age of Reform*; and Paul Johnson, in "Buggery and Parliament: 1533–2017," have definitively adjusted the timeline, confirming without doubt that peaks of intense persecution of men for sodomy during the nineteenth century had taken place and that this persecution continued for decades, earlier than the Wilde trial.[67]

That crucially important history should be known not just by specialists and their readers, but by every reader; indeed, by every high school student.

The primary documents that undergird these works, though many people are unfamiliar with them, do indeed, as these scholars argue, confirm a lost history; in which severe punishments—dozens of executions up until 1835, and in the years after, sentences of long years of hard labor, penal servitude for life, and transportation to penal colonies—were meted out to men who loved men, and even to young boys, for decades in Britain before Wilde's famous sentencing.

And what happened to men who loved men in Britain cast a chill over all of Victorian letters, and over society as a whole.

PART III

The State Regulates Desire

CHAPTER 7

Formative Scandals

In 1858, Symonds was at Harrow, close to graduating. The fag system at Harrow remained brutal: "pretty" boys were given female nicknames, and the prettiest boy in each house was passed around to older boys as the "house tart." Alfred Pretor, a friend at Harrow, sent Symonds a letter in which Pretor confessed to a sexual relationship with the school's headmaster, Dr. Vaughan.[1] Vaughan had outwardly disapproved of the same-sex relationships at Harrow but had nursed a passion for Pretor for eight years, since the boy was eleven years old. Symonds had no problem believing that Pretor and Vaughan were involved with each other: Dr. Vaughan had earlier made a sexual approach to Symonds himself.

Nothing came of this revelation to Symonds until that autumn, when Symonds enrolled at Balliol College in Oxford. While out on a ramble, Symonds confided the story to the Corpus Christi College professor of Latin, John Conington, who was also homosexual. Conington, perhaps worried about his own future as an academic at Oxford if he kept the secret, insisted that Symonds disclose the information to his father. Feeling torn, Symonds complied. He did show his father Alfred Pretor's letter and gave the elder Symonds additional information about the rumors of Headmaster Vaughan's sexual contact with other students at Harrow.

Symonds's father—who may have been particularly adamant about the situation because by now he suspected that his son too was a homosexual—reacted by essentially blackmailing the headmaster. Dr. Symonds offered Dr. Vaughan the choice between immediate resignation from his position at Harrow or public exposure. In September 1859, Vaughan abruptly decided to retire.

Vaughan was then offered the bishopric of Rochester. At first he accepted the position. But a day or two later, under continued pressure from Dr. Symonds, Vaughan withdrew his acceptance of that post as well.

In spite of these two victories, Dr. Symonds did not let up. As the priest tried to go from position to position, the doctor pursued and hounded the man. The former headmaster eventually managed to restore his distinguished career, but he was never free of the threat of blackmail from Dr. Symonds. Vaughan asked in his will that the posthumous "life"—the reverential biography commonly issued upon the death of a distinguished Victorian leader—never be written.

So, as a teenager, Symonds saw—from within his own family circle—how the most respectable of men could be blackmailed, and his life ruined, by letters revealing male-male intimacy. The trauma of this experience was complex. Symonds's loyalty to his father also cost him valuable friendships. Unsurprisingly, Alfred Pretor believed that his friend had betrayed him unconscionably; he never spoke to Symonds again. Symonds's two closest school friends also cut off all contact with him.

What Dr. Symonds had done—using private letters for the purpose of blackmail—was becoming common. A thriving market for "purloined letters," to be used as blackmail, was developing. Anyone in Britain, but especially those with the most to lose in terms of position, could be compromised or ruined by letters that fell into the wrong hands. A private letter could suddenly, horribly, turn public, with life-altering results. So documents once considered a nearly valueless means of personal communication now became chits in a lucrative economy centered on threats and public shame. Sodomy was a crime, and private correspondence could provide evidence for it.

And sentencing marched ahead. In 1858, several convictions were handed down at the Old Bailey, not for the act of sodomy but simply for "the attempt" at sodomy. This wording may not have always referred to confirmed actual attempts to commit sodomy; rather, in some cases there likely wasn't enough physical evidence to convict for sodomy. As the Old Bailey Records database explains it, "[D]ue to the difficulty of proving this actual penetration and ejaculation many men were prosecuted with the reduced charge of assault with sodomitical intent [. . .] This charge was [also] leveled in cases of attempted or actual anal intercourse where it was thought impossible (or undesirable) to prove that penetration and ejaculation had actually occurred."[2]

In another development, as Charles Upchurch points out, consensual sex between men was being recorded as "assault" or "indecent assault."[3] New emotive language appeared in legal documentation as well: "THOMAS JOHN DAVEY (15) AND WILLIAM WILLMAN (28) were indicted for a detestable crime."[4] The conviction of men and boys for "the attempt" now entered the Proceedings of Old Bailey records more frequently, suggesting possible efforts at entrapment on the part of the municipal police, who might be looking to fill their quotas. "JAMES STEVENS (26), B—y" is found "GUILTY of the Attempt.—Confined Twelve Months."[5] And, for the first time in that record, men were tried for simply meeting each other: "CHARLES RICHARDS (32), and DANIEL PATCHING (23), were indicted for unlawfully meeting together with intent, &c. [. . .]"[6]

Men's social encounters with other men, and even their thoughts about sex with other men—without any accompanying sex acts—were becoming criminalized. Perversely, through this expansion of the law (as philosopher Michel Foucault has pointed out), a new modern category of people was being defined. What, now, were men who had thoughts, among many other thoughts, about desires for men? Or meetings, among many meetings, with men whom they might desire? They were criminals.

This development in the law had obvious implications for literature. If just thinking about sodomy and just meeting a man whom one might desire could result in a trial, then writing a poem about love and desire between men was clearly now a legal risk.

In 1859, Symonds, now at Balliol, having loved and, as he claimed in the "Set Apology," renounced his love of "W.," began to write "In Memoriam Arcadie."

In spite of the grief about the purported end of the affair that the long poem records, Symonds found inspiration and reassurance in his assigned college reading. The literary and historical heritage of classical Greece was a source of redemption for him. A conventional education at Oxford and at Cambridge at this time centered on "the Greats"—the classical texts of Greek and Roman antiquity. For many students who were attracted to men, essays from this period represented their first encounter with a mirror reflecting positively their own emotions. Symonds too had felt a sense of liberation upon first reading Plato's essays "Phaedrus" and "The Symposium." Both are essays on love: "And when the other is beside him, he shares his respite from anguish; when he is absent, he likewise shares his longing and being longed for, since he possesses that counterlove which is the image of love, though he supposes it to be friendship rather than love, and calls it by that name" ("Phaedrus").[7]

In these essays, Plato invokes a love very different from what Symonds saw as the sordid lusts of his Harrow schoolmates.[8] For Plato and other writers of classical antiquity, loving relationships between men were not only accepted but also admired, and considered far more emotionally fulfilling, and socially valued, than were relationships between women and men: male-male relationships inspired stirring discussion, the appreciation of sensuous beauty, and the discovery of one's ideal self. By contrast, the primary role of a wife in ancient Greece was procreation, and female courtesans were for sex—though some were skilled at music, and also at conversation. The Spartans perceived male-male relationships as a source of the manly virtues: love spurred warriors to courage in battle. (This tradition of accepted male-male sex and emotional attachment continued among Roman aristocrats as well.)

This Hellenistic inheritance gave Symonds's generation a means of talking safely about love between men. The critics Linda Dowling, in *Hellenism and Homosexuality in Victorian Oxford*, and Stefano-Maria Evangelista, in *British Aestheticism and Ancient Greece: Hellenism, Reception, Gods in Exile*, have established conclusively that classical antiquity became a code for homosexuality in Britain, especially at Oxford and Cambridge. "Arcadia," and classical Greece in general, let homosexual Victorian men find, as Symonds had, a culturally authoritative validation of their love for men.[9]

Symonds's college friend G. H. Shorting, for example, described himself in a letter as sharing Symonds's "'Arcadian' tastes."[10] "Hellas" was, for Symonds and for his contemporaries, an imagined dimension in which to understand their own sexuality without self-loathing.

Christianity could not offer this. "Lord make me pure before I die," Symonds had written in his eventually mutilated love poem. But "Phaedrus" and other classical texts offered, to male students who loved men, a balm for such self-hatred.

In spite of the classical texts that Symonds was reading in the Bodleian Library or in his tutors' quarters, the drumbeats in the morning papers echoed through the common rooms. The same year, sentences handed down at the Old Bailey for "the attempt" at sodomy started to extend in length, from a year to eighteen months. And teenagers were now convicted more often: indeed, that year, fourteen-year-old Thomas Silver was "indicted" for "an unnatural offence." [. . .] "GUILTY—Death recorded."[11] The result was not death but, according to Digital Panopticon, the youth served two and a half years at hard labor.

This is the first time in a search that the phrase "unnatural offence" entered the Proceedings of the Old Bailey records.

Then the language changed again in this archive, and the highly charged biblical word "abominable" appeared in the formerly matter-of-fact court record: "RICHARD ROCHE (34), was indicted for unlawfully committing, with William Clements, an abominable crime [. . .] GUILTY of the attempt—Eighteen Months Imprisonment."[12]

Symonds, still in his late teens and apparently pursuing and then grieving the end of his love affair, could easily have read about what happened to teenagers when word about their intimacy with other boys got out.

Between 1858 and 1860, sodomy sentences in the Proceedings of the Old Bailey database got longer. Now "the attempt" at sodomy was punished by sentences of at least eighteen months and up to two years in prison. Forty-three-year-old William Mepham, for instance, was "indicted for b—y [. . .] GUILTY of the attempt." He was sentenced to two years.[13] Twenty-seven-year-old William Dunlop also was "indicted for an unnatural offence [. . .] GUILTY of the attempt";[14] Dunlop received a sentence of eighteen months. Sentencing became even more aggressive: John Spencer, a sixty-year-old man, was tried three times, accused of "b—y" with three different men. The first two times, he was acquitted; for the third, his sentence was "GUILTY—Death recorded."[15] Digital Panopticon reports the outcome as "imprisoned."

Even as Symonds and "W." walked together on the towpath along the Cherwell, or lay on the grass next to one another, watching the scudding clouds, in one of the meadows near Christ Church that slopes down to the river, Symonds must have been aware that youths of his and "W."'s age were being sentenced to prison, and even sentenced to years at hard labor, for just such love.

CHAPTER 8

Calamus: "Paths Untrodden"

In 1859, Walt Whitman lost his final editing job, at the *Brooklyn Times*. Now unemployed, he was never to return to a staff position in journalism.

He was still a *flâneur*—a walker of the streets. Those critical of him described him as aimless, a "loafer." He could often be found in Pfaff's famous "bohemian" beer cellar at 653 Broadway, in Manhattan's Bowery. The novelist Allan Gurganus describes Pfaff's as countercultural: "Pfaff's was the Andy Warhol factory, the Studio 54, the Algonquin Round Table all rolled into one."[1] When Whitman was a habitué, radical personalities such as the actress Adah Isaacs Menken and popular talents such as the actor Edwin Booth drank the large glasses of champagne that Charles Ignatius Pfaff, the owner, poured there and enjoyed the lavish breakfasts he offered.

Whitman also returned to the manuscript of *Leaves of Grass*, which had been through two editions—in 1855 and 1856. In March 1860, he traveled to Boston to meet with his new publisher, the firm of Thayer and Eldridge, which was preparing a major edition of two to five thousand copies, a vast expansion over the print runs of the first two editions.

This edition looked dramatically different yet again—various cloth bindings, in orange, green, and brown, contained the pages. Font sizes and styles varied; there were line drawings around some of the titles and added to the beginnings and ends of poems. Illustrations such as a globe emerging from a cloud—and a sunrise—were dispersed throughout.[2]

To this version Whitman added two provocative sets of verses: one was the "Calamus" cycle of poems, also called the "Live Oak" cycle; it portrays romantic and physical love between men. (A calamus plant, or *Acorus calamus*, is a water plant with a distinctly phallic shape.)

The second notable set of new poems was called "Enfans d'Adam" ("Children of Adam").[3] "Enfans d'Adam" graphically describes heterosexual eroticism. With these two sets of poems, Whitman went even further than he had in 1855 and 1856 to sanctify the explicitly sensual.

Just before this third edition came out, Whitman also visited the eminent Ralph Waldo Emerson. Without the elder writer's permission, Whitman had earlier emblazoned Emerson's letter of endorsement on the very cover of a second 1855 edition of *Leaves of Grass*. Emerson had by now forgiven the younger man for this self-promotional use of his letter. Now Emerson warned Whitman that he should remove the explicit "Enfans d'Adam" poems before publishing the volume. Whitman flatly refused.[4]

The "Calamus" poems start with a mission statement. Whitman is "[n]o longer abashed." He insists, with language like a trumpet blast, that he at last will "tell the secret of my nights and days." His soul, he declares, "rejoices only in comrades."[5]

> [. . .] *in this secluded spot I can respond as I would not dare elsewhere,*
> *Strong upon me the life that does not exhibit itself, yet contains all the rest,*
> *Resolved to sing no songs to-day but those of manly attachment [. . .]*
> *Bequeathing, hence, types of athletic love,*
>
> [. . .] *I proceed, for all who are, or have been, young men,*
> *To tell the secret of my nights and days,*
> *To celebrate the need of comrades.*[6]

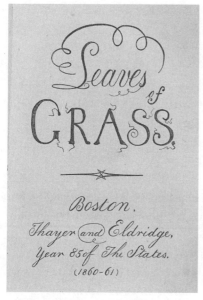

Title page, 1860 *Leaves of Grass*.

The calamus plant, or sweet flag.

According to Whitman scholars Kenneth Price and Ed Folsom, "In giving voice to this new camaraderie, Whitman was also inventing a language of homosexuality."[7]

This edition included titles such as "Poem of Procreation" and provocative passages like this one:

> *The wrestle of wrestlers, two apprentice-boys, quite grown, lusty, good-*
>> *natured, native-born, out on the vacant lot at sun-down, after work,*
> *The coats and caps thrown down, the embrace of love and resistance,*
> *The upper-hold and under-hold, the hair rumpled over and blinding*
>> *the eyes;*[8]

The sexual and romantic attraction presented in this homoerotic wrestling match is vividly reminiscent of scenes from classical antiquity that portray youths wrestling. But this match is not set in a long-ago time and a faraway place. Rather, the wrestlers face the reader directly. Whitman's youths are transported to everyday America, just down the street, in fact—a "vacant lot at sun-down." In a touch of humor, the strigils and laurel wreaths of classical times become "coats and caps," and the gymnasium a common workaday scene in America. What is transpiring between them, frankly, is "love and resistance." Whitman's refusal to assume literary "cover" was part of the shocking freshness he represented to readers such as Symonds.

> *From my own voice resonant—singing the phallus,*
> *Singing the song of procreation, [. . .]*
> *Singing the bedfellow's song, (O resistless yearning!*
> *O for any and each, the body correlative attracting!*
> *O for you, whoever you are, your correlative body!*
> *O it, more than all else, you delighting!) [. . .]*
> *the smell of apples and lemons [. . .]*[9]

The "Calamus" poems describe exuberant male-male sexuality, but they also tenderly limn scenes of quiet, even domestic love between men. Whitman describes a relationship between male lovers playing out in social spaces where no one is horrified or shocked by their love:

> *He whom I love travels with me, or sits a long while holding me by*
>> *the hand [. . .]*

I walk or sit indifferent—I am satisfied,
He ahold of my hand has completely satisfied me.[10]

Later in this sequence, the narrator hopes that his lover will not "content himself without me." The poet grieves that the lover—described as "him"—is "far away." In conclusion, the narrator claims, "(I am ashamed—but it is useless—I am what I am)." This declaration—"I am what I am"—could not have escaped the young Symonds once these astonishing new verses made their way to England.

The simple and direct word choice of the "Calamus" poems suggested to British readers a new world in which same-sex love could be as undisguised as it was in Whitman's language. In "Poem 13," Whitman writes:

CALAMUS taste
(For I must change the strain—these are not to be pensive leaves, but
    leaves of joy,)
Roots and leaves unlike any but themselves,
[. . .]
Love-buds, put before you and within you, whoever you are,
Buds to be unfolded on the old terms,
If you bring the warmth of the sun to them, they will open, and bring
    form, color, perfume, to you,
If you become the aliment and the wet, they will become flowers, fruits,
    tall branches and trees [. . .]
NOT heat flames up and consumes [. . .]
Myriads of seeds,
wafted, sailing gracefully, to drop where they may,
Not these—O none of these, more than the flames of me, consuming,
    burning for his love whom I love! [. . .][11]

In "Poem 19," Whitman's archetypal male lover becomes even more real. This relationship is situated somewhere in New York in the middle of the nineteenth century; the couple heads to recognizable urban destinations—the street, a bar; later, the man is kissing his lover on the deck of a ship:

Yet comes one, a Manhattanese, and ever at parting, kisses me lightly on
    the lips with robust love,

And I, in the public room, or on the crossing of the street, or on the ship's
     deck, kiss him in return [. . .]
We are those two natural and nonchalant persons [. . .][12]

A particular section of this *Leaves of Grass* especially outraged British
reviewers:

Receive me and my lover too—he will not let me go without him.

I roll myself upon you, as upon a bed—I resign myself to the dusk.

Darkness! you are gentler than my lover! his flesh was sweaty and panting,
I feel the hot moisture yet that he left me. My hands are spread forth, I
     pass them in all directions,
I would sound up the shadowy shore to which you are journeying.

Be careful, darkness! already, what was it touch'd me?
I thought my lover had gone, else darkness and he are one,
I hear the heart-beat, I follow, I fade away.

O hot-cheek'd and blushing! O foolish hectic!
O for pity's sake, no one must see me now! my clothes were stolen while
     I was abed,
Now I am thrust forth, where shall I run? [. . .]

I feel ashamed to go naked about the world.
I am curious to know where my feet stand—and what this is flooding
     me, childhood or manhood—and the hunger that crosses the
     bridge between.

The cloth laps a first sweet eating and drinking,
Laps life-swelling yolks—laps ear of rose-corn, milky and just ripen'd;
The white teeth stay, and the boss-tooth advances in darkness,
And liquor is spill'd on lips and bosoms by touching glasses, and the best
     liquor afterward.[13]

The book would not make it to Symonds's nation, or into his own hands,
without a ban.

The Customs Consolidation Act of 1853 had made it illegal to import the first edition of *Leaves of Grass*, but not to print and distribute it domestically in Britain.[14] By 1860, though, direct distribution of *Leaves of Grass* in Britain had also become illegal. Nonetheless, several enterprising British publishers used the plates of the American volume to print illegal editions for British distribution. At times, pages from the American edition of *Leaves of Grass* would be rebound into covers marked with a British publisher's imprint, producing a small number of pirated copies. Horsell was one such publisher; Trubner, later, another.

The publishers added misleading title pages to obscure what the books actually contained. To protect themselves from prosecution, the publishers who produced these doubly illicit copies (illegal to distribute in Britain; produced without paying royalties to Whitman) would "tip in"—that is, interpolate—fake title pages. Sometimes the title page would be left completely blank; at other times, the actual publisher would glue an inaccurate attribution to another publisher onto the title page. The American *Leaves of Grass* became a cult object to many readers, including many of Symonds's contemporaries. Owning, reading, and referencing this little book had become a crime, but sharing the book also became a way to identify one's own identity to another potential reader. The book spoke for British readers when speech became problematic.

When copies of the now-illegal American editions of *Leaves of Grass* began to be distributed in Britain, its status as taboo literature did not go unnoticed. Several British publications dragged the topic of censorship law into their reviews. A London magazine, the *Leader and Saturday Analyst*, addressed the issue with the anonymous piece "Walt Whitman and His Critics": "Among American authors there is one named Walt Whitman, who, in 1855, first issued a small quarto volume of ninety-five pages [. . .] which, it appears, the author had printed himself and then 'left to the winds of heaven to publish.'"[15] That comment is a wink to the reader about the missing publication information on some of the books' title pages. The unnamed author of the review reflects on the difficulty of procuring a "Whitman" but notes that it is possible, with some difficulty, to secure one. The reviewer calls the author "rough." Another review describes the "indecencies" of the book and warns readers away from it:

Here is a thin quarto volume without an author's name on the title-page; but to atone for which we have a portrait engraved on steel of the notorious individual who is the poet presumptive. This portrait expresses all the features of the hard democrat, and none of the flexile delicacy of the civilized poet. The damaged hat, the rough beard, the naked throat, the shirt exposed to the waist, are each and all presented to show that the man to whom these articles belong scorns the delicate arts of civilisation. The man is the true impersonation of his book—rough, uncouth, vulgar [. . .] Is it possible that the most prudish nation in the world will adopt a poet whose indecencies stink in the nostrils?

"The depth of his indecencies will be the grave of his fame," the reviewer concludes.[16] The reviewer notes that he can't (for legal reasons) even cite the passage that so upsets him, but that the unspeakable, unquotable content should condemn the poet: "The very nature of this man's compositions excludes us from proving by extracts the truth of our remarks; but we, who are not prudish, emphatically declare that the man who wrote page 79 of the 'LEAVES OF GRASS' deserves nothing so richly as the public executioner's whip."[17] This kind of attack was soon not to be just a turn of phrase. The review of a book was fast becoming a legal threat.

The passage so upsetting from the 1855 edition that it was left uncited is indeed somewhat excessive. It is also quite moving, as it describes an unbounded attraction to human beings as a whole, and a specific attraction of the male poet to a man, and it honors the sexuality of both women and men. The scene begins with a man whom the poet admires: "[A]ll who saw him loved him [. . .] you would wish long and long to be with him . . . you would wish to sit by him in the boat that you and he might touch each other." The poet goes on to speak about how pleasing it is to be among crowds of people of both genders and "to touch any one . . . to rest my arm ever so lightly round his or her neck for a moment [. . .] I swim in it as in a sea."

He goes on:

[L]oveflesh swelling and deliciously aching,

Limitless limpid jets of love hot and enormous . . . quivering jelly of
*   love . . . white-blow and delirious juice;*
Bridegroom night of love, working surely and softly into the
*   prostrate dawn,*

Undulating into the willing and yielding day,
Lost in the cleave of the clasping and sweetfleshed day.

This is the nucleus . . . after the child is born of woman, the man is born
*   of woman,*
This is the bath of birth . . . this is the merge of small and large, and
*   the outlet again.*

Be not ashamed women . . . your privilege encloses the rest . . . it is the
*   exit of the rest,*
You are the gates of the body and you are the gates of the Soul.

The female contains all qualities and tempers them . . . she is in her place
*   . . . she moves with perfect balance, [. . .]*
The fullspread pride of man is calming and excellent to the soul; [. . .]
The man's body is sacred, and the woman's body is sacred . . . it is no
*   matter who [. . .]*[18]

Unlike charges of "filth" or "lewdness," accusations of "obscenity" now had a legal valence, with real penalties attached.

A review in the *Spectator*, also anonymous, suggests that Whitman's language is the moral responsibility not only of the poet but also of the other "gentlemen" involved with the book's production—and that the obscenity is so obvious that it practically spills out to "infect" the cover art and the author photograph: "The paper, print, and binding are indeed superb; but one thing these gentlemen have forgotten: where are the phallic emblems, and the figures of Priapus and the Satyrs that should have adorned the covers and the pages of this new gospel of lewdness and obscenity?" The reviewer also asks why Whitman is depicted in a clothed portrait, and not naked, in the act of "making love."[19]

The prestigious *Literary Gazette* refers explicitly to the threat to publishers posed by the recently passed Obscene Publications Act, and to the legal risk undertaken by the booksellers now distributing the volume. The words "criminals" and "verdict" are invoked, along with a new category: actual "literary judges." This is a resonant and chilling phrase as the times were changing in distressing ways. Literary critics, whose former remit was to express well-considered opinions, now came to be empowered as "literary judges"—who could send to prison the writers of whose work they did not approve. Traditional "literary judgment" could now precipitate a "legal judgment."

The same review refers to the even more "disgusting" quality of the 1860 edition and jokes that if the reviewer can think of worse things to say, he will "print them in a second edition." This is a joke that depended on readers' knowledge that the 1860 edition was "dirtier" than that of 1855.

> We are rather surprised that with John Lord Campbell on the wool-sack, and a certain act of his still unrepealed on the statute-book, Mr. Walt Whitman should have found a London vendor for his uncleanly work. This is more decided language than we generally employ, and our readers may ask us for some justification of it. Let us remind them of Lord Macaulay's description of Wycherley, which we can certainly apply to Walt Whitman. "His indecency is protected against the critics as a skunk is protected against the hunters." It is safe because it is too filthy to handle, and too noisome even to approach. There are certain criminals whom even literary judges must try with closed doors, and our readers must deduce from our verdict that "the evidence is unfit for publication." We say, then, deliberately, that of all the writers we have ever perused, Mr. Walt Whitman is the most silly, the most blasphemous, and the most disgusting; if we can think of any stronger epithets, we will print them in a second edition.[20]

In spite of the serious penalties for obscenity and sodomy, identifying ways to get around the censorship of Whitman's volume amounted to a parlor game in some literary circles. An anonymous review in the *London Review and Weekly Journal of Politics, Society, Literature, and Art* cautiously does just that. It declares that "[c]omparing this volume with the earlier editions of the 'Leaves of Grass' we find that [. . .] all is retained, including some things that might better have been omitted."[21] The anonymous author directly states his appreciation of the new law: "We are not [. . .] maintaining that a poet may run counter to every social and religious belief and law."[22] Then, safe from any suspicion that he might endorse such a work, he goes on to share a little gossip, explaining how the book was being removed from bookstalls, which only increased the demand; *Leaves of Grass* could now be found "on the shelves of second-hand book stalls in side places in the city."[23] If a "curious person" finds it, "the stall-keeper will ask him treble its first price."

The *London Review* referred, also with a wink, to the volumes of *Leaves of Grass* that were being smuggled into Britain and pirated: "So far as the title page of the well-printed volume furnishes any information it is written by and published by New York, and doubtless such is the case."[24] The writer is wryly suggesting that readers knew that printers of a potentially obscene book would, on occasion, assign to a pirated edition inaccurate provenance, or else none at all.

Yet British readers continued to take the risk of buying, reading, and sharing this exhilarating criminal text.

The year after the "Calamus" cycle was published, a new anti-sodomy law was passed in Britain: the Offences Against the Person Act[25] of 1861 consolidated all sodomy law into one modern, unified statute. This streamlined statute took the chaos of existing common law—which could mean leniency toward offenders, as we saw, if juries and judges had discretion—and made it uniform.[26] Lest there be magistrates not sufficiently bothered by the crime of sodomy between men, this law took away any judicial discretion in sentencing related to it. This new act defined sodomy as a nationwide civil offense and assigned hard labor for no less than ten years and for as long as a lifetime for the act.

> Whosoever shall be convicted of the abominable Crime of Buggery, committed either with Mankind [. . .] shall be liable, at the Discretion of the Court, to be kept in Penal Servitude for Life or for any Term not less than Ten Years. Whosoever shall attempt to commit the said abominable Crime [. . .] shall be guilty of a Misdemeanor, and being convicted thereof shall be liable, at the Discretion of the Court, to be kept in Penal Servitude for any Term not exceeding Ten Years and not less than Three Years, or to be imprisoned for any Term not exceeding Two Years, with or without Hard Labour [. . .]

The court no longer needed to prove that ejaculation inside another man's body had taken place—now "Proof of Penetration" was the only evidence needed to prosecute: "Whenever, upon the Trial for any Offence punishable under this Act, it may be necessary to prove carnal Knowledge, it shall not be necessary to prove the actual Emission of Seed in order to constitute a carnal Knowledge, but the carnal Knowledge shall be deemed complete upon Proof of Penetration only."[27]

This act abandoned the death penalty, still on the books though not enacted, and enshrined in its place penal servitude,[28] ranging from a minimum sentence of ten years and up to life for the crime.

The Offences Against the Person Act of 1861 did indeed boost arrests in some archives. The Proceedings of the Old Bailey records from the 1860s show dozens of convictions and consequential sentences of penal servitude. The numbers may have in fact been higher, since many sentences were suppressed and left unrecorded. In the two decades following its passage, my review of the Proceedings of the Old Bailey records shows that sentences for the crime of sodomy between men increased alarmingly.

That year, thirty-three-year-old Joseph Mead was sentenced to a year and a half of penal servitude for "the attempt" at "b—g—y."[29] Thirty-five-year-old John Griffiths received a sentence of ten years of the same for an "attempt" at "B—g—y."[30]

In 1861, too, the twenty-one-year-old Symonds took out the notebook that held his long love poem and added his "Set Apology"—which frantically puts on the record a presumed disavowal of his love for "W."

British reviews now directly condemned *Leaves of Grass* as obscene and therefore as a matter for the police. In the *Westminster Review*, Wathen Mark Wilks Call did so using the very words of the 1857 Obscene Publications Act: "If Mr. Walt Whitman's 'Leaves of Grass' had been printed on paper as dirty as his favourite topics—if the book itself had presented the general aspect of that literature which usually falls under no other criticism than that of the police office, we should have passed it by without notice, as addressing only such a public as we have no concern with."

But, he went on, the volume contained "more obscenity and profanity" than was to be found in polite circles. For this reason, he concluded, it was deadly.[31]

The Morgan Library preserves one of the rare extant pirated volumes of *Leaves of Grass*, with the "Horsell interpolation," the page with the British publisher's pasted-in imprint. This once contraband book is now considered a treasure: Sotheby's recently advertised a *Leaves of Grass* with the Horsell interpolation for $160,000.[32]

If you ask for the earliest copy there of *Leaves of Grass*, you will be brought this volume and be with met with its dry aroma. If you turn to the frontispiece, there indeed is the "tip-in." It is a scrap of paper a quarter of an inch wide and two and a half inches long, pasted on over where the publisher's mark would typically be printed. Depending on your perspective, the little paper scrap is a fig leaf covering the shame of the book having had no licit British distributor; or it might be a falsified passport stamp that allowed the volume to travel across many borders and awaken many minds.

The Victorian label shows a slight puckering caused by the organic nature of its adhesive, which survives from the world before petrochemicals.

Holding the volume is like holding something of inestimable value retrieved from a burial site—from the grave of someone who had never truly died.

Or rather, it is like holding something still entirely new that has been retrieved intact—from the grave of someone with millions and millions and millions of living descendants.

CHAPTER 9

Symonds's Second Scandal

In 1862, a second scandal involving Symonds proved again that literature could now leap out into the world from the page and attack the author.

After his final year at Balliol, Symonds was awarded a prestigious fellowship at Magdalen College. That college was a short walk but in some ways a whole world away from his undergraduate college.

The architecture of Magdalen is more romantic than that of Balliol, and more self-enclosed. Balliol looks out over Broad Street, a wide avenue where, since the Middle Ages and into the nineteenth century, livestock markets were held. From the moment you step outside Balliol it is impossible to ignore the contemporary world: tradesmen and farmers, piles of vegetables and droves of cattle, would have surrounded Symonds the moment he ventured out through the Porters' Lodge.

Magdalen, in contrast, is situated outside of time. It is nestled beside a bridge that arches over the ever-rushing River Cherwell, and the ancient, wealthy college owns land on both sides of the river. To the left, as you enter and pass the medieval buildings closest to the Porters' Lodge, are immense groomed lawns. Situated here and there on these greenswards are marble-columned buildings that look like Greek temples. In the famous deer park, which the temples overlook, soft-coated deer wander at will.

To your right is a simple wooden bridge that crosses the Cherwell. On the opposite side of the river, you enter a wilderness—a series of overgrown meadows, densely shadowed with thick-trunked, heavy-leafed trees; the park is an island between the branches of the rivers. On both sides of the river, paths meander.

Students can wander together on the groomed side of the river, but they are in view of the college. But when they cross over to the wilderness side, they can walk the rough paths together without scrutiny. Shielded, by foliage and crenellated walls, from the judgment or attacks of the outside world, they are free to hold hands, kiss, or embrace. In that bit of

Carving on exterior of Magdalen College.

uninflected wilderness sheltered by ancient ramparts, it is easy to imagine the construction of new worlds.

Magdalen has its own surreal and magical—nearly pagan—set of traditions, which Balliol and other more pragmatic colleges lack. At 4 a.m. on May 1, "May Morning," for instance, the boys' choir assembles on the Magdalen tower overlooking the bridge and sings psalms to celebrate spring, while nearly all of Oxford gathers beneath, in a hush, to listen.

Balliol is famous for producing statesmen. Magdalen produces visionaries. It is not a surprise that the privileged, protective, wild-and-civilized landscape of Magdalen produced the two men who would envision a society in which all kinds of love would be safe—Symonds and, later, Oscar Wilde.

But in spite of Magdalen's secluded landscapes, the rules of the mid-Victorian world did, Symonds found, still bear down on him. Trouble began with G. H. Shorting; Symonds was Shorting's instructor. Symonds described Shorting as "vain, possessive and strong-willed," a flirtatious young man with curly yellow hair. Symonds became infatuated with him. Shorting had, however, been pursuing—"pestering"—the teenage choirboys at Magdalen. Symonds wished to keep Shorting away from one specific choirboy. So Symonds, motivated perhaps by jealousy, insisted that tutorials with Shorting take place in Shorting's Balliol rooms, rather than at Magdalen. (Entrance to a college at Oxford was not, and still is not, allowed without an invitation from a member of that college.)

Symonds's restriction on Shorting's access to Magdalen and its choirboys infuriated the younger student. In retaliation, Shorting issued "hysterical threats" that he would ruin Symonds; he sent poems written by Symonds to six fellows of Magdalen College, the authority figures who managed the academic and moral lives of the students.

Shorting claimed to the fellows that Symonds had encouraged him to approach the boys in the choir. He submitted to them extracts from Symonds's personal letters. He had edited and arranged them to give the impression that Symonds had also been pursuing choirboys sexually. Shorting, in a daring confrontation, directly told the fellows that Symonds shared his own sexual tastes.[1]

Faced with an investigation into his writing and his sexuality, Symonds was forced in turn to collect letters testifying to his moral character and to write a letter himself in his own defense.

Symonds was summoned before the fellows of Magdalen College—he knew that many of them were homosexual. They eventually acquitted Symonds of soliciting sex from other male students, but it took a general meeting of the College of Magdalen for the entire cadre of fellows to make the decision. They concluded their investigation by censuring two of Symonds's incriminating personal letters.

In the end, Symonds was not "sent down" from Magdalen, but he spent the next year of his tutorship under a shadow. At this young age, Symonds had been humiliated by a group of men who were essentially his colleagues, who undertook a highly public investigation of his private sexual life. He felt that this permanently affected his reputation among many of the Oxford University gatekeepers; he would always be suspected of "sexual guilt."[2]

Symonds's health was already compromised; his lungs, as well as his mental resilience, were weak. The stress and shame of this episode led to the first of several psychological breakdowns. Dr. Symonds sent his son away from college altogether, to a hotel in the part of the Swiss Alps frequented by British tourists, in an attempt to help the young man recover his health and mental equilibrium.

There Symonds met Janet Catherine North, known as Catherine. She was three years older than he. An intelligent, well-educated young woman with a certain seriousness of purpose, she was highly regarded by those who knew her. She came from the respectable upper middle class, as did Symonds; their families were on friendly terms.

Catherine was flattered by the attentions of this young man. She thought him brilliant, a young man with a promising future.

Catherine represented a possible future for Symonds—but one he had never chosen.

CHAPTER 10

"Goblin Market":
Attraction and Aversion

W as Whitman's liberationist message troubling to some female readers and exhilarating to others? The ones who resisted had good reasons to do so.

Christina Rossetti was the daughter of a well-known Italian nationalist and Dante scholar, Gabriele Rossetti, and the former Frances Polidori, a scholar in her own right; the couple were well connected to London's poets and revolutionaries. The family's Bloomsbury salon was filled with artists, musicians, poets, and democracy activists during the four siblings' childhoods; all of the Rossetti children grew up radically, in different ways, to innovate.

Christina Rossetti showed brilliance as a poet when she was still a young teenager and printed a volume of her poetry at seventeen. She was

The Rossetti family: Dante Gabriel Rossetti, Christina Rossetti, Frances Rossetti, and William Michael Rossetti, 1863.

the only woman to have contributed, in 1850, to the iconoclastic magazine the *Germ*, which caused a sensation in literary London.[1]

The group of young artists and writers who contributed to the *Germ* chose the name Pre-Raphaelite to express their opposition to the staid Royal Academy's celebration of the Renaissance; they re-valorized medieval iconography. These young people also opposed the conventional genre paintings and classical subjects considered most elevated at the time. They were revolutionary, too, in addressing contemporary social issues, such as prostitution and adultery, in their work. In the early 1860s, Christina Rossetti's siblings Dante Gabriel and William Michael were growing in prominence as, respectively, a major painter/poet and a critic; a sister, Maria, had taken orders as a nun.

Symonds was aware of the Pre-Raphaelite Brotherhood; its innovations and challenges to received authority were reported in the journals that he read. He was friendly with supporters and allies of the Pre-Raphaelites—the art critics John Ruskin and Walter Pater were mentors of his, and the poet Algernon Charles Swinburne, whom Symonds knew, was a correspondent of William Michael Rossetti's. But the Pre-Raphaelites' leading figures, notably Dante Gabriel Rossetti, were viewed as socially avant-garde in the extreme, and many had unorthodox living arrangements. Symonds watched from afar; he was younger, and already settled in a much more conventional mode of life.

Just as Symonds was aware of the Rossettis, Christina Rossetti was likely aware of *Leaves of Grass*, not least because her brother William Michael was so moved by the volume that he would eventually edit a version of it himself. The siblings' letters reveal that the three of them closely followed one another's reading and contributed to each others' editorial processes.[2] Christina Rossetti was also reading the *London Review*, the *Saturday Review*, and the *Athenaeum*—the kinds of literary publications that followed the Whitman drama—so it is very likely that she was aware of the furor caused by the "small, queerly-shaped volume."[3]

The contrast between Christina Rossetti and her robust brothers, who were both in different ways pushing the boundaries of expression, is striking. Photographs and paintings from this time present an ascetic-looking, pale woman; she appears in her brother Dante Gabriel's paintings and drawings as a model for various religious figures, including the Virgin Mary. Her biographer Jan Marsh believes that Christina Rossetti had a breakdown at fifteen, involving both hysteria and depression; Marsh speculates that

Christina Rossetti may have suffered a sexual trauma of some kind as a teenager, as her personality changed dramatically, from outgoing and confident to contained and introverted.[4] Other scholars speculate that the extremely thin, pale woman may have been anorexic.[5]

Though she may indeed have suffered such experiences, many of her contemporaries describe her apparent fragility as deceptive; she had a powerful analytical mind and a steely will.

Christina Rossetti passed up several times the chance to marry. As a single woman living at home, with no source of income, she had little choice but to accept a dependent, outwardly conventional life. The female poet had no scope for the kind of experimental life of the appetite that her brother Dante Gabriel was pursuing. Renunciation became the hallmark of her work, and in some ways of her life. She had, in short, none of the options of adventurous self-determination that were available to her bohemian brothers. In contrast, Dante Gabriel was by 1860 a successful painter; he was free to seek out "stunners," working-class women who modeled for painters, and who typified his ideals of female beauty. He was experimenting not only with genres, but with unorthodox affairs of many kinds.

Warnings about what a woman would face if she didn't maintain a conventional social role were abundant in Christina Rossetti's time and place. Christina Rossetti saw vividly what became of young women who responded to the seductions of sexual temptation. The consequences, she knew, of embracing the vision of sexual freedom in *Leaves of Grass* were different for women readers than for men. Though the two poets never met, the shaggy-bearded democratic visionary and the self-judging, exacting poetess seem to be in a kind of dialogue through their poems. Where Whitman invited, Christina Rossetti, speaking from a vulnerable female perspective, said no.

In Whitman's world, nature is all-embracing. In "Song of Myself," he offers rapturous descriptions of ripe, red fruit: "At the cider-mill, tasting the sweet of the brown squash—sucking the juice through a straw / At apple-peelings, wanting kisses for all the red fruit I find."[6] In Christina Rossetti's world, nature also often serves as a metaphor for erotic potential, but this potential is blighted: "I, figtree, fruit-unbearing," mourns her poem "Ash Wednesday."[7] In her poem "I Know You Not," composed in 1856, a year after the first edition of *Leaves of Grass*, the natural world is as eroticized as it is in Whitman, but the Beloved is not a human man, but the safer figure of Jesus:

Stronger than Lebanon Thou Root,
Sweeter than clustered grapes Thou Vine; [. . .]
And ruddier than the ruby Thou [. . .]
I thirst for Thee, full Fount and Flood.[8]

And in her series of poems titled "A Daughter of Eve," surely a response to Whitman's scandalous "Children of Adam," it is possible to see her making the case that, for Daughters of Eve in mid-Victorian Britain, the fruits that Whitman blithely offers are far more dangerous to accept.

It's reasonable that Christina Rossetti, possibly provoked in part by Whitman, might wish to warn women about the dangers posed by sexual temptation: she had witnessed, within her own family circle, the social vulnerability of sexually compromised women. Her brother Dante Gabriel's lover, Elizabeth Siddal, had suffered for years because of their unconventional relationship.

At twenty, Siddal had been working as a milliner in London; she supplemented her meager income by working as an artist's model as well. Dante Gabriel had met her through another painter, Walter Deverell; he was captivated by her gaunt, pale beauty and by her mass of coppery hair. Dante Gabriel became obsessed too with the way that her unusual beauty manifested his own developing iconography, which mixed avatars of spirituality with a sense of earthly emotion and physicality. Over the course of his career, Dante Gabriel created more than a thousand images of Siddal.

By 1851, Siddal had become Dante Gabriel's model and was sexually involved with him as well. By 1852, she had moved to his lodgings in Chatham Place. For a young Victorian woman, there was no turning back from such a step. She was thenceforth "ruined," no longer considered respectable. Marriage to Dante Gabriel Rossetti would be Siddal's only chance at social redemption.

As a model, Elizabeth—"Lizzie"—was observed obsessively by the men around her, but the gaze was not necessarily compassionate. Her lover's friend, John Everett Millais, painted her, famously, as the nearly drowned Ophelia. She was made to lie on her back, fully dressed, in a half-filled bathtub in order to model the image. Millais kept painting as the weather grew colder and colder, and though he normally heated the bathtub water with lamps, the lamps went out one day. Millais was too preoccupied with his canvas to notice. Lizzie did not complain, but the experience left her ill with pneumonia.

Her health was always precarious. She experienced periods of acute depression over the course of the decade that she lived with Dante Gabriel Rossetti; she expected he would eventually leave her for another, younger, muse. She also became dependent on the opiate chloral. Eyewitnesses described her with empathy during these years—a gifted woman and a talented artist in her own right, but so frail from her drug habit and poor health that she could barely move from the sofa; haunted by dependency on her lover, she appeared restless and uneasy when he left the room and could relax only when he reentered it to sit beside her.

Siddal was not wrong to worry about her lover's level of commitment: she was forced to tolerate Dante Gabriel Rossetti's many ill-concealed infidelities. Over the years, she was unhappily aware of other "muses," many of them from backgrounds similar to her own, as they became the focuses of his canvases and his erotic life.

Finally, though, Dante Gabriel did marry Siddal, in May 1860. Lizzie gave birth to a baby that was stillborn. Traumatized, grieving, Lizzie suffered apparent hallucinations. She sat beside an empty cradle, warning visitors not to disturb the baby's sleep.[9]

On February 11, 1862, Siddal, now Mrs. Rossetti, died from overdosing on an opiate; she had been married for less than two years. Diaries of contemporaries, such as that of the daughter of the Rossettis' doctor, discussed her death as having possibly been self-inflicted, after her husband had gone out to meet another woman, his voluptuous model Fanny Cornforth.

Overwrought with guilt, Dante Gabriel placed into his wife's coffin a collection of his poems—which he had been preparing for publication—and buried them with her body in Highgate Cemetery. (Seven years later, gruesomely enough, he obtained permission to exhume his wife's coffin in order to retrieve them; the book was worm-eaten in part but still mostly legible. Gossips spoke of the red hair of the deceased Mrs. Rossetti as still intact. In 1870 the poems would be published from "the exhumation proofs.")[10]

Perhaps in reaction to this appalling drama, with its waste of human life and potential, Christina Rossetti turned her attention to helping other women who had been exploited sexually by men and made outcasts by society. She became an activist, in her own quiet way. At St. Mary Magdalene House of Charity, a refuge in the London neighborhood of Highgate, she worked with prostitutes, so-called "soiled doves," who were seeking to leave the profession. Serving as a volunteer, Christina Rossetti garnered firsthand knowledge of the difficult, disease-ridden lives of prostitutes. She wrote her famous poem "Goblin Market" about a character named "Lizzie" and her sister "Laura" in order to read it to the prostituted women whom she was assisting.[11]

Many scholars of the Pre-Raphaelites today tend to stereotype Christina Rossetti as a pious single woman who was unconscious of the sexual content in "Goblin Market." But that is a gross misunderstanding of the poet's intentions. Indeed, in her firm, directive letters to her publisher, Alexander Macmillan, she indicated that she was well aware of the sexual nature of the material in her poem.

Christina Rossetti's *Goblin Market and Other Poems* was published in 1862, the year Lizzie died. The book was rapturously received by the public. Women readers in general understood from the first that "Goblin Market" was about sexual temptation and its danger to women.[12] In the poem, one sister—Laura—is tempted by the luscious, juicy fruits held out to her by disturbing, aggressive "Goblin Men."

> *"Lie close," Laura said,*
> *Pricking up her golden head:*
> *"We must not look at goblin men,*
> *We must not buy their fruits:*
> *Who knows upon what soil they fed*
> *Their hungry thirsty roots?"*[13]

But Laura is mesmerized in spite of Lizzie's warnings: "Their offers should not charm us, / Their evil gifts would harm us." Laura greedily tastes the fruit and becomes addicted to it. Christina Rossetti uses Whitman's precise sexual iconography of root and sap, juice and sunlight, red fruit and kisses, while precisely inverting the moral: these fruits, she warns, at least for women, are toxic: "O Laura, come; / I hear the fruit-call but I dare not look: / You should not loiter longer at this brook." But this warning came too late:

> *She dropped a tear more rare than pearl,*
> *Then sucked their fruit globes fair or red:*
> *Sweeter than honey from the rock,*
> *Stronger than man-rejoicing wine,*
> *Clearer than water flowed that juice;*

She never tasted such before,
How should it cloy with length of use?
She sucked and sucked and sucked the more
Fruits which that unknown orchard bore;
She sucked until her lips were sore;[14]

Lizzie chides her sister, in a passage redolent of the lusciousness of female sexual desire, but Laura scoffs:

"Nay, hush, my sister:
I ate and ate and ate my fill.
Yet my mouth waters still [. . .]
You cannot think what figs
My teeth have met in,
What melons icy-cold
Piled on a dish of gold
Too huge for me to hold,
What peaches with a velvet nap,
Pellucid grapes without one seed:
Odorous indeed must be the mead
Whereon they grow, and pure the wave they drink
With lilies at the brink,
And sugar-sweet their sap."[15]

There are consequences. After her feast, Laura becomes pale and languid. In 1862, venereal diseases—especially gonorrhea and syphilis—were rife in the British population, and no effective treatment was available. (Venereal diseases at the time were misunderstood as spread by women's sexual fluids—not by those of men.) Sufferers indeed grew pale and languid. Lizzie had warned Laura of a mutual friend of theirs who was also tempted and succumbed:

"Do you not remember Jeanie,
How she met them in the moonlight,
Took their gifts both choice and many
Ate their fruits and wore their flowers
[. . .]
She pined and pined away;

Sought them by night and day,
Found them no more, but dwindled and grew grey;
Then fell with the first snow, "[16]

Appalled at her sister's similar decline, Lizzie sacrifices herself. She goes to confront the Goblin Men. In a quasi-rape scene, they press their fruits against her face and mouth until she is smeared with their juices.

Lashing their tails
They trod and hustled her,
Elbowed and jostled her,
Clawed with their nails,
Barking, mewing, hissing, mocking,
Tore her gown and soiled her stocking,
Twitched her hair out by the roots,
Stamped upon her tender feet,
Held her hands and squeez'd their fruits
Against her mouth to make her eat.
[. . .]
Though the goblins cuffed and caught her,
Coaxed and fought her,
Bullied and besought her,
Scratched her, pinched her black as ink,
Kicked and knocked her,
Mauled and mocked her,
Lizzie uttered not a word;
Would not open lip from lip
Lest they should cram a mouthful in:
But laughed in heart to feel the drip
Of juice that syrupped all her face,
And lodged in dimples of her chin,
And streaked her neck which quaked like curd.
At last the evil people,
Worn out by her resistance,
Flung back her penny, kicked their fruit
Along whichever road they took,
Not leaving root or stone or shoot [. . .]
In a smart, ache, tingle,

Lizzie went her way;
Knew not was it night or day;[17]

Lizzie returns to her ailing sister. She cries, "Hug me, kiss me, suck my juices" and allows Laura to lick off the juice that the Goblin Men had smeared on Lizzie's face. This revives and heals Laura.

The two sisters end up, improbably, in a scene of domestic tranquility, never venturing out again to encounter the Goblin Men or the temptations they might proffer. The luscious apples and other fruits of the landscape present to women a treacherous seduction that only self-discipline and self-sacrifice can allay.

By writing a poem to read to prostitutes, Christina Rossetti was not addressing a subculture, but rather tackling a major issue central to many women's daily lives. Historians confirm that Victorian prostitution wasn't segregated as it is today; it wasn't a discreet subculture that most of society never encountered. Rather, it was a porous realm that lower-income young women continually and casually entered and left. Many young women working as milliners, factory girls, shop girls, and servants often had to, or chose to, make arrangements to trade sex for money in order to supplement their extremely low wages. Many female agricultural workers would enter prostitution for a few years in order to save up money for a small business or to prepare economically for marriage.[18]

So the issue of young women trading sex for money confronted people everywhere. Prostitution was at the time visible in nearly every area of London and was rife in towns as well. Victorian male commentators wrote openly about the fact that prostitutes operated actively at all times of the day and night, soliciting them in full view of their "respectable" wives and daughters.

Christina Rossetti, having surely read Whitman's romantic, inspiring vision of sexual self-determination—and having seen the ravages left by similar autonomous sexual choices made by women—wrote a warning, but indirectly, as a dream. Why do two young women in the poem get into a conflict with weird animal-like men who have rats' tails and cats' faces? Why do those vicious creatures smash ripe fruit against the face of a young woman trying to redeem her sister, who is wasting away, addicted to "goblin fruit"? Why this convoluted storytelling at a time when there was no shortage of realistic novels and poems?

Christina Rossetti's publisher, Alexander Macmillan, and possibly Macmillan's legal counsel, would have known that a poem about women and sexual temptation was unpublishable in 1862. A tale about seduction, various kinds of kisses, and the threat of untreatable venereal disease would certainly have been actionable at the time for its potential effect of "corrupting" the innocent. But an allegory about mysterious "goblin men," delicious plums and peaches, and a vague wasting away after succumbing to temptation could be published without legal risk to Christina Rossetti—or to Alexander Macmillan.

Some scholars of Christina Rossetti's work read the sexual subtext in this poem as if it is welling up from the subconscious, in spite of the author's conscious intention. Those who ignore the power of censorship law at this time are, I would say, reading the poem ahistorically.

To work around the 1857 obscenity law, British writers were now forced to layer a veneer of allegory over sexual material. The editorial decisions that Macmillan made and that Christina Rossetti actively debated, negotiated, and finally endorsed show that "Goblin Market" was positioned to be a mass-market bestseller, with overt moralistic messaging about female sexuality for its Victorian audience.[19]

Christina Rossetti asked her brother Dante Gabriel to design a frontispiece for the poem: "your woodcuts are so essential to my contentment that I will wait a year for them if need is—though (in a whisper) six months would suit me better," she wrote to her brother.[20] The illustrations were, like so many of Dante Gabriel's commitments, imperfectly delivered; they were completed late. By the publication date of *Goblin Market and Other Poems*, the erotic nature of much of Dante Gabriel's paintings and engravings was already well known, and controversial. Christina Rossetti understood exactly what she was commissioning and awaiting.

Dante Gabriel Rossetti's frontispiece illustrations are direct about the poem's sexual content. Christina Rossetti openly approved them; her stylized "CR" logo is embedded in the corner of the woodcuts. She wasn't the stereotype of the virginal poetess dreamily allegorizing material she didn't consciously understand; rather, she owned this book, deciding on its exact shape, cover, and layout with her publisher, and she bestowed her imprimatur upon the images.

One of the two engravings depicts Laura cutting her "golden curl" as the Goblin Men crowd around her. It features an owl-like Goblin Man holding a pomegranate, which startlingly enough resembles labia, up toward Laura's face. The fruit has anatomically correct but botanically incorrect folds on either side of the vertical opening. The goblin nuzzles the pomegranate while seeking to make eye contact with Laura. The pomegranate as a symbol for "forbidden fruit," which Dante Gabriel Rossetti used in erotic contexts in other works of his, derives from the myth of Persephone.[21]

Other sexually graphic details are also clear. In the upper left corner, a ratlike creature beckons to the fleeing Lizzie, who carries an intact vessel seemingly to safety. The rat carries a phallus-shaped staff from which a bunch of grapes is suspended. A catlike creature kneels before Laura, who

"Buy from us with a golden curl." Dante Gabriel Rossetti frontispiece of "Goblin Men," 1861, in Christina Rossetti's 1862 *Goblin Market and Other Poems.*

is kneeling as well. He has wrapped her long golden hair around his neck and is caressing a strand of it, with an ecstatic expression on his face. The phallic tail of this creature, which is wearing a typical Victorian man's jacket and trousers, rises up from between the creature's legs. A platter of fruit, including two figs, extends from this creature's lap and rests between Laura's thighs. Dante Gabriel Rossetti's vision is one of riotous sexual innuendo. Lest the warning in the poem be missed, the spots on the froglike creature in the upper right corner may suggest the lesions of venereal disease.

"Goblin Market" consciously warns the female reader not to embrace the seductive natural world or the temptation of experimental, out-of-bounds sexuality. It can be read as an angry and politically alert feminist rejoinder to the siren lure proffered by *Leaves of Grass*—a rebuttal written by a woman reflecting on the life and death of another woman who had said yes to illicit sexuality and the lure of intoxication, but who was then broken by male infidelity, disease, addiction, and maternal loss.

CHAPTER 11

The State Seizes the Female Body

U ntil the early 1860s, British medical understanding of venereal diseases was not precise. Syphilis and gonorrhea, for instance, were thought to be two manifestations of the same disease. But in 1861, Jonathan Hutchinson, who worked at the London Hospital as a surgeon, identified the epidemiology and characteristics of congenital syphilis.[1] This discovery had a far-reaching effect on women, as it gave the state yet another rationale for colonizing the bodies of some of its citizens.

Christina Rossetti may have seemed defensive or even reactionary in 1862 in warning women about the dangers of sexual temptation and its possible consequence, venereal disease, rather than joining the activist resistance against sexual double standards represented by her friend Barbara Bodichon; by Josephine Butler, a prominent activist against the abuse of women seen as prostitutes; and by other women recently radicalized around what we would understand today as feminist issues. But Christina Rossetti wasn't wrong to focus on these dangers; indeed, she was prescient. For the state was soon to stage mass arrests of women for their sexual activity, using disease as a pretext.

The colonies of the British Empire were sites of experiment in social control. Laws tested in the management of empire, when proven effective, were then brought home.[2] Whether this was consciously intended by administrators or not, the British colonies became a legal laboratory for testing new methods of managing possibly restive modern populations; the laws that worked overseas were reissued and reinterpreted domestically for use on populations in Britain and in Ireland. To manage sexually transmitted diseases among military men serving in British India, administrators were supported by parliamentary legislation that permitted the rounding up, examination, and incarceration of women identified as prostitutes in that particular colony.[3]

One series of laws that was brought home to Britain from the laboratory of empire included the four Contagious Diseases Acts. In 1864, in response to the War Office and the Admiralty's concern about the high incidence of venereal diseases among soldiers, and its possible impact on military effectiveness, Parliament passed the first of the domestic Contagious Diseases Acts.[4] These acts were ostensibly passed to help in the pursuit and quarantine of diseased prostitutes in garrison towns and seaports.[5] In effect, the laws allowed the state to seize any woman and make her submit to a forced vaginal exam. If a doctor thought she was infected, she would be imprisoned.

. Those women arrested after 1864 were often factory girls walking home from a late shift after dark, or young women who had stayed out a bit too late, perhaps to have a drink. Other women were taken into custody while walking in the evening with male companions or beaus—or even with male relatives. The wording of the acts allowed police to arrest women who looked as if they might be prostitutes. Of course, like the definition of "obscenity," the definition of who looks like she might be a prostitute, especially in an era when working-class young women often moved in and out of situations in which they sold access to sex, was open to a policeman's subjective interpretation.

Just as the earlier problem of tainted water had allowed the state to exploit a newly imagined "commons" and weaken the traditional British notion of private space, so the very real problem of venereal disease allowed the modern state to invent its own role in policing a sexual "commons." In this case, it invented a role in deciding who was a sexually transgressive woman. The Contagious Diseases Acts allowed any undercover policeman to arrest any woman in Britain if she looked too sexually experienced, acted too flirtatiously, seemed too flashily dressed, was too drunk, was out too late—or was simply having too much fun in male company.[6]

If a magistrate agreed that a woman brought before him was indeed a prostitute, she was forced to submit to a vaginal inspection. Doctors, or casually employed nurses with no formal medical qualifications, performed the examinations, and they used the same unsanitized speculum for all the detained women. If the medical staff thought a woman might be infected with a venereal disease—for which there was at that time no definitive test—she was sent to a "lock hospital" for nine months to a year.

Incarceration suspended a woman's civil liberties until the time of her release. When they were unfortunate enough to be swept up in these arbitrary arrests, women lost their jobs, could not care for their children, and suffered ruined reputations, whether or not they were what we would today call sex workers, or whether or not they had ever in fact been infected with any disease. If a woman who was initially detained refused to be examined and refused to go into the hospital when the physician said that she must, she could be imprisoned at hard labor for up to a year.[7]

The prisoners, for their part, had to endure such exams every week or two. If a prisoner did not cooperate in undergoing a vaginal exam, she was physically forced to do so. If she refused to go along with the rules of the hospital in general, she was punished with one month's additional imprisonment for the first act of resistance, and two months' more for each time she continued to disobey.[8]

Like most of these new laws to police the sexual and verbal commons, the reach of these laws metastasized over time. The 1866 version of the Contagious Disease Acts extended these regulations to eleven British cities and forced all "prostitutes" in certain areas to submit to regular inspections. And the 1868 version of the acts only changed details of administration. An 1869 version added seven new garrison towns and seaports to the areas in which women could be arrested. It enlarged the region encircling these cities in which women could be arrested, extending it from five miles to fifteen.

The acts were deployed, at first, quietly; the government avoided press scrutiny. When the public slowly became aware that women were being rounded up by the government, at first the response was supportive. Parliamentary spokespeople represented these mass arrests as the only way to protect the health of the nation. But soon public protests mounted, due to the fact that accounts were emerging of how brutally the vaginal exams were conducted, and the fact that "respectable" women were also being arrested and outraged in this way. Josephine Butler and other middle-class women and their allies began to call publicly to cease these arrests and examinations.

The main treatment for women in lock hospitals who were diagnosed with syphilis was—in addition to moral instruction—mercury delivered via an "inunction rub." Dr. Anne Hanley, who studies Victorian sexually transmitted diseases, explained that for the "inunction rubs," mercury paste was rubbed all over a woman's skin; she was then wrapped in cloths and rubber sheets and left in a heated room to sweat, forced to inhale the toxic fumes of mercury. "The paste," says Hanley, "was allowed to absorb into the skin. The idea was that this would slow the development of symptoms. Symptoms would subside, but this was because the mercury paste had induced heavy metal poisoning. Heavy metal poisoning kills syphilis symptoms—but over time it kills the patient too."[9] The patient might alternatively be given the mercury to drink in the form of dosed castor oil, or she would have to swallow mercury in tablet form.[10]

Over time, the mercury would cause symptoms such as acute salivation, fetid breath, loss of hair and teeth, and constipation. It also eventually caused insanity; indeed, the phrase "mad as a hatter" derives from the mercury poisoning that accompanied hatters' work using mercury to treat fur for making felt. Finally, mercury poisoning could cause a painful death.[11]

Doctors treating women in "lock hospitals" often assumed that when a patient died, the cause was syphilis—or mercury poisoning.

Yet a woman arrested for wearing a pretty dress, or having a drink with a beau, had no choice, if arrested, but to face these horrors.

To this day, of course, Western women often feel that they are in danger of losing the state's protection if something bad happens to them when they are "out too late," or if they are seen as having "too much" sexual experience to deserve the state's protection, or if they are perceived by police or accused in a judicial proceeding of being "dressed like a slut." To this day, judges in rape cases adjudicate on the basis of, and public debate engages with, the question of how a victim was dressed and whether or not her level of prior sexual experience affects the level of protection the state is willing to give her. To this day, many Western women often feel particularly nervous when they defy rules and resist authority and expect amorphously to be punished in some way that is gendered.

From where do these irrational expectations descend?

They descend to us, if we live in the West, from this period and these laws. If we live in former British colonies, they descend from the imposition of similar laws.

With the four Contagious Diseases Acts, the secular modern state got into the business of separating "bad" women from "good" ones. And these acts joined censorship law and sodomy law in giving the modern state tools to subjugate its potentially unruly citizens.

The philosopher Michel Foucault points out, in *The History of Sexuality*, volume 1: *An Introduction*, that the modern bourgeois capitalist state invented proliferating discourses about sexuality as a way to control and manage citizens.[12] The way that the Contagious Diseases Acts joined the Obscene Publications Act and the Offences Against the Person Act to create this role for the modern state offers a perfect set of illustrations supporting Foucault's insight.

We are used to the state arrogating to itself the right to censor certain non-violence-threatening words, to monitor adult citizens' consensual sexuality, and now to do whatever it deems necessary to the commons of digital communications or the environment. We take for granted that the modern state has a role in deciding policies regarding abortion and even vaccination. We don't tend to question the modern state as the only appropriate overseer and manager of these affairs. Debate, when it occurs, focuses on fine-tuning or somewhere drawing a line restricting the rights of the state. We tend to ask, *Which* words shall the state censor or police? *Which* consensual sex acts shall it punish? *Which* boundary of the body shall be the limit of state intrusion, and at what point? But we don't tend to question the very right of the state to police the body, to invade the body, to engage with our most private consenting sexual acts, or to surveil and police our words.

But the more historically informed question is this: What right does the modern state have to involve itself in this kind of policing *at all*?

The modern state—both the government itself and the satellite of elite interests that always orbits it—invented these "rights" because a concatenation of government leaders, policymakers, and administrators, encouraged by influential and wealthy people and powerful interests, benefited from their invention. State power overseas and at home was boosted via the state asserting and expanding these roles and then persuading citizens that this power grab was necessary for their own protection.

But it left to us, the heirs of this Western legacy today, the irrational ways in which we are expected to think about good and bad women when women are caught up in the criminal justice system; it left to us modern women our fears that if we are out too late or drink too much or look too "slutty," we will lose the protection of the state if something bad happens to us.

And it left us our too-unquestioning acceptance of the state's self-claimed role in management of our speech—and the state's decisions overall about whose adult consensual sex acts are licit, and whose are illicit.

PART IV

Love and Literature Driven Underground

CHAPTER 12

"I Will Go with Him I Love"

As Christina Rossetti was warning her female readers about the dangers of sexuality, and as the college student Symonds was recording for posterity his apparent renunciation of his first great love, Walt Whitman was forced to turn his attention beyond personal relationships and beyond poetry in order to face his nation's great struggle. The Civil War—then called, in the North, the War Between the States—had begun in 1861. Whitman's brother George had enlisted and been wounded in battle. In December 1862, Whitman traveled to Fredericksburg, Virginia, to find George and care for him. He located his brother and stayed with him for two weeks in the military camp where the soldier was convalescing. The suffering around the poet made a powerful impression on him.

Whitman didn't head back north after he left Virginia. He decided to remain in Washington, D.C., the engine room of the war. The city was also the location of many military hospitals to which thousands of injured soldiers were continually being transported from the battlefields. Whitman found part-time work in an army paymaster's office, doing accounts, and he spent much of his time outside work visiting the wounded.

Whitman's compassion for these wounded young men led him to learn to nurse. He spent hours every week cleaning soldiers' wounds or seeking to comfort the young men, many of them just teenagers, who were gravely injured or dying. He wrote to their families on their behalf. He solicited funds to buy the soldiers in his care oranges and tobacco. He distributed his treats and gifts for the soldiers from a haversack that became a familiar, welcome sight in the hospital wards.

Whitman was beloved in this role. Many contemporaries spoke of Whitman's radiant personal presence, and he used this warmth tenderly to care for the young men in his charge. Their letters to him reveal the love that he inspired: "We loved you from the first time we spoke to you," wrote one soldier.[1] "May god bless you forever," wrote another; "I cant find words to tell you the love their is in me for you. I hope you & I may live to meet again on this earth, if not I hope we shall meet in the world where thier [*sic*] is no more parting."² Whitman for his part felt deeply attached to his charges as well: "I cannot bear the thought of being separated from you," he wrote to one young soldier named Elijah Fox. To his own mother he wrote, "I believe no men ever loved each other as I & some of these poor wounded, sick & dying men love each other."³

Whitman wrote about how such love and caring helped the men recover or at least deal better with their injuries and trauma. "The men feel such love more than anything else. I have met very few persons who realize the importance of humoring the yearnings for love and friendship of these American young men, prostrated by sickness and wounds. To many of the wounded and sick, especially the youngsters, there is something in personal love, caresses, and the magnetic flood of sympathy and friendship, that does, in its way, more good than all the medicine in the world. Many will think this mere sentimentalism, but I know it is the most solid of all facts."⁴ In doing what he felt was his part to address where he could the human wreckage of the Civil War, Whitman was gathering evidence of the redemptive power of love between men, what he would later call "adhesiveness."

But his self-sacrifice took a toll. Exposure to viruses and infections, and his witnessing of amputations and deaths, wore down Whitman's physical resistance and strained his emotional health. He retreated from the havoc of Washington and spent seven months in Brooklyn, preparing his patriotic collection of verse, *Drum-Taps*, for publication. He then returned to Washington, where he took up a new position at the Indian Affairs section of the Department of the Interior.

Secretary of the Department of the Interior James Harlan, however, discovered that his new employee wrote frankly about sexuality. Whitman was quickly fired. The following day, sympathetic friends in the Attorney General's office hired Whitman.

Wide press attention followed his firing by the secretary of the Department of the Interior. Whitman's friends prepared and published defenses of the poet, including a book of hagiography, *The Good Gray Poet*. This volume, which helped recast the poet's reputation, positioned Whitman as a kind of ultra-patriot and poet-martyr. Factions were forming now in America, as they already had for years in Britain, blasting and counterblasting around *Leaves of Grass*.

As Edwin Haviland Miller, editor of Whitman's letters, puts it, "The fight of a book for the world" had, in yet another country, now begun.[5]

As Whitman faced negative press attention and professional battles in wartime Washington, Symonds was experiencing a second near-total breakdown of his mental and physical health.

In the autumn of 1862, Symonds was back and forth between London and Oxford, trying to recover from the scandal involving Shorting and the fellows of Magdalen College. (We know this only because some unknown hand saved Symonds's own private account from censorship: in the manuscript of Symonds's memoirs, for instance, the names "Vaughan" and "Shorting," as well as others, are heavily scored through, as if someone—probably Symonds's literary executor, Horatio Brown—had tried to delete them, but the overscoring has been smudged or erased by yet *another hand*, so as to reveal the names once again.)[6] Though he had had "a complete acquittal," Symonds felt that his "name is soiled with an unbearable suspicion; my usefulness in the College is destroyed, and Oxford is made an impossibility."[7]

In December, he and a friend, W. R. W. Stephens, began a trip to Belgium, almost losing their lives when their steamer broke down near Calais; they had to be rowed to shore in "tremendously high seas."[8] Symonds's "nervous malady," which had caused him general malaise his whole life, now manifested with trouble "in the brain and eyes" and also with "a terrible [unnamed] disturbance of the reproductive organs."[9] He also realized that he had "begun to be consumptive." His mental suffering was acute: "Scorpion-like [his mind] turned round and round in a circle of fire."[10] He won the Oxford Chancellor's Prize for an essay but was too depressed to enjoy this honor: "I did not care about the prize."

His journal records Symonds setting up house in London—but also suffering from a range of physical symptoms: life was "adverse" for him, as he put it. He reflected on his mental and physical breakdown, believing it to be connected to his suppressed sexuality: "Nature bade me indulge my sexual instincts, but these were so divided that I shrank alike from the brothel and the soldier."[11] Burned by now several shameful semi-public scandals, Symonds sought, in every way he could, to redirect his passions toward women:

> I thought that, by honest endeavour, I could divert my passions from the burning channel in which they flowed to [friend] Alfred Brooke,

and lead them gently to follow a normal course toward women. I
neglected the fact that poetry and power of expression and the
visionary pomp of dreams awoke in me only beneath the touch of
the male genius. I wanted to do right. To be as one I loved and hon-
oured, the nobler men I knew around me. Therefore in all simplicity
and sober diligence I addressed myself to the task of stimulating a
romantic feeling toward women.

These secret papers disclose the crushes he tried to whip up toward
alluring or compelling women around him. His friend, the activist Josephine Butler, tried to flirt with him: she "exercised her unhealthy spiritual
fascination (a mixture of religious fervor and flirtation) and her really
brilliant physical influence, upon me in vain." She "failed to win" the young
man, he wrote, though "she did her best to do so," taking risks herself, as
she was married.

The famous Swedish singer Jenny Lind—the "Swedish nightingale"—was another female friend on whom Symonds sought to project an
attraction he simply did not feel. Though men around the world were falling
passionately in love with the singer, Symonds wrote that "I respected her
[. . .] I admired her as a comrade."[12] Jenny Lind roused his "devotion." He
explored through these friendships an intellectual curiosity about women
but could not elicit in himself a shred of desire for women. His struggle to
do so makes for painful reading, and Symonds detailed the absolute lack
of desire he felt for these compelling, alluring women as evidence, using
himself as his test subject, that exclusive sexual attraction to men was, at
least for him and many others whose lives he wished to explain and defend,
innate and unchangeable.

The two women, he wrote, "affected my character" and "prepared me for
my wife," but in spite of his best efforts to feel passion for them, "[n]either
of them touched my sex."

None of the women around him stirred what Symonds called "the
sluggish coals of my emotion." "It is much to feel that a woman is my
ideal," wrote the young man in his journal; his older self would comment
that no "real lover" of women would ever write such a sentence. "Difficult
and abused," he concluded in his secret papers, "is the way of a young man,
who willfully is forced to warp his inclination." Finally he concluded that
the efforts were pointless. "[F]or the main purposes of life, it might have
been better if I had got me to a brothel, and tried all its inmates by turns.

What I needed was the excitation of the sexual sense for women, and the awakening to their sexual desirableness, combined with the manifold sympathies, half brutal and half tender, which physical congress evokes."[13]

In Germany, that same year, new conversations were being initiated. Karl Heinrich Ulrichs, a lawyer and writer, disclosed to his family and his close social circle that he was a man who loved men. Under a pseudonym, he wrote "Studies on the Riddle of Male-Male Love" and coined the term "Urnings" to describe such loves. He argued that such love was part of the natural order. He even coined a term for women who loved women as well as innovating terms for people whom today we would call bisexual and transgender.[14]

But this nascent European conversation did not affect British views.

Symonds's father insisted that Symonds travel again for his health, so in 1863, with male friends from college, he journeyed through Reims and Strasbourg in France to Interlaken in Switzerland. He became enamored of a fifteen-year-old peasant girl named Rosa Engel—a flirtation that came to nothing. In March 1864, there were more excursions, this time to Germany: Nuremberg, Bamberg, Dresden. There he met Arthur Sidgwick, who would become a lifelong friend and interlocutor. Arthur, brother of Henry Sidgwick, also a friend to Symonds, came from a family of six siblings that would produce distinguished reformers and educators. (Henry Sidgwick would become a moral philosopher and an advocate for women's education, helping to found Newnham College, the first women's college in Cambridge. Arthur Sidgwick would eventually marry, but for the rest of his life as a classics professor at Oxford, he would remain preoccupied with the magic quality that he felt all-male friendships and educational spaces possessed—communities that he identified with classical antiquity.)[15]

"I had heard a great deal [about Arthur Sidgwick] from Rugby and Cambridge men—of his personal beauty, graceful manners and acute intelligence," wrote Symonds in his journal. The friendship between Symonds and Arthur Sidgwick was "heightened for many years by a romantic admiration on my part. It was not quite wholesome for me at that crisis, for Arthur was enthusiastic about what I called 'Arcadia'; and this worked my feelings back again into their old channels."[16] Symonds felt magnetically drawn to Sidgwick and tempted overwhelmingly by Sigdwick's commitment to "Arcadia."

Sidgwick met Symonds again in Cologne and then traveled onward with him. Symonds eventually returned to England, but his father sent him back again to the Continent, continually anxious about his son's health and concerned about his psychological torment. Symonds didn't come back to England until the early spring of 1864.

In Clifton then, he met another formative friend: Henry Graham Dakyns, called "Graham," an assistant master at Clifton College, which had been recently established, and a friend of Arthur and Henry Sidgwick. Dakyns, who had been born in the West Indies, was also the son of a large, affluent family of six sons. Dakyns "was physically robust, athletic at football, courageous and spirited [. . .] Gentle exceedingly and sweet in converse—[Symonds writes here in Greek, a phrase that translates as "longed for by his friends"]—; Masculine to the backbone." A photograph of Dakyns in his mid-twenties, as a master of Clifton College in 1865, a few years after he and Symonds met, shows him to be powerfully built, bearded, and tall; he wears black masters' robes and mortarboard and gazes at the scene before him with a serious, even worried expression.

Symonds returned to London and roomed with his friend Rutson, sharing accommodations at 7 Half Moon Street. He dabbled with studying the law at Lincoln's Inn, socializing with students and London intellectuals, and dining at his club.

His daily life grew increasingly excruciating: a physician named Dr. Bowman arrived at his home every day to apply "deleterious caustic"—a burning substance—under both of his lower eyelids. And then Symonds had to sit for hours in a darkened room, listening to hired readers, as his eyes were too weak and inflamed to allow him to read.

Symonds's father, now very concerned, brought his son to the famous Dr. William Acton. Acton was the author of the influential textbook *The Functions and Disorders of the Reproductive Organs* (1857), which famously held that "the majority of women (happily for them) are not very much troubled by sexual feelings of any kind." Dr. Acton had a practice of cauterizing the sex organs of both men and women who practiced masturbation. To "cauterize" is to burn the skin with either a heated instrument or a caustic substance. Dr. Acton dealt with Symonds's unnamed "sexual disturbances"—perhaps Symonds's arousal by fantasies relating to men—by cauterizing the young man's penis with a heated surgical instrument; he did so via the urethra.

Still another physician, Sir Spencer Wells, met with Symonds. Sir Spencer advised Symonds to take a "hired mistress" or get married. As Symonds noted, "I felt that if I hired a mistress, or took a wife on calculation, I should be running counter to my own deepest and most powerful instincts; shutting myself out from passion and ideal love, neither of which had been indulged, although my whole being panted for them [. . .] If instinct had to be followed, I must have found its satisfaction in male friendship. But this was just what I had resolved to suppress and overcome."[17]

Soberly, Symonds consulted with his father and their family friend Sir Edward Strachey, who was a magistrate and a man of letters. The three men—two distinguished, one young and suffering—decided that Symonds should simply force himself to marry. "Then, as by inspiration, the memory of Catherine North returned to me [. . .] To her I felt that I must turn."

Resolved, Symonds met with Catherine's family at 3 Victoria Street, in London, where the Norths lived. Symonds asked if he might follow them on vacation in Pontresina. In 1864, he traveled to meet them. He went "in quest of Catherine," in August, to the Hotel Krone in the Alps to overtake her and her family. "This was earnest business on my part, charged with misgivings, not of her, but of myself [. . .]"[18] At this time of crisis, with no clear way forward unless he married a woman, Symonds continued to court her. The young people made a habit of meeting on a certain bridge and walked daily by a little lake near the village of St. Moritz, picking up their long conversations from their previous time together. "The more I saw of her, the more I felt for certain that she was the woman whom I ought to marry—for my own sake."[19] He expressed "emotional sympathies" that led him to "seek a woman for my life comrade" but also revealed that "I had treated the purely sexual appetite (that which drew me fatally to the male) as a beast to be suppressed and curbed, and latterly to be down-trampled by the help of surgeons and their cautery of sexual organs."

In spite of his misgivings about himself, Symonds was successful in his persuading of Catherine. On a day when snow was falling, Symonds asked Catherine to marry him.

He described the sweetness of the friendship and accord the two felt. But secretly he wrote, "It would endure till death, I knew. But I missed something in the music—the coarse and hard vibrations of sex, those exquisite agonies of contact, by whch [*sic*] the God in man subsumes into himself the beast and makes that godlike. The vibrations I had felt in dreams for male beings [. . .] Not discovering them now, some qualms came over me."[20]

Symonds's friend Charles Knight was also at Pontresina; he gave Symonds a warning about the step he was preparing to take: "The one thing in marriage is passion; without passion no man has the right to make a woman his wife." Symonds conceded this in his secret journal: "And while I had everything else, and have always had everything else to give Catherine—if needful, I would die for her willingly—I could not so conquer the original bent of my instincts as to feel for her the brutal unmistakable appetite of physical desire [. . .] [A]ll the difficulties of my subsequent life, and a large part of hers, have come from our not having originally started with a strong sexual attraction on either side."[21]

Catherine North recorded details of the courtship in her own journal. She noted, on the one hand, the deep love that the two felt for each other. But she also tellingly described how the two of them stood on the bridge, looking at two rocks near each other, in the eddies. She pointed out to "Johnny" that there was a gap, a few inches of distance, between the two rocks that nothing could ever erase. A perceptive young woman, she asked if in any way he saw the scene as similar to their own case. "Johnny," in response, asked her not to talk about it, as the subject was "too near."

It seems from both journals that Symonds tried to explain himself to Catherine, as clearly as he could, using the language available to him, and that Catherine accepted him, understanding overtly that while his deep love for her would make her happy, his lack of physical passion for her would always also cause her grief.

Photographs of Janet Catherine North are few; the ones that do remain reveal her to have had dark eyes with an expression of keen intelligence, and strain; she had straight dark hair, a firm set to her mouth, and a windblown complexion, as if she spent time outdoors—unusual for a lady of her era. She wears, in one image, the high-necked black silk dress of her station, but also a rakish, gypsy-like embroidered-lace cap—a woman who is compelling, yet hard to place into either a conventional or bohemian cliche.

John Addington Symonds married Janet Catherine North on November 10, 1864, in a ceremony in the picturesque village of Hastings, in Sussex— where Lizzie Siddal and Dante Rossetti had also married, just two years before. The couple honeymooned in the seaside holiday town of Brighton.

In his secret papers, Symonds wrote about his wedding night:

I shall not forget the repulsion stirred in me by that Brighton bedroom, or the disillusion caused by my first night of marriage. Disagreeable as it is, I cannot omit to tell the truth about these things [. . .] I had never had anything at all to do with any woman in the way of sex. I had only a vague notion about the structure of the female body. I had never performed any sex act with anyone, and I did not know how to go about it. I firmly expected that some extraordinary and ecstatic enthusiasm would awaken in me at the mere contact of a woman's body in bed, although I was aware that the presence of a woman did not disturb my senses in the ballroom or a carriage. I also anticipated that nature would take care of herself when it came to the consummation of marriage.

To my surprise and annoyance, I felt myself rather uncomfortable [. . .] at the side of my wife, oppressed with shyness, and not at all carried away by passionate enthusiasm. Dearly as I loved her, and ardently as I desired through marriage to enter into the state of normal manhood, I perceived that this thing which we had to do together was not what either of us imperatively required. I felt no repugnance at first, but no magnetic thrill of attraction. A deep sense of disappointment came over me when I found that the

Corps féminin, qui tant est tendre,
Poli, souef, si précieux

Did not exercise its hoped-for magic. What was worse, nature refused to show me how the act should be accomplished. This was due to no defect in me. The organ of sex was vigorous enough and ready to perform its work. My own ineptitude prevented me for several nights from completing the marital function, and at last I found the way by accident—after having teased [bothered] and hurt both my wife and myself, besides suffering dismally from the humiliating absurdity of the situation.

[. . .] I also discovered that the physical contact of a woman, though it did not actually disgust me, left me very cold. There was something in it nauseous, and cohabitation in my case meant only the mechanical relief of nature.[22]

Symonds and his new wife found lodgings in London near Hyde Park. Then they moved to a gloomy townhouse in Norfolk Square, furnished it, and settled down for a life of propriety. On October 22, 1865, their first child, Janet, was born. A nurse who was tending the baby heard the father's incessant coughing and commented, without tact, that Symonds suffered from what was called "a churchyard cough." At Christmas, his father concurred: he diagnosed Symonds with serious tubercular trouble in his left lung and told his son to abandon all hope of a traditional professional career such as the law, which Symonds had briefly considered. From now on, the young man could write and teach, but he had to rest, travel to more healthful climates than that of Britain, and take care above all in protecting his health.

Seeking a better climate for Symonds, the little family traveled to Menton, on the Riviera, then to Florence, Ravenna, a series of other warmer destinations, and back to Clifton in July.

Graham Dakyns, still a master at Clifton, married as well: a woman named Margaret Elsie Pirie. The young men of "Arcadia" were giving up any alternative futures—as indeed, there were none—and settling down, if with difficulty and emotional pain for all concerned, into the marriages and families expected of them.

But this socially sanctioned "cure" of marriage, for what was "wrong" with Symonds, proved, of course, to be no cure at all. Marriage, and even fatherhood, did not solve the problem that Symonds called "the wolf"— his powerful homoerotic desires. He felt compelled to sneak out to visit the public baths, to gaze surreptitiously at naked men. Even as he made these furtive journeys, Symonds tried to resist acting on his feelings: he did not wish to jeopardize the trust of his wife or the secure home of his baby girl. The marriage, he wrote secretly, "remained what it had been before—a union of feeling and fellow service, rather than one of passion or of *hefti[n]g liebe* [violent love]. The serious fault in it on my side has always existed, and could not be eliminated, because it belonged to the very groundwork of my nature. I was born with strong but slowly matured sexual appetites and these were incapable of finding their satisfaction with a woman. Nuptial intercourse developed them by the exercise of the reproductive organ. It did not and could not divert them from their natural bias toward the male."[23]

A year into his marriage, and its strain and disappointment, Symonds found Whitman.

Symonds was visiting a friend, Frederic Myers, at Cambridge University. Myers, who shared Symonds's feelings of attraction to other men, took an illegal 1860 *Leaves of Grass* from a shelf and began to declaim lines from the "Calamus" section, in which the love relationship is unambiguously romantic and the pronoun of the Beloved is male. Myers read:

One who loves me is jealous of me, and withdraws me from all but love,
With the rest I dispense—I sever from what I thought would suffice me,
   [. . .]
I heed knowledge, and the grandeur of The States
And the example of heroes, no more,
I am indifferent to my own songs—I will go with him I love,
It is enough for us that we are together—We never separate again.[24]

The phrases deeply stirred the twenty-five-year-old husband and father. Symonds began to implore his other friends to read the poet who had written these galvanizing lines. His friends did so, and they in turn asked Symonds to track down American or pirated British copies of *Leaves of Grass* for them to keep for themselves.

In 1865, in Washington, Walt Whitman met a man who would be one of the loves of his life: Peter Doyle, his "beloved comrade." Doyle, an Irish immigrant, was an eighteen-year-old tram conductor. Doyle described the scene when he first met the poet—Whitman was the only passenger on the tram, and a storm drenched the vehicle: "We were familiar at once—I put my hand on his knee—we understood. He did not get out at the end of the trip—in fact went all the way back with me."[25]

Though during the next decade Whitman's journal records his meeting and sleeping with "dozens" of young men, Doyle was foremost in his emotions. The two men took walks together along the Potomac River during this period and met at least weekly.

When the two were apart, Whitman wrote Doyle letters filled with endearments: "Dear Pete," "dear son," "my darling boy," "my young & loving brother."

A year after Symonds first heard the "Calamus" poems read aloud, he, and the literary world in London, witnessed yet another explosive literary scandal. In 1866, the first book of poems by twenty-nine-year-old Algernon Charles Swinburne, *Poems and Ballads*, was published by Edward Moxon. Moxon was no stranger to controversy; twenty-seven years earlier the publisher had stood fast against the outcry that greeted his publication of the poet Percy Bysshe Shelley's *Queen Mab*, a radical work on societal evil.

Now the public was once again horrified. Swinburne made overt, hypnotically cadenced references to sadomasochism, flagellation (Swinburne was himself addicted to being whipped), Sapphism—the Victorian term for sexual relations between women that today we would call lesbianism—and even cannibalism.[26]

I feel thy blood against my blood: my pain
Pains thee, and lips bruise lips, and vein stings vein.
Let fruit be crushed on fruit, let flower on flower,
Breast kindle breast, and either burn one hour.[27]

Many reviews of *Poems and Ballads* were hostile in literary terms, but some also invoked, like earlier reviews of *Leaves of Grass*, the terms of the Obscene Publications Act of 1857.[28] An article titled "Swinburne's Folly," published in the *Pall Mall Gazette*, castigated the book as "publicly obscene" and attacked its "lewd ideas and lascivious thoughts."[29] The *Athenaeum* declared that Swinburne was "unclean for the sake of uncleanness," and the *London Review* charged the poet with being "utterly revolting." The *Times* actually called for both the poet and the publisher to be prosecuted under the obscenity laws.

While some influencers, such as William Rossetti, supported Swinburne—understanding that a great deal more was at stake than some steamy or outrageous verses—others distanced themselves.

This time, under such a barrage, the formerly courageous Moxon lost his nerve. With this storm of attacks on the purported indecency of *Poems and Ballads*, he feared a second prosecution.[30] Moxon had reason to quail; the law had changed so much since 1839.

So Moxon canceled the planned print run of a thousand copies. In the context of any literary marketplace, whether 150 years ago or today, an abandoned print run is a catastrophe. The cancellation represented a loss of several thousand pounds to the publisher and made it unlikely that Swinburne would ever be published again. Swinburne's reputation and career prospects were in ruins.

Swinburne wrote furiously to a less reputable publisher, J. C. Hotten, explaining that his agreement with Moxon was at an end. The poet strategized with Hotten about purchasing the copies that had already been printed, which Moxon now refused to distribute. Swinburne even tried to concoct a way for a third party to purchase these copies, identifying them "as waste paper"—a complicated scheme, explored presumably to avoid prosecution.

Swinburne wrote:

> [Moxon's] nonfulfillment of contract has robbed me. . . . [But] I do not wish to drag the matter before a law court. . . . [Moxon] does not deny the contract which he refuses to fulfill; he simply said [. . .] that on hearing there was to be an article in the Times attacking my book as improper, he could not continue the role. As to the suppression of separate passages of poems, it could not be done without injuring the whole structure of the book, where

Algernon Charles Swinburne, around the time of the publication of the scandalous *Poems and Ballads*, circa 1865.

> every part has been so carefully considered and arranged as I could manage, and under the circumstances, it seems to me that I have no choice but to break off my connection with the publisher [. . .] Now to alter my course or mutilate my published work seems to me somewhat like deserting one's colours [. . .] One may or may not repent having enlisted, but to lay down one's arms, except under compulsion, remains intolerable.[31]

Hotten did agree to take on the risk of publishing the abandoned book. More of a strategist than Moxon had been, Hotten mobilized supporters. At Hotten's invitation, William Michael Rossetti rushed a defense of Swinburne into print. Rossetti lamented the fact that due to the "holy water of morals," Swinburne's book had been withdrawn from its planned publication; commentators for the highbrow literary periodicals had "exorcised" it:

> As to blasphemy, Swinburne is certainly a pronounced anti-Christian. And something very closely resembling an atheist; I consider that he is right in entertaining these or any other speculative opinions which commend themselves to his own mind and expressing them as freely as Christians, Mohammedans etc. express [theirs] [. . .]

As to indecency, [I do not think] his writings are likely to do any harm to anybody fitted by taste and training to admire them.[32]

William Michael Rossetti thus addressed the two main legal issues now facing booksellers and writers. He went on to protest any possible legal action against the book with the same argument that opponents of the censorship bills had used in Parliament: by making the case that it was un-British to suppress debate. And he invoked a class of readers who couldn't possibly be influenced negatively by reading the text—their elite education, he argued, protected them from any such harm.

Swinburne, for his part, now sought to rush into print his own fervent defense of his book. Hotten asked William Michael Rossetti to urge Swinburne to temper his intended discussion of censorship. So Rossetti wrote to Swinburne. In a difficult-to-read—perhaps deliberately indirect—paragraph, the critic urged the poet to make revisions that would keep Swinburne and his publisher out of prison and ended by requesting cuts to two sections. By this time, as this passage reveals, British publishers sometimes had to negotiate with their own writers to ensure that the writers did not mention prosecution in a way that might bring down prosecution on the publishers:

> [Y]ou wd probably be disposed to take into careful consideration the [note] which shows [Hotten's] own preference on a point which concerns himself personally i.e. he wd be gratified if you were to make the change there indicated rather than retain the reference to threatened prosecution [. . .] Indictable offense he hoped wld be changed if the reference to prosecution is (as he hopes) cancelled [. . .] He wld like the same fate to befall the "suppression of Common Sense" &c. here—& thinks there is some peculiar virulence in "Company" printed at full length [. . .][33]

Swinburne's final version of the essay defending *Poems and Ballads* is turgid and hardly readable. He laboriously explained that by "passion" he had actually meant suffering, not sexual passion; he claimed that he was interested in setting out a philosophy of "moral passion." This quatrain from his poem "Faustine," however, seems a far cry from the essay's argument:

Stray breaths of Sapphic song that blew
Through Mitylene

Shook the fierce quivering blood in you
By night, Faustine.[34]

Swinburne tried to persuade his readers that this racy poem was merely "symbolic and fanciful." His apologia sounds as tortured as Symonds's "Set Apology"; both writings undertake an awkward mission by means of awkward language.

By now, British writers had to say in print that what they wrote wasn't really what was written, that they hadn't meant it, that it was not intended to be understood as it sounded, and that even if it did sound a bit indecent, it referred to something else that was perfectly innocent.

Literature now had to go out into the world bearing letters of reference.

Nonetheless, Hotten's risk paid off: he immediately sold out five printings of the volume. In the wake of the scandal and the attacks, Hotten inserted into the next printings of *Poems and Ballads* slips of paper meant to prop up Swinburne's moral character. They read: "He is a young poet with sterling qualities, and the outcry that has been made over this volume is not very creditable to his critics."

But other writers saw this scandal, and many of them slowly backed away from Swinburne. The painter and critic John Ruskin, for instance, was a friend of Swinburne's from Oxford; Ruskin had been a mentor to and supporter of Dante Gabriel Rossetti and the Pre-Raphaelite painters. Indeed, he had been one of the few to recognize Lizzie Siddal's own artistic talent, in spite of her sexually compromised status, and had given her, before her marriage, 150 pounds in exchange for many of her drawings and paintings.

But in spite of his earlier progressive mentoring of these brilliant and disruptive young people, times were changing. Ruskin had previously thought it unwise for Swinburne to publish *Poems and Ballads*. Now that the volume was out, Ruskin was intimidated by the accusations of indecency in the press.[35] Like many influencers at the time, he equivocated. On the one hand, he refused to support those who wished to prosecute Swinburne's publisher. On the other hand, Ruskin sent a letter to Swinburne, distancing himself in terribly personal terms; "there is assuredly something wrong with you," he told his former friend.

Perhaps this declaration of a friend's moral wrongness—or possible insanity,—was influenced by the current legal climate. Its possible subtext was "Don't contaminate my reputation, lest they come for me." Writers were creating by necessity what lawyers today call "paper trails"—written evidence that they had opposed the publications now being targeted as obscene. Writers might use these "paper trails" as a form of defense if they were ever swept up in an obscenity trial.

Meanwhile, according to the Proceedings at the Old Bailey, sodomy trials marched on, with long sentences at hard labor: "SAMUEL KETCH (22) and JOSEPH SLADE (60) were indicted for b-g-y. [. . .] SAMUEL KETCH—GUILTY. Twelve Years' Penal Servitude. JOSEPH SLADE—GUILTY. Fifteen Years' Penal Servitude."[36]

CHAPTER 13

Regina v. Hicklin:
"To Deprave and Corrupt"

In 1867, a year after the scandal of Swinburne's *Poems and Ballads*, an appeal was brought under the Obscene Publications Act. The case, *Regina v. Hicklin*, "Queen [Victoria] against Hicklin"—centered on an anti-Catholic pamphlet. In the ruling, Lord Chief Justice Alexander Cockburn wrote an interpretation of obscenity that would change Western literature for a century.[1]

Eleven years before, Lord John Campbell had criminalized the authorial imagination and intention: according to the 1857 act, a work was criminal if it had been "written for the single purpose of corrupting the morals of youth and of a nature calculated to shock the common feelings of decency in any well-regulated mind."[2]

But now Lord Cockburn criminalized the reader's reception of the text. A decision of his led to the "Hicklin test," which involved an appeal by a critic of Catholicism, Henry Scott, whose anti-papist pamphlet had been confiscated as being obscene. Benjamin Hicklin, a court official, revoked the order of destruction. Hicklin maintained that Scott's intention had been not prurient but civic-minded—to reveal corruption within the Catholic Church.

Yet Lord Chief Justice Alexander Cockburn, to whom the appeal was made, did not agree. He concluded that the author's intention did not matter in evaluating whether or not a publication was obscene. Lord Cockburn decided that whatever an author had intended, it didn't matter: a work was obscene, he stated, if it had a "tendency [. . .] to deprave and corrupt those whose minds are open to such immoral influences, and into whose hands a publication of this sort may fall."[3] The *Regina v. Hicklin* decision had the important effect of allowing judges to assess a work out of context: if even a single part of a book or poem could be judged as obscene, the whole text could be destroyed and the author, printer, and publisher imprisoned.

The question that determined whether a crime had been committed was no longer "Is the text disturbing the king's peace?" (pre-1857) or "Did the author intend for this to be obscene?" (1857–68). Rather, it was "Could an innocent person open to corruption experience any part of this as obscene, no matter what else is in it or what the author intended?"[4]

The term "obscene" had not been defined in Lord Campbell's act of 1857, opening the door to subjective interpretations. Just as unhelpfully, Lord Cockburn left the phrase "to deprave and corrupt" equally ill-defined. Though the phrases "a well-regulated mind," "common feelings of decency," and "deprave and corrupt" were not new to society, they were new to the law and to legal precedent.

These vague terms had an immediate dampening effect on literature. They made the more conventional literature a safer avenue for writers. If readers reacted with bland approval, a writer was less likely to be prosecuted for the contents of a given work. On the other hand, any sort of heightened or disturbed reaction on the part of readers might subject an author's writing to scrutiny, possibly resulting in criminal proceedings. It became truly dangerous to express unusual, original, arousing, or socially challenging thought. Doing so could drag down writer, publisher, and bookseller alike.

For the next century, Balzac, Flaubert, Joyce, Lawrence, and scores of other writers whose work is now part of our literary treasure house would be banned, expurgated, or censored in Britain through the application to literature of the principles of the *Regina v. Hicklin* decision.

Now, in a kind of expanding Venn diagram, older 1857 censorship law and 1861 sodomy law overlapped with the 1868 *Hicklin* ruling and created another force in the shaping of modern homophobia. A work of literature that elicited conventional, mainstream responses to romantic or sexual situations posed little threat to "a well-regulated mind" and "common feelings of decency" and could be defended against a charge of "depraving" or "corrupting" vulnerable minds. Writers and readers with minority sensibilities, however, including those who experienced non-mainstream arousal, found themselves in a curious position: "always already" a criminal. Now texts that spoke to non-mainstream arousal were criminal even while being imagined, and even while being read, if the reader subjectively found them arousing and if the reader experienced them as making an impression. (This decision echoes through today's society when men, whatever their sexuality, fear being inadvertently aroused by homoerotic scenes, images, or texts; you can also see its legacy in the focus that contemporary conservative groups have, on policing the "influence" of gay male teachers or role models on the impressionable young.)

The *Hicklin* decision did not identify explicitly whose minds might be "open to such immoral influences" or how precisely they might become criminally inflamed. Over the course of the nineteenth century, this hypothetical reader came to be defined by age, amount of experience, gender, and class. A work of literature's level of obscenity could be "measured" by the impact it might have on the mind of an innocent young girl, or one's servants. Critics for the next century would ruminate on whether a publication or play "raised a blush" on the cheek of a hypothetical virginal lady. This preoccupation did not arise spontaneously; it reflects an engagement with the actual wording of the legal decision. The virgin's blush, after *Hicklin*, had actual legal valence.[5]

Judges now assessed obscenity based on the hypothetical effect specific passages might have on "impressionable" minds, stressing three questions: First, does the material arouse "impure thoughts"? Second, does it "encourage impure actions"? Finally, does it erode previously established standards of public morals? Any one of these three was enough to convict.

With Lord Campbell's earlier ideas about obscenity now recodified by Lord Cockburn, an author's personal morality became a legal issue, and it posed a legal risk to the author him- or herself. For this reason, reviews of sexually controversial books and poems in popular publications such as *Cornhill*, the *Athenaeum*, the *Academy*, and the *London Review* began, from about 1868 right up to the great censorship trials of the following century in Britain, to address exactly what "the common feelings of decency in a well-regulated mind" might be. These periodicals were taking a legal risk if they reviewed too-graphic material using too-graphic terms.

The revised Obscene Publications Act allowed judges to permit police to use force to break into bookstores, publishing houses, or writers' private homes and to search those homes and businesses. Police could order the immediate destruction of books and prints found to be obscene, and they could follow that destruction with prosecution.[6] This meant that a publisher could face immense losses if a judge took a disapproving view of the state of mind of the writer whom the publisher had commissioned. This moral scrutiny of British writers could cost publishers thousands of pounds and could end an author's literary career. Once a writer's work was confiscated as obscene, he or she would likely remain unpublishable.

The vagueness and thus the danger of the statute is clear in the legal historian Colin Manchester's analysis of the history of obscene libel: "The

definition [of obscenity] in *Hicklin* [. . .] was to be subject to varying interpretations, for the exact meaning of the formula is by no means clear."[7]
Manchester gives an example from a particular case: "Cockburn [. . .]
emphasized the tendency of the pamphlet to arouse impure thoughts, for
it would 'suggest to the minds of the young of either sex [. . .] thoughts
of an impure and libidinous nature.'" Manchester goes on to explain how
courts, after the *Hicklin* decision, were advised that the author's intention to
corrupt must be considered a fact simply because the obscene material had
been published—even if the author did not deliberately intend to "deprave
and corrupt" by writing the book.

This Catch-22 about authorial intention may have been one reason
why many authors, including Symonds and Wilde, became interested in
making the case that the author's intention was *not* to corrupt—or to go so
far as to try to set the work of art free from the author's intention entirely.
Walter Pater, for instance, would create the famous phrase "art for art's
sake," which came to denote a philosophy of art that does away altogether
with moralizing about the author's or artist's intent.

These attacks on writers had different effects on literary men and
literary women. Women such as Christina Rossetti now tended to stress
their own religiosity, morality, and sexual chastity—in other words, their
respectability. Male writers who loved men emphasized the uplifting nature
of male-male friendships and the cultural authority of Greek ideals when
they wrote, even in veiled ways, about homoerotic subjects.

To this important insight I would add that classical antiquity now had
legal utility for such men. By stressing how inspiring and ennobling male-
male love was, the writers defended themselves from the *Hicklin* caution
concerning the author's wish to "corrupt and deprave." Ancient Greece
formed a shield for male Victorian writers who loved men, safeguarding
them against possible post-*Hicklin* arrest.

As the law began to criminalize the literary imaginations of men who loved
men, as well as that of others who may have wished to write about sexuality,
Symonds began to compose in earnest a secret set of poems.

One of the most significant of them, in his own assessment—Symonds's
secret "John Mordan" poem—has been lost, but we know from his letters
and journals that he started composing this epic accounting of male-male
love in history in 1866 (he would keep revising it until 1875).

In January 1866 Symonds wrote to his then-closest friend, the now married Graham Dakyns, that "a second part of John Mordan" was "locked up beyond my reach" and that "Catherine holds the key."[8] This peculiar arrangement—in which Symonds tasked Catherine, essentially, to keep him from himself—and many other instances offer evidence that Catherine and Symonds were good friends, and that they trusted each other profoundly, though they could not be passionately physically involved.

Symonds was now under strict instructions from his physicians, and his own father, to rest and try to recover his lung function. The Symonds family spent the winter of 1866–67 with Catherine's family, the Norths, in Hastings; Catherine's father had become a member of Parliament for the area.

It is likely that Symonds brought along his copy of the 1860–61 edition of *Leaves of Grass*. Perhaps it was during this winter that he highlighted these lines in the "Calamus" cluster: "I meant that you should discover me so, by my faint / Indirections." Next to them Symonds wrote, "This is the true method wh I have failed in."[9]

On February 12, 1867, the twenty-seven-year-old Symonds wrote to Graham Dakyns that he wished to share with his friend a copy of *Leaves of Grass*; it would have been the illegal 1860 edition, which included the "Calamus" poems. But he did not risk putting the illegal text in the mail; he planned to hand-deliver it. "I cannot send you 'Calamus.' Wait till I come."[10]

In March, Symonds caught a terrible cold and did not readily recover. By May, his father insisted that once again Symonds travel for the sake of his health; his sister Charlotte was to join him, and Catherine was left behind with the toddler, Janet. Catherine was now also pregnant with the couple's second child.

From Rouen, Caen, and Dieppe, Symonds wrote to Catherine, describing the scenery, services in old churches, and the weariness of the journey. But he also tried to disclose more to her: he wrote that if he had to choose a flower, he would choose the columbine, as he had so many associations with it: "The lilac flowers in Leigh Woods, out of which I once wove a crown for the dearly loved friend of my adolescence, 'W.'"[11] He confided to his wife, too, that he prayed that his "perpetual weakness of the body" would not keep him from doing the nobler things to which he aspired.

He didn't share everything, though, with his unusually sympathetic wife. In his private notes he recorded the fact that with Charlotte, in a public garden in Coutances, he met two elderly ladies accompanied by a young male relative. Symonds noticed "the passionate suppression of the boy, alert f[o]r adventures and eager to taste love's forbidden fruit . . ." He went on: "[A]ll the while his liquid eloquent eyes were asking me: 'do you want nothing? Is there nothing to give, nothing to get?'" Symonds mourned: "But the young man and I, we wanted to be comrades, if only for a day or two in passing [. . .] to embrace and exchange experiences; to leave a mark upon each other's memory to part at last as friends with something added each to each. And things are so arranged that this may not be, though I cannot, for the soul of me, see why they should not be."[12]

He returned to England; he felt worse than he had before the trip. The summer of 1867 was hot, and he longed for Switzerland. Poems poured out of him—all of them on the subject of male-male love. He continued work on "John Mordan." Other secret poems were titled "Diego" and "Love and Music."

He recorded in his secret papers that "I entirely misunderstood my own case." His health was deteriorating: "What was really happening was that I was pining away through the forcible repressions of my natural inclination for the male sex." He was living now, he wrote, as a bachelor within his marriage. Catherine had expressed "repugnance" for the marital bed before she had, probably reluctantly, gotten pregnant for the second time; in an age before reliable contraception and before safe childbirth and anesthesia, this aversion to intercourse even within marriage was not uncommon among women. The couple's second daughter, Charlotte, called Lotta, was born on July 30, 1867; after Lotta's birth, both members of the couple tried to avoid having intercourse.

It was now a sexless, emotionally attenuated marriage, though both husband and wife were trying their utmost to be kind to each other and to meet each other's needs. But as Symonds wrote in his secret papers, "I was in a perpetual fever [. . .] Early in the morning I used to rise from a sleepless bed, walk across the Park, and feed my eyes upon the naked men and boys bathing in the Serpentine. The homeliest of them would have satisfied me; and I wrote my feelings out in a prose poem [. . .] Sometimes the literary expression of my incurable malaise assumed an almost hysterical force [. . .] Give me love, love; to taste love, such as I imagine it, at length [. . .]"[13] In a secret poem titled "Song of the Cyclades," he wrote, in clumsy imitation of Walt Whitman, "The morning of seeing young swimmers, of bursting my heart for love of them."

Benjamin Jowett, a revered tutor at Oxford and master of Balliol, a translator of Plato and Thucydides, asked Symonds to translate some Aristotle; so by day, Symonds was peering at tiny Greek letters and referring to dictionaries, though his eyes were still continually inflamed. With dogged, even self-destructive determination, Symonds finished the translation even as this inflammation became chronic, and only then flung the manuscript away.

His work was tedious, his eyes and lungs hurt, and Symonds's emotional misery was intense. "I recognized the fact that I was not truly living or alive, nay that I was very seriously dying [. . .] But I had not arrived yet at the point when passionate experience could be freely inconsiderately attempted [. . .] It was nearly three years before the clouds began to roll away under the keen breezes of what I still condemned as a sin."[14]

In September the family crossed the Channel, accompanied by servants. They entered Switzerland, where Symonds felt "infinite peace."[15] Symonds had always breathed more easily in the Swiss Alpine air, and he now felt better immediately. The Symondses stayed in Glion for a month. Then the family went sightseeing in wet weather—Geneva, the Rhone, Grenoble, Avignon, Nîmes, Arles. Henry Sidgwick came out to join the group.

At Cannes, Symonds's health again declined. He sprained an ankle, and no doctor could treat it properly; his "nervous irritation" felt at times like "insanity," in his words. He was in "a devil's cauldron," he wrote secretly, assailed by "[a]ll the evil humours." Severely depressed, Symonds felt beset by sorrow about his "disappointment of the sexual sense in marriage," by the feeling that there was no moral basis for society, and by the worsening condition of his lungs.[16]

Now that he was done with the Aristotle translation, he wrote something he kept secret—something entirely new: "I composed the first draft of an essay on Greek Love." This essay, as we will see, remained in manuscript for some time.

Symonds, in his misery, felt the urge to connect with the reassurance and inspiration that Whitman represented. He wrote to Graham Dakyns that he would seek an introduction to Whitman's friend, the American physician and Whitman evangelist Moncure Conway, who was then in London: "From him I hope to learn something more about the innovator. I shall not omit to ask him questions about the substance of Calamus—as adroitly as I can [. . .]"[17]

Fights raged, still, about Whitman in literary Britain. But now they couldn't be waged outright. By this time, the post-*Hicklin* legal landscape was affecting the language used in literary reviews. Just as we saw tangled grammar protecting Swinburne's self-defense in 1866, now impossible-to-follow grammar became a hallmark of the few positive reviews of Whitman's work: "[A] careful perusal of these remarkable productions has convinced us that the vague impression we have now and then encountered that Walt Whitman is a kind of 'learned pig' is far from correct; we cannot pretend to name his species exactly, but it is certainly winged."[18]

The strange, roundabout wording reflects the fact that periodicals, reviews, and newspapers could now face legal action for printing any kind of open discussion of what was being censored in this erotic text. Even the journalistic discussion of censorship and the editorial assessment of sexual content had to be censored. In the midst of the swirling if oblique debates over what should and should not appear in print, John Hotten made another extraordinary decision. He asked William Michael Rossetti, who had been such an adroit ambassador for Swinburne's *Poems and Ballads*, to serve now as an advocate for an even more dangerous book: a British edition of *Leaves of Grass*.

Hotten, William Michael Rossetti, and Swinburne met to discuss the legal risks of publishing an unexpurgated *Leaves of Grass*. The men concluded that there were indeed serious risks—an unexpurgated volume could not be published without everyone involved facing potential prosecution. Nonetheless, Rossetti agreed to edit the manuscript for an expurgated version, though he did so reluctantly. He hoped that it would pave the way for British audiences to accept, in time, the real thing. Rossetti's determination to complete this task—even while at the very same time, critical brickbats, aimed at Swinburne, flew past his ears—is a little-known act of heroism in the history of publishing.

In a letter to his British-based friend and passionate advocate, the abolitionist minister and radical writer Moncure Conway, Whitman commented on Hotten's proposed publication. He wanted, he wrote, for Hotten to "sell his English publication of my Poems" on the condition that Whitman would receive a shilling per copy. Whitman also asked Conway to send him "noteworthy" British criticism of the book. The poet recognized that he had a potent advocate in William Michael Rossetti: "I wish to send my sincerest thanks & personal regards to Mr. Rossetti. To have had my book, & my cause, fall into his hands, in London, [I] consider one of the greatest pieces of good fortune."[19] Whitman's assessment was prescient.

William Michael Rossetti knew that he was undertaking a contradictory literary task by assembling this collection. He selected the poems that would not offend the Obscene Publications Act and discarded the others—while hoping that this maimed volume would give Whitman's renegade voice at least a place in Britain's literary landscape.[20] Rossetti asked Whitman for his permission to take out what he called "venereal sores or discolorations" and "any degeneracy of young men." Rossetti himself acknowledged that he bowdlerized Whitman in 1868 in order to save a version of the poet, and a version of his poetic voice, for publication for an English audience:

> As some of Whitman's poems are regarded as indecent, and others (though quite unconcerned with indecent subject-matter) contain phrases open to the same objection, I went on the principle of omitting everything to which any such imputation, major or minor, can attach. The consequence is that I excluded several of the compositions which are the most characteristic and (apart from this single and sometimes disputable objection) the most praiseworthy. Let me say here that I wholly dissent from the idea that Whitman is an immoral writer; but I amply agree with people who think that some of his writings, in whole or part, put certain matters with a downrightness and crudity or even coarseness of expression which is rightly resented on the grounds not only of decorum and delicacy but also literary art.[21]

The bowdlerized Hotten edition of *Leaves of Grass* came out in 1868. William Michael Rossetti had cut many of the most important of Whitman's poems.[22] Most of the "Calamus" poems were missing entirely; "Song of Myself" and "Children of Adam" did not appear. The "degeneracy of young men" was indeed scrubbed from this volume. In fact, about half of the poems were left out. In this sad and deceptive guise, Whitman finally entered polite British society.

There was now no need to import *Leaves of Grass* secretly or pass it in silence from hand to trusted hand. You could buy this edition openly. But for Symonds and others, who had been deeply touched by the original, it must have seemed that the heart had been cut out of the book.

Hotten, writing in the *Examiner* on April 18, 1868, promoted the safe, cut-up volume he had managed to produce: "It seems as if it would have been easy for Mr. Rossetti to have done his work much better, but he did well in putting in a shape available to English readers the best, and some of the most characteristic, writings of Walt Whitman."[23] Hotten's readers would have understood that one meaning of "a shape available to English readers" was "a text that conforms to British obscenity laws." Hotten referred to Whitman's material as "crude" and "coarse," a hat-tip to the law, but then exonerated Whitman by invoking his almost Christlike origins as a "carpenter." He compared Whitman's doctrines to those of the apostle Paul. This overdone spiritualizing was meant to frame the publication in an "uplifting" manner, to circumvent *Regina v. Hicklin*, and to forestall any legal challenge relating to "corruption."

. William Michael Rossetti, for his part, protected himself from legal attacks by warning readers in his introduction about the "very serious faults" in the original work. In a twenty-seven-page introduction, the editor explained and justified what he had deleted and not deleted. He had made the decisions, he wrote, to edit out the sexual material in Whitman by a process of "omit[ting] entirely every poem which could with any tolerable fairness be deemed offensive to the feelings of morals or propriety in this peculiarly nervous age." The echo of the wording of *Regina v. Hicklin* was clear. He had culled all "indecencies or improprieties" to suit a British audience. Still, he wrote, awkwardly nonetheless defending the poet, the "deforming crudities" of the original were part of the poet's voice, and "to call them immoralities would be going too far."[24] This introduction could have been dictated by a barrister. Stuffy footnotes accompany various poems, and little was left to either offend or to liberate anyone.

Christina Rossetti is likely to have carefully followed her brother William's work on expurgating the book. She knew he would face danger if his pen was too careless. The Rossettis were far from wealthy; a criminal defense could ruin them. Did the furor surrounding the unexpurgated Swinburne and her brother's balancing-act effort to create a carefully censored volume of Whitman affect her own voice and persona?

From this year forward Christina Rossetti primarily presented herself as a writer of religious verse. She turned away from the themes of passion and appetite, both physical and spiritual, that had previously preoccupied her. Now her collections of verse focused on purely spiritual themes. The "lover" and the "Beloved," from that year on, are almost always the bridegroom Jesus. This rebranding worked.

Her religious verses after 1868 were often repetitive and conventional. They lack the strangeness, sensuality, and fire of "Goblin Market." Few people read them today. But after this abrupt change in her voice, Christina

Rossetti became increasingly popular and widely published in her own lifetime; she was at length almost sanctified in popular culture.

After the scandals that she witnessed from a vantage point so close to home, she managed to secure an unassailable position. In the battlefield that publishing had become, she was honored, compensated, and safe, known as the "Poetess of Purity."

The publication of Hotten's tepid *Leaves of Grass* was a success. The establishment smiled.

The influential *Saturday Review* loved Rossetti's edition of this work. It bemoaned the fact that the earlier American versions that had found their way to England had been "indescribably filthy." But the new version, the magazine was pleased to announce, was at last suitable to be offered "to the British public in a comely form."[25] But was it indeed "a comely form"—with half of the poems left on the editorial cutting-room floor?

Does any manuscript, hewn by censors and not by the author and editor, retain any organic shape, any breath of life? Reading the 1869 bowdlerized *Leaves of Grass* beside the original 1860 version is to experience anew the miracle of reading and also to see anew the damage that censorship really does: it maims a relationship. A reader accompanies a writer on what is, ideally, an oddly transformational journey together, undertaken side by side. Censoring the text interrupts that intimate movement forward together in time.

Whitman, in his later letters, referred to the Rossetti edition as "the horrible dismemberment of my book."[26] Yet this "dismemberment" was the only version of *Leaves of Grass* published legally in Britain during Whitman's lifetime. Whitman—strategically?—put it on the record that he was unhappy about the excisions, but at the same time, he did not take any action to prevent them.[27] Each man involved in the publication played his role in getting this curtailed version into British hands.

Even though Whitman had allowed William Michael Rossetti to publish this bowdlerized *Leaves of Grass*, he had insisted that the original frontispiece remain: that provocative, open-necked portrait. But the image was not reproduced as the poet requested. In Britain, the iconic image of Whitman himself was cropped, leaving out most of the poet's body.[28] It accompanied the equally disembodied text.

That year, more teenage boys than ever before were sent to the dark and brutal courthouse, the Old Bailey according to the Proceedings.

Fifteen-year-old Stephen Alexander received a six-month sentence at the Old Bailey for "the attempt" at sodomy: "GUILTY of the attempt. Recommended to mercy [. . .] on account of his youth."[29] Another adolescent, fifteen-year-old William Tibble, was also convicted for "the attempt" and received a sentence of a year's imprisonment.

As these young boys were taken from their families in the courtrooms after sentencing and escorted to prison cells, the "dismembered" *Leaves of Grass* went on sale. With its buttoned-down revised image of the author, who now looked exactly like every proper Victorian gentleman, it was freely available in bookstalls across England.

No one who picked it up, though, or bought it could even know to ask what "Calamus" meant.

In 1868, the Symonds family was still itinerant: Monaco, Bordighera, Corsica, northern Italy, then Germany and back to Clifton. Marcus Aurelius and Walt Whitman, Symonds wrote secretly, "are my companions." In April, with friends, including the writer and artist Edward Lear, the family journeyed through Tuscany: "[T]he congenital bent of my temperament was perpetually causing me uneasiness. All kinds of young men—peasants on the Riviera, Corsican drivers, Florentine lads upon Lugarno in the evenings, facing at Venice [. . .]—used to pluck at the sleeve of my heart, inviting me to fraternize, drawing out of me the sympathy I felt for male beauty and vigour. The sustained resistances to these appeals, the prolonged reversion to mere study as an anodyne for these desires, worried my nerves; and sometimes I broke out rebelliously into poems of passionate longing." He described Catherine as being at his side, "lovingly waiting on my irksome moods and illnesses"—even as his intense frustration and despair led him finally to a state of "indifference" to the demands of his passionate inner nature.[30]

Secret poems continued to pour out of him. One of these poems Symonds titled "Phallus Impudicus." That is the Latin name of a phallic-shaped fungus called the "common stinkhorn," which has a revolting stench:

> *At a touch [. . .]*
> *The strange thing vibrated, and lewdly thrust*
> *Up from the gloom its mimicry of lust;*
> *For here had nature, in a freakish mood,*

Of mud and water framed a filthy brood:
Symbols priapic, phallic, prurient, crude
Of human needs and yearnings unsubdued.
Poisonous and loathsome both to touch and smell
Rotten and rotting, reeked the spawn of hell
emblem of heat unhallowed, foul desire [. . .][31]

Truly, in its description of a phallic natural growth that represents unhallowed desire—a description filled with repugnance that continues for several pages—Symonds had written the anti-"Calamus." But he concluded, in a sudden about-face, defiantly:

—Do you loathe me?
Curse me? I smile and care not. Spurn and shun me?
Let all the world be sane; count me as a madman!
Have I not seen, felt, fingered, tasted? Lo,
Ye are the madmen; it is I am sound.[32]

He wrote in his secret journal, "Being what I am, the great mistake—perhaps the great crime of my life, was my marriage[.] I did not overcome abnormal passions [. . .] There is no word of blame for my wife here. She has been at every point a good, true, honest, loving and devoted wife to me. She is a woman whom better and happier men than I might have worshipped with sex-generated passion [. . .] But I shall go to the grave with an unsatisfied desire."[33]

The Symonds family returned from the Continent, and Symonds started teaching at Clifton College. They settled at 7 Victoria Square in Bristol; Symonds's father-in-law was reelected once again as member of Parliament for Hastings.

In December his third daughter, Margaret, was born. The family called the baby "Madge."

Catherine was keeping house and overseeing the household staff; the couple was occupied with the local community, with their two young daughters, and with the new baby girl. But Symonds's restlessness within did not abate. In July 1868, he wrote Dakyns that an "Essay"—probably *A Problem in Greek Ethics*—had joined the secret poems in the locked metal box.

That summer, Symonds first wrote to William Michael Rossetti. He politely but insistently asked the editor exactly which poems from the British edition of *Leaves of Grass* had been excised and why this "purgation," as he called it, had taken place. Symonds wanted to know if Whitman himself had authorized the excisions. He especially missed "Calamus," he told the editor: "May I be permitted, [to] ask you on what account you have omitted Sleep-Chasings and A Leaf of Faces [. . .] Is it because you would not submit them to the necessary purgation for English readers? I remember that one passage in the latter poem moved Tennyson's wrath in particular [. . .] I should also have liked to see the poem Calamus (old edition) the more so perhaps because it has been omitted in the last edition by Whitman himself. Do you happen to know what induced him to suppress it?"[34]

William Michael Rossetti didn't answer directly. He couldn't.

Rossetti had, of course, suppressed the "Calamus" poems. But just as Symonds couldn't legally spell out his specific question about "Calamus," even in a private letter, Rossetti couldn't legally explain to a reader—even in a private letter—why "Calamus" was no longer to be found.

CHAPTER 14

Dangerous Poems

The topic of "Greek love" continued to provide psychological shelter for Symonds. His specialty at Clifton College was a series of lectures in which he instructed young ladies in the same core classical texts that had awakened him too as a student: Plato and Socrates, the *Iliad* and the *Odyssey*.

While his days were filled with respectable family life and with lecturing, he reached out to some of the most advanced thinkers of his time. He was a skillful flatterer, liked to be in touch with influential people, and could initiate a lasting epistolary friendship with a letter or two.

His 1869 letters reveal that Symonds was developing rich friendships with powerful people outside his Clifton milieu. He saw political opposition to the Contagious Diseases Acts crystallize. Quakers, Methodists, and Anglicans all began to speak out against them. Two main activist groups—the National Association for the Repeal of the Contagious Diseases Acts and the Ladies' National Association for the Repeal of the Acts—were formed, with the purpose of changing the laws. These organizations could be called the first nationwide formal feminist political action groups.

And Josephine Butler was now, as Symonds, her friend, watched, becoming the leading voice in the land against these acts. In speeches and in opinion pieces, she sharpened her argument. She was a model of courage in the face of hostility; when she spoke in public, for instance, members of the audience often pelted her with rotten fruit, but she kept on speaking. Butler and her fellow activists endured other kinds of ostracism and abuse as well. But she, and they, persisted.

Butler used Britain's own most authoritative documents to bolster her argument: She protested that the acts violated the Magna Carta and its guarantee of due process of law. She used morally based reasoning, turning upside-down the rhetoric that justified as moral the arrests of these "immoral" women: the state, she said, was the party that was behaving immorally. Its cruel treatment of women assaulted, she said, "[t]he feelings of those whose sense of shame is not wholly lost, and further brutaliz[es] even the most abandoned." She highlighted, as many feminists then did, the sexual double standard, which punished women and left heterosexual men alone; she argued that it was "unjust to punish the sex who are the victims of a vice, and leave unpunished the sex who are a main cause, both of the vice and its dreaded consequences."[1] Other well-known women, such as the influential journalist, travel writer, and reformer Harriet Martineau, in a kind of tipping-point aggregation, joined forces with Butler. These women presented a petition against the acts to Parliament.[2]

John Addington Symonds was well aware of the price that his friend paid for her dissent. She was taking action on a difficult-to-discuss sexual issue and the state's unfair persecution of women, carried out by violating their bodies. But he also saw her remain steadfast and pursue her campaign in the face of hostility; she organized effectively, changed the terms of the conversation about arrests of women, and gained ground with Parliament. Is it possible that Symonds's experience of observing this model of persistent, strategic activism planted a seed that could bear fruit later in his own advocacy, and with his own circle of friends?

Perhaps in part because of the daring examples set by correspondents such as Josephine Butler, Symonds became increasingly frustrated by his domestic setting and his predictable life.

The young father and college professor was hired to prepare a student for matriculation at Oxford. The student's name was Norman Moor. Photographs of Moor show a handsome, dark-haired man who looks physically powerful; with full lips, he smiles mischievously at the camera. Symonds, in spite of his commitment to shunning "the wolf," could not help but fall deeply in love with his student. In Symonds's letters to his closest male friends, Moor soon became, simply, "the Beloved." Symonds's almost-daily letters to Graham Dakyns, for instance, were filled with updates about the relationship. It was the first enduring sexual relationship with another man in Symonds's adult life.

The love affair would last for four years. It occupied Symonds's imagination; for the first time as an adult, he expressed the deep emotions that up to this point he had managed to repress. He even left Catherine and the girls behind to take Moor on a journey to Italy and Switzerland. When he came home to his wife and his houseful of small children, he still pined for

Moor, and for the more open societies of Venice and Naples. "Had I wanted to live a poem, I should have chosen Venice, and not Clifton," he wrote.

In his letters to his trusted male friends, he described new experiences of sexual intimacy with Moor—though both men felt conflicted about some of the acts they sought to share. On May 16, 1869, for instance, Symonds wrote to Dakyns about his unhappiness that Moor "has not come tonight, [which] was to have been one of our sacred nights."[3] He complained that Moor "does not by any means feel strongly toward me. It is I who baise [kiss] and he who tend la joue [holds out the cheek]." Symonds worried that he was no longer a novelty to the younger man: "Only I have asked so much & so passionately & have shown such intense desire that I feel I ought in self-respect to leave him now to give of his free will," he wrote. "[. . .] I seem to see him saying [Greek: 'Why do you tempt me, Satan?']."[4]

The men had private meetings in the family home even while Catherine was present, and Symonds's letters suggest intimacies when she was away. In March 1869 Symonds wrote to Dakyns, "I am dazzled by a pair of wrists & upturned hands."[5] Several lines from Theocritus, in Greek, follow. Translated, they read, "O enviable Komatas, you, in very truth, should experience delights here [. . .] But, beloved, concede to these nonsenses of mine." This use of Greek as code and tactic was not now unusual: educated homosexual men had started to translate certain phrases in their letters into Greek. These sentences could make it through the mail and into a private home with reasonable safety; the maids who might tidy up a desk generally lacked a classical education.

Under the pressure, perhaps, of his frustration, Symonds composed a series of illicit poems about male-male desire. Into them he poured all of the things he could not say in letters, including the emotions and physical feelings involved in love affairs between men; he described sodomy as the consummation of a relationship. But even as his inner life as an artist was flourishing, he maintained stern control over how and to whom he communicated about this inner life. He tested the relationships around him, reaching out in oblique terms to see which of his friends might be trusted with the secret that he wished both to keep and to share. His letters from this time are painful reminders that a rebuke from a friend was not just socially embarrassing; it might also present terrible legal danger.

On April 1, he wrote to Henry Sidgwick about a long love cycle, "Eudiades," which he was composing. Set in classical antiquity, it concerns a beautiful Greek youth, Eudiades, and his older male lover, Melanthius. The centerpiece of the poem is Melanthius's intense longing for the intimacy of anal sex, and his extreme regret, and fear of ostracism, after attaining it. Symonds finally showed Henry Sidgwick "Eudiades" and shared other secret poems, all of them focused on homoerotic love scenes and all hidden in the locked cache in Symonds's study. Symonds also sent Graham Dakyns a copy of "Eudiades."

Dakyns challenged Symonds, pointing out that it was dangerous for either of them to harbor the secret poems that included scenes of sodomy. "As to my cycle," Symonds responded, "I determined in August to suppress these poems; and now the deed is done. I shake from my wings those drops of morning dew. What matters it if ephemerals such as Eudiades perish? This brain holds a dozen Eudiadeses. And you were quite at liberty, so far as I am concerned, to burn it."[6]

But Symonds couldn't stop there. He went on to defend what he had written: "[A]bout Eudiades, I still have something to say. The poem was written with an attempt to realize an historical situation. You asked me what I meant by the temptation of the lovers. I chose to depict one of those young men of Plato's *Phaedrus*, who recoil from acts which were permissible in Hellas. But I admit there is an element of pathos in the poem, which makes it what you call 'Orectic' [focused on appetite] and therefore inartistic."[7]

Symonds defended his lovers' desire to unite in an act of anal sex as something that had been "permissible in Hellas," that validating reference. And yet he had to put onto paper a condemnation of his own "pathos"— that is, his own sympathetic depiction of the lovers. Because the story of the lovers uniting in the act of sodomy was told without disgust, it was against the law. It was, Symonds was forced to agree—with a homosexual friend who may have felt forced to say it—that the poem was too "Orectic," too sensual, too positive about this forbidden act of the body.

Several months later, on October 2, 1869, the relationship with Moor was likely consummated in this most dangerous of ways. Symonds continued to need to tell his close friends about his consuming love affair, though always in code. He sent Henry Sidgwick a quatrain, half in Greek:

> . . . *[the beast in us] rose and roared last night*
> . . . *[the child] was petulant and longed for play*
> . . . *[the god] kept silence seated far away*
> . . . *With good intentions lost & out of sight.*[8]

Henry Sidgwick was appalled, as Dakyns had been, at receiving this disclosure, and he too warned his friend again about the potential consequences of showing verse such as this to anyone.

To Graham Dakyns, Symonds wrote later: "I have not meant to be silent. I wrote you a long letter & tore it up because it was a chocked [choked] confused incoherent of what cannot must not may not be expressed [. . .] Tear this up," he concluded.[9]

But Symonds could not, did not, end the affair. A year later, his diary entry of January 28, 1870, recorded that "I stripped him [Moor] naked and fed sight, touch and mouth on these things."

A month after that, Symonds wrote a clumsily satirical letter to the college's literary magazine, the *Cliftonian*.[10] In the guise of having stumbled upon scraps of paper from the wastebaskets of famous poets, Symonds wrote pastiches of Swinburne, William Morris, and Tennyson. One of the satirical poems was a pastiche of "Walter Whitman, Esq.":

> *Who are you? Come forth. Whoever you are, I will unmask you.*
> *Forth from the broadcloth and gaiters, from the starched shirt and*
>   *shaven chin, from the creaking boots and spectacles, from the*
>   *worsted gloves and well-brushed hat.*
> *Wriggle and twist as you like. I am inexorable. You shall not elude me.*
> *British Philistine! Let others despise you. I will not despise you.*
> *Things in their places are good, and things not in their places are good*
>   *also. I do not despise you. I commiserate you.*[11]

It was a remarkable verse for Symonds to publish in a local journal— one that was read by his wife, many of his neighbors, and his coworkers at Clifton College. The *Cliftonian* is a chatty, smugly cliquish publication, in which satire and former-public-schoolboy inside jokes mingle with hearty reports of cricket games and sports scores. Through the veil of satire, the writer announced to the Clifton community his refusal to "despise" what we would call homosexuality, and addressed the painful dilemma presented by suppressing true desire: "Wriggle and twist as you like. I am inexorable. You shall not elude me."

The following year, the secret poems became a touchpoint among Symonds's friends. Edward Clifford, one such friend, asked Symonds in October 1870 if he might see the "unpublished productions."[12] It may have alarmed Symonds that friends who had only heard of the poems through others contacted him, asking to see them; it meant that word was getting out. To T. E. Brown, another master at Clifton College, Symonds wrote in November, "All these poems of mine are about to proceed on a long journey—illic under negate etc [to that place whence they deny etc.]." This phrase meant that Symonds knew that the poems would never be published and that he was planning somehow to do away with them.[13]

Still concerned about the risk they presented to the entire group of friends, Henry Sidgwick continued to try to persuade Symonds to destroy the "dangerous" poems. As Symonds wrote later, his friend "thoroughly investigated the subject of my poems on Eros. His conclusion was that I ought to abandon them, as unhealthy and disturbing to my moral equilibrium. I assented. We locked them all up in a black tin box. Having done this, Henry threw the key into the river Avon."[14]

What Symonds threw into the swirling eddies of the Avon in 1870 was not merely the "key," or the access, to his suppressed emotions; he was also destroying part of the evidence of a crime. Because of the terms of the Obscene Publications Acts, literary self-expression and legal self-incrimination often amounted to the same thing. And because "In Memoriam Arcadie" and the verses in "Eudiades" dealt frankly with lovers who wanted anal sex, the poems could also be used against Symonds as evidence in a sodomy trial, and the sentence could be a lifetime at hard labor or transportation.

But—how thorough was Symonds's self-purgation? In that private ceremonial, Symonds allowed Henry Sidgwick to throw only the *key* to the box into the rushing river. He could not bring himself to actually throw the box *itself* and destroy his work. Could there be a more vivid metaphor for the conflict between his need to suppress and his stubborn longing, at whatever risk to himself, to express?

In February 1871, Symonds once again came under scrutiny triggered by rumors about his sexuality. He had written to a friend that he had found "genius marked" on the face of one of his Clifton College students; word of this reached the student's father. The father was one of a number of parents upset over the Clifton headmaster's investigation into the possibility of homosexual activity among Clifton College's teachers.[15] In a twisted return of his own adolescent history, Symonds had to face the young man's outraged father, who demanded clarification of the letter.

Frightened by this near-exposure, Symonds tried still harder to purge his study of incriminating content. He wrote to Graham Dakyns that he and James, his servant, had carried down into a courtyard "great loads of [. . .] letters & burned them all."[16]

A month later, nonetheless, the relentless Symonds wrote to Dakyns, "I send you some verses. Five or six stanzas want cutting out. I have marked which they are."[17] To Henry Sidgwick, he wrote, "I send a poem of mine which escaped burial in November by accident. Please return that I may burn it."[18]

In a reprise of Symonds's method—throwing away the key but retaining the box that it unlocked—the young man of letters now dramatically burned his letters yet still ensured that a few copies would somehow escape the flames.

PART V

The Laboratory of Empire

CHAPTER 15

Six Signs:
"The Anus and the State"

W hen the new decade of the 1870s began, Symonds and Moor had been together for two years. Catherine was now apparently aware of the attachment.

But a new fear was gripping Symonds and his circle, based on yet another political development that could endanger them. The British state, as we've seen, had perfected the bureaucracy for arresting "deviant" women and inspecting them intrusively, with the result of intimidating all women. The state's next target was the men whose sexuality it had found to be unruly, or "deviant." Its new mission was similarly to invade and punish the bodies of these men, by means of a new pseudoscience and a quasi-medical industry.

In sodomy trials, the state had begun to seek out testimony from a new breed of medical men. They claimed to be able to determine, by means of intrusive examinations, whether a man had been anally penetrated in an act of sodomy. Their field of study was called "venereology."

There is a modern meaning for this term; it refers to the field concerned with treatment of venereal diseases. In 1870, though, the field included the study of venereal diseases but also a lucrative and socially influential sideline. Its practitioners worked with criminologists, the police, and the courts to confirm who was a virgin, who was a prostitute, who had been raped, and who had had anal sex. In rape cases, these physicians asserted that they could even identify "virginal" breasts.

This supposed "science" descended to British criminal justice from Auguste Ambroise Tardieu, a French physician who had in 1857—that force-field year of rule-making—written a forensic medical treatise, *Étude Medico-Legale sur les Attentats aux Moeurs* (*Forensic Study on Offenses against Morals*). In it, Tardieu alleged that a physician or other investigator could positively identify a prostitute by examining her vagina, and a passive sodomite by examining his anus. Tardieu had listed what he called the "six signs" of anal penetration that inevitably, he wrote, would reveal whether passive sodomy had occurred.[1]

As Scott Long, an activist for international human rights and a legal historian, points out in his important essay "When Doctors Torture: The Anus and the State," according to Tardieu, these "six signs" included "excessive development of the buttocks; funnel-shaped deformation of the anus; relaxation of the sphincter; the effacement of the folds, the crests, and the wattles at the circumference of the anus; extreme dilation of the anal orifice; and ulcerations, hemorrhoids, fistules." Tardieu maintained that of all of these, the funnel-shaped anus was "the unique sign and the only unequivocal mark" of passive sodomy. Men who practiced active sodomy, Tardieu insisted, had penises that were correspondingly altered in shape: either a "slim, attenuated member" or a glans tapered like "the snout of certain animals."[2]

These "six signs" were, unsurprisingly, debunked decades later. Dr. Lorna Martin, professor of forensic pathology at the University of Cape Town, South Africa, terms Tardieu's theories "bizarre and antiquated rubbish," adding that "it is impossible to detect chronic anal penetration; the only time the [forensic anal] examination could be of any use is for acute non-consensual anal penetration, when certain injuries may be seen."[3] In other words, on the basis of an *imaginary* taxonomy, by 1870, British men could be brutally examined and sent to prison.

The state's campaign had begun abroad in the 1860s. In the colony of India and in North African colonies as well, British colonial administrators had found Tardieu's taxonomy useful. The Indian Penal Code of 1860 had codified anti-sodomy laws abroad, criminalizing male-male sex acts in parts of the British Empire that had never singled out such intimacy for outraged attention, let alone prosecution. British forensic medical experts justified the arrests by citing Tardieu. They used his imaginary "six signs" of the anus as metrics in arresting, examining, and convicting colonial subjects who had been accused of being "catamites." Officials found that arresting subjects for what had been private acts was an effective tool. It helped keep vast subject populations under the control of a small group of British colonial administrators. Expanding this arsenal of tools was a priority.

Populations in Britain were targeted next. In the 1860s the role of official adviser to the state on "medical forensics" had been instituted, bringing medical forensics to the state on a national level; at this time, the discipline was becoming professionalized.

The toxicologist Alfred Swaine Taylor had published *Manual of Medical Jurisprudence* in 1844, and he reprinted and updated it over the next two decades; later editions include Tardieu's "six signs" of sodomy. Designed to help officials understand how to apply the law to evidence retrieved from appraising actual bodies, bedding, fluids, and so on, the book makes some extraordinary statements that would have far-reaching effects. Taylor's tone is dry but utterly confident. The 1866 edition reads: "The late professor Amos remarked that for one real rape tried on the circuits, there were an average twelve pretended ones!"[4] Taylor also calmly explained that the law allows an adult man to have intercourse with a girl above the age of ten, as that was the age of consent for girls—a subject about which we will hear more later.

That edition also explained clearly that now only penetration was enough to condemn the accused sodomite: "It shall not be necessary, in the case of rape, sodomy or carnal abuse of a child under the age of ten years, to prove the actual emission of seed [. . .] but the carnal knowledge shall complete upon proof of penetration."[5] In other words, now evidence of semen, confirmed under a microscope, was no longer what was required to convict; attention shifted to the condition of the anus. Taylor's certainty likely assuaged any fear, among judges and police, of a false accusation or conviction caused by a "misreading" of the anus (there is no less odd way to describe this). After offering this basis of proof, which he presents as definitive evidence, Taylor acknowledges uncertainty that is related to blackmail and false accusations, which he admits were common: "Trials for sodomy and bestiality are very frequent [. . .] It is punishable by penal servitude for life, under the 24th & 25th Vict. C. 100, s 61. There cannot be the slightest doubt that false charges of sodomy are more numerous than those of rape, and that this is too often a successful mode of extortion [. . .] [I]t is especially deserving of notice that these accusations are very frequently made by soldiers and a mad class of policemen."[6] So, paradoxically, at the same time that Taylor asserted that the state of the anus was definitive proof of sodomy, he conceded that false accusations of sodomy were commonplace.

And, in a twist on the idea that you can't really rape a woman if she doesn't somehow invite the assault, Taylor asserted that there was no such thing as rape by one man of another; all sodomy, he wrote, implied consent: "[The] slightest resistance will suffice to prevent its [sodomy's] perpetration."[7]

Thus, forensic exams for sodomy were given a firm "scientific" underpinning by Taylor and Tardieu, and British police forces, who had quotas of arrests to fill, adopted them.[8] The subsequent minute scrutiny of the bodies

of men required special technology. By 1870, the typical British venere-
ologist used "a rough sphincterometer" to assess the anus of the accused.[9]
Venereologists reported to the police and the courts a specific measure of
millimeters of the anus's dilation. If there was an opening of "4 to 5 cm in
diameter," then the man under investigation was deemed guilty.

The historian of sexuality Ivan Crozier points out that this methodology
reduced the suspect to that part of his body: "If the anus was 'perfect,' then
there was no forensic medical evidence that penetration had taken place, and
hence other proof of criminal activity had to be found. In such instances,
the body refused to plead guilty. If the anus showed signs of being 'abused'
then the suspect was liable for the full penalty of the law. In a very real sense
the body of the sodomite was equated with the condition of the anus."[10]

At this time, the whole field of medicine was in a struggle to establish
its authority: doctors wanted to be seen as part of a prestigious and skilled
profession, rather than just as the traditional "sawbones." The court's reli-
ance on this kind of medical testimony boosted the status as well as the
profits of those in one branch of medicine—medical forensics, specifically
venereology. Certain Victorian physicians developed reputations for expertise in this kind of assessment, and courts started to call on them during
sodomy trials. As hard as it may be for us to believe, some men risked
being sentenced to hard labor when the venereologists found that they
had what the venereologists called an "infundibuliform," or funnel-shaped,
anus. Like the equally mythological witch's marks that characterized earlier
hunts targeting women, in the anti-catamite hysteria of the 1860s and
1870s, fantastical beliefs about men's bodies and how they "revealed" guilt
were used to incriminate men.

Assessment of the male body by means of allegedly visible and interpre-
table signs could confirm this criminality.

Scott Long takes Michel Foucault's explanation of the power relations that created the modern category of "homosexual" an important
step further. Long explains that these exams, and the court's claim on
the "evidence" they produced, helped "create" the category of the modern
criminalized homosexual.[11] Long uses the term "moral panic" to describe a
crucial innovation of modern statecraft: whipping up fears of "degeneracy"
as a way to control populations. That dynamic is critical in understanding
how legal homophobia was codified in Victorian Britain at a time when the
state sought to consolidate its control. The form of homophobia produced
in this crucible still endures.

Here is another legacy of the period. The Victorians focused medically on the passive recipient of sodomy as being the more visibly guilty party. And the passive recipient of an act of sodomy is often seen, according to the modern homophobic point of view, as "more guilty" than the active partner.

With the advent of these forced anal exams, the state aligned homosexual men with the far-less-than-equal category of women.

In Britain before the 1860s, men who committed sodomy were certainly not celebrated for doing so, but the wish to do so was seen as arising from contexts of intense or exclusive masculinity. Before the 1860s, a man's inclination to commit sodomy, or even his reputation as a catamite, by no means necessarily made him "less manly" or in any essential way "more like a woman."

But in the 1870s, by treating the bodies of men accused of sodomy just as it treated the bodies of women arrested for unruly sexuality, the modern state codified and compartmentalized the modern association of the category of men who had sex with men alongside that of the hated, invaded, managed feminine.

The trauma of this Victorian venereological test is still experienced by men in countries ranging from Egypt to Zimbabwe. They inherited anti-sodomy statutes from nineteenth-century British colonial administrators, and authorities there still avail themselves of the long-debunked "medical jurisprudence" based on Tardieu's "six signs" in examining accused homosexuals. Contemporary activists such as Scott Long, who report from these countries, document the fact that these anal examinations, with their state-imposed humiliation and torture of men who love men, continue to this day.

An aspect of modern homophobia is the fear among many straight men that gay men's sexuality will somehow affect them, and thus harm them. But why should one man's sodomy in any way affect another man who is not sexually involved with him? Some straight men inherit this histrionic fear from the general culture—they are anxious about being "mistaken for" gay men. These straight men often feel the need to continually pass a "test" of straightness, to demonstrate to the world that they are not gay, as in the joke about how straight men embrace when they greet one another, each slapping the shoulder of the other three times: "I'm. Not. Gay."

But why would anyone have to "prove" anything about "not being gay"? Why is the "gayness" of some men to this day seen as threatening or as encroaching upon straight men, while "straightness" is not seen as something that might malign, threaten, or "infect" gay men? These irrational but persistent aspects of modern homophobia aren't part of the natural order; they aren't historical constants.

Do these stubborn, illogical, but widespread anxieties descend at least in part from this traumatizing period in British history, when men's bodies had to "prove" that the men weren't sodomites—from a time when jail and hard labor could be the punishment when a male body failed to pass this "test"?

News reports during the 1870s sensationally documented some venereological examinations. An arrest for "conspiring" to commit sodomy could now involve a public shaming that could also generate a conviction. A conviction for sodomy could arise from a letter, a social association, or a poem; that letter or poem could now lead to an exam focused on minute physical variations, and particular minute physical variations could now sentence a poet or essayist to penal servitude for decades and/or to transportation.

Adding to this fresh pressure on Symonds and his friends, during the 1870s the Society for the Suppression of Vice in Britain became even more formidable. (The newly established American Societies for the Suppression of Vice were organized along parallel lines and used similar strategies to suppress "low and vicious" publications.)[12] The society raised funds from wealthy patrons and from the public to hire undercover agents, who then posed as book buyers in order to arrest offending booksellers and publishers. Arrests of booksellers were reported in regional British newspapers up and down the island, including in Scotland and Wales. Most resulted in sentences of two to three months at hard labor.

The society created a secret army of informers, which resulted in nerve-wracking working conditions for booksellers. Any customer asking for an out-of-the-way title might prove to be an undercover agent who had the power to arrest the bookseller and to confiscate or destroy the booksellers' inventory of books. These agents had the authority to go after publishers as well, and to destroy type and even printing presses. In 2013, I read through the British Library regional newspapers database for "obscene publication" mentions; a search of 1857–95 shows dozens of booksellers' arrests and convictions, involving bookstores across the British Isles, with an average sentence handed down of three months at hard labor. Booksellers suffered prosecution or served time for peddling a range of works, from literary titles such as Baudelaire's *Les Fleurs du Mal*, to practically worded pamphlets about how to limit family size, all the way to the crudest pornographic woodcuts.[13] The society made no distinction on the basis of literary merit.

In an unusual arrangement with the courts, these prosecutions were subsidized: the voluntary societies paid for them.

In 1868, Karoly-Maria Kertbeny, Viennese-born, Austro-Hungarian journalist, added to the discourse in Europe, extending the discussion that Karl Ulrichs had begun regarding "Urnings." Kertbeny coined the term "homosexual" as he sought to change anti-homosexual law. In the 1870s, in Europe, a great deal of discussion about same-sex love began to animate society.[14]

Kertbeny, as Ulrichs had done, made the case that these feelings were inborn and innate.

Britain, though, remained unyielding. Indeed, its criminal justice system grew even more punitive toward "sodomites."

A search of the Old Bailey Proceedings online showed that from 1869–70, there were twice as many convictions for sodomy in that court as there had been in that archive for the preceding decade.[15] Another teenager, Richard Farmer, and his twenty-one-year-old friend, Alfred Biggs, were both sentenced, to eight and to twelve months, respectively, at the Old Bailey, for attempting "to commit B—y."[16] The phrase "unnatural offence" now entered the Old Bailey court records consistently: "ALEXANDER CAMPBELL (40), and ARTHUR FISK (21), were indicted for attempting to commit an unnatural offence."[17] Thirty-two-year-old Isaac Church was sentenced to six months "for a like offence."[18]

As you recall, before 1827, court descriptions of sodomy were matter-of-fact. You weren't supposed to commit sodomy, but it wasn't usually described as "unnatural." This bears thinking about, as the idea that love between men is "unnatural" descends to us today in the terms of modern homophobia. Sodomy had been proscribed in the Hebrew Bible and later in ecclesiastical law as well, as we saw. But many acts that are prohibited by both Judaism and Christianity are not considered in any way "unnatural." Even the Hebrew Bible doesn't describe men lying with men as "unnatural." Leviticus 18:22 states, "Thou shalt not lie with mankind, as with womankind; it is abomination." But the Hebrew word for "abomination" here is the same one used for acts that were considered ritually impure, such as uniting in a mixed marriage, eating certain kinds of seafood, and worshipping idols. Those are proscribed, but they are not "unnatural."[19]

The Hebrew Bible frowned as well, we should bear in mind, upon many things that men and women naturally do; it forbade, in similar terms, adultery and masturbation; it advised, for example, that the men of a city should stone a daughter to death if she could not prove her virginity.[20] But human beings' temptation toward these sins was seen by the Abrahamic religions as, indeed, all too natural. Graham Robb notes that "the term 'unnatural' was as 'capacious' as the term 'sodomy.'"[21]

"Unnatural" is a vexing term to introduce into the law—it gives power to the entity charged with defining the "unnatural." For what indeed *is* the "unnatural," and how can this nebulous term be defined? And once a man who loves a man is defined as "unnatural," how can he possibly rebut such a damning yet unclear charge?

CHAPTER 16

Criminalizing "Effeminacy": The Arrests of Fanny and Stella

In 1870, London authorities arrested two charismatic, beautifully dressed women—who turned out to be men.

The 1870 arrest and the 1871 trial of Ernest Boulton and Frederick Park brought home to London, in a sensational context, a way to showcase anti-homosexual legislation and to further unite two concepts that had not really been brought together in the public mind—sodomy and effeminacy.

Boulton and Park were two young men, both from a lower-middle-class background, who enjoyed dressing as stylish women. Some sources state that they had performed in theatricals dressed as women during the 1860s and had developed a following of admirers. The two had the habit of enjoying the gardens and boulevards of the capital together, dressed in elaborate gowns and delicately trimmed bonnets, their gloved hands carrying parasols. They also dressed in women's clothing when they went out to pubs and theatricals in the evening. Photographs show a striking couple: "Stella" was slender and conventionally pretty, with masses of dark hair looped up in the height of fashion. She had the haughty gaze of a society beauty. "Fanny," in contrast, had a more substantial build and heavier features; in photographic portraits she nestles devotedly against Stella. (I use "she" and "her" when Fanny and Stella are presenting themselves in their female personae, and "he" and "his"

Frederick Park (*right*) and Ernest Boulton (Stella and Fanny), 1869.

when they are in masculine attire, to reflect the contemporary historical accounts, and also because there is no definitive account of which gender the two people preferred to use in referring to themselves generally.)

One evening in 1870, the two visited the Strand Theatre. A third young man, Mr. Hugo Mundell, who had been captivated by Stella, accompanied them. The three men were arrested. As Graham Robb explains: "Unfortunately, their 'giggling and chirruping' attracted the wrong kind of attention [. . .] they were observed to light their cigarettes 'with gestures of unnecessary flamboyance.' [. . .] Worst of all, when her lace came unpinned one day at the Strand theatre, Fanny availed herself of the facilities."[1]

Fanny and Stella did not directly solicit sex that night. The arrest was triggered when Fanny entered the ladies' restroom. Police awaited her on her return.

Fanny had gone into the ladies' restroom and had asked the attendant for help with her dress.[2] Middle-class and wealthy women in 1870 struggled under a very complicated set of fashion demands. Women's fashion that year had abruptly changed: the immense, unwieldy hoop skirt of the 1850s had evolved into a bell-shaped hoop skirt for the duration of the 1860s. Neither was easy to manage (indeed, both might catch afire if the wearer stepped for warmth too close to a fireplace or coal fire), but both were far simpler than the style of dress popular in 1870. It's interesting that right after the first feminist political success—the campaign against the Contagious Diseases Acts—women's fashion abruptly became extraordinarily cumbersome and constricting.

A lady's fashionable dress involved a tight jacket cut closely along the upper arms and tailored to the upper body. This was attached at the waist to an overskirt, which looped up on the sides and was piled in a heap behind. The bunched-up fabric in turn was arranged over a cage made of netting to form a bustle, which was sometimes strengthened with horsehair padding. The fabric of the overskirt often looped down behind the lady's bustle in additional folds, which in turn were sometimes trimmed with tasseling; all of this sometimes ended in a train.

A second visible skirt, sometimes in a contrasting color—indeed, at the start of the 1870s, fashion abruptly included three or four different colors and various different fabrics in a single outfit—underlay the overskirt. The underskirt was drawn tightly across the lady's hips and pelvis, restricting her movement: "another curious device to attract the male sex was the scarf swathed either around the knees to suggest that the woman was, as it were, 'tied up' and at his mercy, or in suggestive fashion [the scarf was tied] round the sexual region," writes one historian of fashion.[3]

Beneath the underskirt were petticoats, some of them trimmed with lace. Under the petticoats a lady wore muslin chemises; indeed, this decade invented the shaped undergarment, which was cut to fit closely to a woman's body. Over the chemises, the maid would tightly lace whalebone- or steel-stayed corsets. Think of Scarlett O'Hara's Reconstruction-era gown made from green velvet curtains in the film version of *Gone with the Wind*.

After the mounting successes of the fight against the Contagious Diseases Acts, it is hard not to see the influence of politics on women's fashion. Not only could women barely move due to restrictions of the limbs or breathe due to constriction of the waist; the sheer weight of their clothing was oppressive: "Owing to the multitude of layers and the substitution of woolens for silks, the total weight of the clothing was considerably increased" in the early 1870s.[4] That was the level of fashion complexity that well-dressed women in Britain and in the United States had to manage that year.

A ladies' room attendant often helped women pin up these elaborate skirts, tassels, and folds. But in this case, Fanny's request for help from the ladies' room attendant proved to be one social transgression too many.

One newspaper exclaimed, "There is one peculiar trait in the evidence which stands out in bold and audacious relief [. . .] We refer to the entrance of Park into the retiring room, which is set apart for ladies at the Strand Theatre, who had the unblushing impudence to apply to the female attendant to fasten up the gathers of his skirt, which he alleged had come unfastened."

The police were summoned. Boulton and Park, having dared to dress like women, were treated like women—that is, like women of the evening. The young men were brought to the precinct office and compelled by the police officers there to undress. A Charing Cross surgeon then performed an anal examination on both men. The fact that these exams took place was reported in the London and regional press.

Having forcibly removed the young men's dresses, the police confiscated them, along with their stays, petticoats, stockings, knickers, shoes, wigs, and jewelry. Then the prisoners were forced by the police to get dressed again—but this time as "men." Mundell, for his part, told the police that he had been duped; he had assumed that both of the men were women. Whether this was true or not, he was given the benefit of the doubt and released.

The media followed the two young men in prison and reported the progress of their case. And at first the press coverage had an amused tone—almost
affectionate; some papers dubbed them "the funny He-She Ladies."The early
newspaper reports and penny pamphlets were appreciative of the drama:
"The Lives of Boulton and Park. Extraordinary Revelations."[5] Coverage
wasn't particularly respectful, but neither was it tinged with fear or aversion.

The masses rather liked these transgressive men. Huge crowds and
immense press interest in the men who insisted on being dressed as
women at their trial continued without pause. Once again, the state forced
the men to dress in men's clothing, this time when they appeared again
before the magistrate.

The initial charge against the men—dressing in the "wrong" clothing
for their gender—was only a misdemeanor. But as the hearings progressed,
the state produced evidence of more serious wrongdoing. It became clear
that the men's arrest hadn't been a spur-of-the-moment action; the two had
been under police surveillance for quite a while.

So the prosecutor left behind the issue of what the two had worn that
one night and went deeper into the details of the men's personal lives, and
further back in time, to make a damning case about more serious crimes.
Women who worked as domestic cleaners in the rooms where the men
kept their ladies' clothing, cosmetics, and accessories were summoned one
by one to the court to testify. A household servant told the court endless
details about the men's crinolines, petticoats, false curls, rouge and powder,
chemises, and kid boots. There were fifteen such hearings.

Park's lawyer sought, at trial, to depict the men's dressing up as a form
of theatrical performance. He called it a joking display, "a frolic." He
summoned witnesses, including Park's mother, who stressed how often
Park had enjoyed amateur theatricals, along with the whimsical costuming
that was a normal part of performance. A man's intention for wearing the
petticoats, the curls, the corset determined his legal status. If he had "meant
it," the cross-dressing was a crime. But if it was all fun and games, or better
yet, a parody of women, then no harm had been done.

The police solicited testimony from the men's landlady concerning intimate details of the men's lives: their habits, schedules, grooming practices,
bedding, and sleeping arrangements. Her testimony went beyond clothing and cosmetics and offered to the court evidence of the men's sexual
practices. The details were sufficiently scandalous to merit a more serious
charge: conspiracy to commit sodomy.

Police had seized a set of intimate letters in which Stella wrote of a close connection with a young aristocrat, Lord Arthur Clinton, who was about the same age as Stella and Fanny—also in his twenties. (Dangerously for Lord Clinton, he was also a Liberal politician and a member of Parliament.) Indeed, in some of the letters, Stella was referred to as Lord Clinton's "wife." Just before Lord Clinton was compelled to appear on the witness stand to explain to the nation and the magistrate what these letters meant, the young aristocrat killed himself, according to some reports; other sources stated that Lord Clinton died of scarlet fever. Whatever its cause, this death was also widely covered.[6]

Fanny and Stella were ultimately acquitted. The prosecution was unable to prove that they had committed any homosexual offense or that the wearing of women's clothing by men was an offense under English law. "The trial was a disaster for the police. They had gone to court, caused a sensation, then failed to secure a conviction."[7] But though the state had lost its case, the charge did in fact set a precedent for police and magistrates: "effeminate" intent alone, subjectively defined, might now lead to a sodomy witch hunt. Thus a note, a glance, a joke, a flirtation, a conversation, an accessory, a hairstyle, a stance, or the state of a bedroom that might cause gossip among housekeepers, in reference to a man whom a member of the municipal police might perceive as "effeminate," could now enmesh that man in a charge of having conspired to commit sodomy. "Effeminacy" as the starting point of a crime had now been brought into a British courtroom. But what is "effeminacy"? The famous trial explicitly linked effeminacy and sodomy.

In his memoirs, Symonds struggled to refute this assumed link between sodomy and "effeminacy." Refuting Ulrichs, and his theory that some "Urnings" possessed feminine souls in masculine bodies, Symonds wrote, "I do not recognize anything which justifies the theory of a female soul. Morally and intellectually, in character and taste and habits, I am more masculine than many men I know who adore women. I have no feminine feelings for males who rouse my desires. The anomaly of my position is that I admire the physical beauty of men more than women, derive more pleasure from their contact and society, and am stirred to sexual sensations exclusively by persons of the male sex."[8] This clearly expresses his attitude toward masculinity and male-male desire.

The trial of Fanny and Stella—and the fact that the state could not prove a case against the two men for their "effeminacy"—may have affected the push to codify effeminacy as a crime. Just before the Offences Against the Person Act was passed in Britain, a statute was passed to support the same kind of outcome overseas: anti-sodomy laws to police the British Empire were subjected to the same kind of systematizing and streamlining that similar ones had undergone concurrently at home. Chapter XVI, Section 377, of the Indian Penal Code had introduced to British India, in 1860, the criminalization of sexual activities "against the order of nature," including homosexual sexual activities.[9]

The Indian Penal Code of 1872 reaffirmed Section 377:

377. Unnatural offences: Whoever voluntarily has carnal intercourse against the order of nature with any man, woman or animal shall be punished with imprisonment for life, or with imprisonment of either description for a term which may extend to ten years, and shall also be liable to fine.

Explanation: Penetration is sufficient to constitute the carnal intercourse necessary to the offence described in this section.[10]

This code, titled "Of Offences Affecting the Human Body," restated the offense, defining "unnatural offences" as "carnal intercourse against the order of nature with any man, woman or animal."[11] It stated further that "[p]enetration is sufficient to constitute the carnal intercourse necessary to the offence described in this section." The Indian Penal Code proposed as a penalty a sentence of up to ten years for "penetration" "against the order of nature." Part of "the order of nature" now, stated the law, was vaginal intercourse involving a man and a woman—any man and any woman having intercourse were lawfully "part of the order of nature." But outside "the order of nature"? The state put in writing that the least penetration of one man by another could result in ten years' imprisonment, and the statute left room to define additional male-male offenses against "the order of nature" as time passed and need for more elaboration emerged.

(To get a sense of how male heterosexual privilege was defended in this same penal code, a few pages earlier this "exception" to the law against the rape of women is spelled out: "Exception: Sexual intercourse by a man with his own wife, the wife not being under ten years of age, is not rape."[12])

The statute also removed categorically the right of the accused to use the results of a microscope test to prove that ejaculation in the body had not taken place. Accused men had resorted to this access since microscopes had become more widely available in the 1850s and '60s.

As activists, including Symonds and current supporters of gay rights, have had to point out again and again, sexual preference is generally experienced as innate, and male-male sex acts are found "in nature."

But why should anyone have to make such arguments? Because the counterclaim was invented by the Indian Penal Code and exported to the parts of the world under British control starting in 1860. The Criminal Tribes Act of 1871 went further; it didn't stop with defining sex acts between men as outside the "order of nature," as the 1860 act had done. It rigorously policed adherence to conventional gender norms; indeed, it took a class of people who had had an accepted social role in India—*hijras*, or eunuchs who dressed in female clothing—and actually kept a register of them. It also specified that their cross-dressing was now illegal:

> Penalty on registered eunuch appearing in female clothes. Any eunuch so registered who appears, dressed or ornamented like a woman, in a public street or place, or in any other place, with the intention of being seen from a public street or place, or dancing in public, or for hire [. . .] may be arrested without warrant, and shall be punished with imprisonment of either description for a term which may extend to two years, or with fine, or with both.[13]

After Fanny and Stella had defeated the effort to criminalize their female dress, the state found a way to make sure that would not happen—at least overseas. This statute brought the criminalization of cross-dressing into communities in which it had had cultural value. In many Indian communities, for instance, *hijras*, or eunuchs who dressed as women and assumed traditionally feminine social roles, had long had a valued role in society.[14] But *hijras'* gender fluidity in self-presentation challenged the British colonial consciousness. Again, the definition of the offense was left unstated in the statute. What did it mean to be "ornamented as a woman"? This vague prohibition was easy to violate by accident. Was a man with long hair "ornamented as a woman"? Was he a criminal if he had short hair but wore it in a wavy style, or if he wore a waistcoat that was brocaded? If a man was wearing cosmetics, was he "ornamented as a woman"?

With the 1871 Criminal Tribes Act, men who were perceived as not presenting themselves in a masculine enough way could be seen as criminals, and, in turn, the law linked effeminacy with sodomy. At the same time, an updated Vagrancy Act criminalized people in Britain for any perceived deviance from community norms; "rogues" were punished and indecent displays even in private spaces targeted.[15] But what did it mean to be a "rogue"? Britain was known for its long and noble history of loving its eccentrics and its "rogues": from its veneration of John Milton, with his defense of divorce, privacy, and free speech, the *Aeropagitica*; to its appreciation of Lady Georgiana Cavendish, Duchess of Devonshire, with her racy private life, her political activism, and her addiction to gambling; to its fascination with Lord Byron, who was "mad, bad, and dangerous to know," according to Lady Caroline Lamb.[16] Though "incorrigible rogue" had been a legal term in Britain since the seventeenth century, this network of Victorian laws gave new teeth to the idea that conforming to social norms was not only desirable, but it also kept one on the right side of the criminal justice system.

But defending these British values of original thought, right to privacy, and freedom of speech and association seemed too radical now that new millions could read, write, own property, and vote.

So British law, with new masses to manage, swerved away from its long-held core values that for centuries had preserved such rights for its cherished eccentrics and its "rogues and vagabonds." New civil social norms developed as a kind of character within the drama of the law, and British law gave that "Mrs. Grundy" the power to determine social norms, to point fingers, to shame people, to ostracize—and to convict.

Until 1872, men in every culture, including cultures in the West, had always worn color and adornment. For thousands of years of recorded visual history involving the representation of human beings, prior to the 1870s in the West, men everywhere wore every bit as much color, trimming, and ornamentation as did women; long deemed the superior sex, they often wore *more* color and adornment.

This has been true of the recorded fashion history in the West. In the Middle Ages, men who could afford to do so wore tunics in glowing hues, hats shaped like cones or cylinders, shoes with long pointed toes, trains, and trailing sleeves. Renaissance men with the financial means to do so wore lace cuffs, ruffs, and collars, jewel-toned velvet jackets, dramatic codpieces, and luxurious fur capes. In the seventeenth century, Royalist men signaled their political view by flaunting long curled locks; in the eighteenth century, elite men from all professions wore powdered wigs, tight silk stockings, brocaded vests, slippers with high heels, face powder, beauty patches, and rouge. This taken-for-granted ornamentation of men extended right through the first half of the nineteenth century, when "dandies"—men who wished simply to stand out—played with fashion, too, with pastel-colored gloves, tightly fitting breeches, deep-green swallowtail frock-coats, and boutonnieres. The modern restrictions around "manly" color and style are an extreme historical aberration.

It can be argued that the trauma induced by the Victorian laws connecting effeminacy and sodomy still affects the consciousness of many Western men, perhaps giving rise to some of the common male anxieties today around gender norms. By age three, almost every young boy in the West is naturally playing dress-up; most boys in our culture today learn soon after that if they wear pink or lavender, they will be mocked; by four they have a phobic aversion to these colors. By seven, a boy will often push bright trinkets and colorful frocks—even too-colorful shirts—away with horror. Try telling a modern eight-year-old boy that he looks beautiful; he will make a gagging sound.

Male culture today provides "safe" spaces to play with "effeminacy" in dress, such as Harvard's Hasty Pudding Club Theatricals. But if a man who wishes to be seen as heterosexual dares to wears cosmetics or a skirt in "real life," it is often perceived as a confounding transgression.

Scott Long points out that after the mid-nineteenth century, the role, style, and attitude of the "dandy"—a term previously used for a man of any sexuality—were collapsed into the role of the homosexual. After the anal examinations that shamed "sodomites," and after the penal codes that united the two generally unrelated social transgressions of sodomy and "effeminacy," men's fashion entered a state of rigid conventionality and lack of color from which it has really not, in many influential circles such as finance and law, recovered.

In these mid-Victorian decades the modern "business suit"—black or dark serge—was invented, and it has changed very little from that day to ours. Invented too at this time were the identical top hats worn by men of business, also in solid black. Lithographs of this period show men of the educated classes dressing virtually identically—while women of the same classes continued to dress in riots of color. It is from these decades that we inherit the certainty that fashion and dress are feminine preoccupations, or are the interests of men who are not "manly men"—that "real men" don't wear color, don't adorn themselves, and must be sentenced to a life of uniformity in self-presentation and to a narrow, tedious range of acceptable dress.

Since this prejudice and magical thinking are so much a part of our cultural heritage, we don't pause to consider that this tradition is only 150 years old—and that it overturns a Western tradition of thousands of years, characterized by intensively adorned, colorfully attired, fashion-conscious men of all sexualities and from every walk of life.

This historical trauma may have helped to instill in Western men a fear of "effeminacy" in self-presentation. The common masculine fear of style and variation, let alone of sentiment and vulnerability, is really, if one is human, a constantly renewed fear of certain aspects of the self. This fear, such an essential part of many Western men's lives that many can rarely even examine it, may have been entirely invented. It may well descend to us from the time, not so long ago, when the state arrested, violated, and sentenced playful and colorful men.

Even if the Boulton and Park trial was front-page news in both highbrow and lowbrow publications, the young men arrested and imprisoned were still at one remove from Symonds. Though the two were more affluent and educated than were the farmers, laborers, artisans, and sailors who made up the majority of those arrested for same-sex offenses, they were not of Symonds's elevated social class.

But the elite economic class was losing the power to protect Symonds and his companions.

Simeon Solomon, a gifted painter, was a close friend of Symonds and of the literary and art critic Walter Pater, who was based at Brasenose College in Oxford. Symonds and Pater were friends as well. Solomon was charming, magnetic, and privileged. The scion of a wealthy Jewish merchant family based in London, he was also a sought-after member of the Pre-Raphaelite circle. Solomon's early exhibits, in the 1860s, in prestigious London galleries and exhibition halls had been praised by Pater and celebrated by other cultural gatekeepers as well. By the early 1870s, his star was ascendant.

Photographs show him looking extraordinarily modern. He lounges. He had, if we can read the sepia photographs correctly, deep brown eyes, soft black hair, and tawny skin. Confidently, he played visual games with his Semitic identity. In some images he poses for the camera dressed in a quasi-biblical or Turkish costume. In one photograph, a white turban binds his hair, and his thick black mustache and glossy beard are on splendid display.

Solomon had created the illustrations for Swinburne's poem "The End of a Month" for an outré Oxford journal titled *The Dark Blue*.[17] Swinburne in turn had written in the same issue an appreciation of Solomon's artistry.

Solomon's paintings had become increasingly provocative. In 1869, he had painted a portrait called *An Italian Youth*, which spoke plainly of his appreciation for male beauty. *Sleepers and One That Waketh*, from 1871, can also be read as a provocation, with its three classically beautiful figures pressed closely together—idealized beings of indeterminate gender. The three embracing figures, with their long, curling locks, soft glances, and smooth skin, could be men, but they could also be women—or some combination of these genders. They might depict brothers, sisters, friends—or lovers. The only gender-related certainty about the figures in *Sleepers and One That Waketh* is that the image plays tricks on an audience's assumptions

Simeon Solomon, *Sleepers and One That Waketh*, 1871.

about the genders of those who love. Solomon clearly intended to create this effect.

Then there was his 1867 *Bacchus.* This painting portrays the god of wine and of release from societal rules and restrictions. Solomon depicts the god as a young man of great beauty and athleticism; his dark hair curls back from a broad, fair forehead; he has an eager, energetic expression; his lips are red and full; he appears not bound by social rules. The sensuality and allure of the image of a male figure, as painted by a man, is unabashed. The image was confrontational to male as well as female viewers; it irresistibly invited any and all to share in Solomon's unmistakable enjoyment of the lush masculine beauty of this deity.

Solomon was exhibiting these paintings in prestigious venues such as the Royal Academy. He added to his exhibits a drawing titled *Love Bound and Wounded* (1870). A beautiful youth is tied to a tree, suffering from arrow wounds. The figure echoes Renaissance images of St. Sebastian, similarly bound and wounded—a favorite subject drawn and painted by homosexual artists of the Italian Renaissance such as Michelangelo Buonarroti and Leonardo da Vinci. Solomon's title was provocative. Was this "love" a reference to Cupid—"eros"? Or to another, more transgressive kind of love? Was *Love Bound and Wounded* a critique of social persecution?

Solomon's defiance of public norms went too far, and the drumbeats were increasingly audible. In 1871 the critic Robert Buchanan, writing under the pseudonym Thomas Maitland, published in the *Contemporary Review* an explosively worded, impactful attack on the Pre-Raphaelite group in general. It was titled "The Fleshly School of Poetry." He singled out those writers and artists who were, he claimed, guilty of excessive sensuality. The critic included Solomon—along with Swinburne and Dante Gabriel Rossetti. Buchanan used metaphors drawn from the 1868 obscenity law to level his attack on the men and their work's "fleshliness," which, he argued, "was unwholesome when there is no moral or intellectual quality to temper or control it."[18]

At this time more was at stake than bruised reputations. An attack like Buchanan's could expose an artist or writer to criminal prosecution. Buchanan's essay certainly put these men on the political and legal map as possible targets for arrest.

CHAPTER 17

"My Constant Companions"

All of Britain was a site of persecution. Where was Symonds to turn for direction? He looked westward.

On October 7, 1871, Symonds, who was with his family in Clifton, for the first time sent a letter directly to Walt Whitman in America.[1] "My dear Sir," he began. "When a man has ventured to dedicate his work to another without authority or permission, I think that he is bound to make confession of the liberty he has taken," he wrote, almost flirtatiously, then went on obsequiously:

> This must be my excuse for sending you the crude poem ["Love and Death: A Symphony"] in [which] you may perchance detect some echo, faint and feeble, of your Calamus [. . .] I cannot refrain from saying that since the time I first took up Leaves of Grass in a friend's rooms at Trinity College, Cambridge, six years ago till now, your poems have been my constant companions. I have read them in Italy by the shores of the Mediterranean, under pine trees or caverns washed by the sea—and in Switzerland among the alpine pastures and beside the glaciers. At home I have found in them pure air and health—the free breath of the world—when often cramped by illness and the cares of life. What one man can do by communicating to those he loves the treasures he has found, I have done among my friends.[2]

Then he continued, using coded phrasing: "As for the poem I send you—it is of course implicit already in your Calamus, especially in 'Scented herbage of my breast.' I have but set to an old tune the new divine song—: for you know that on this side of the Atlantic people most readily listen to old tunes." He meant that in order to tell the story of male-male love, he needed, in Britain, to set it in classical antiquity. "I fear greatly I have marred the purity and beauty of your thought by my bad singing.—I am an

JAS, paterfamilias.

Englishman, married, with 3 children, and am aged 30.—"He added his marital status, and the fact that he was a father, probably to avoid legal dangers related to what he had just set out in code. He continued, "Answer to this I scarcely expect, as I certainly do not deserve it." Then he restated, again likely for the legal record, that he meant nothing personal in his approach: "The poem I send is due for the reasons already set forth." In conclusion, he said, "It is a printer's proof at present and no more"—meaning that it is not yet that actionable thing, a book.

After he sent this letter and waited for a response, poems passed from his hands to the hands of others with even greater secrecy and intensity. Some poems served Symonds as emissaries for new relationships. With those he sent to his friend Edward Clifford, he speculated flirtatiously, "I wonder whether my poems of Antinous & Diego would shock you!" Clifford, though, brutally repudiated them, and Symonds scrambled to put on the record statements that would, if necessary, exonerate him: "What you say about the effect of my poems on you is intensely painful to me," he wrote. "They shall not be published: I will not cause so much offense." Mindful of *Hicklin*, Symonds argued, "Yet how the Upas Tree & Caligula could be to anyone tempting poems beats my comprehension." And he concluded, as he did so often now, with the request that Clifford burn the document: "Will you please then consign this second pamphlet to the fire?"[3]

For a second time Symonds began to gather up his homoerotic poems in order to burn them. He asked Henry Sidgwick to return a poem "which escaped burial in November by accident"—meaning it escaped the bonfire—and he asked his friend once again, "Please return it that I may burn it." Yet he couldn't help stating—as the writer in him impulsively defied the state—"I think in style it is the strongest I have written."

He started to retrieve from his whole circle of friends poems that he had sent them, in order to burn them. He told his friends not to even write to him about the poems: "Don't write again about these poems but burn them."To his friend Mrs. Arthur Hugh Clough, who had also harshly rejected his secret homoerotic poems, he wrote, "Burn them. Delenda est Carthage. [Carthage must be destroyed.] As for burning, you cannot object to burn what is partly repulsive & partly mediocre."

Yet in spite of this beseeching, he could not help but lament the need continually to undo what he had done: "I am become a real Penelope of literature—weaving subtle embroideries of verse and then unravelling what I weave."[4]

When Graham Dakyns asked him only weeks later about the secret poems, Symonds wrote back in a letter full of self-loathing: "Poems—? Verses? *Des Vers?* Yes, worms—a wormy writhing putrescent entanglement of low animal lives bred in the decaying depths of my gangrened Soul. Lots of them—some 2000 lines—2000 wriggling loathsome worms, [which] I hate; the evil birth of wasted hours; forgotten now and abandoned with wringing hands and my Soul crying ah, ah! To little purpose."[5]

Yet in spite of this forced conflagration, in spite of the serious danger so very near to him, Symonds kept trying, stubbornly, to find a way to express his truth about love, about sexuality. This is one reason why Symonds's story, in the context of the history of censorship and the history of homosexuality, is so remarkable. The man just would not be silenced.

Whitman was still in Washington, D.C., working as a clerk in the Solicitor's Office of the Department of Justice. His relationship with Peter Doyle remained strong.

He had prepared and submitted the fifth edition of *Leaves of Grass.* A collection of his essays, *Democratic Vistas and Passages to India,* also appeared in 1871; it cast "adhesiveness" between men as part of the renewal of democracy. (Symonds's copy of this book is in the Morgan Library—with his sharp dual vertical lines of emphasis scored next to passages in which the poet spelled out this philosophy of love between men.) Whitman's prestige in America was at an apex: he was invited to speak at mainstream events such as the American Institute Exhibition in New York. He was also receiving fan mail from readers around the world.

One of these came from a friend of Symonds's, the British widow of an editor in his circle: the writer Anne Burrows Gilchrist. Unbeknownst to Symonds, she too had fallen passionately in love with the poet; she had done so after, in 1869, having read the Rossetti edition of *Leaves of Grass,* lent to her by the editor, William Rossetti himself. At about the same time that Symonds was peppering the poet with letters, begging Whitman to reveal the meaning of "Calamus" to him, Anne Gilchrist, on a separate track of correspondence, was offering her own sexual love to the poet, including an offer to bear the poet's child—offers that Whitman eventually sidestepped with gentlemanly diplomacy. His friends gently sought to redirect her ardor for a man she believed was "the tenderest lover" into literary support for the poet: she wrote anonymously the essay "An Englishwoman's Estimate of Walt Whitman" in 1870—making a female reader's case for the value to women of the words of the radical poet.[6] Truly, everyone who looked found his or her Whitman.

In January 1872, Symonds finally received an answer from Whitman himself. The poet told his admirer that he appreciated the "Beautiful & elevated 'Love & Death'" and stated to Symonds that the "letter was most welcome to me. I should like to know you better [. . .]" He described with satisfaction his work in a government office, asked Symonds not to "think hard of me" for not writing earlier, and stated, "I have thought of you more than once, & am deeply touched by your poem."[7]

Symonds, understandably, was elated by this warm and even slightly flirtatious reply. He sent a fervid missive in return on February 7: "Your letter gave me the keenest pleasure I have had for a long time [. . .] [W]hat you say has reassured me nearly as much as if I had seen the face and touched the hand of you—my Master!"[8]

For many years I have been attempting to express in verse what in a note to Democratic Vistas (as also in a blade of Calamus) you call "adhesiveness." I have traced passionate friendship through Greece, Rome, the medieval & the modern world [. . .]

It was while engaged upon this work [. . .] that I first read Leaves of Grass. The man who spoke to me from that Book impressed me in every way [. . .] I did learn confidently to believe that the Comradeship, which I conceived as on a par with the Sexual feeling for depth & strength & purity & capability of all good, was real—not a delusion of distorted passions [. . .] but a strong & vital bond of man to man.

Yet even then how hard I found it—brought up in English feudalism [. . .] to winnow from my own emotions [. . .] all husks and affectations and aberrations and to be a simple human being. You cannot tell quite how hard this was, & you have helped me.[9]

He burst out effusively with his central question:

I have pored for hours over the pages of Calamus [. . .] longing to hear you speak, burning for a revelation of your more developed meaning, panting to ask—is this what you would indicate?—Are the free men of your lands really so pure & loving & noble [. . .] Most of all did I desire to hear from your own lips—or from your pen—some story of athletic friendship from which to learn the truth [. . .] Shall I ever be permitted to question you & learn from you?

What the love of man for man has been in the Past I think I know. What it is here now, I know also—alas! What you say it can & shall be I dimly discern in your Poems. But this hardly satisfies me—so desirous am I of learning what you teach.[10]

Symonds concluded beseechingly: "Some day, perhaps, in some form, I know not what, but in your own chosen form—you will tell me more about the Love of Friends!"[11]

And yet: Symonds also carefully put it on the record that he was "on a tour with my wife." And he included a photograph of the "little girl [who] is my youngest daughter." But after adding these documents confirming his apparent domesticity, he added his own photograph, with the telling note that he wished that Whitman might know "my face."[12] On February 25, seemingly unable to manage his impulse to communicate with the famous man, he went further still: he sent Walt Whitman a poem, "Callicrates," which had a homosexual theme.

Whitman's friend and eventual biographer Horace Traubel thought that it was because Symonds pushed so aggressively about the homoerotic content in his work that Whitman was reluctant to reply.[13]

Symonds received a response to this outpouring from Whitman, but it was noncommittal; it contained only a clipping of a poem of Whitman's printed in a Washington newspaper. To this neutral gesture, Symonds wrote back with even more fervor: he insisted that "I must exchange my token for yours," and he enclosed what he called "a study of Greek friendship."[14]

What did Whitman think when he received the draft manuscript from this importunate young man, now thirty-three years old, who had sent him a manifesto about the nobility of the love of men for men—a manifesto that was illegal to send through the British mail?

Symonds had titled his work awkwardly: *A Problem in Greek Ethics: Being an Inquiry into the Phenomenon of Sexual Inversion, Addressed Especially to Medical Psychologists and Jurists.* He had turned the handwritten draft into a forty-eight-page pamphlet, which he privately printed.

In addition to sending it to Whitman, he circulated the text among a few carefully selected friends. In the introduction, Symonds wrote:

> For the student of sexual inversion, ancient Greece offers a wide field for observation and reflection. Its importance has hitherto been underrated by medical and legal writers on the subject, who do not seem to be aware that here alone in history have we the example of a great and highly-developed race not only tolerating homosexual passions, but deeming them of spiritual value, and attempting to utilise them for the benefit of society [. . .] It is the feature by which Greek social life is most sharply distinguished from that of any other people approaching the Hellenes in moral or mental distinction. To trace the history of so remarkable a custom in their several communities, and to ascertain, so far as this is possible, the ethical feeling of the Greeks upon this subject, must be of service to the scientific psychologist. It enables him to approach the subject from another point of view than that usually adopted by modern jurists, psychiatrists, writers on forensic medicine.[15]

Remember that "modern jurists" were at this time sending adult men and even teenagers to hard labor for the set of behaviors and emotions so lauded in ancient Greek society. Symonds—presumably with some fear—wrote this secret defense of these feelings, arguing that they had been an accepted part of a highly evolved and much-respected civilization. He went on, even more assertively and romantically, by quoting Maximus Tyrus, who distinguished between base and elevated forms of "Greek love": "The one love is mad for pleasure; the other loves beauty. The one is an involuntary sickness; the other is a sought enthusiasm. The one tends to the good of the beloved; the other to the ruin of both. The one is virtuous; the other incontinent in all its acts. The one has its end in friendship; the other in hate. The one is freely given; the other is bought and sold. The one brings praise; the other blame."[16]

By seeking to draw a distinction between a Greek love that was noble and honorable and sentiments that were "incontinent," Symonds tried to establish a duality that let him reject and bracket the aspects of male-male love that sodomy laws and sodomy discourse had reinforced.

Nonetheless, in spite of this defiant reframing of forbidden love, the pamphlet of *A Problem in Greek Ethics* was likely among the papers that Symonds kept so carefully in the locked black metal box in his study. Though Whitman now had a copy overseas, Symonds wrote about the pamphlet's existence only obliquely to his British friends, and he did so in terms confirming that he despaired of its ever seeing the light of day in his home country.

Did his correspondence with Whitman empower Symonds, even just a bit? In his secret papers, he confides that it did, that his passion became manlier, more direct. In May 1872 Symonds rethought the desperate campaign of the year before of burning all of his homosexually oriented verses. He acquired two new boxes, in which he kept the forbidden texts, and he kept their keys secure. Simultaneously he was carefully hiding the texts but also seeking access to them in order to revise them. From a journey on the Continent, he wrote to Graham Dakyns:

> On receiving this will you be so kind as to go to my study & look in the china flower pot on the left hand bookcase just as you enter the door—it has a thermometer and some fuse boxes in it—& take out & send to me at once 2 small keys that are in it? They ought to be at the bottom of the vase. I am sorry to give you this trouble. But I want them much.
>
> At the same time would you see whether 2 iron boxes, one on the chair close by the door (called "Board of Health") & one on the ground behind it as it opens, are locked—& if they are not will you take them home & keep them for me?
>
> [. . .] Please do it yourself & send the keys to me at the Union Club [. . .][17]

Catherine Symonds by this time fully understood her husband's true orientation. Catherine's letters, and his own letters to and about her, reveal that she had accepted her situation, sadly for herself but without evident rancor toward her husband. She seemed to view her husband—who was a caring, if rarely passionate, companion to her and a devoted father to his girls—with both empathy for his tortured inner life and regret for what it meant for their union.

By hiding his work away so thoroughly, with a secure cache that is now not one tin box but two iron ones, under a false "Board of Health" label—with the keys in the china pot hidden under a thermometer and some fuse boxes—Symonds was protecting himself, but he was protecting his family as well. Given the trope of "infection" related to sodomy, it is fascinating that Symonds kept his homoerotically themed poems in a box labeled "Board of Health." Was this an unconscious mimicry of how the health authorities handled infectious materials? Or was it possibly unconscious satire about how "poisonous" to others such thoughts and feelings were seen to be?

A locked set of boxes could not, however, contain the writer's desire to communicate, at whatever risk. Symonds sent his illicit poems in December to the ever-controversial Swinburne. Symonds was immediately ashamed. After hearing nothing from Swinburne for two days, Symonds wrote miserably to Dakyns: "I sent off my letter & a lot of poems to Swinburne. Here, after two days, it seems like a stupid thing done in a third rate dream. He will certainly despise me for bothering him instead of being out with it all to the public."[18]

Meanwhile, the Old Bailey convictions progressed.

In 1873, a decade of penal servitude was handed down to sailor Andrew Sobolski as a sentence for "B—g—y."[19] Charles Casebow, age thirty, was indicted for an "unnatural offence" and sentenced to seven years of penal servitude for "the attempt."[20]

CHAPTER 18

Comstock:
Censorship Crosses the Atlantic

B y 1873, the British Society for the Suppression of Vice was at the peak of its powers. Its wealthy patrons provided deep coffers, which paid for its army of private snoops. These "trusty and intelligent paid agents" who went undercover to entrap booksellers were privately funded because, as the society's records note, "there are no funds at the disposal of Government" for the purpose.

The society's minutes document confiscation of a vast number of "obscene" books and prints. The relatively new technology of photography, and its ability to produce images of live female models, was causing additional headaches. According to the minutes,

> This society, instituted in 1802, has laboured unremittingly to check the spread of open vice and immorality, and more especially to preserve the minds of the young from contamination by exposure to the corrupting influence of impure and licentious books, prints, and other publications, its difficulties have been greatly increased by the application of photography, multiplying, at an insignificant cost, filthy representations from living models, and the improvement in the postal service has further introduced facilities for secret trading which were previously unknown.[1]

The minutes also elaborate on the tremendous rate of confiscation:

> This society has been the means of suppressing the circulation of several low and vicious periodicals. Within the last two years it has also been the means of bringing to punishment, by imprisonment, hard labour, and fines, upwards of forty of the most notorious dealers

[. . .] Within a few years [the society] has seized and destroyed the following enormous mass of corrupting matters:—140,213 obscene prints, pictures, and photographs; 21,772 books and pamphlets; five tons of letterpress in sheets, besides large quantities of infidel and blasphemous publications; 17,060 sheets of obscene songs, catalogues, circulars, and handbills; 5,712 cards, snuff-boxes, and vile articles; 844 engraved copper and steel plates; 480 lithographic stones; 146 wood blocks; 11 printing presses, with type and apparatus; 81 cwt. of type, including the stereotype of several works of the vilest description.

The numbers, though self-reported, are staggering. Forty booksellers were arrested by the society in just two years it asserted. The society claimed to have destroyed an average of 70,000 images and 10,500 books and pamphlets annually. The thousands of "vile articles" probably included con-traceptive devices such as condoms and pessaries—a form of diaphragm.

In two years the society said that it had destroyed eleven printing presses, including handcrafted, expensive lead type. The destruction of a printing press would have been a financial catastrophe for its owner. At the time, a single printing press cost fifteen to twenty thousand pounds sterling.

If a voluntary society could destroy even one printing press—let alone eleven in two years—that meant that it could destroy a newspaper's, print-er's, or publisher's primary asset and close down the business altogether. The purity societies' intense and effective campaigns against literature increas-ingly pitted writers against their own newspapers, editors, and booksellers, and vice versa. In place of the usually collaborative relationships among these parties, now writer, editor, bookseller, and publisher could each betray, abandon, or ruin the others.

For the censors now made headway in America too. Whitman's formerly freer New World was quickly emulating Britain.

In the 1870s, a powerful alliance was forged in America among aboli-tionists, public health reformers, temperance reformers, and certain feminist advocates for women to become what the historian David J. Pivar calls "the social purity alliance."[2] Up to this point there had been no US federal statute criminalizing speech—not even obscene speech, which, as we have seen, was why *Leaves of Grass* was publishable there.[3] The First Amendment of the Bill of Rights deterred any attempts to create such a law.

But the American social purity campaign was extremely successful in passing censorship regulation at the state and local levels.[4] The reformers there established their own newspaper, the *American Bulletin*, and formed their own umbrella group, the International Purity Federation. Based in New York City, the federation had effective branches in Boston, Philadelphia, and other cities.

The clamoring of the American purity societies may have also made it more difficult for Whitman to keep his job as a clerk in the Solicitor's Office of the Department of Justice—and perhaps jeopardized his health.

Washington was experiencing a Reconstruction-era expansion. New commuter tramlines extended all the way to the northwest of the city. New neighborhoods of wooden homes fronted with wide porches and bright white-and-yellow-brick Queen Anne–style homes with steep steps and elegant bay windows proliferated along the transportation lines, and the construction put development pressure on what had been the rural villages of Friendship Heights and Tennalley Town, now reincorporated as Tenleytown.

A plaque near a Best Buy now commemorates Whitman's years in D.C., identifying the area where he lodged—in one of these northwestern villages near Tenleytown. It marks a street of modest wooden houses with lilac-shaded porches and sweet pea–tangled gardens, almost unchanged since Whitman's time.

While Symonds was finding a sense of inner liberation by imagining his hero untrammeled in the rugged expanses of the New World, Whitman was commuting daily to his mundane place of work. Such are the uses of poetry: Whitman's actual situation was unimportant compared to the imaginative transference of the poet into an archetype that could shelter the emotional and creative growth of Symonds, and of other English men and women who needed him in this role.

In January 1873, while Whitman was by himself at night in his workplace, he suffered a serious stroke. In addition to his companion Peter Doyle, he had a close community in Washington, from many parts of society. They looked after him with devotion.

Whitman never fully recovered from his stroke. As the poet lay stricken, activity related to obscenity began closely to parallel that of Britain. The American Society for the Suppression of Vice was established the same year—with powerful patrons, just as in Britain. This group began to mimic the British model by sending agents to undertake surveillance of newsstands so that offending booksellers and distributors could be prosecuted.

Anthony Comstock, a US postal inspector, was an ardent Christian active in the Young Men's Christian Association. In 1873, Comstock founded the New York Society for the Suppression of Vice. Later that year, moving quickly, he successfully lobbied Congress to pass what became known as the Comstock Law, which criminalized mail transport of any "obscene, lewd, and/or lascivious" materials.[5] The nominal target of this law was material related to abortion. But it soon swept up material related to contraception, and then to sexuality in general. Over the course of his various campaigns, which would last for decades, Comstock would boast of destroying fifteen tons of books, 284,000 pounds of printing plates, and almost four million pictures. He prosecuted nearly four thousand booksellers. He was at least as diligent as his British counterparts. His obituary would note, "Mr. Comstock had caused the arraignment in state and federal courts of 3, 697 persons [. . .] fines were imposed to the extent of $237,134.30 and imprisonment to the total of 565 years."[6]

This law immediately affected sales of *Leaves of Grass*. A bookseller in any state might order books from a Boston or New York publisher, who would ship them across state lines. But since mail was now closed to certain texts, even though it was legal in America to publish an "obscene" book such as the 1855 and 1860 versions of *Leaves of Grass*, it had become effectively illegal to distribute them unless you could transport them personally by hand. Comstock destroyed the marketplace for such books.

Whitman, who depended on sales of *Leaves of Grass* for part of his meager income, never regained full use of his left arm and leg. Nonetheless, he returned to work in April 1874, on a part-time basis. Having come so close to death, Whitman wrote a will—which named Peter Doyle, along with his mother and his disabled brother Edward, as his heirs.

His mother did not outlive him; in May of that year, she died, her final words a farewell to her cherished son "Walt." When the poet came back to Washington after her funeral, he asked for and was given a two-month leave of absence from the Solicitor's Office. Still suffering from neurological symptoms such as weakness and pain, the poet was beset by depression. He expected to die of his symptoms.

With US censorship activities coming to a peak, Whitman, like his British friends, felt he had to construct a literary bonfire. He piled upon it masses of his personal letters and manuscripts. We will never be able to read the poems and essays by Whitman that were consumed in this conflagration of 1874.

The spring continued to be difficult; Whitman experienced a terrible pain in his left lung. (After his death, physicians discovered that a chest abscess had caused the complete collapse of this lung.) By July 1874, as prosecutions under the Comstock Law increased, Whitman lost his job altogether. He had been working for one of the chief lawyers in the land; he himself was now a potential criminal. Officialdom in Washington was unlikely to continue taking the risk of employing a staffer who represented a possible scandal.

Whitman, sick and partially paralyzed, was now unable legally to send out his books through the mail. So Comstock won; this writer of "obscene" material now struggled for basic survival and had no steady income.[7] No disability pay or unemployment benefits existed for civilians at that time in America.

On both sides of the Atlantic, the scrubbing of visual images of transgressive "obscenity" and the stern state determination of which images were permitted, and which ones were not, continued apace. The next target was a hoary London tourist attraction. Dr. Kahn's Anatomical and Pathological Museum was a waxworks display. For years it had been a fixture on the round of London sights that out-of-towners of all kinds would visit. For a few shillings they could marvel at the decorative waxworks, which showed how people were put together just under the skin. They could also learn about general human anatomy and basic human reproductive functions.

By viewing models of the human body open at the abdomen and also at the level of the reproductive organs, visitors could get a rudimentary sense of human sexual anatomy and learn about pregnancy and childbirth. Displays also showcased the depredations of venereal diseases, although the most explicit exhibits were not shown on the days when ladies were invited.[8]

Dr. Kahn had profitably used the museum as an intake point for his treatment clinic for men suffering from venereal diseases. His success in this field had impinged on the businesses of established physicians, who formed a professional group and tried to shut down the museum and clinic, but failed. But with the advent of obscenity law, they were able to enlist the Society for the Suppression of Vice—and thus achieved their goal. In 1873 the society used the 1857 obscenity law against Kahn's clinic and museum.

London police, directed by the society, broke in and confiscated several expensive "Venuses" and "Samsons," as well other life-size figures. The society had also hired the prosecutor, Mr. Collette, who was present at the raid. Mr. Collette asked the Metropolitan Police for the "privilege" of personally destroying the wax figures. Flanked by police inspectors, he took a hammer to the finest of the anatomical waxworks. The *Times* noted that the models that had been destroyed "were of the most elaborate character, and said to cost a considerable sum of money."[9] The defendants, who had to stand by helplessly and watch this spectacle of destruction, were handed the pieces.

After reports of the destruction of Kahn's Anatomical and Pathological Museum appeared in the London newspapers, police closed similar anatomical museums in Liverpool and Manchester.

From then on, anatomical displays were classified as obscene in British courts. Women of childbearing age were especially affected by this crackdown on anatomical displays and by the war on information about contraception being transmitted through the mails. These had been among the very few widely available sources of information for women concerning how conception worked, and how it might be prevented.

Education about human anatomy was now restricted to students of medicine—who were overwhelmingly affluent and male. The human body and its sexual and reproductive functions would become mysteries once again—that is, to those who did not hold social power.

But though visual displays able to empower and inform women and men of various social classes were now forbidden, other images of the human body escaped the investigator's hammer and the censor's confiscation warehouse. As the exhibit "Exposed: The Victorian Nude" at the Tate Gallery (2001–2002) made clear, in 1873, nudes painted for the pleasure and appreciation of affluent heterosexual men were successfully exhibited and sold well.[10] So clearly it was not just the nudity that "crossed a line," but whether the observer was, ideally, heterosexual, male, and in power. A deciding factor as to an image's acceptability was whether it reinforced or critiqued things as they were.

In this climate, the publisher Smith, Elder and Company commissioned Symonds to write a two-volume summary of the poets of classical Greece: *Studies of the Greek Poets*.[11] This project followed on the success of the translation Symonds had done for Benjamin Jowett. The first volume of *Studies of the Greek Poets* came out in 1873. At the time Symonds told a correspondent not to assume that he wished to preach to this or the next generation.

But did he in fact wish to speak to a younger generation? His books about the Greek poets did exactly that.

The volumes—essentially textbooks—did overtly address the established classical practice of an older man taking a youth as his lover. But at the same time, Symonds carefully avoided certain lines of study. For instance, the poet Apoxyomenos of Lysippus had written: "Blessed is he who, being in love, practices gymnastic exercises / Then, coming home, sleeps all day long with his handsome boy [. . .]"[12]

But Symonds, as he told his friend Graham Dakyns, censored these lines, even while seeking to explain the practice of male-male union among Athenians in the fifth century BCE. He did so lest a "malevolent critic," as he put it, might guess at "what the ending of that couplet is." Symonds explained to Dakyns that he wished "not [to be] too timid, yet not wantonly to offend." He wanted the book to tell at least some of the truth about the homoerotically oriented lives of the Greek poets—yet to do so in a way that protected him from prosecution.[13]

The set was critically well received; it was widely assigned to schoolboys and to university men studying the classics, or "Greats," including those at Oxford.

PART VI

Countercampaigns and Resistance

CHAPTER 19

The Arrests of Simeon Solomon

In 1873, the same year in which Symonds's first volume of *Studies of the Greek Poets* was published, the artist Dante Gabriel Rossetti, who was now immensely sought after by collectors, was enmeshed in a tumultuous romantic triangle with Jane Morris, the skilled embroiderer and his muse, and her husband, the renowned Pre-Raphaelite designer, muralist, and painter William Morris.

William Morris was aware of his wife's affair with Rossetti, though he was not happy about it. Reluctantly, he agreed that the three, along with the Morrises' children, should share a house in the countryside. Morris even knew that his wife and her lover would be together while he traveled on a research trip to Iceland.

In the 1870s, sexual infidelity and even heterosexual erotic chaos such as this were managed and even tolerated as long as they stayed behind closed doors. But the members of the Pre-Raphaelite group of artists and writers who were homosexual, such as Simeon Solomon, did not have that luxury of private personal indulgence hidden by a public management of appearances.

While Solomon's paintings faced a declining market, Dante Gabriel Rossetti had put together a thriving atelier in Chelsea and become skilled at producing images that were quite similar to Solomon's in their focus on the physical beauty and seductiveness of the subjects. Rossetti enjoyed his peak earning years during the 1870s, as he attracted a steady stream of clients who had new wealth. But Rossetti's more commercial portraits of seductive women were designed to suit the marketplace; they were often commissioned by collectors who were heterosexual men.

Dante Gabriel Rossetti dressed his female models in rich fabrics and situated them in biblical or Renaissance scenes, creating thematically uncontroversial set pieces. The 1873 *Blanzifiore*, for instance, is a typical portrait: Jane Morris decked in a deep-green gown. She is holding snow-drops; she turns to the viewer with a sultry gaze; her long white neck is bared. All in all, *Blanzifiore* is a beautiful object for a male collector's display and enjoyment. Rossetti painted Jane Morris in this painting—valuable from the moment it was completed—with lips that are as full, and as scarlet, as those of Simeon Solomon's disgraced *Bacchus*.[1]

In 1873, Simeon Solomon was arrested in a public urinal near the thoroughfare of Oxford Street, London, and was accused by the municipal police of having sought to solicit an act of sodomy.[2] He was fined a hundred pounds; but he was not at that time sentenced to prison. Word of the scandal, though, tore through the same polite society that was the source of his exhibits and of his patronage.

In 1874, Simeon Solomon was arrested again. This time, the event took place in Paris. He was caught in a public urinal with a male prostitute named Henri Lefranc. The artist was charged with *outrage public à la pudeur* (outrage to the public decency, or modesty). Though consensual sex between men in private was legal in France, Solomon had broken the law by soliciting sex in a public setting.

He was convicted and served three months in a Paris jail.[3]

When he returned to Britain, his career did not recover its former luster. Few patrons sought him out, but within the small circle of those who shared his sense of beauty and his orientation, he became a cult figure. Symonds, Wilde, Pater, and others who felt themselves to be in alignment with him quietly began to collect and privately to display his work.

At the Morgan Library, Ms. Molestina produced a copy of the first volume of Symonds's *Studies of the Greek Poets*. It wasn't just any copy; it had been the personal property of the undergraduate Oscar Wilde. When Wilde first held this book at age twenty-four, he was older than most of his peers. He had graduated from Trinity College, Dublin, and was at Magdalen College on a scholarship.

This was one of the very first texts to transmit homosexual history from an older generation to a younger one. Thirteen years after Symonds, as a student himself, had evidently relinquished his own love, Symonds crafted these volumes validating the love of men for one another, which would be assigned to a new cohort of students who might find that such "lives" resonated with them.

This first edition physically signals its "Greek" identity: it is bound in royal purple, with a border suggesting Greek keys across the top and bottom of the fabric. Wilde wrote his name on the inside flyleaf in confident cursive: "Oscar O'Flahertie Wilde."

In spite of Symonds's self-censorship, the volume described the Socratic ideals of male beauty as a noble inspiration to the male viewer. Symonds used code here, as he had learned to do by this point in his life. The title page reads: "Im Ganzen Guten Schönen / Resolut zu Leben." This means, roughly: "To live with determination in the whole, the good and the beautiful."[4] This seemingly opaque couplet could have provided Symonds with a legal defense, if needed, against a criminal charge. If the overt goal of his volume was to encourage people to "live with determination in [. . .] the good," it would be difficult to accuse him of evil or corrupting intentions, as per *Hicklin*.

Wilde marked certain passages with vertical lines in the margin. (This was the way Victorians tended to highlight text, rather than underlining, as we now do.) The passage Wilde highlighted reads: "The 'beautiful human heroism' of Achilles, his strong personality, his fierce passions controlled and tempered by divine wisdom, his intense friendship and love that passed the love of women, above all, the splendour of his youthful life in death made perfect, hovered like a dream above the imagination of the Greeks."[5]

"Love that passed the love of women"—the phrasing echoes 2 Samuel 1:26, in which David laments the death of his beloved friend Jonathan: "You have been very pleasant to me; your love to me was wonderful, surpassing the love of women." Slid stealthily into Symonds's exposition of long-dead Greek poets, these words validated the emotions that students such as Wilde may have felt. Wilde also made a nearly three-inch pencil mark alongside a passage describing the physical beauty of the male athlete: "The athlete, tall and stately, tired with running, lifts one arm, and with his strigil scrapes away the oil with which he has anointed it [. . .] Of this sort are the two wrestling boys at Florence, whose heads and faces form in outline the ellipse which is the basis for all beauty, and whose strained muscles exhibit the chord of masculine vigor vibrating with tense vitality."[6]

Symonds brings that historically distant image of two young Greek men "vibrating with tense vitality" right into the fields and lakes familiar to student readers such as Wilde: "If we in England seek some echo of this melody of curving lines, we must visit the fields where boys bathe in early morning," he wrote, "or [. . .] the banks of the Isis when the Eights are on the water." The Cherwell, a tributary of the Isis, ran below Wilde's own window at Magdalen.

Just as Whitman in *Leaves of Grass* had brought the loving, struggling wrestlers of antiquity into the present moment and relocated them to the grassy
summertime lot on a New York City street, so Symonds was insisting that
such a sensibility could be found not only by looking long ago and far away,
but also by opening one's eyes to what was close to home, right now.

Symonds also described a statue he called "The Genius of Eternal Slumber." In this statue, he wrote, the male figure was "reclining with arms folded
above his head, upright against a tree . . . . To judge by his attitude, he might
be Bacchus, wine-drowsy [. . .] Looking at his long tresses, we call him Love
[. . .] His stately form, not unlike that of Phoebus, makes us exclaim [. . .]"[7]
Wilde marked the passage with both a line and a check mark.

After public opprobrium had erased Simeon Solomon's images—the
beautiful *Bacchus*, the dreamy, ambiguous *Sleepers and One That Waketh*—from
the center of the culture, now that it was risky for Pater to keep *Love Bound
and Wounded* visibly displayed on a wall in Oxford lodgings, it seems that
authors such as Symonds turned to using words to describe male-male desire
represented in works of art. If these words didn't exactly replace that disgraced
and marginalized visual imagery, at least they spoke up for other examples of it.

By invoking these visual works of art, presumably from classical antiquity, Symonds was able to speak to Wilde and other students. By using
the pronoun "we," he invited readers to share his gaze, and his conclusion:
"we call him Love." In a two-volume set masquerading as a rather tedious
assignment for university undergraduates about a long-dead civilization,
Symonds had hidden wonderful treasures.

A new pedagogy was in the world, for those who knew how to look for it.

Symonds now applied for the prestigious professorship of poetry at Oxford.
He was father of three girls: Janet, Charlotte, and Margaret. And in 1875 a
new baby girl, Katharine—the couple's last child—was born.

While a committee of fellows deliberated on Symonds's application,
he left Britain and his family behind to make one of his now-habitual
escapes to Italy. He also, rather courageously, purchased two pictures from
the now twice-disgraced Solomon. "[I]t touches me to the quick," he wrote
to his friend Horatio Forbes Brown, "to hear that a really great artist is in
difficulties because no one will exhibit his pictures."[8]

En route to Italy, he fretted: he had not heard from Whitman for some
time and was worried that the older man had lost interest in corresponding

with him. Then, in May, he wrote from Rome to Graham Dakyns to tell him that he had finally heard from the poet. Whitman had managed, in his poor health, to send Symonds a brief note. "W. W. Still unwell & paralyzed, but up & around," wrote Symonds, with some self-absorption. "I am glad he has not forgotten or got to hate me, as I thought he had."

Given Whitman's fragile state as he made a slow recovery from his stroke, Symonds's next letter, even pushier than earlier ones, seems almost rude; he sent the poet yet another missive asking him to explain what the "Calamus" poems really meant. Symonds pointed out, in a somewhat needling way, that he himself was still assuming the burden of publicly supporting the American poet, and facing the brickbats involved: "Time does not diminish my reverential admiration of your work, nor do the unintelligent remarks of the British press deter me from giving expression to the same in print," he wrote. "It was about three years ago, I think—[I] sent you a poem called 'Callicrates' and asked you questions about 'Calamus.'" Symonds suggested that he was glad that his importuning had not caused Whitman to cease communication.[9]

But now the partially paralyzed, impoverished man was facing adversarial legal headwinds in the United States. After trying one last time to be reinstated in his former job at the Justice Department, Whitman had given up on Washington and returned to Camden, New Jersey, to live in a tiny wooden house that he was able to afford, near family members who could help look after him. In spite of his weakness, he managed to issue another edition of *Leaves of Grass*—one that cut the sequence "A Passage to India." (This sequence greatly affected the next generation; E. M. Forster's 1924 novel *A Passage to India* took its title from it.) The sequence posits the soul as seeking a "Comrade perfect" through time, over continents, and even through lives, and it describes a transcendentalist reunion of the soul with the divine in terms of brothers uniting in an embrace:

> *O Thou transcendant! [. . .]*
> *(O pensive soul of me! O thirst unsatisfied! waitest not there?*
> *Waitest not haply for us, somewhere there, the Comrade perfect?) [. . .]*
> *Reckoning ahead, O soul, when thou, the time achiev'd,*
> *(The seas all cross'd, weather'd the capes, the voyage done,)*
> *[. . .] frontest God, yieldest, the aim attain'd,*
> *As, fill'd with friendship, love complete, the Elder Brother found,*
> *The Younger melts in fondness in his arms.*[10]

While critics stepped up their attacks in London—assailing Whitman in the *Saturday Review*—negative criticism now ramped up in the United States: the *New York Tribune* denounced him, as did other American publications. The American censure was more consequential to the impoverished, disabled poet.

As in Britain, some members of the American literati stepped forward to support him; others went into retreat. The Boston literary eminence Henry Wadsworth Longfellow made a pilgrimage to Camden. Other well-known American figures, though, kept their distance. But the poet was focused less on the politics of reputation and more on survival; he was trying to rehabilitate himself physically. He often bathed in a nearby creek in Camden, attempting to strengthen his muscles. He had a new attachment to a dark-haired young man with sunburnt skin and a hypnotic gaze, Henry Stafford. The poet often visited Stafford's family in the countryside, which he believed improved his overall health.

His British supporters heard of his sufferings, and the fact that he now had no income from a job. They sent him a "subscription"—which meant a sum of money, pooled from their public solicitation of charity for the poet. The public nature of their solicitation embarrassed Whitman, and accepting the funds made him uneasy, but he had no choice.

In January 1876, Symonds started a seductive epistolary friendship with a new acquaintance, the wealthy poet, memoirist, and critic Edmund Gosse. Symonds had to approach this new friend gingerly, and he used Whitman to help him do so. He wrote that he saw himself and Gosse as both "having the root of Calamus within our souls." If the letter fell into the hands of the average magistrate, this sentence was unlikely to provoke suspicion. Gosse understood, though, and responded warmly.

Back in Oxford, meanwhile, Whitman was also on the mind of the student Wilde. He daringly discussed the poet with his Oxford supervisor. As Wilde wrote to his friend William Wardin, he had "nipped up" to his viva, his main oral exam, where "in Aeschylus [meaning in relation to Aeschylus] we talked of Shakespeare, Walt Whitman and the Poetics."[11] Whitman, like "Greek love," like "Phaedrus," was now among the coded signals used at Oxford, as elsewhere, between men who loved men. Was Wilde mentioning Whitman to signal his own orientation to his examiner? Was he perhaps even mentioning Whitman to flirt with William Wardin?

Wilde's generation was chafing outright at the constraints that Symonds's own generation could themselves scarcely bear.

In the Morgan Library, if you turn to the second of Wilde's two volumes of Symonds's *Studies of the Greek Poets*, you will see that the last essay is a defense of the Greeks' homosexuality. Symonds used language directly echoing the wording of the 1873 Indian Penal Code and its judgment on sex acts between men as being "against the order of nature." Symonds stated clearly, using the Greeks as pretext, that the practice of sexual love between men was not "unnatural"; he defended this love on the basis of what he called its "organicity."

The second volume of the series came out two years after the first. Wilde had had time to mature, and to consider the legacy of writers such as Whitman and Symonds. This time around, Wilde added his name on the title page of this second volume, in even more baroquely confident loops of script:

Oscar F. O'F W. Wilde
Oxford May '76.

Across two open pages in this book, you will see an arc of dark drops. They are still a deep purple in color.

Wilde was known already at college as a legendary conversationalist who gestured with his hands as he spoke. Are these purple spots faded wine stains, flung by the hand of the young Oscar Wilde?

Could Wilde have splashed wine as he read, perhaps aloud, to friends, Symonds's words from an assigned textbook—one that quietly slipped the information to students that in classical antiquity it was perfectly "natural," and even warmly admired, for men to love other men?

In spite of Walter Pater's own painful earlier exposure, in 1876 Pater went out of his way to address the painting *Bacchus*, by Simeon Solomon, and to publish a positive review of it in the *Fortnightly Review*. By now, Swinburne, always somehow the first in retreat, had repudiated his own former friendship with the daring young painter.[12] But Walter Pater had a close friendship with the painter, and where Swinburne retreated, Pater stepped forward.

In 1867 and 1868, Pater had purchased two images from Solomon. One was *Chanting the Gospel,* one of Solomon's early artistic triumphs, now lost. The other was *The Bride, the Bridegroom, and the Friend of the Bridegroom.* Solomon had inscribed the image visibly, at the bottom of its border, to

Pater. This artwork is now in the Birmingham Museum of Art. It is a "platinotype laid down on card."[13]

It is a rather stunningly confrontational visual statement about the nature of the intimacy among the three figures. The bridegroom, a radiant Christlike figure who is heroically tall, broad-shouldered, and Apollonian in his beauty, inclines toward his "friend," at whom he gazes lovingly, a gentle smile on his lips. The "friend" is slighter of build and not as tall. He is dressed in the medieval garments that the Pre-Raphaelites admired. The "friend" is leaning into the bridegroom, nearly resting his head on the bridegroom's shoulder, and he is holding the bridegroom's hand up to his mouth, to bestow a tender kiss upon it. His expression is concentrated, devoted. The bride, though bedecked in veil and garland, hovers anxiously, or possibly irritably, behind the male couple. At first sight it is difficult to read whether her arm is linked with that of the bridegroom. But when you look closer, you see that it isn't; the bridegroom's right arm simply holds a bough of a tree—mirroring the sheaf of flowering branches held by the friend.

The bride is slightly bent, looking insecure, following behind the two men. The men's feet, in contrast, are on the same plane. The bride is technically present, but emotionally and physically, she is on her own.

Simeon Solomon was making a visual statement about such uneasy threesomes that were so prevalent in the Victorian era, when social convention required a man to marry a woman, even if he loved other men.

Now the painter of this image was in trouble, and Pater came to his friend's aid. In his public defense of Solomon, he singled out an especially vivid homoerotic image, the painting *Bacchus*. In his review, "A Study of Dionysus," Pater lauded the god of wine and release and used his Greek name, Dionysus. Solomon's painting of Bacchus, or Dionysus, explained Pater, "inspires; he explains the phenomena of enthusiasm, as distinguished by Plato in the Phaedrus, the secrets of possession by a higher and more

Simeon Solomon.

energetic spirit than one's own, the gift of self-revelation, of passing out of oneself through words, tones, gestures."[14] What code words was Pater using in his praise of "the gift of self-revelation"?

By reading "Phaedrus," as we saw, thousands of British schoolboys first encountered the idea that there had been a civilization in which men loved men. Pater also invoked Michelangelo—known by Symonds's circle to have been homosexual—and Michelangelo's painting of still another Platonic character, Charmides. Charmides was often invoked, by men in Symonds's world, to signify homoerotic desire.

Pater described two famous characters from a key text of classical antiquity, in close physical connection: "The head of Ion leans as they recline at the banquet, on the shoulder of Charmides."[15]

In the Platonic essay by that name, Socrates is introduced to the beautiful, popular youth. Socrates asks his host if the guests may encounter the young man's "naked soul" to see if it is as beautiful as "his comely face and body" and proceeds to engage in a dialogue with him about the nature of the good. At a certain point in the dinner, as Charmides seats himself, his robe falls open. Socrates is so overcome with desire that he struggles to maintain self-control.

Pater ended his defiant but coded essay by defending the "Hebrew painter" of the beautiful Bacchus. Everyone in Pater's circle—Christina Rossetti, William Michael Rossetti, Dante Gabriel Rossetti, William Morris, Algernon Charles Swinburne, and Symonds himself—read the *Fortnightly Review* and would have known exactly which disgraced "Hebrew painter" Pater had meant, even though the critic stopped short of actually naming the man.

Others, though, feared to emulate Pater's courageous praise of the outcast painter. After this essay, critical commentary on Simeon Solomon's work remained muted.[16]

Solomon could not adapt. Defiance was in his essential personality and in his artistic makeup. Though he was only thirty-three, he believed that his career was over; many previous sponsors and supporters withdrew.

CHAPTER 20

Annie Besant
and Charles Bradlaugh

It wasn't enough to censor publishers and imprison artists, writers, and booksellers. In 1876 the British state claimed even more power by fining importers of paintings, lithographs, photographs, and books considered offensive.

Parliament passed the Customs Consolidation Act 1876, which strengthened penalties against distributors of obscene materials imported from overseas. The law empowered customs officials to board ships, break locks, open boxes, and seize cargo without warrants. Seized material could be dragged off to warehouses owned by the queen. The importer of such material would be fined a hundred pounds.[1]

Just as a patchwork of sodomy statutes had been streamlined in the Offences Against the Person Act of 1861, now what had been a motley and sometimes improvised, if powerful, campaign of harassing booksellers at the behest of private organizations morphed into a centralized, fully funded censorship bureaucracy administered at the national level "on behalf of the Home Office."[2] It no longer was possible to smuggle into Britain from America the unexpurgated *Leaves of Grass*—or at least not without great risk.

Newspapers that year widely publicized still another obscenity court case. Symonds's circle saw that someone whom they knew socially could lose more than liberty or livelihood for having published the wrong kind of text. Now they saw that even a woman's custody of her own young child could be at stake.

Annie Besant was the estranged wife of a clergyman, Frank Besant. She had married him at age twenty, during a phase of intense religious feeling, but she soon found marriage stifling. She and her highly conventional husband were not compatible: "we were an ill-matched pair," she wrote later, "my husband and I, from the very outset—he, with very high ideas of a husband's authority and a wife's submission [. . .]"[3] After living under the strictures of Victorian domesticity, she discovered that "under the soft, loving, pliant girl there lay hidden, as much unknown to herself as her surroundings, a woman of strong dominant will, strength that panted for expression and rebelled against restraint, fiery and passionate emotions that were seething under compression [. . .]"[4]

The couple had a son, Digby, and a daughter, Mabel.

Even as she cared for her children and kept up appearances as a Victorian "Angel in the House," her restless intelligence led her to keep questing, until she came to realize that she was an atheist, as well as being wholly unsuited to a self-effacing domestic life.

By 1874, she had separated from her husband. A friend who was also a "freethinker" brought her to "a Freethought hall," where she heard the atheist and populist activist Charles Bradlaugh speak. She was twenty-six. Bradlaugh was forty.

After the speech, the two activists met in person. She felt, she said later, an instant sense of recognition. Within two days, she was visiting Bradlaugh in his home. Soon they were lovers, and inseparable.

Besant also began to speak in public about free thought. Female speakers were still a rarity and the young woman had great powers of communication. She was also, press reports often noted, well dressed and shapely. As fairly new forms of mass media sought for sensational content, Annie Besant became a celebrity.

In 1877, a Bristol publisher, Henry Cooke, who sold pornography under the counter, issued a volume called *The Fruits of Philosophy*. (Cooke had already served one prison sentence—of two years—for selling what was considered to be obscene literature.) *The Fruits of Philosophy* had been written by an American doctor, Charles Knowlton, decades before. It assembled

Annie Besant, radical activist for women's reproductive rights, mid-1880s.

information about various contraceptive methods—including coitus interruptus, the pessary, and the "French letter," or condom. The book had been published in Britain in 1832 and had sold steadily since then without drawing any official attention.[5]

Cooke, though, pushed his luck by publishing an edition that included how-to illustrations about methods of contraception. Officials identified them as obscene. The London police joined in, buying a dozen copies to examine. Cooke faced legal action once again.

Cooke reached out to Besant and Bradlaugh for help. A common argument that Besant was now making in her speeches was that spreading information about contraception could help alleviate poverty.

The activists decided to make the book a test case. They alerted the police to where they would be offering the pamphlet for sale. The police duly arrived and arrested Besant and Bradlaugh for distributing an "indecent, lewd, filthy, bawdy, and obscene book." The two were charged with the crime of obscene libel.

The indictment accused the two activists of encouraging "obscene, unnatural, and immoral practices" and bringing youth and others "to a state of wickedness, lewdness, and debauchery."[6]

At a time when no woman played an official role in the enactment, administration, enforcement, or adjudication of the law, the defendants served as their own attorneys. The trial began on June 18, 1877. According to eyewitness reports, twenty thousand people stood outside the court throughout the four-day trial of the two activists.

Besant, dressed at the height of demure fashion, wearing tight corseting and a bustle, with her curled hair piled high in an elaborate coiffure in the back of her head as befitted an upper-middle-class gentlewoman, used the conventions of ladylike demeanor that she knew so well in order to challenge convention. She objected to the coarse wording of the charge against her. She knew the law was based on the "intent" of the distributors of obscene material. If her "intent" was not lewd, she pointed out, the authorities would have to acquit: "The intent in a medical book must be taken to be the very essence of the character of the book [. . .]—it does not conduce to morality to say that these [medical] men shall not spread knowledge, because that knowledge may be made impure by the impure minds that read it. Every book, however good the book may be—any of your old classics [. . .] may be read for the vilest purposes, if the impure mind is to be permitted to characterize them and put upon them the shame that comes from its own obscene impurity [. . .] [M]edical books have no tendency to arouse sexual feelings."[7]

The two activists later published a transcript of Besant's rebuttal, which is a tour de force. She argued with wit, understatement, sentimentality, irony, and subversion of stereotypes that it was indeed moral, rather than immoral, to distribute such material, and that those who would keep women in ignorance and force them to bear "starveling," "ricketty" children were in fact the ones who were morally corrupt. She explained that instead of London having a lower death rate than two decades previously, the death rate was now higher. She told stories to the magistrate to dramatize the sexual injustice of women's lives—including the suffering and ignorance addressed by the book that she had distributed. Young wives of all backgrounds, she told the magistrate, merely wanted to, and deserved to, know how to limit their pregnancies.[8]

She broke all social convention about how women should speak in public by daring to invoke her desire to control her own body and her own conception. She argued that the real issue with the distribution of Knowlton's book might be that, since it cost only sixpence, information that had been restricted to the upper and upper-middle classes would now be accessible to the working classes and the poor. "I shall call upon you, gentlemen, to return a verdict of 'Not Guilty,' and to send me home free, believing from my heart and conscience that I have been guilty only of doing that which I ought to do in grappling with—that terrible poverty and misery which are around us on every hand."[9]

The assembled audience burst into applause at her conclusion, which court officials suppressed.

The Lord Chief Justice then instructed the jury to decide whether the book "has a tendency to excite unholy desires" and to consider whether it "outrages decency and tends to corrupt public morals." That jury delivered a guilty verdict, and the judge sentenced the two to six months' imprisonment and a fine. Each defendant was to pay two hundred pounds sterling. In February 1878, due to a legal technicality, the guilty verdict was reversed. At that point, Annie Besant and Charles Bradlaugh were permitted to retake possession of the confiscated copies of *Fruits of Philosophy*, books that were now stamped "recovered from the police."

But then, after this apparent victory, Besant was told that she had lost custody of her eight-year-old daughter, Mabel, to her estranged husband. He had accused his former wife of "heretical opinion" and of blasphemy.

Mabel Besant, 1878.

Though Judge Jessel acknowledged that Annie Besant took good care of her daughter, in his decision to take a child away from her mother, the activist's notoriety was used against her.

Her account of how Mabel was taken from her care is wrenching: "A messenger from the father came to my house," she wrote later, "and the little child was carried away by main force, shrieking and struggling, still weak from [a] fever [. . .] [N]o access to her was given me [. . .] I nearly went mad [. . .] [T]he loneliness and silence of the house weighed on me like an evil dream."[10]

Her appeal to regain custody of Mabel was denied; a reason for the denial was her public support for "obscene" literature. She appealed the loss of her child. But Judge Jessel again explained that because Besant had distributed obscene literature, she was not fit to be a mother. She was not even allowed to visit her children.

This tragic conclusion was one that the national press covered with avid attention.

Besant ultimately won her war of words in the courtroom, and she certainly won in the court of popular opinion. But she lost access to the beings most precious to her.

Besant had crossed yet another newly demarcated line around obscene speech. As Symonds and his friends and colleagues read day after day in the newspapers that covered these events, the state in response claimed the power to take away from a mother the child who was in her care, and to keep her from even seeing her young children.

CHAPTER 21

"The Greek Spirit"

In 1877, Symonds was lecturing in London, giving what he called "very dull" lectures at the Royal Institution in Florence, Italy. Standing in the icy draft of the lecture hall, he caught a cold that turned into bronchitis, after which he returned to Clifton. He traveled alone in the spring to Lombardy but fell seriously ill again at Turin; with the last of his strength he made it home again to Clifton and his family, where he collapsed with "a violent hemorrhage from the lungs." His wife, whom he called "a ministering angel," fed him, spoonful by spoonful. He was, agonizingly enough, still being considered for the professorship of poetry at Oxford. But two years had made a huge difference in his reputation. His *Studies of the Greek Poets*—even though it had so recently been considered proper enough to be assigned to Oxford undergraduates—was now thought quite indecent.

The Reverend Richard St. John Tyrwhitt, rector of the Oxford church of St. Mary Magdalen, wrote a damning essay in the *Contemporary Review*, titled "The Greek Spirit in Modern Literature." The essay singled out Symonds's musings at the end of his book on the beauty of a young Greek athlete (the same essay on which young Wilde had made his annotations).[1]

Tyrwhitt coined the term "English decadence." It derived, he asserted, from the less-than-wholesome aspects of Greek culture, and he claimed that Symonds was seduced, as well, by the prurience of Greek sculpture. Symonds, warned Tyrwhitt, in praising the ancient Greeks, was calling for "the total denial of any moral restraint on any human impulses" and was rejecting Christianity, the sense of sin, and decency in general.[2] The churchman went on to chastise Symonds for acknowledging that he had been influenced by Walt Whitman, "whatever on earth Mr. Symonds means by it."[3]

Symonds was taken aback. He wrote to Edmund Gosse that he could hardly bring himself to read the attack: "Of course it was meant to be galling to me & damaging to my reputation."[4] He told Graham Dakyns that the essay was "a fierce onslaught on me." Once again, Symonds's own sexuality was publicly invoked as a way to undermine his career.[5]

That year, eighteen-year-old George Wright received a sentence of ten years' penal servitude, according to the Proceedings of the Old Bailey, for the crime of sodomy, and an older man who was with him, James Smith, was sentenced to a lifetime of penal servitude. Wright's sentence represented a new high point concerning severity of punishment for a teenaged offender in that archive and the sentence of life imprisonment for his lover also marked a new extreme.[6] Thirty-three-year-old John Sweeting was sentenced to a decade of penal servitude.[7] Twenty-five-year-old Charles Gurr received a sentence of ten years at hard labor as well.

Children continued to be sent away from their families and set to hard labor. Fourteen-year-old Frederick Parker was sentenced to a decade at hard labor. A group of young men was tried together, for the first time according to these records: "JULES MANNETT (22), FRANCIS DEEKES (15), and HENRY HERBERT CUBEY (25), Unlawfully attempting to commit an unnatural offence. GUILTY. MANNETT and CUBEY—Ten Years' Penal Servitude. DEEKES [the fifteen-year-old]—Twelve Month' Imprisonment."[8] According to the digital archive of the Proceedings of the Old Bailey, Francis Deekes was the eleventh adolescent in twenty-two years to be sentenced for "sodomy" or "the attempt."[9]

By April, after Tyrwhitt's direct public attack, Symonds had given up hope of an English academic career. As he had expected, the assaults on his reputation had done their job. The position would not go to Symonds.

He concluded that "[i]t was impossible to think of remaining in England." His doctor recommended the Alps and the family, consisting of Catherine, Charlotte ("Lotta"), and Janet, traveled there with him. The two youngest, Madge and Katharine, were left with their nurses and their grandparents in Clifton.

On August 7, Catherine, with Madge and Janet, all returned home to England and to the smaller girls, and Symonds arrived alone in Davos, Switzerland, which was then a small, charming village with a nascent tourism industry attracting wealthy invalids. Expatriates with respiratory problems visited the tiny Alpine town, as the thin air was considered healthful for the lungs. Tuberculosis was still, in 1877, incurable; rest, a nourishing diet, and "good air" were the limited treatment options available.

Symonds settled in at a sprawling rented house and remained for the winter, soothed by the remote beauty of the place. Yet in spite of these surroundings, it seems as if he suffered a crisis. His letters speak of a deep depression. His loneliness was intense. He loved and missed his daughters, and in his own way, he loved his wife. He missed England.

But he could not live with his wife and children without pursuing a double life. He could not bear the temptation of "the wolf" without responding to it. In the snows of the Alps, he faced that crisis.

From this little town, Symonds wrote to Whitman to say that a signed photograph of Whitman was "framed and hangs in my bedroom."

Where was Symonds's country, and who was his family?

Symonds's own father had forcefully rejected and even persecuted the kind of "unnatural" attractions that his son felt. Symonds addressed Whitman, in contrast, as an accepting, benevolent father: "To me as a man your poems—yourself in your poems—has been a constant teacher and loved companion [. . .] I seem to know you as a friend and father [. . .] And those who love me best, make me gifts recalling you."[10]

CHAPTER 22

"Were I as Free":
The Secret Sodomy Poems

In 1878, Davos became the site of Symonds's rearranged family life. Catherine and all four girls came to join him, to live together in a series of hotels. This began what would be a permanent exile for Symonds and his family.

And yet he periodically traveled alone from Switzerland and his brood to Italy, for his other life, with other men. Italy was where he found a homosexual community. His friend Horatio Brown, who had Italian relatives, was often there, traveling with his mother. By 1879, the Browns had taken a permanent villa in Venice, the Palazzo Balbi Valier on the Grand Canal. They hosted visitors from England—many of them homosexual.

Brown had been in a relationship with a local man, "his friend Giuseppe Erba." When Erba died, Symonds wrote to Graham Dakyns that the death "has been a terrible blow to [Brown]. Giuseppe was truly loveable; & Brown had made him the sheet anchor of his heart."[1]

Symonds traveled in the spring to Milan and to Lago de Como, in Italy, by himself and then back to Davos for the summer to be with Catherine and the girls. An autumn trip took him once more back to Italy, and then by November he had returned to Davos. There, he and his family settled down at the Hotel Buol; he developed a warm friendship with the Buol family, longtime inhabitants of the town, who ran the hotel. His letters idealized what he saw as the robust, thoughtful Swiss workingmen from families such as the Buols'.

Symonds's letters from Davos to Graham Dakyns from this time contain messages from Catherine, describing one of the small Symonds daughters prattling about Dakyns's own baby, Bo, who had come to visit Davos with his family earlier; she also sent greetings to Dakyns's wife, the similarly situated Maggie Dakyns. The two fathers of young families, friends who shared passionate descriptions of their inner lives and described to each other courtships and sexual affairs, also conscientiously sent greetings at the ends of letters to the other's wife, as well as kind wishes for the health of each other's children. (Edmund Gosse had also married, in 1875, to the Pre-Raphaelite painter Ellen Epps; he had a baby girl, Emily Theresa.)

Symonds now wished to publish a privately printed collection of homoerotic-themed poems, *Rhaetica*.[2] He again wrote to friends, asking which poems from the collection could be published without repercussions. His friends, including Henry Sidgwick, once again warned him to destroy the pamphlet altogether. The poem "Rhaetica" and the other secret poems wouldn't just incriminate the author: they could now, Sidgwick warned, ruin his friends as well. But Henry Sidgwick was seemingly as conflicted as the poet himself. Even though Sidgwick asked Symonds to destroy the manuscript so as not to incriminate him as a reader, Sidgwick did in fact read it, and even offered suggestions as to which poems to cut in order to prepare the manuscript for publication. In spite of their commitment to this task of censorship, the two men spoke of literary excision in terms of castration.

Symonds released an edited selection of verse, *Many Moods*. He included some poems related to sexual desire but changed the male pronouns in poems in the locked iron boxes in his study to female ones, so that the poems could enter the world of readers.

Symonds's textual veilings in *Many Moods* took a toll on his voice. He experienced self-loathing as a man when he expressed the impulses he called "the wolf," and he also felt self-loathing as a writer when he repressed or censored these feelings on the page. As Symonds's biographer Phyllis Grosskurth put it, "He believed that he had never been able to attain complete self-fulfillment because of the constant façade he was forced to maintain. A man hidden behind a mask, a writer who never attained first-rank, he suffered the tormented struggle of a homosexual within Victorian society."[3] Even with the re-dressing of almost all the male love objects in the garb of female gender, Symonds could not help but include a few references to male-male love. In "Love and Death," for instance, he invoked the great lovers of antiquity, stressing the price they paid "for love made sure":

Did not Patroclus die, Achilles pay
Though goddess–born, his life, a little price
For love made sure [. . .]?[4]

But overall, *Many Moods* feels false and stifling to read. On the surface, it is a collection of rather banal verse—but also, as we will see, if you look at it another way, it is a puzzle waiting to be solved through death and through time.

The mere hints of homosexuality in *Many Moods* were enough to outrage the critics at home, who had doubtless also heard of the scandalous rumors connected to Symonds. Many wrote reviews condemning the book as "unwholesome." The ostensibly sterilized *Many Moods* was composed in a year when, according to the Proceedings of the Old Bailey, twenty-nine-year-old Martin Manetti received a life sentence of penal servitude for "s—y." Marcus Manuel, who was only fifteen, received a sentence of ten years' hard labor—*after* the sentence took his youth into account. Manuel was the twelfth teenager sentenced there for "the offence" since 1855 according to the Old Bailey archive.

Thwarted by critics who bayed for blood at the least hint of improper emotion, and yet unwilling—seemingly unable—to leave the "black iron boxes" of illicit poems alone, Symonds took the secret poems and self-published them, to give them in printed, rather than handwritten, form to the very friends who had begged him never to reach out to them as possible readers. He tasked a printing house—not a publisher—to create a tiny print run of "Eudiades" and another of the secret poems, probably written during the 1870s. "Dead Love," like so many of his secret verses, mourned a renounced relationship. Yet another secret poem hidden in the black box was titled "The Tale of Theodore."

Even though these secret poems were bound, self-published, between covers, Symonds made use of coded pagination. That is, as with "In Memoriam Arcadie," he interpolated unpaginated pages among paginated ones; the pages with sexual material are identified by letters rather than by numerals. If illicit pages had to be cut out hastily, the book would show no break in pagination.

The secret sodomy poems have additional codes. There is no publisher or publishing house on a title page. On page 12, at the bottom of the page, is "Arrowsmith, Printer, Quay Street, Bristol, 'Poems.'" This is an unusual location for publication data, which is usually, of course, on the title page. The printer is hidden, in other words, on an interior, random page.

Symonds showed his characteristic ambivalence about publication of dangerous sexual material. Though he had arranged to print a few dozen of these pamphlets, he personally destroyed most of them.

After Symonds's death, his second executor, Edmund Gosse, would write, on the recto page, in pen: "Of the pamphlets here bound together, [. . .] J.A.S. destroyed the greater part of even these small editions, and some may be considered almost unique. Of these pamphlets some were presented to me by the author, the rest, after his death, by H. F. Brown [. . .]" Gosse confirms that the handwritten notes on "Dead Love" and "The Tale of Theodore" are in Symonds's hand. In the upper right corner of the page of "Dead Love," Symonds wrote, "N. B. The Whole of the [sequence] forms part of my Diary [1860–1863]. 'The Tale of Theodore' was written in 1862 in order to explain the state of my mind to my father."[5]

"The Tale of Theodore," first drafted at the same time as "Set Apology" at the front of "In Memoriam Arcadie," and based on journal entries covering the same period of Symonds's seemingly annihilated affair with "W.," is actually an uncensored sexual and romantic version of the exact same love story that Symonds had told more publicly, using some of the same language, in the restrained, etherealized, and finally disavowed "In Memoriam Arcadie."

Symonds probably did show his father "In Memoriam Arcadie," with its clear disavowal. But there is no evidence that Symonds ever did show "The Tale of Theodore," with its uncensored echoes of that earlier poem— or "Dead Love," or anything like it—to Dr. John Symonds Sr. Though Symonds wished "to explain the state of my mind to my father"—indeed longed to share his inner life, to the extent of creating dozens of pages of verse, now locked away—it is unlikely that he ever did.

Other secret poems in the privately printed collections center on sodomy as a test of love and as a moral turning point in a love relationship. In "Eudiades," the poem from the locked black iron boxes that Symonds seemed most compelled to share, the act of anal sex serves as a culmination of love, but also as a crisis in the narrative. Melanthius, an older man, as we recall, fell in love with the beautiful youth Eudiades. "[. . .] 'Make full broad thy bed, / For henceforth we together shall be laid,'" exclaims Melanthius.[6] In a characteristically overwrought passage about the lovers' night together, Symonds wrote:

> [. . .] *yea, and he [Eudiades] trembled with the passionate pain*
> *Of those white winding arms, whose eager strain*

Yet made him flutter like a bird just caught,
Who in the fowler's hands most gently brought
Must struggle still and pant and long to be
Once more at large in woodland liberty.

After the lovemaking, Melanthius suffers self-loathing and regret:

[. . .] Swords too on his heart like lead
Lay with a dull unapprehended dread.
This passion was so new, so terrible [. . .]
The good thing
Which he had longed for with such sorrowing,
How all untried, immeasurable, full
It was of wild pain and joy wonderful! [. . .]
His flesh quaked with the fierce tongues of desire . . .
. . . 'Twere well to shun
The sweetness that brings shame.[7]

Even as Melanthius advised his conscience that " 'twere well to shun /
The sweetness that brings shame," he testified to the beauty and goodness
of the love that he experienced.

In the morning, wrote Symonds, "Up rose Melanthius, and the boy
could see / His beauty naked in the mystery [. . .]" Eudiades now "knew
what passion was"; as the two men built a relationship together, "the joy
that grew between them wove / Their very bodies in a web of love [. . .]"
But the swooning lyrics give way again to moralizing; love becomes a form
of temptation, and at the same time, a path to certain death. Symonds
compared love's temptation to "coals of fire," a biblical metaphor for shame.
Male-male desire was "a sly snare."

The "fierce and fiery thing" and the "flames, a shape of dread" threatened
to kill the lovers, to "shrivel their young veins in dry decay."[8]

Yet the alternative to this deadly temptation was just as terrifying.
Symonds used the pomegranate of the Persephone myth as a symbol for
forced heterosexual intimacy. But instead of the sweet, richly colored fruit
that Dante Gabriel Rossetti painted again and again to represent the vulva,
in "Eudiades" the feminine fruit was "harsh and bitter," with a "shell" that
suggests falseness. Symonds described with aversion the "furnace-breath of
that fierce mouth."[9]

In contrast, the male lovers' longing for the most damning form of union—sodomy—grew, along with their emotional closeness. Eudiades "learned to long" and Melanthius was "[n]ursing the fever of a hidden want." And yet the poet asked, "Why from the fruits should they their hands withhold / Which strewed the paths of loving men with gold?"[10]

Eudiades, using Christlike sacrificial language, offered his lover this form of connection:

Nay, take [. . .] fear not to shed my blood;
For I will die to do thee any good,
Or in my body bear thy mark of shame
To all men visible, cherish the blame
That falls on me for blessings![11]

These lines reflected the way that Tardieu's "six signs" of sodomy, promoted in courtrooms throughout Britain, affected the consciousness of homosexual men. These signs allegedly were a "mark of shame / To all men visible." Symonds's secret poetry here suggested that he either believed, or feared to believe, that the act of sodomy will be permanently imprinted on the body of the receiving lover, a visible and dangerous "mark of shame."

The deed was done; the lovers were left

Lying with passionate tears tired in the grey
Light of the weeping dawn. Felt love so sore,
So tested in the fiery furnace-core,
That nought might stand between them any more.[12]

In this fantasy's outcome, Eudiades disclosed the nature of his love to his father, Ameinas. Ameinas "turned and read / The boy's face like a book" and "searching his soul found neither spot nor shame."[13] After the boy was "bold" with the truth, wrote Symonds, "the mighty wing / Of Love spread broad above him."[14] The formerly judgmental father yielded to "the strength of Love," and "kissed the boy, and blessed him." In Symonds's imagination, the rejecting father he had actually faced, in his own youth, was transfigured into an idealized, nurturing father who felt only acceptance for his son's happiness in finding love.

The fantasy ended with a traditional comedy's ending—a marriage scene celebrated by the community, "the press / Of men crowd round to greet their goodliness."[15] A hundred and thirty years before the movement for gay marriage, Symonds painted the scene of this joyful outcome—a wedding uniting two bridegrooms: "Lie in union, youth and boy [. . .]"[16]

But there was nowhere for the narrative to continue, for the marriage to proceed to the next stage of life: a social context. Eudiades, wounded in battle, died in his lover's arms. This death, and Melanthius's suicide soon after, solved—if not persuasively—Symonds's narrative problem. How could Symonds, in the nineteenth century, have imagined a "happily ever after" domestic life for his two male protagonists, to follow his fantasy of homosexual marriage?

The narrator added a "Postludium," in which he saw himself as being "[b]orn out of time"—"by cross fate cast upon / A sandy tract of sloth [. . .]"[17] The "cross fate" put the narrator at cross-purposes with his historical moment. His fate of being born at the wrong time was also the narrator's "cross" to bear. He longed for something that doesn't exist yet—something he could barely name:

> *A stony sadness cleave*
> *Here to my heart, and for some unknown good*
> *I pine, perplexed with pain and solitude [. . .]*[18]

The narrator addressed his own literary creations, a devoted male couple, as if they were real people—friends fading into the dimming of the scene at the end of the story:

> *Farewell Melanthius! Eudiades*
> *Farewell! You fade, and fading filch away*
> *Some portion of my heart, that still must stay.*[19]

Symonds took his family to Milan, and they moved on from there to Venice. To that seductive city, though, Symonds returned after his family left for Davos. He spent time apart from his domestic circle and continued to embrace friendships with the community of younger men centered on Horatio Brown and his villa—men who were more open about their sexuality than his own generation had been. During his time with this community, the content of Symonds's private writings shifted from his usual crippling self-hatred and shame regarding "the wolf" to a measure of at least internal acceptance: "It would be an ideal condition of existence were I as free from the dread of human law and custom as I am conscience free before God and nature in the matter of my passions," he wrote.

But by the middle of the summer, when the humid Venetian air was considered unhealthful for Symonds, he returned to his family in Davos.

In 1881, "indecent assault" entered the record of the Proceedings of the Old Bailey—an example of how the offense of sodomy was being codified as a violent crime even if it was consensual, between adults.[20] As in the case of John Clayton: "JOHN CLAYTON (38). Unlawfully attempting to commit an abominable crime with Alfred Henry Kimble [. . .] for an indecent assault [. . .] unlawfully inciting, &c [. . .]—Fifteen Month's Hard Labour."[21] John Clayton received a sentence of fifteen months' hard labor for "inciting"—that is, for *asking* for—sodomy, rather than attempting or completing it.

Witnessing this from afar, with nowhere further to go in writing about his true subject, Symonds turned his frustrated pen to travel writing. He published in England an anodyne travel journal based on his Italian other life. He drew on the many journeys he had taken away from his family of wife and four girls, who remained in the snows and propriety of Switzerland. This Italian journey had taken him into a subculture set along Venetian canals, into a sensuous world of men with men. Taking a history-teacher-ish, touristy angle, he directed English readers' attention to the churches and monuments along his way, obscuring altogether the reason he took these journeys.

He gave the book a bland title: *Sketches and Studies in Italy and Greece.* It was extremely well received.[22]

But for those who knew how to read the unspoken, he had included, opposite the title page, an engraving of "The Ildefonso Group," a classical sculpture "[F]rom the Museum at Madrid." It depicted two beautiful young men, both nude, each leaning toward the other; they face the viewer, embracing.

PART VII

The Next Generation: Symonds, Whitman, and Wilde

CHAPTER 23

"Love at First Sight"

In 1881, Symonds and Catherine built in Davos what would be their last home—an imposing, boxy estate, with white plastered walls, fit for a late-Victorian paterfamilias, servants, wife, and daughters; the family named the estate Am Hof.

But despite being so settled, Symonds couldn't, or no longer wished to, keep himself from seeking out his other life. He returned to Venice for a few days.

Horatio Brown now lived permanently in Venice; the Brown family had bought a beautiful villa on the Zattere, called the Ca Torresella. Brown kept a type of small, sleek boat called a *sandolo*. He named it *Fisole* and decorated it with orange sails adorned with a fleur-de-lis. Symonds loved drifting through the lagoons on the bright vessel. Brown also arranged one of the tacitly understood threesomes that were so common in this era: his "close friend" Antonio Salin, who was a gondolier, lived in the Ca Torresella, along with his wife and family.

On a warm day in May, Symonds and Brown were sitting in the garden of a restaurant in that shimmering city, and Symonds saw the man who would become the love of his life: a twenty-four-year-old gondolier named Angelo Fusato. This poised young man, with sleek black hair and a mustache, wore the broad black hat that was a mark of his profession. He was a servant

Venetian gondolier Angelo Fusato: "love at first sight," circa 1881.

working for an expatriate general. Two days after meeting Fusato, Symonds wrote about him in his secret papers: "He was tall and sinewy, but very slender [. . .] he was rarely in repose, but moved with a singular brusque grace [. . .] Great fiery grey eyes, gazing intensely, with compulsive effluence of electricity—the wild glance of a Triton. [. . .] He fixed and fascinated me."[1]

Symonds described his feelings as "love at first sight." He wrote that the fascination was "sharp" at first but became "durable" as a "steady friendship" grew up between the men. "My good sense rebelled, and told me that I was morally a fool and legally a criminal. But the love of the impossible rises victorious after each fall given it by sober sense. Man must be a demigod of volition, a very Hercules, to crush the life out of that Antaeus, lifting it aloft from the soil of instinct, and appetite which eternally creates it new in his primeval nature."[2] He sought out Fusato the next day; the two met in the evening, and Symonds took him back to his rooms. A dreamy sonnet commemorates their first night together.

> *Yes, he was here.*
> *Our four hands, laughing, made*
> *Brief havoc of his belt, shirt, trousers, shoes:*
> *Till, mother-naked, white as lilies, laid*
> *There on the counterpane, he bade me use*
> *Even as I willed, his body.*[3]

Fusato was, like Brown's beloved, also a married man. But, as Catherine Symonds had done—and as Maggie Dakyns, and Antonio Salin's wife, had also done—Fusato's unnamed wife accepted, or had to find a way to accept, her husband's almost immediate and constant connection with the Englishman.

Symonds and Fusato began a domestic, deeply intimate relationship. But Symonds concealed its true nature by employing Fusato as a manservant. Fusato traveled back to Switzerland with Symonds. Symonds wrote to Sir Henry Layard that Fusato was a good gondolier and an able servant; he described needing Fusato to look after his children's troublesome little dog, overexplaining rather awkwardly.

The Symonds family moved into Am Hof in September 1882. Catherine and the girls often managed without Symonds. He was frequently away, traveling with Fusato, but when he was home, he remained a devoted father to his girls and a caring friend and partner to his wife.

Horatio Brown visited Symonds's family in Davos, and Symonds wrote to him afterward that "when you ever seek me here again, I trust you will find a pigeon-hole of your writings, under lock and key, with a separate division of my cupboard to yourself." He was sharing a room, among his locked boxes, for the additional forbidden, locked-away writings of others for whom he cared, and whom he could trust.

In 1881, James Osgood, the foremost publisher in the United States, who was based in Boston and whose stable of writers included Longfellow, Hawthorne, and Emerson, brought out a new edition of *Leaves of Grass*. This publication was one that Whitman believed would herald his "break-through as a poet."[4] Whitman again designed the cover, providing for it an image of a butterfly resting on a hand. He prepared for the publication with excitement and traveled to Boston personally to oversee it.

But there was trouble. On May 1, 1882, Oliver Stevens, the district attorney of Massachusetts, urged on by the New England Society for the Suppression of Vice, wrote to Whitman's publisher: "We are of the opinion that this book is such a book as brings it within the provisions of the Public Statutes respecting obscene literature and suggest the propriety of with-drawing the same from circulation and suppressing the editions thereof."

Stevens specifically wished to remove the poems "A Woman Waits for Me" and "To a Common Prostitute," and he asked for changes to "Song of Myself," "From Pent-Up Aching Rivers," "I Sing the Body Electric," "Spontaneous Me," "Native Moments," "The Dalliance of the Eagles," "By Blue Ontario's Shore," "Unfolded Out of the Folds," "The Sleepers," and "Faces."

Osgood forwarded this alarming letter to the poet. "We are . . . naturally reluctant to be identified with any legal proceedings in a matter of this nature," he wrote. Cutting the manuscript so that the list of "obscene" poems that the district attorney had taken the time to identify would possibly, he implied, save the print run. Without the excisions, Osgood was unwilling to risk publication.[5]

Whitman replied fiercely: "The list whole & several is rejected by me, & will not be thought of under any circumstances."[6] He would change phrases here and there, he conceded, but steadfastly refused to alter or omit entire poems.

Soon afterward, Osgood wrote to say, sadly, that "there seems no alternative for us but to decline to further circulate the book." He returned the plates of the new edition of *Leaves of Grass* to Whitman.[7] He also sent back the portrait, the dies, and about 225 copies of the book, in the form of unbound sheets. Luckily, Whitman had the skill to reuse these chaotic bits and pieces. And he had help. David McKay, of the Philadelphia house Rees Welsh and Company, had heard of the canceled print run and approached the poet; his publishing house bought the plates, dies, portraits, and sheets.

McKay wisely capitalized on the "censorship" of this edition to boost sales. The first printing of this "suppressed edition" was released on July 18, 1882. It sold out in one day.

But printer and author had to take care. They showed defiance, yet also careful planning. One thing they changed was the portrait of the author. The lithograph Whitman had chosen in 1855, in which he wore an open-collared shirt, had accompanied every US edition of *Leaves of Grass* up to that point. But in 1882, given perhaps the serious risk he was facing, Whitman added a new image to replace that of the virile, provocative body, which had been read by both genders as inviting. In the new image, the poet was presented only from the chest up, wearing a sober dark coat. His hair is white and his beard is full; he inclines his head thoughtfully.

The persona had evolved: he was now a mature, meditative sage, adorned with a Santa Claus–like beard. For the remainder of Whitman's public life, he offered this image to American readers: the patriarchal wise man, a chronicler of American history and its military mythology.

Whitman also reproduced, in the opening pages of the volume itself, in a copy held in the Berg Collection, a long, positive interview from the *Boston Globe*. This *Leaves of Grass* came into the world not sauntering with ease, as in 1855 and 1860, but armored, defended: "In a small inner room connected with the printing establishment of Rand, Avery, & Co., Walt Whitman the poet was reading by a table [. . .] No, he had no objection to entering into a conversation which should be given to the public [. . .] he was here, he said, to look over the proofs for his new 'Leaves of Grass' [. . .]"

The reporter compared *Leaves of Grass* to "one of those old architectural edifices" that have been "hundreds of years building [. . .] There have been seven different hitches at it [. . .] the book has been built partially in every part of the United States; and this Osgood edition [reprinted by McKay] is the completed edifice."[8]

Whitman was using the validating *Boston Globe* article to fend off any suspicion that the book might shock a reader. Rather, it was a hoary old edifice many years a-building, a firmly fixed part of the American landscape.

Censorship law in the United States had caught up with Whitman. Now his formerly declarative voice, so clearly trumpeted in his introduction to the 1855 *Leaves of Grass*, took on the syntactical contortions that marred Symonds's prose. Whitman concluded the interview with a rather astonishing redirection of his audience's attention: he insisted to the *Globe* reporter that *Leaves of Grass*, the great love poem, was in fact a poem about war: the "whole book turns on the Secession War," he declared.[9] Whitman had selected the Civil War to serve as his cultural validator, just as ancient Greece had done for Symonds.

The *Globe* reporter asked Whitman whether the poems "are to appear entire in the new edition of the book."[10] Readers would have known that the reporter was asking about the "Calamus" and "Enfans d'Adam" poems, among others. Whitman's answer sounds, on the surface, defiant, but it is in fact equivocal: "All the objectionable passages which were the cause of so much complaint at the time of their appearance will remain. Not a word is to be changed, nothing omitted, except for the sake of conciseness. The great difference is, that whereas in the first issue they made a main portion, here they occupy but five or six pages out of nearly four hundred."[11]

Whitman's several strategies to direct attention away from the more contentious poems—the newly conservative packaging around his radical message—worked, at least with law enforcement. District Attorney Stevens did not, finally, decide to prosecute Walt Whitman.

This version went through five printings of one thousand copies each. By December, McKay was able to give the poet a royalty check for a thousand dollars.[12]

The poet's courageous gamble had succeeded—for the time being.

CHAPTER 24

Pilgrimage to Camden

Symonds had written textbooks, possibly as a way of entrusting his experiences and observations to future generations. Whitman also greeted and in his own way mentored the best-known emerging "Greek" voice of the next generation—Oscar Wilde.

By 1881, Oscar Wilde was a well-known young writer and personality. He had completed his studies at Oxford, moved to London in 1879, and begun to write journalism; he'd also published a much reviewed, if unoriginal, volume of verse, titled *Poems.*

In the 1880s, the machinery of modern celebrity was gearing up; newspapers were able to reproduce photographs now in addition to engravings, and literacy was far more widespread up and down the economic scale, as two generations of students had benefited from public education. A network of fast trains made daily media updates possible. In both the United States and Britain, hundreds of newspapers and tabloids filled an ever-expanding appetite for news, scandal, and gossip about these larger-than-life personalities.

And individuals were being elaborated into national celebrities, including the society courtesan Lillie Langtry and the actress Sarah Bernhardt. Such celebrities posed for endless photographs, and columnists followed their careers and social lives. The industry of advertising boomed alongside the popular media, and famous people made money by lending their names to products for sale.

Oscar Wilde, who came of age as these industries were creating the foundations of modern media, understood this landscape far better than did his older influencers. As the Wilde scholars Dr. Michèle Mendelssohn and David Friedman both point out, Wilde took the persona of poet-critic out from behind the ivied walls that had sheltered the work and lives of men such as Walter Pater and Benjamin Jowett and remade it into something entirely new: the poet-critic as mass-media star. He was perhaps the first

British writer successfully to manipulate the modern media machine, and he did so from the beginning of his career. Of course, the voracious public attention that resulted would prove to be double-edged.

As part of his platform, Wilde began to elaborate on the theory that others had started to refer to as Aestheticism. Walter Pater had developed these ideas, and the French novelist and critic Joris-Karl Huysmans, in his novella *À Rebours* (*Against Nature*), would elaborate them as well. At the core of Aestheticism was the notion that art did not serve any social or utilitarian function—utilitarianism itself was suspect; according to Pater's famous dictum, "to burn always with this hard gemlike flame, to maintain this ecstasy, is success in life." One should above all, he wrote, as mentioned earlier, pursue "art for art's sake."[1] In a religiously self-important, materialist era, the Aesthetes declared that it was sensation and beauty, not religious morality or materialism, that were the proper ideals of a well-lived life—a radical premise indeed, in any era.

It seems clear to me that the climate of censorship, the related trials and convictions, and the wording of *Hicklin* all influenced the formation of Aestheticism. When an entire nation's judiciary has become obsessed with art as a cause of a specific moral effect in real life—and when proof of that cause and effect can send an artist to prison—it seems inevitable that a philosophy would arise created by artists and writers, entirely to decouple art from life, making the claim that art has no responsibility for morals whatsoever.

As a journalist and poet-about-town, the young Wilde played up his striking physical attributes. Wilde was over six feet tall; he grew out his thick, dark locks until they fell across his wide forehead and swept down almost to his shoulders, like the hairstyle of a medieval page. *Patience: Or, Bunthorne's Bride*, a play by Gilbert and Sullivan that became a hit, made gentle fun of a Wilde-like character—and Wilde embraced the notoriety. He was virtually a household name—an early mass-market "brand."

Richard D'Oyly Carte, the stage promoter who had produced *Patience*, contacted Wilde and offered him a major American tour. Wilde sailed for the New World from Liverpool in 1881 and stayed through 1882.

Early in the tour, when he was based in a New York hotel, Wilde posed for the photographer Napoleon Sarony, who was known for his portraits of theatrical performers.[2] Wilde brought a number of costume changes to the studio and experimented with props that were already there. The critic-lecturer wore a velvet jacket, a cape, a cravat; he held a walking stick and a broad-brimmed felt hat. For some images he wore his famous fur-lined coat over conventional long trousers. In one, we see the same coat and a fur hat; in another, though, he wears equally remarked-upon knee breeches and silk stockings; in still others, he lounges at ease in conventional white tie, with a black swallowtail jacket and a white waistcoat.

In an 1877 photograph, Wilde had actually worn a Greek national costume—clothing of the nineteenth-century Greek peasantry, that is. Wilde could hardly have created a more amusing way to wink at the viewer, hinting at his admiration for all things "Greek."

The Sarony photographs were reproduced all over America. They appeared in highbrow and mass-market contexts. The pop-culture image of Wilde showed up in cartoons, in popular songs, and in ads for soap. As Dr. Mendelssohn has proved, even in minstrel shows, white actors wearing blackface pretended to be like Oscar Wilde.

Sarony Image Number 18, in which Wilde leans in toward the camera, with his long dark hair flopping about his face, became so familiar to American readers of news and advertising that it became the subject of a famous copyright infringement lawsuit. (Sarony took the lawsuit all the way to the Supreme Court and successfully established the photographer's right to copyright photographs in America.)

On the road, for stage appearances, Wilde also dressed theatrically: he wore tight black knee breeches, buckled shoes, black silk stockings, and "Byronic" white shirts with immense ruffled sleeves. He carried kid gloves and a cane. His dark hair fell in soft locks on either side of his face.

Wilde's appearance and dress were much discussed in virtually every American interview with him or feature about him. Reporters seemed fascinated by the extremes of gender stereotypes that they saw as intermingling in Wilde's self-presentation. They often remarked on how "massive" and "strong" he was, how firm his manly grip; they also described his taste in clothing as delicate and feminine. They dwelt on his lush fur coat and his lounging pose. The tone of the interviews with Wilde revealed that this mélange of gender stereotypes was powerfully appealing—at least to the stream of male reporters, often equally young, who visited the celebrity in his various regional hotel rooms. And in turn, their enthusiastic reports made this mélange, and the celebrity himself, appealing to readers of all backgrounds throughout the country, from the coasts to the heartland. Wilde was, in 1881–82, a media darling in America.

Provocatively, Wilde played with the shock value of the fresh lilies, violets, or other flowers on display in his hotel room. He often called

One of Napoleon Sarony's portraits of the young celebrity Oscar Wilde, during his American tour, 1882.

attention to them in the presence of the press: "'Where's that camellia that was presented us at Reno? [. . .] Bring them violets,' he yelled [. . .] to the valet."[3] His courtship was successful: he rather astonishingly well succeeded in seducing mainstream, mostly heterosexual America. But what appeared charming and novel in American popular newspapers ran close to the legal line at home in Britain, where "effeminate" self-presentation was proscribed. From the British perspective, Wilde's American success was threatening because he had made the obviously "Greek" aspects of his message appealing. This recast "Greek" inclinations in an acceptable and benign, though admittedly quirky, light.

Wilde didn't just deliver playful innuendo to male reporters. He risked more. He deliberately declared his interest in visiting his own lodestar, Walt Whitman. In many interviews Wilde spoke about his admiration for Whitman, a public figure even better known then in America than Wilde, and who had, just before Wilde's arrival, been targeted by the legal establishment in Massachusetts.

Wilde gave an interview to the *Philadelphia Press* in which he claimed that his mother, Lady Wilde, who was a well-known Irish nationalist poet herself (whose pen name was "Speranza"), had read Whitman's poems aloud to him when he was a child. He told reporters that he and his Oxford student friends used to carry Whitman along with them, to read "on their rambles."[4] This was a knowing reference to the way Whitman acolytes would read the poet outdoors in the natural world. Without being asked about him, Wilde mentioned Whitman more than a dozen times in press interviews during the 1881–82 US tour.[5] This can practically be read as a campaign.

The Philadelphia reporter asked Wilde about influences upon him: "What poet do you most admire in American literature?" Wilde replied directly: "I think that Walt Whitman and Emerson have given the world more than anyone else [. . .] I admire [Whitman] intensely—Dante Rossetti, Swinburne, William Morris, and I often discuss him. There is something so Greek and sane about his poetry; it is so universal, so comprehensive."[6] Wilde used every name-dropping option available, invoking the best-known members of the Pre-Raphaelite Brotherhood: Dante Gabriel Rossetti, Algernon Charles Swinburne, and William Morris. This statement can be read as a stealthy tactic to wrap the poet, who was still a target of the American vigilance societies and US attorneys general, in the protective cloak of Old World cultural prestige. It's a moving moment; just as Symonds had sought to use the American poet's validation of the "Calamus" poems to protect British poets in England, now the younger British man was trying to protect the beleaguered invalid American poet. But shielding Whitman with these powerful public statements could endanger Wilde, especially if word of this campaign got back to Britain.

The American poet now lived on the volumes of his verse that he managed to sell by hand, and meager royalties. Photographs of the upstairs bedroom—which also served as a sitting room—in the little house in Camden, New Jersey, where he now lived, show a book-cluttered space with unpainted walls, simple wooden furniture, and a scuffed wooden floor. Whitman was still ill and often bedridden.

Though Wilde was surrounded by the wealthiest hostesses in each city and housed in America's costliest hotels, he wanted nothing more than to detour to Whitman's humble out-of-the-way home in Camden.

Wilde wrote to the older poet, asking to see him; Whitman wrote back to welcome the younger man. On January 17, 1882, Wilde wrote proudly to a local society hostess, "I go to see Walt Whitman, at his invitation, tomorrow."[7]

Wilde left his luxurious hotel room in Philadelphia and went, in the company of his friend the publisher J. M. Stoddart, on a ferry across the Delaware River to Camden; Wilde wore brown velvet trousers in the icy weather. After the men hired a carriage to bring them to Whitman's small house, Wilde announced at the door:

"I come as a poet to call upon a poet."

"Go ahead," replied Whitman.

"I have come to you as one with whom I have been acquainted almost from the cradle," the young man continued. Inside the little, untidy house, he described more details of his attachment to Whitman. He repeated his story about how his mother had given him William Michael Rossetti's edition of *Leaves of Grass* when he had been a teenager; he and his friends, he continued, telling the poet what he had earlier told a reporter, used to take the book with them and declaim from it out in the countryside.

Whitman, delighted, retrieved a bottle of homemade elderberry wine from a cupboard, and the two men drank together. Stoddart, tactfully, went for a walk to give them privacy.

Walt Whitman, imaged as an elder statesman, late 1880s–early 1890s.

"I will call you Oscar," said the sixty-two-year-old invalid.

"I like that so much," replied the twenty-seven-year-old celebrity.

Whitman replied that the men could speak to each other on "thee and thou" terms. They had an argument about beauty—Whitman had reservations about Aestheticism. But at last the older man gave his blessing: "You are young and ardent, and the field is wide, and if you want my advice, [I say] go ahead."

At the end of the visit, Whitman's blessing was even more direct. He gave Wilde a portrait of himself, and as he said goodbye at the door, said, "God bless you, Oscar." Later, Wilde would tell British friends, "I have the kiss of Walt Whitman still on my lips."

On the return to the ferry, Stoddart tried to make fun of the humble elderberry wine, but Wilde replied, "If it had been vinegar I should have drunk it all the same [. . .] for I have an admiration for that man which I can hardly express."[8]

After the visit, Wilde described it in gossipy letters for readers in literary London. Wilde also wrote sweetly to the American poet himself, "Before I leave America I must see you again. There is no one in this wide great world of America whom I love and honour so much."[9]

Wilde's personal visit to Whitman was more than a literary pilgrimage. It was, it seems clear in context, an act of political identification. But the young man also, he seemed to feel, had received a blessing from a kind of secular guardian angel; perhaps this blessing was part of what would support him in trials to come.

Not everyone of Wilde's acquaintance exhibited such brave effrontery that year.

Swinburne's about-face movement to reject the elderly poet escalated dramatically.

In 1859, Swinburne had been one of Whitman's greatest British admirers, as he wrote to his friends. In 1868, he publicly compared Whitman to

Blake. In 1871, he had written an ode to Whitman in *Songs Before Sunrise*, titled "To Walt Whitman in America": "O Strong-winged soul with prophetic / Lips hot with the bloodbeats of song [. . .]"[10]

But times had changed, and the record suggests Swinburne wanted to make public his distance.[11]

On March 1, 1882, Algernon Charles Swinburne put on record, in a letter to Wilde in America, his "admiration" for Whitman. But he added an equivocation: "He [Swinburne] also wished Whitman to know that he believed him to be at his best when he speaks 'of great matters—liberty, for instance, and death.'"[12] In other words, the former lyricist of flagellation, lesbianism, and sadomasochism wanted it to be known that he admired Whitman not for anything with sexual content, but for his poems that centered on noble, abstract themes. Wilde forwarded this somewhat queasy-making letter to the poet.[13] But, as if that guarded gesture had spent all of Swinburne's available generosity, Swinburne wrote to an acquaintance a hostile letter about Wilde. "[T]he only time I ever saw Mr Oscar Wilde was in a crush [casual party] at our acquaintances," wrote Swinburne, putting social distance between himself and the self-dramatizing young star. "I thought he seemed a harmless young nobody," he went on. "A letter which he wrote to me lately about Walt Whitman was quite a modest, gentlemanlike, reasonable affair, without any flourish or affectation of any kind in manner or expression."[14] "Flourish or affectation of any kind in manner or expression" by this time was clear enough, if coded, language for what had become unsayable.

While Whitman was enjoying the visit of this younger acolyte, and its after-echoes, Symonds was engaged in apparently censoring and slicing up his own poems for a new collection, to be called *Animi Figura*.

Symonds once again asked his friends to help him apparently to censor this volume, which he intended to self-publish; this time he enlisted Horatio Brown. "And then you will come to the final decision as to omissions, etc.," he wrote to his friend. Once again, he mourned what had been excised—that the censored volume would remain "fragmentary, imperfect and obscure."[15] He succeeded in masking the nature of his attractions, and again, most of the poems were moribund. Symonds knew that when the censor's pen flattened his voice, he was dying as a writer though he remained physically alive.

Animi Figura was eventually properly published, by Smith and Elder in London, in 1882. And, as Symonds had predicted, it made barely a ripple in literary London. The bowdlerized poems in the volume are trite and bland.

No one, not even his closest friends, knew that this collection too was a puzzle set up for the future to unlock. The poet had buried in the conventional little volume a secret history of his mature love.

When you open one of the volumes of *Animi Figura* in the Morgan Library's collection, it shows an inscription from Symonds to his eldest daughter, Janet. In his nervous hand, in black ink, on the upper right corner of the title page, the author wrote:

> *Janet Harriet Symonds*
> *From her father the*
> *Writer of this book*
> *Davos July 1882*

The book itself is dedicated to
H. R. F. B (Horatio Brown)
"Amico Dilectissimo"—*Most beloved friend.*

Startlingly, out of this volume that the author had inscribed to his adult daughter, a folded note, also in his hand, falls out. It reads:

> P.S. You will probably like to know that the abbreviations at the foot
> of some of the sonnets may be interpreted:
> S. A. = Schatz Alp
> H. B. = Hotel Buol
> M. G. = Mer de Glace

And in Janet's copy of the book, all of the poems do have the conventional notations that apparently Symonds reminded her that she would recognize: "H B" for "Hotel Buol," the note "Clifton"—sites of family memories and family life.

But Janet had additional information from her father, buried in her copy of the book: when the reader gets to the poem titled "L'Amour de l'Impossible"—"The Love of the Impossible"—Janet's father has annotated the page with a maelstrom of spiderlike scribbling of notes: expostulations, revisions, and a pronounced year in pencil, 1881. This was the year he met Angelo Fusato.

"L'Amour de l'Impossible" is about a tormented male narrator trying to ignore the drive of what he calls "Chimaera." The poet describes a young man marrying, loving his wife, kneeling by a cradle of his firstborn —but then "Rises Chimaera [. . .] We pant. Thought, sense rebel. And swoon desiring things impossible [. . .] They crave one shrill vibration, tense, ideal."

The narrator struggles to fulfill his family commitments—though another kind of love also draws him away:

> *Chimaera, the winged wish that carries men*
> *Forth to the bourne of things impossible*
> *Their hearts with vague untameable longing swell [. . .]*
> *Who love what may not be, are sick of soul.*

"L'Amour de l'Impossible" is followed by poems with titles such as "Self-Condemnation" and "Amends."

> *Nothing is real but thirst, the incurable,*
> *Thirst slaked by nought save God [. . .]*[16]

Was Symonds trying to talk to his beloved adult daughter Janet about the conflict he felt in loving her, her sisters, and her mother—and yet feeling powerless not to pursue the "thirst [. . .] incurable"? Was he trying to explain to her his absences to Venice and the timing and context of the great love affair that had brought him to his true partner—who was not Janet's mother? Was he trying to account to his adult daughter for his real inner life and explain to her the love affair that had transformed it?

It's possible, but what Janet could not have known was that yet another story was embedded in the seemingly bland volume as well, waiting for the alchemy of the future to decipher it.

In 1884 Symonds self-published another secret collection: *Fragilia Labilia*. This, too, seems like an anodyne vanity publication—a banal anthology with indeterminate pronouns, or feminine ones, for the Beloved:

> *The stately ships are passing free*
> *Where scant light strikes along the flood:*

Gaunt Winter scowls o'er field and wood:
Oh, who will bring my love to me?[17]

But it had secrets buried within.

Were there even more secrets encoded in this bland text?

One of the four copies in the Morgan Library of this very rare printing has a nearly transparent cover that folds over a more substantial inner paper cover. The outer cover has the name *Fragilia Labilia* printed on it in brownish-red ink. The brittle outer cover is of paper that has been made to look like vellum. The outer cover has a title but no author; the inner cover has an author and a title. The outer cover was at one time attached to the spine but was only glued lightly; it could easily have been removed. This is a book that can assume or shed its author's identity as required. Symonds chose this shape for his book.

The outer cover even bears a smudged, unreadable postal mark, suggesting that it may have been sent through the post as if it were a personal letter rather than that actionable thing, a "book." Most of the love poems have had their pronouns changed, unconvincingly: "Here on the cool green sward my fancy drew / A group of ladies [. . .]" But some do not.

The title page reads:

Fragilia Labilia

by

John Addington Symonds

(Written Mostly Between 1860 and 1862)

TWENTY-FIVE COPIES PRINTED FOR THE AUTHOR'S USE

1884

So the very body of the slight volume is full of elisions and even lies. The "Twenty-Five Copies Printed for the Author's Use" allows Symonds, or his friends, to say that this is not a "book" and it wasn't "published." And the dating is a deflection. Symonds claims that these poems were written when he was just out of college—and before he was married.

But were they?

In fact, the last poem in the sequence, titled "The South Wind," is about a man who masters the ocean, a male "Sea-Lover." To the left of the text of the first paragraph, in Symonds's hand, in pencil, is the word "Davos."

DAVOS   *Over this prison*
Where suns new-risen
Can yield no vision
Beyond our vale
The South wind, winging
His way, and bringing,
Echoes of singing,
Doth lightly sail:
That rippling burden
Full oft I've heard on
The waves he stirred on
Italian sea,
Oh light land-rover
Oh soft sea-lover,
Soul of the South, I am fain for thee!

Then the next two stanzas have the words "Omit" and again "Omit" to the left of the text:

Thou fickle stranger
Blithe ocean-ranger
From dread and danger
And man's doubt free
Thy wings enfold me,
||OMIT|| *Thy whispers hold me;*
What hast thou told me
Of Venice and thee?
A vault of thunder;
Two lives thereunder,
That clasp and sunder
In gloom and glare. [. . .]

For though years carry
Their load, and tarry
On hearts that marry
With frore despair;
Still 'neath thy pinion,
E'en misery's minion

||OMIT||
Scorns her dominion,
And smiles at care.
These lips with kisses,
Where love still misses
Hope's crown of blisses,
Are faint and fain:
For thou hast sought me,
Thy breath hath brought me,
Lips of light loving above the main. [. . .]

[. . .] Yet, O my master,
Through all disaster
Thrills fast and faster
||OMIT||
Thy yearning strain!
I pine and sicken;
[. . .]
These dry roots quicken
'Neath winter's bed!

His notes stated: "OMIT. OMIT."

But he *didn't* actually omit these verses, which tell the world of love for an "ocean-ranger" who was connected with Venice, who was his "master," whose kisses renew his sense of vitality and hope, and the memory of whom makes "DAVOS" feel like "this prison." Symonds is very unlikely to have written this poem "between 1860 and 1862," when he was a young unmarried man.

He is more likely to have composed it in the early 1880s, after he met the gondolier Angelo Fusato in Venice, when, living with his wife and children in snowy Davos, he missed his lover on the "Italian sea."

In November 1884, Symonds wrote to Whitman from Am Hof. His letter reached an ailing man. The poet had managed to buy himself a new home, also in Camden, but it was no more comfortable than the one out of which he had moved; it was another small two-story wooden house. His sunbathing and river bathing had not provided the cure for which he had hoped. He still had difficulty walking, hearing, and seeing.

Symonds's recent silence, the Englishman wrote, hadn't been "for want of love of you, not because I am not always in communion with you—that

I am, and so are all my friends." Rather, he explained, the delay in writing was due to the death of a young man, the son of an expatriate neighbor "whose mother brought me back today a copy of Leaves of Grass which I had lent him and which had been his constant companion [. . .]"[18] The bereaved mother, by this gesture, may have been sharing information about her deceased son.

Though Symonds had pestered Whitman for over a decade about "what Calamus means," this letter doesn't contain a single word to the poet, his self-described heart's interlocutor, about the happiness that was finally his in his personal life with Angelo Fusato.

Symonds went on to mention, formulaically, his "wife and children around me." He ended the letter conventionally.

But then he added in the postscript his eternal, nagging question: "I always feel Calamus more deeply than any part of your work; and the reason why I have not published much that I have written about your poems, is that I cannot quite get to the bottom of Calamus. I wish I had your light upon it!"[19]

CHAPTER 25

The Labouchere Amendment: "Gross Indecency"

Symonds and Fusato, now often in Davos together, in a semi-open ménage alongside Symonds's family, were at least physically safe. Catherine Symonds traveled often—visiting friends in other cities and going on rural retreats on the Continent. Apparently she created for herself, by necessity, a separate life. Photographs from the 1880s show a woman whose expression is steadfast yet resigned.

Symonds's letters to Whitman reached him at a home where he often remained bedridden. Friends collected money to buy the poet a horse and a small carriage so that he might not be entirely housebound. Since the end of the 1870s, Whitman had at times traveled halfway across the country, when he had enough bookings, to give his well-received lecture on President Lincoln. Now he could travel only short distances; he gave "the Lincoln lecture" in Elkton, Maryland, in Philadelphia, Pennsylvania, and in other nearby states. As the wheelchair-bound poet with the unsteady income directed his public energies to becoming the memorial voice of the Civil War and the mourner-in-chief of the assassinated president, the threat of persecution, which had temporarily gained momentum in Massachusetts, died away. The famous American painter Thomas Eakins painted Whitman's portrait. His reputation evolved again, transforming him into a national patriotic muse.

A fierce campaign, led mostly by feminists, was underway in the first half of the 1880s in Symonds's abandoned Britain—and once again feminist groups were loudly targeting heterosexual men's sexual excesses and what they described as these men's immorality. In a major industry, heterosexual men were buying young girls to use for sex.

Adult men's purchase of sex with female near-children was, in the early 1880s, completely legal. In 1861, the Offences Against the Person Act had criminalized "carnal knowledge" of girls younger than *ten*, as we saw, and in another category had criminalized adult men's intercourse with girls younger than twelve. In 1875, the age of consent for girls was raised to just thirteen.

So for the same two decades that saw the consolidation of modern homophobia, adult heterosexual British men were perfectly at liberty to purchase sex with girls age eleven, twelve, and thirteen. The network that paid parents for such girls, and trafficked them, was extensive in every city.

By the early 1880s, well-organized groups of female advocates turned their attention to this widespread trafficking of such young girls for sex with adult men. The feminist groups sought to raise the age of consent for girls.

In 1885, the newspaper publisher W. T. Stead, who had an instinct for the sensational, published an exposé, "The Maiden Tribute of Modern Babylon."[1] Stead demonstrated how easy it was in London to buy a girl-child for purposes of prostitution: to prove his point, he actually purchased a thirteen-year-old girl himself and described the transaction in lurid prose. He added: "The victims of the rapes, for such they are to all intents and purposes, are almost always very young children between thirteen and fifteen. The reason for that is very simple. The law at present almost specially marks out such children as the fair game of dissolute men. The moment a child is thirteen she is a woman in the eye of the law, with absolute right to dispose of her person to any one who by force or fraud can bully or cajole her into parting with her virtue [. . .] The law, indeed, seems specially framed in order to enable dissolute men to outrage these legal women of thirteen with impunity."

Stead made a good point about the devious construction of the existing law. According to it, a rape was not a rape if the victim was ignorant of the nature of the act, and he made the case that the young girls thus trafficked were intentionally kept in the dark about what was to happen to them upon their first violation.[2]

Stead's piece created a furor. In reaction, Henry Labouchere, a wealthy and progressive politician, former journalist, and diplomat, sponsored a bill to raise the age of consent. (Ironically, Labouchere represented the same constituency as the radical activist Charles Bradlaugh, who was now also an MP.)

The bill did raise the age of consent for girls—to sixteen. A second material victory, brought about when women raised their voices politically, could be seen by all.

But it did more.

The Labouchere Amendment, which was a few pages written almost in passing and added to the bill to raise the age of consent, expanded the scope of the state to police the private lives of homosexual men.

The amendment spelled out these stipulations: "'Outrages on decency': any male person who, in public or private, commits, or is party to the commission of or procures (a) or attempts (b) to procure the commission by any male person of, any act of gross indecency, shall be guilty of a misdemeanor, and being convicted thereof shall be liable at the discretion of the court to be imprisoned for any term not exceeding two years, with or without hard labour [. . .]"[3]

This piece of legislation is often misunderstood. The thirty-year history of locking up boys and men with sentences of hard labor for years or even decades for same-sex offenses—and of executing dozens of men, before 1835, for sodomy—is very little known. Therefore many readers interpret the Labouchere Amendment as representing a new high point of persecution, especially because it would form the basis for the arrest and conviction of the century's most famous homosexual writer, Oscar Wilde for gross indecency.

Labouchere was a progressive MP, and scholars have been puzzled by his sponsorship of this amendment. But if you understand the history of persecution of men for same-sex offenses preceding 1885, in some ways the Labouchere Amendment can be read as representing a "reform." Since it restricted sentences for "gross indecency" to two years at most, it captured sex acts that had been penalized by the sentences of five, ten, or fifteen years that had been handed down in the second and third quarters of the nineteenth century.

In other ways, though, as Paul Johnson argues, the amendment markedly intensified the danger to homosexual men. The definition of the offense was widened, and the wording "public or private" did away with all privacy for men who loved men. It criminalized all sexual contact between men: "'Gross Indecency' [. . .] even if the misconduct is in private, an offense notwithstanding is committed [. . .] One class of cases which this section would meet is where men have been guilty of filthy practices together, which have not been sufficiently public to have constituted indecent exposure, or which have not had sufficient direct connection with a more abominable crime to allow an indictment for conspiring or for soliciting one another to commit an unnatural offence."[4]

The offense of "gross indecency" was defined so loosely, in such vague phrasing, that everything men who were intimate did together was actionable. The offense could be applied far beyond sodomy itself to any male-male sex act, any private act of love, or even any public "commission," such as inviting another man for a date if it resulted in sex, or introducing a man to another man, if the two men introduced later got together.[5]

From 1827 to 1885, as we saw earlier, fellatio and mutual masturbation between men, while considered unacceptable in Britain, had been difficult to prosecute if the acts were committed in private. With some important restrictions, the general right to a homosexual male private life, apart from publicly proved "attempted sodomy," or other same-sex acts, existed in Britain before 1885. The rise in policing had made public spaces, however, subject to surveillance and intervention, and it was a crime, and terrifying, to be caught soliciting sodomy itself. Yet homosexual men had had some private space for sexual relations until 1885—as long as they kept evidence of their sexual behavior out of the public eye. But the wording of the amendment did away with this.[6] The state was finally in the bed itself.

It was no longer what a man actually did with another man sexually that could send him to jail: it was not if he ejaculated inside another man (1832); it was not if he wrote about homosexuality (1857, 1868); it was not if he ejaculated inside or outside of the body of another man, or else barely penetrated him (1861); it was not if he was "effeminate" or wore clothing that was not considered "masculine" enough (1871)—a man was possibly committing a crime when he anything he did or said caused another man to be intimate with a third.

This amendment had a chilling effect on the tropes a homosexual man might be mulling over for a poem, the notes of social engagements in his journal, a joke in a letter. It cast a shadow on a painting of a beautiful man carrying a bunch of grapes over his shoulder, or a poem in a student journal—such as "Two Loves," by Lord Alfred Douglas, Wilde's lover, the origin of the phrase "the love that dare not speak its name." It criminalized in new ways reading those poems, sharing those poems, or even referring to the poems when speaking to someone who had never read them. The amendment further moved speech about homosexuality—which had already been criminalized as obscene—into the realm of a trial for sodomy or for "gross indecency," far more serious crimes.

And poetry and novels now didn't even have to be obscene to be actionable, as we have seen—they just had to be proven to lead to third-party homosexual contact.

The young and vulnerable reader whose need for protection had been invented by Lord Campbell in 1857, and further "protected" by Lord Justice Cockburn in 1868, morphed into this law's hypothetical innocent and naive observer of men romantically enjoying the company of other men, who could thus, by merely observing, be corrupted by the articulation or demonstration of the attractions of "gross indecency."

Into the twentieth and twenty-first centuries, we see bills such as California's 1978 Proposition 6, which sought to keep gay teachers, administrators, aides, and school employees out of classrooms lest their ideas and their homosexuality "infect" students; we see the Boy Scouts of America, until 2014, prohibiting "any known or avowed homosexuals" from becoming scout leaders.[7] The wording of Labouchere planted this very modern, very recent idea—that words about homosexuality or positive examples of homosexuality can, and indeed are likely to, criminally seduce the young.

In addition to inventing the hypothetical innocent witness, who must be protected from the allures of male-male attraction, the Labouchere Amendment further codified the tone of heterosexual aversion, polished it up, and added "disgust" to the developing construct of modern homophobia.

Before the Labouchere Amendment, sodomy wasn't described in public debate in Britain as "gross"—a term whose definition expanded from "of conspicuous magnitude" or "thick" to include "glaring, flagrant, monstrous." "Gross" joined earlier heightened and fairly recent terms used to describe homosexual desire, such as "vile" and "morbid," which were encircling homosexual men.

Now heterosexual people, and the institutions purportedly made up of them, were described as having an "instinctive" aversion to sodomy, or at least they ought to manufacture such an aversion. Through this stipulation, heterosexuality became, like homosexuality, codified—that is, now something was wrong with heterosexual people if they could not demonstrate *sufficient* aversion to men who had sex with men, if they couldn't tell what "gross indecency" was, or if they were not sufficiently bothered by it.

The ill-defined phrase "gross indecency" helped to define male homosexuality in the West, in general, as being a practice whose test is that it makes heterosexuals, especially heterosexual men, recoil. This heterosexual reaction is presented as something that is not learned, but rather inborn. Doesn't everyone automatically know what "gross indecency" is? Doesn't everyone know what "filthy practices together" are?[8]

This amendment was passed at a time when women were starting to say in public, in lurid detail and very effectively, that it was "grossly indecent" and a "filthy practice" for adult heterosexual men to purchase female children to, in effect, rape them for sexual gratification. But the Labouchere

Amendment directed society's attention away, once again, from that genuine horror to something else: consensual acts in private between adults. British citizens were asked to redirect their attention to these consensual practices between adults, and away from the industrial-scale rape of young girls, as being the truly "filthy" and horrifying deviancy.

This development, of course, echoed the campaigns against heterosexual men's sexual perfidy that led to the passage of the 1857 Matrimonial Causes Act. Women's activism had spurred the passage of that law too. But when women targeted the sexually abusive practices of heterosexual men, the outcome was a backlash by the heterosexual male establishment. These men directed society's attention at that time, too, toward the purportedly *greater* and more threatening sexual immorality practiced by homosexual men.

In August 1885, the Society for the Suppression of Vice merged with the National Vigilance Association. After passage of the Labouchere Amendment, key public figures started backing away from discussing any issue with even a whiff of what was defined as sexually marginal, "indecent," or "vile."

Nonetheless, Symonds collaborated by mail with the researcher Havelock Ellis to bring out a biography of the playwright Christopher Marlowe. Marlowe attracted Symonds in part because of the playwright's relationships with other men, so Marlowe joined other historical figures, including the Renaissance sculptors and artists Michelangelo Buonarroti and Benvenuto Cellini, on the shelf of biographies that Symonds wrote or translated, a mission that we today would call a reclamation of queer history. The volume was published by Henry Vizetelly, an elderly publisher who made a living on the fringes of London's publishing industry by reissuing translations of Continental fiction and nonfiction, all of it high to middlebrow, but some of it racy.

In 1887, prosecutions under the Labouchere Amendment had begun. Swinburne, having authored lascivious verses in *Poems and Ballads* and other works, was now at risk himself of prosecution under the new legal definition of gross indecency. He moved to protect himself by escalating his earlier critiques of other "deviant" writers into full-blown attacks. Seemingly out of the blue, he decided to mount an aggressive assault on his former hero, Walt Whitman.

Swinburne's essay "Whitmania" appeared in the *Fortnightly Review*.[9] It excoriated the poet for producing literary "filth." He compared Whitman to "Adamites," members of an obscure ancient sect who during sacred rites wore no clothing. He compared lines of *Leaves of Grass*—ones he had once so publicly admired—to diarrhea: "If nothing that concerns the physical organism of men or of women is common or unclean or improper for literary manipulation," Swinburne wrote, then writers may as well now detail the excreta caused by laxatives.[10] Whitman was, according to Swinburne, like "a drunken apple woman, indecently sprawling in the slush and garbage of the gutter amid the rotten refuse of her overturned fruit-stall."[11]

The gorgeous, lush fruits that not only Whitman but also Swinburne himself had described, in the freer atmosphere of the 1860s, had now become "rotten refuse." The well-established commons that must now be kept pure was being polluted, Swinburne charged, with the American apple-seller's "slush and garbage of the gutter."

Whitman did not respond to this attack. An anonymous rebuttal to the essay appeared in the *Fortnightly Review* on August 5, 1887: "The Literary World: Mr Swinburne on Whitmania." Though it seemed friendly to Whitman, it expanded on Swinburne's metaphors of infection via "filth": it compared Swinburne's concern about obscenity to a concern about "diseases," "rabies," and an "epidemic."

Symonds jumped in to defend his hero in an essay titled "A Note on Whitmania." But the text reveals a conflicted response: Symonds conceded that Whitman used a "very low" tone.[12] At the end of the essay, Symonds completely backed away from supporting the American poet, writing that he "will not" defend Mr. Whitman's treatment of sexual matters, which, he declared—surely with at least mixed emotions?—was in his view "far too physiological."[13] Symonds was in the ring for Whitman, sort of, but had bound one of his hands behind his back.

If the attacks and counterattacks in the literary reviews seem repetitive, they were: the "fleshly" writers and painters were continually under siege at this time and could not let any of the many assaults in the literary journals go unanswered. Too much was at stake.

What did "Calamus" mean? Surely it did not mean publicly sabotaging a mentor and a friend.

Also in 1887, Symonds and his family suffered an appalling tragedy. Janet had inherited her father's weakness of the lungs and died after a long struggle with tuberculosis. Her death plunged the entire family into a long period of mourning; Symonds experienced nearly unbearable grief.

CHAPTER 26

Prophets of Modernity

Whitman's final published essay, "A Backward Glance O'er Travell'd Roads," appeared in 1888.[1] In it, the poet argues against efforts to censor the sexual material in his own work and makes a case against censorship in general. Ironically, though, by this time the cloud of censorship had settled on America, affecting its writers, even Whitman: double-speak prevails in this essay. Whitman's original title had been "A Backward Glance O'er My Own Road." The final title, "A Backward Glance O'er Travell'd Roads," lacking the personal pronoun, distances Whitman from his own journey.

Oscar Wilde again defended Whitman, comparing self-censorship to ill health: "Literature," he wrote, "is always calling in the doctor for consultation and confession, and always giving evasions and sweeping suppressions in place of that 'heroic nudity' on which only a genuine diagnosis can be built."[2]

That same year, Parliament passed the Indecent Advertisements Acts, which even more minutely defined which texts could be considered obscene and therefore criminal. These acts expanded the range of publications that could land a writer, publisher, or bookseller in legal trouble. Now advertising was added to that list, and promotion of condoms or other contraceptive devices could be prosecuted, with penalties of one to three months at hard labor.[3]

That year, too, yet another acquaintance of Symonds's was prosecuted and sent to prison for the crime of publishing literature. The National Vigilance Association brought proceedings against Henry Vizetelly, the elderly London bookseller who had published Symonds's Marlowe book; the bookseller was already in poor health.[4]

Vizetelly sold inexpensive translated editions of Émile Zola's 1880 novel *Nana*, among his other avant-garde fiction.[5] His customers included not only British readers but those overseas. Their reasonable cost made these editions accessible to various economic classes and both genders. The sentencing of the bookseller was big news—it was reported in English-language newspapers as far away as China.[6]

Zola's subject matter posed a challenge to British censors. On the one hand, the novel could be read as highly moralistic: *Nana* told the tale of the degradation of an eighteen-year-old music hall performer and prostitute in Paris, during the Second Empire. The heroine was based on Valdesse de La Bigne, a beautiful *grande horizontale* of the period. At this time, sales of four thousand copies were considered successful; this novel sold half a million copies. (Zola himself had narrowly escaped prosecution in the past, even in more liberal France. In 1865, after he had published *La Confession de Claude*, the French police investigated him, and as a result he lost his job at the respected publishing house Hachette.)

In *Nana*, Zola, the realist, took his readers into the bedrooms and dressing rooms of the prostitutes, whom he described with a documentary level of detail. He narrated unflinchingly the "bestial" lust of the men who hired these prostitutes. Zola's description of Nana's debut onstage, and a later scene of her admiring her own nudity in a mirror, provoked the British censors. These passages certainly violated *Hicklin*, as they are clearly written to arouse:

> Venus made her appearance. A shiver of delight ran round the house. Nana was stark naked.
>
> With quiet audacity, she appeared in her nakedness, certain of the sovereign power of her flesh. Some gauze enveloped her, but her rounded shoulders, her Amazonian bosom, the rosy points of which stood out straight and stiff as lance-heads, her broad hips, which swayed to and fro voluptuously, her thighs—the thighs of a fully-fleshed blonde—her whole body [. . .] could be divined, nay, discerned, in all its foamlike whiteness of tint, beneath the slight fabric she wore.[7]

Zola offended the moralists with his prurient descriptions, yet at the same time he served their purposes: Nana dies hideously, of smallpox, at the end of the book. In 1880, Zola had heard rumors that the police wanted to prosecute him for *Nana*. But by now, 1888, he had powerful protectors, which made the French prosecutors tread lightly.[8]

But Britain was a different matter. Did the novel's moral framework, which might be seen as punishing the protagonist for her "crimes," outweigh the obscenity? To make a living, Nana has sex with men in exchange for money. How would a post-*Hicklin* publisher censor such a novel correctly, or adequately? With sex, arousal, and the just punishment of the transgressor mixed together throughout its pages, *Nana* was bound to provoke action as soon as translations made their way to London in significant numbers. The British censorship machine awaited them.[9]

So Henry Vizetelly was arrested and successfully prosecuted. He was sent to Holloway Prison. But for reasons unclear to the senior management of the prison, the elderly bookseller was transferred to Pentonville, a far more brutal prison. There, Vizetelly was forced to sleep on bare boards and was subjected to continual surveillance. He died not long after his release. Though he was in prison for only three months, the experience broke him, according to his family.

The London literary world paid serious attention to the trial, to Vizetelly's sufferings, and to his demise.

In this context, Symonds began writing his memoirs. It was, he confessed, "a foolish thing to do." It was also an extraordinarily moving act. In them he recorded his struggle to reconcile his homosexuality with his professional and familial identities. He told the truth about his life.

In 1889, as he wrote, he reviewed what were now eight contented years with Fusato: "I can now look back with satisfaction on this intimacy," he wrote. "Though it began in folly and crime, according to the constitution of society, it has benefited him and proved a source of comfort and instruction to myself [. . .] And all this good, good for both Angelo and myself, has its tap-root in what at first was nothing better than a misdemeanor punishable by the law and revolting to the majority of human beings."[10]

Symonds wrote this first whole account of his life knowing that he would live and die without bringing it into the light of day. He wrote the book for a type of future he could not be sure would ever exist. He wrote these unwieldy hundreds of pages as an act of pure faith in the power of books—and the possibility of change.

He wrote his memoirs when no publishers or readers could legally produce or consume such material. But he began and ended his labors believing that one day a world would emerge in which new readers would be born, grow up, and be free to encounter his words.

CHAPTER 27

"The Life-Long Love of Comrades"

S till domiciled in a committed relationship with Fusato, Symonds was aware of others who were insisting on speaking out more clearly about same-sex love—some with what he saw as informed analysis, others cloaking the issue in what he saw as nonsense.

In 1886 the heterosexual explorer and Orientalist Sir Richard Burton published "The Sotadic Zone" as an essay at the end of his bestseller, *The Book of a Thousand and One Nights and a Night*, his translation of *The Arabian Nights*. Sir Richard argued that homosexuality was prevalent in a geographical band across the globe, among certain cultures affected by climate and location: "Within the Sotadic Zone the Vice is popular and endemic [. . .] while the races in the North and South of the limits here defined practice it only sporadically amid the opprobrium of their fellows who, as a rule, are physically incapable of performing this operation and look upon it with the liveliest disgust."[1]

The book was printed privately to avoid obscenity arrests; nonetheless, it had an influential readership, and the popular circulation of this way of explaining male-male love must have maddened Symonds.

The work of Karl Heinrich Ulrichs was also becoming more widely reclaimed in the 1880s; Ulrichs had proposed in the 1860s, as we saw, the idea of the "Urning." He had defined this as a man who loved men from earliest consciousness, but he argued that such a man had a feminine soul housed in a masculine body. This too was an idea that Symonds, with a number of his close friends, strongly contested. Symonds burned to better inform these emerging, if marginalized and still often secretive, debates about same-sex love.

In 1889, Dr. Richard von Krafft-Ebing, a Viennese psychiatrist, brought out *Psychopathia Sexualis*, a volume that was closer to Symonds's heart and aligned in part with his arguments in *A Problem in Modern Ethics*.

Krafft-Ebing argued that there were two groups of men who loved men—those who were born with those impulses and those who were affected by outside influences.

In 1890, Symonds met the attractive young doctor and essayist Havelock Ellis, who had earlier, in print, praised Symonds's criticism. Ellis now praised Whitman, in his book *The New Spirit*. He offered the poet to Britain in a redeemed role, as a Christlike figure and as an archetype of the man of the future. He sent a copy of the book to Symonds.

When Symonds questioned him about Whitman's homosexuality, he received from Ellis an affirmative response.

Symonds felt that he may have found his collaborator at last; he began to discuss Ellis's planned sexological book, using his own secret notes, and with a joint byline. That arrangement, he thought, would let him both safely and truly speak.

By 1889, Whitman's health was so poor that the nearly destitute poet's medical needs outstripped his income. Horace Traubel, a young acolyte who came often to visit and help him, set about raising money again from Whitman's admirers to pay for doctors and nurses.

In July 1890, Whitman's health deteriorated further. He was maintaining an active correspondence, though, and welcoming guests. He wrote to his friend Richard Maurice Bucke that Symonds had sent him "his (formidable) finely printed 'Essays Speculative & Suggestive,'" which included an essay devoted to the poet: "Democratic Art, with Special Reference to Walt Whitman." Symonds had become captivated by the argument that Whitman had made in his 1872 collection of essays *Democratic Vistas*. It defended a new embrace of male-male "adhesiveness"—a recognition of the redemptive nature of the "love of comrades," which would be powerful enough to renew democracy itself. (Symonds's carefully marked-up volume of the book, which highlights sentiments about "adhesiveness," can also be seen in the Morgan Library.)

The poet commented dryly to Bucke, however, that Symonds at this late date was still skirting the central issue: "Have run it over & a few other pages—I guess there is meat in the vols. But I doubt whether he has gripped 'democratic art' by the nuts, or L of G. either." Bucke agreed: "The whole article is stale, flat and unprofitable [. . .] dealing with the hull, the shell, the superfices, never for one line [. . .] penetrating to the heart of the business."[2]

In a letter dated August 3, 1890, Symonds finally asked his idol definitively to "come out," as we would say, about the meaning of the "Calamus" poems. He had done so, more gently, repeatedly over the course of a dozen years.

Why was Symonds still pushing? He was too sophisticated a critic to believe that a poet should be pressed to say literally what any passage of poetry means. Was Symonds imploring Whitman to declare publicly "what Calamus means," so that someone else—someone notable, writing outside Britain and thus safe from prosecution there—would at last make a declarative statement about male-male love? One that Symonds could use, perhaps, to challenge the Offences Against the Person Act and the Labouchere Amendment?

And Whitman once again refused.

Indeed, in a famous letter, he went further.

Whitman rebuffed the British critic in odd, irate language. The draft is dated August 19.

"Yrs of Aug: 3rd just rec'd & glad to hear f'm you [. . .]." The poet then offers to send Symonds a new photograph of himself. But he goes on, with a sharp change in tone:

> —A b't the questions on Calamus pieces &c: they quite daze me. L of G. is only to be rightly construed by and within its own atmosphere and essential character—all of its pages & pieces coming so strictly under that—that the calamus part has even allow'd the possibility of such construction as mentioned for such gratuitous and quite at the time entirely undream'd & unreck'd possibility of morbid inferences—wh' are disavow'd by me & seem damnable. Then one great difference between you and me, temperament & theory, is restraint—I know that while I have a horror of ranting & bawling I at certain moments let the spirit impulse, (?demon) rage its utmost [. . .] I end the matter by saying I wholly stand by L of G. As it is, long as all parts & pages are construed as I said by their own ensemble, spirit & atmosphere.[3]

Whitman, understandably, described to his able-bodied British demander of battle-action his own physical debility: "sight & hearing half-and-half," the power in his legs almost gone. He conceded that his earlier life had been "jolly, bodily, and probably open to criticism—[.]"

Then he made yet another abrupt turn in subject: "Tho' always unmarried I have had six children—two are dead—One living southern grandchild, fine boy, who writes to me occasionally. Circumstances connected with their benefit and fortune have separated me from intimate relations."

He signed off curtly: "I see I have written with [. . .] too great effusion. But let it stand."[4]

Many critics have been puzzled or affronted by Whitman's reply to Symonds. Some wonder if this outburst against Symonds demonstrated what we would today call internalized homophobia on the poet's part. But in light of the legal context by then prevailing in America, this exchange should not be so mystifying.

First, there is the garbled syntax that writers in both nations were using to describe taboo sexual material. There is no active subject. The "construction" of what "calamus" means "as mention'd" is "terrible"; the "inferences" are "disavow'd by me" and "seem damnable." None of this is actually, of course, a rejection of "calamus." Yet this tangled syntax does provide legal cover. Then, in apparent contradiction, the poet circles back to insisting that he "wholly stand[s] by L of G."

The last part of the letter is startling. Six illegitimate children? Southern grandchildren? No biographers have ever found confirmation of any such relationships.

So what does this letter mean? The poet's response is so outlandish that it is best read as a coded, satirical rebuke to Symonds. "I have six children" could be read as Whitman's signal to Symonds that he is putting Whitman in an impossible position by demanding an illegal explication of a potentially illegal text, and that he should stop asking for the impossible. The sign-off, in which Whitman lists his six probably imaginary children and "one [. . .] grandchild, fine boy," could be Whitman's irritated satire on Symonds's letters. Over the years, as he pressed the poet for a declaration of "what Calamus means," Symonds often signed off self-protectively by referencing his wife and four daughters.

Whitman's letters to Symonds in 1890 show that he was losing patience. Symonds was now living in a comfortable manor replete with servants in Switzerland, and visiting friends in Renaissance palazzos in Venice. Whitman was poor, half-paralyzed, and forced to beg for help to meet the costs of his nursing care. The poet may have felt nearly done with the privileged Symonds, who refused to go out into the front lines of the battle himself but insistently tried to push the much older, poorer, sicker man into the fray.

In spite of the poet's frustration with his British correspondent, he retained a grudging respect for him. In *With Walt Whitman in Camden*, the book Horace Traubel made from his notes of the time, he stated that Whitman was reading Symonds's collected essays in 1890. Whitman commented to the younger man that Symonds was not among the greatest writers of his generation, but he was a great critic. Whitman even advised Traubel to read Symonds and referred to Symonds in a friendly way about a dozen times over the course of that year.

In December 1890, for example, the same year when he had earlier sent the angry letter rebuffing Symonds, Whitman described Symonds to Traubel as among "those literary men of a high type" who "yet in a sense belong to us too."[5]

Who is "us"?

In this conversation with his young acolyte, did Whitman mean "we Americans"? Did "us" mean simply "we men who share an admiration for the love of comrades"? Or could "us" also have referred to "those of us, from whatever walk of life, who are stubborn, tough, and demanding seekers of a better world"?

Whitman and Symonds continued their conversation to the ends of their lives: indeed, each spoke to the other, or about the other, from the death-bed itself.

In 1891, Whitman issued the final version of *Leaves of Grass*; biographers refer to it as the "death-bed edition." A housekeeper and friend, Mary O. Davis, a widow, was now living in his house, in exchange for her lodging, to care for him and look after the housekeeping. By then Whitman was completely bedridden.

But weak as he was, Whitman arranged to send to Symonds this final edition of *Leaves of Grass*.[6]

Whitman died of pleurisy—an infection of the lungs—on March 26, 1892.

The poet was buried in Harleigh Cemetery, in Camden, New Jersey.[7]

CHAPTER 28

A Problem in Modern Ethics

By 1892, the year Whitman died, Symonds had taken the most daring step of his career yet and firmed up his imagined co-publication with Havelock Ellis. With Whitman's death, perhaps he felt that there was no one left to speak for him or instead of him.

Letters were now traveling between him and Ellis about how their book would address homosexuality. "[I]t is a field in which pioneers may not only do excellent service to humanity, but also win the laurels of investigators & truth-seekers," wrote Symonds, courting his potential collaborator, who, being heterosexual, had less at stake personally in the subject.

Their collaboration, though, was not smooth. Ellis tried to warn Symonds away from engaging with any social issues outside the narrow scope of scientific observation. These limited parameters appalled Symonds, who of course wanted nothing more than to address and change society. Symonds also fiercely opposed the "morbidity" theories of influential psychiatrists, which Ellis too espoused. Symonds acknowledged that neurosis might sometimes accompany "inversion," but he felt that discrimination was the cause of any psychological issues that some homosexuals may have suffered.

In the summer of 1892 Symonds's health was unrecoverable. As if sensing that he had little time left, he filled his calendar with frantic traveling. Symonds took Fusato on a six-week journey to Britain: to London, to country homes in the north of England, and to Scotland. We can only conjecture how the couple was received and understood in the drawing rooms and at the theatrical evenings that Symonds and Fusato attended. Symonds was still presenting Fusato, publicly at least, as his serving man, and not essentially as his longtime spouse. But those who knew, knew.

On that journey, Symonds canceled a planned meeting in London with Ellis. Ellis still allied himself with the theory of homosexual men's "neurosis"; Symonds continued to lobby him in letters to abandon that point of view. Symonds may have intuited that the collaborators would not resolve their differences easily.

In the fall, Symonds was back in Venice, but there was a shadow over him. He wrote to Horatio Brown that he had had a vision in which he waited for death—indeed longed for it—in a room filled with spectral music. Brown was alarmed by this communication.

In the face of his increasing frailty, Symonds wrote to the publisher Charles Elkin Mathews, proposing an unexpurgated British edition of *Leaves of Grass*. "I should be glad to undertake an edition of Whitman's poems [. . .] I have most of the editions of Leaves of Grass, but I shd want the 2nd, that of 1872 [1856] [. . .] if I were to undertake a complete and critical work [. . .] pray enter at some length into the question of Whitman's poems."[1] That imagined edition was meant to bring the "Calamus" poems intact to England. He clung to this possibility almost as if clinging to life itself.

In December 1892, he brought his life's true subject to his daughter Madge, as he had to her now-deceased older sister Janet, and as he had to his wife.

This self-disclosure is unusual for several reasons: for one, few men of that class and era typically addressed their adult daughters, let alone their wives, with such seriousness of purpose and such relative personal openness.

Symonds wrote to Madge, who was in England, that he felt his life's most important book was now complete. "If I were to publish it now, it would create a great sensation. Society would ring with it. But the time is not ripe for the launching of 'A Problem in Modern Ethics' on the world. The MS [manuscript] lies on my table for retouches; & then will go to slumber in a box of precious writings, my best work, my least presentable, until its day of Doom."[2]

But despite once again declaring a manuscript dead—Reader, he published it. The next year, the last year of his life, Symonds printed fifty copies privately, in pamphlets consisting of 104 pages. He sent them out to close friends and asked that they make comments in the wide margins.

The physical pamphlet itself shows the tensions involved in "publication" of such material. It is a large pamphlet, about twelve by fourteen inches, bound in gray cardboard—so not technically "a book"—and printed in two volumes. The title page has the full name:

A Problem in Modern Ethics:
Being an Enquiry into the Phenomenon of Sexual Inversion
Addressed Especially to Medical Psychologists and Jurists

·But there is no publisher's imprint or author's name on the title page. Written there in pencil, in Symonds's hand, in one copy, are the words "By John Addington Symonds." A second copy, in the same library, the Morgan, has no such identification.

Before the text begins, there is a "List of Books Consulted." One of these is *A Problem in Greek Ethics*. Even in this list, the author's name is absent. Yet Symonds's hand has added an asterisk to the line and written in pencil at the bottom of the page, "The Author was J. A. Symonds himself." Symonds was handing this volume to his friends with literally nothing printed in it to identify himself. Yet he could not bear for his authorship of both essays to be unremarked. So the same pamphlet has two costumes: naked and clothed. The book could go out into the world either with or without an author's name upon it, depending on the reader to whom it was being entrusted.

And the name-identified pamphlet at the Morgan Library has other writing in it as well: the handwriting of the man to whom it was given, probably by the author. It has the penciled inscription in a bolder hand, on the flyleaf: "Ed Carpenter."

Carpenter was a philosopher, a poet, and also an early activist for what we would today call gay rights. He was far more radical, in some ways, than Symonds. Carpenter was a Socialist, a friend of Havelock Ellis's, and also of Walt Whitman himself. He had recently met the man who would be the great love of his own life, a working-class man named George Merrill.

A page in Symonds's pamphlet deals with rebutting the traditional argument that licit sexual attraction must be reproductively fruitful. Symonds points out that "legislation does not interfere in sterile intercourse between men and women." Next to this sentence, in the wide margin evidently designed by Symonds for comments from his friends, Carpenter made this firmly worded annotation: "Nor does legislation interfere with sterile intercourse between women and women."

Symonds's work shows virtually no interest in the question of lesbianism, a term that didn't legally then exist—even as late as 1893, British law showed its disrespect for women's love for other women by completely ignoring it. But this penciled note by an even more radical and expansively thoughtful younger friend of Symonds gives a reader the remarkable sense of seeing the very beginnings of what someday will be a fully theorized gay and lesbian rights movement. This note may be the first text by an activist arguing for lesbian intimacy to be legally protected, alongside arguments for legal protections for homosexual men. Unsurprising at this time, Symonds did not take the note into account in his revision of the argument; lesbian love remained literally marginalized in all the drafts of this essay.

But in the start of this quiet argument, no doubt echoed by other quiet arguments and conversations between women and women, women and men, and men and men, it becomes possible to see one very early correction of focus, anticipating what will someday be a far-reaching set of ideas, debates, and emendations to include the many kinds of love that we now identify as part of the LGBTQ+ movement

What did John Addington Symonds actually say in what may be the first gay rights advocacy text in the English language? The pamphlet summarizes the historical instances of cultures in which men loved men; it argues systematically against the Labouchere Amendment; it also categorizes men who seek intimacy with other men into groups—those who are attracted to other men from birth, and who have absolutely nothing neurotic or degenerate in their inborn attraction; those who are not exclusively attracted to men, but who engage in sodomy when environments, such as a prison or the Navy, make other men the only or main possible sexual outlets; and a third group of men who over time become oriented to other men due to moral influences. Symonds resoundingly issues a full and fluent rejection of any "unwholesomeness" or degeneracy in the category of love of men who are born with innate attraction to other men. He also appeals to jurists to change the law, arguing closely from examples of other countries, including France and Italy, in which laws did not punish consensual male-male love between adults—and this state of affairs did not threaten civilization there.

Symonds sent a copy of *A Problem in Modern Ethics* to Graham Dakyns and asked for his response: "I am eager about the subject for its social & juristic aspects," he wrote. "You know how vitally it has in the past interested me as a man, & how I am therefore in duty bound for an elucidation of the legal problem." Symonds also sent copies to Sir Richard Burton and tried to get Ulrichs to help him with what he imagined as a legal campaign to follow—eventually—the publication of his pamphlet. He was spurned, and remarked, "[O]nly I fear that a free legal course with social sympathy attending, will not be given to my brethren—the Urnings."[3]

As *Leaves of Grass* had done thirty-seven years earlier, *A Problem in Modern Ethics*—that "unpublished" pamphlet of 1893—passed from hand to hand and "aroused furtive, excited interest."[4] Henry James read it and called it "remarkable." James saw its flaws but nonetheless assigned

Symonds a place among "the great reformers," calling him "the Gladstone of the affair"—that is, the leading statesman of a planned campaign for homosexual legal rights. The conversation had been launched. The next year, 1894, Carpenter wrote his own manifesto: *Homogenic Love, and Its Place in a Free Society.*[5]

Letters from homosexuals, describing their tormented lives, now flooded into Am Hof. As Symonds was contemplating this urgent response from readers to his "unpublished" pamphlet, he turned anew to his work with Havelock Ellis. By January 3, 1893, they established parameters for their collaboration, and a book was underway.

Symonds, though, just at this promising juncture was suffering again from symptoms of tuberculosis. He grew too ill to give a planned lecture in Florence in April. But in spite of his poor health, he invited Madge on an April pilgrimage to many of his favorite locations in southern Italy; the father and daughter visited Paestum and climbed Mount Vesuvius. Then, in Rome, Symonds alarmed Madge by his feverish talking and ceaseless motion. Madge later described his frantic activity—her father bringing her to see sketches by Dürer, picking wildflowers with her by the side of the road, and even climbing into a carriage to ascend a hill, where he pointed out the spectacular vista. The way he shared his emotions, and his appreciation of the world as he saw it, may explain the acceptance and even devotion with which members of his family treated him.

An influenza epidemic swept through Rome; on Sunday, April 16, Symonds told his daughter that his throat was sore. The next day his condition worsened. Madge called in Dr. Abel Munthe, a local physician. A poultice was placed on the patient's throat, and the doctor said there was no cause for serious concern.

But on Tuesday, Symonds was much weakened. Madge was faced with the miserable reality that Catherine too was now ill, in Florence, and unable to travel.

Symonds wrote to his long-suffering wife a final letter: "I am fallen here at Rome." He continued, in writing that reveals that his hand was shaking:

There is something I ought to tell you, and being ill at Rome I take this occasion. If I do not see you again in this life you remember that I made H F Brown depository of my printed books. I wish that legacy to cover all Mss Diaries Letters & other matters found in my books cupboard, with the exception of business papers. I do this

because I have written things you could not like to read, but which
I have always felt justified and useful for society. Brown will consult
& publish nothing without your consent.

Madge and Angelo Fusato were left, then, as the only people, both of
them effectively family members, available to care for the patient in Rome.
We can only imagine the dialogue and the collaboration between the
daughter and the unacknowledged spouse in attending to the man whom
they both loved.

The thoughts of the invalid began to drift. He seemed to be speaking
to himself, traversing memories of his life. By the next day he had difficulty
breathing and was extremely weak. But Madge reported in her notes that
his face was transformed: the habitual lines of care and exhaustion somehow had smoothed out, and he looked again like a young man.

The daughter cradled her father's head in her arms. Eventually he rested his
head against her shoulder. Finally she noticed that his breathing had ceased.

The funeral was delayed until Catherine and Charlotte could reach
Rome. Symonds was laid to rest in Rome's Protestant Cemetery.

John Addington Symonds was fifty-two.

Even as Symonds's health had been failing, he had prepared his last love
letter to Walt Whitman: a volume of critical appreciation, including a
critical biography of the man, titled *Walt Whitman: A Study*. It went out
into the world after his death in Florence.

In it, Symonds used Whitman's own words as a summary of his own
life's meaning:

> *I will make divine magnetic lands*
> *With the love of comrades,*
> *With the life-long love of comrades.*
> *I will plant companionship thick as trees along the river [. . .]*
> *I will make inseparable cities, with their arms about each other's necks,*
> *By the love of comrades,*
> *By the manly love of comrades.*[6]

In this final tribute to his mentor, the guarded, self-censoring critic
spoke transparently at last. His prose is clear and ringing. The dying man

finally said directly, and for the public, what he had most wanted to say for most of his living days:

> If this be not a dream, if he is right in believing that "threads of manly friendship, fond and loving, pure and sweet, strong and life-long, carried to degrees hitherto unknown," will penetrate the organism of society, "not only giving tone to individual character, and making it unprecedentedly emotional, muscular, heroic and refined [. . .]—then are we perhaps justified in foreseeing here the advent of an enthusiasm which shall rehabilitate those outcast instincts, by giving them a spiritual atmosphere, an environment of recognized and healthy emotions, wherein to expand at liberty and purge away the grossness and the madness of their pariahdom?

At the very end of his life, Symonds finally had had his say about what "Calamus" means.

In his 1910–11 poem "Ithaka," the Greek poet C. P. Cavafy advises readers not to ask about the storied city of Ithaka, but instead to journey there for themselves. He explains that the voyage will be safe if the traveler only understands that the monsters that he or she faces must be fought by rejecting them from "inside your soul":

> *Laistrygonians and Cyclops,*
> *angry Poseidon—don't be afraid of them:*
> *You'll never find things like that on your way*
> *As long as you keep your thoughts raised high [. . .]*
> *Laistrygonians and Cyclops,*
> *wild Poseidon—you won't encounter them*
> *unless you bring them along inside your soul,*
> *unless your soul sets them up in front of you.*[7]

Symonds finally did define "Calamus" for himself, as he located the "madness" and "grossness," which had so preoccupied him, in their proper places at last. The "madness" and "grossness" that had so frenzied his society were not, as he finally declared, inherent in his sexual appetite or in his love. They existed, but their proper location was outside himself: it was in society's mad and gross condemnation of love.

That insight reached the world in his voice only after he died.

But he managed to glimpse Ithaka in his lifetime.

Whitman, of course, never did in his lifetime say what "Calamus" meant. Whitman's withholding, for two decades, of an easy answer forced Symonds onto the painful and risky journey that ended so meaningfully with his advocacy essay *A Problem in Modern Ethics* and with his contribution to *Sexual Inversion*, the sexological treatise that would change the world.

In refusing to speak on Symonds's behalf concerning "what Calamus means," Whitman held his ground as both a poet and a teacher. As a poet, he properly refused to be forced into any simplistic or literal exegesis. And as a good teacher, he wasn't going to provide an answer for a student who would be better served by working out a definition for himself.

And yet it was not enough to set the "monsters" outside the self. In 1895, after three consecutive trials, the playwright Oscar Wilde, at the height of his fame, was sentenced to two years at hard labor for the crime of "gross indecency."

In a series of events that galvanized world opinion, Wilde had tried to accuse Sir John Sholto Douglas, the Marquess of Queensberry who was also the father of Wilde's lover Lord Alfred Douglas, of libel, after that belligerent aristocrat left a note at Wilde's club accusing the playwright of "posing as a Somdomite [*sic*]."[8]

The Marquess of Queensberry offered evidence in his defense that between 1892 and 1894, Wilde had solicited sexual acts from twelve different youths.

Since so much evidence emerged incriminating his own client, on the third day of the first trial, Wilde's lawyer withdrew the libel charges.

With damning evidence emerging that could implicate not just a famous playwright but possibly a prime minister, a second trial was initiated—this one against Wilde, for "gross indecency."

Friends urged Wilde to take the boat train and flee to France, where he would be safe from prosecution. Wilde refused to listen to these pleas. He stayed where he was, awaiting trial. Why did he do so? The reasons remain unclear: a refusal to believe that he had done anything wrong, or the certainty that his wit and charm would sway his audience, as they always had? Or was it the effect of a letter from his mother, Lady Wilde, who herself had faced down threats of prosecution for having written "seditious" verse—a letter in which she told her son in stern language that a gentleman faces battle?

Whatever the reasoning, Oscar Wilde stayed. In a bail hearing, the maids who looked after Wilde's household, as well as a housekeeper in a hotel where the playwright sometimes stayed, testified that they had witnessed young men in Wilde's bed. With echoes of venereological testimony informing the questions put to the women, the cleaning staff testified to having observed fecal stains on the sheets.[9]

Wilde was eventually found guilty of "gross indecency" and sentenced to two years at hard labor. He was taken first to Pentonville Prison, then moved to Wandsworth. On November 20, 1895, he was brought to Reading Gaol as an inmate.

Forced to stand with a jailer in the cold on the railway platform as he was transferred to Reading Gaol, he recorded later that passengers recognized him, and mocked him: "For half an hour I stood there in the grey November rain surrounded by a jeering mob."[10]

Wilde served his full sentence—from 1895 to 1897.

The system at Reading Gaol was designed to keep prisoners apart. Wilde had to wear a "Scottish cap"—a peaked hat that masked the face so that only slits allowed prisoners to see. Each of the prisoners was housed in a solitary cell and allowed out only for exercise and chapel. Even in chapel, they had to sit in cubicles, not pews, so that their isolation was complete. Wilde's cell had a coconut fiber hammock for sleeping and a chamber pot. It had formerly had a cistern for defecation, but this had been removed in order to further punish and humiliate the inmates.

The great playwright and raconteur was set to picking oakum and to turning the hand crank; all to be done entirely in silence.

After his release, he finally fled England. In exile in Berneval-le-Grande, France, in 1897, he wrote "The Ballad of Reading Gaol"—a harrowing account, centered on the execution of a convict, of life at hard labor in prison.

I know not whether Laws be right,
Or whether Laws be wrong;
All that we know who lie in Gaol
Is that the wall is strong;

And that each day is like a year,
A year whose days are long [. . .]
But this I know [. . .]—and wise it were
If each could know the same—
That every prison that men build
Is built with bricks of shame
And bound with bars lest Christ should see
How men their brothers maim.[11]

In 1896, Symonds was three years dead, and Wilde was still in prison, but Symonds's words refused to die. That year, a posthumous print run of *A Problem in Modern Ethics* mysteriously appeared and circulated. Because of its content it was still illegal to publish this volume. Only the words "John Addington Symonds, London, 1896" are presented on the title page, along with "Of this work only 100 copies have been printed." As with the earliest edition of *Leaves of Grass*, the book now stood in for the man. This handmade posthumous edition begins with these words:

> There is a passion, or a perversion of appetite, which, like all human passions, has played a considerable part in the world's history for good or evil; but which has hardly yet received the philosophical attention and the scientific investigation it deserves [. . .] We cannot take up the religious books, the legal codes, the annals, the descriptions of the manners of any nation, whether large or small, powerful or feeble, civilised or savage, without meeting with this passion in one form or other [. . .] The pulse of it can be felt in London, Paris, Berlin, Vienna, no less than in Constantinople, Naples, Teheran, and Moscow [. . .] Endowed with inextinguishable life, in spite of all that has been done to suppress it, this passion survives at large in modern states and towns, penetrates society, makes itself felt in every quarter of the globe where men are brought into communion with men. Yet no one dares to speak of it; or if they do, they bate their breath, and preface their remarks with maledictions.

A Problem in Modern Ethics moves confidently—even aggressively and masterfully—knocking down one fallacious belief after another. The long years of its revisions show in the way it tears down, one by one, the main obfuscations, forms of hysteria, and positings of nonsense regarding the issue of love and sex between men that John Addington Symonds had faced on his journey.

He takes on Tardieu and does away with him quickly, washing the blood of Tardieu's demise off his hands in an impatient rhetorical gesture: "The upshot of the whole matter [. . .] is that the best book on medical jurisprudence now extant repudiates the enormities of Tardieu's method, and lays it down for proved that 'the majority of persons who are subject' to sexual inversion come into the world, or issue from the cradle, with their inclinations clearly marked."[12] He gently annihilates Sir Richard Burton and his theory of homosexuality as being a product of the hot "Sotadic Zone," pointing out that history has confirmed the practice of love between men in the customs of the "Kelts, Scythians, Bulgars, Tartars, Normans, [. . .] and modern Slavs."[13] The essay rebuts the idea that this "passion" is a moral failing. He rebuts as well Krafft-Ebing's theory that it is a "form of inherited neuropathy."[14] Symonds sweeps across all of the main points of Western history, and the West's main religious codes, to argue that "it is illogical" that "an Englishman or a Frenchman who loves the male sex must be diagnosed as tainted with disease; while Sophocles, Pindar, Pheidias, Epaminondas, Plato, are credited with yielding to an instinct which was healthy in their times because society accepted it."[15]

He breaks out, this man who spent a lifetime hedging, into ringing advocacy: "The bare fact that ancient Greece tolerated, and that modern Europe refuses to tolerate sexual inversion, can have nothing to do with the etiology, the pathology [. . .] What has to be faced is that a certain type of passion flourished under the light of day and bore good fruits for Hellas; that the same type of passion flourishes in the shade and is the source of misery and shame in Europe."[16]

He argues that there are several categories of "cause" for same-sex male desire and same-sex male sexual contact. One is when men in general experience forced separation from women, as in the Navy; the second is from simple curiosity-seeking; other categories include conditions of historical acceptance, such as in Greece; but above all, he points out that there is a category of men who have an "inborn instinctive preference for the male" from their earliest consciousness, "and indifference to the female sex."[17]

This category is the one whose identity he wishes at last to define and for whose well-being he wishes chiefly to advocate.

Symonds even invokes "Calamus." What is the conclusion of Symonds's magisterial argument? Change the laws in Britain.

He concludes resoundingly that "[s]cientific investigation has proved in recent years that a very large proportion of persons in whom abnormal sexual inclinations are manifested possess them from their earliest childhood, that they cannot divert them into normal channels, and that they are powerless to get rid of them. In these cases, then, legislation is interfering with the liberty of individuals, under a certain misconception regarding the nature of their offence."[18]

A Problem in Modern Ethics continued to speak for Symonds—though he was gone from the earth.

Like many of those who had spent time at hard labor—from booksellers such as Henry Vizetelly to ordinary men who had been caught with other men—Oscar Wilde, now living permanently in France, had been partly broken by its rigors.

To the dismay of those who cared about Wilde, his lover, Lord Alfred "Bosie" Douglas, intermittently joined him.

Contemporaries tell that Wilde was shunned by expatriate British tourists in the hotels and resorts that he frequented; letters portray Wilde approaching those who were more sympathetic to his plight and more reverential toward his talent to ask for small loans of money.

Wilde's wife, Constance Wilde, died in 1898, not long after Wilde was released.[19] His children, Vyvyan and Cyril, were living with their guardians in Britain. These guardians never allowed Wilde to see his children again. Indeed, the boys were given to understand that their father, like their mother, was dead.[20]

On November 30, 1900, Wilde—still an exile, still poor—did die, in a high room in a shabby hotel in Paris, from meningitis. He was buried in Père Lachaise Cemetery.

Oscar Fingal O'Flahertie Wills Wilde was forty-six years old.

Havelock Ellis had used Symonds's work, with Symonds's willing collaboration at the time, to develop his theories on homosexuality. In 1896, a year after Wilde's trial, Ellis found a publisher in Germany for *Sexual Inversion*. Continental critics gave the book a positive reception.

The British version, when it finally saw the light of day, was much altered, for legal reasons. This edition scrubbed the homosexual author from the sexological treatise about homosexuality. *A Problem in Modern Ethics* appeared, but in scattershot form throughout the book—often reduced to footnotes. Ellis used many of Symonds's case notes, some of them from Symonds's own life, from his unpublished memoirs, but Ellis now minimized his collaborator's role. In the case studies he reduced Symonds's name to "Z." Ellis took his collaborator's name off the title page. Nowhere in the revised English version did Havelock Ellis praise Symonds, or even offer gratitude for his contribution.[21]

By 1901, Ellis was at the height of his career, hailed as a hero. *Sexual Inversion* was eventually a vast success. It went into many printings in dozens of languages, has sold in the hundreds of thousands of copies for over a century, and is still in print worldwide today.

Millions of people today know the name Havelock Ellis and the book *Sexual Inversion*. These have entered the record of history.

Very few people, outside of specialized circles, remember the name John Addington Symonds.

Nonetheless, Symonds finally "won." Following the success of *Sexual Inversion* and other texts that later joined the discussion, the roles of the venereologists, jurists, and medical psychologists, in judging and condemning male-male love, lost status; the new profession of sexology became the main discipline that defined modern ideas about homosexuality.

Today judges unselfconsciously use the language that Symonds pioneered and that Ellis absorbed from him: they generally adjudicate today taking for granted the idea that we all exist on a spectrum of sexual orientations, and notions of blame and of "moral degeneracy" have no relevance at all. Modern judges in the West would face censure if they used, in a decision, Lord Cockburn's language of "poison" or Henry Labouchere's language of "gross indecency" in referring to homosexuality.

From "abnormal" and "indecent" and "morbid" to "natural" and "worthy of respect": the arguments that Symonds had laid out so painfully, so dangerously, in *A Problem in Modern Ethics*, and then contributed to *Sexual Inversion*, are now taken for granted by millions of people, countless institutions, and most legislatures in the West today.

The Labouchere Amendment's criminalization of male-male love and sex was repealed in Britain in 1967 with the passage of the Sexual Offences

Act.[22] Men over age twenty-one, in England and Wales, were now free to be together in private—without any fear of criminal prosecution: "A homosexual act in private shall not be an offence provided that the parties consent thereto and have attained the age of twenty-one years."[23]

Symonds had actually helped to write a new world—one in which he had always believed, though it did not yet remotely exist during his life—into being.

PART VIII

The Memoirs

CHAPTER 29

"As Written by Himself"

S ymonds willed the manuscript of the memoirs he had started writing in 1889 to Horatio Brown, who served as the executor of his literary estate. He was the same dear friend whom Symonds had visited in Venice in 1881 and 1882, on the trip when he met Angelo Fusato. This friend and editor discreetly selected anodyne sections of the memoirs and included them in an 1895 biography of Symonds. But he left out any mention of Symonds's homosexuality.

The widowed Catherine struggled with how to handle the memoirs too. "Are we right in being cowardly and suppressing it?" she asked Brown. But she saw her husband's concerns about contemporary publication as "justified and useful" and finally accepted her role, and Horatio Brown's, as censors.

Brown willed the unexpurgated manuscript of Symonds's memoirs, kept in a "green card-board box tied with strings," along with other papers, to the London Library. Brown set restrictions on the custody of the box, obeying Symonds's wishes. He ensured that the librarian, Charles Hagberg Wright, would restrict readers' access to it for fifty years. In 1895, Brown wrote the obligatory Edwardian posthumous and carefully excluded any references to homosexuality.[1]

After Brown's death, in 1926, Edmund Gosse, Symonds's younger friend, became the executor. Gosse sealed the memoirs in the safe of the London Library, as per Brown's directive. To protect Symonds's posthumous reputation, he also burned many of the other papers and notebooks that had been left with it.

Forty-eight years later, the custodians of the manuscript at the library permitted an American graduate student, Phyllis Grosskurth, to see the memoirs as part of the research for her heavily self-censored 1965 biography of Symonds, *John Addington Symonds: A Biography*, which did identify Symonds as a homosexual. But her treatment of explicit passages in the memoirs had to be circumspect. Homosexuality was still a crime in Britain, as was obscenity. And as she warned in the preface, "the story of Symonds' inner life cannot be revealed in Symonds' own words till 1976"—eleven years into the future from the date of her writing.[2]

As I wrote the first several drafts of this book, as far as I knew, no one but Symonds's two executors, his daughter Katharine, select staff and readers at the London Library, and Phyllis Grosskurth had ever seen the complete unexpurgated memoirs.[3]

In 2016, Palgrave Macmillan changed this. The company announced the publication, at last, of an unexpurgated version. "This edition is the first to reproduce John Addington Symonds' Memoirs in its entirety," read the catalog copy.

In July 2017, the long-suppressed volume was published and a copy was in my hand. I was used to the scraps and tatters of pamphlets in which Symonds had bound his secret thoughts. Now I held a volume that was solidly, beautifully produced: it had a maroon spine, and lettering across the top of the front cover identified the series in which the volume appeared: "Genders and Sexualities in History." A self-portrait Symonds had done in pencil was reproduced on the cover. He had drawn himself with a floppy hat, one like the young Whitman's, covering his eyes.

The man who had bound his own hidden work at nineteen in flimsy, hand-sewn cardboard covers; who had his illicit *Fragilia Labilia* poems bound together under translucent, insubstantial covers that both revealed and concealed; who knew that he could never bring out these six hundred pages during his lifetime, between properly published covers—this insistent ghost had nonetheless made such an intricate deal with posterity, and such a calculated hopeful bet on the future, that he managed to debut his uncensored autobiography in print, at last, 124 years after his body had died.

The title page read:

The Memoirs of John Addington Symonds
As Written by Himself

I read *The Memoirs* with a racing heart. Here was the familiar shape of the life that I thought I knew so well, yet the voice of the author was completely different—at times even unrecognizable to me. In Symonds's other published work, he is verbose, over-careful; even in his secret poems you can feel that tension and hesitancy. The self-obscuring of the man I had studied for so long could be exasperating.

But in those published pages, as you can see from the excerpts I have scattered throughout this book, the same man blazed. He sounded so modern, so urgent—for the first time he actually seemed like someone who could have *been* a friend of Walt Whitman's. The pressure of his need to tell his story is palpable. In fresh, frank, brave prose, the pages spin past. His honesty drives you forward.

Here were all of the familiar events—the scandal over Vaughan; the health breakdown after the Magdalen College investigation; the flight to Davos; the first encounter with *Leaves of Grass*; the publications; the meeting with Fusato, and so on—that I'd read in his letters and reread in Horatio Brown and Grosskurth. But the books in which I had first read about these subjects had all been censored.

This wasn't.

So it felt as if I had known each scene from an album of dusty black-and-white daguerreotypes. And now the same scenes leapt out at me as vivid holograms, clothed in all the colors of the modern world.

The editor of *The Memoirs*, Dr. Amber Regis, of the University of Sheffield, also had an extraordinary journey: she writes in her introduction that the manuscript was made up of six hundred pages of "varying sizes, color and provenance" and included, alongside Symonds's own handwritten accounts, material written by others: his lover and student in Clifton from his early life as a husband and father, Norman Moor; his wife; and others whom he loved. Symonds knew this unwieldy, organic manuscript would "hardly be fit to publish," as he told Horatio Brown; nonetheless, he couldn't help making it as comprehensive as possible.

He left instructions, Regis explains, that the memoirs should survive him intact: they should be, he wrote, "[saved] from destruction after my death." Though his contemporaries left instructions to burn all mention of homosexual affections in papers that survived them, Symonds set specific terms for the preservation of the manuscript—but with limited access, so as not to cause pain to loved ones still living after his death.

As noted, at Brown's death Symonds's friend Edmund Gosse became custodian of the manuscript and chair of the committee tasked with handling the document. He and his colleagues sealed the package in a safe in the London Library—as if it could explode. Ten days later, Katharine Symonds Furse, Symonds's youngest daughter—now a respected author in her own right—tracked down her father's will to look at the terms restricting access to the memoirs.

She had conferred with her bohemian friends—including the writer Virginia Woolf—who had heard rumors of the contents of the memoirs and urged Katharine to read them. "I am trying to write of the 'skeleton in the closet,'" she wrote to Woolf. "To my mind, the more said the better." She thought that she could write a sympathetic biography of her tormented father. Curious about her father's true inner life, she felt that the times demanded honesty about same-sex love and relationships.

What followed, as Dr. Regis recounts it, was an extraordinary standoff between the progressive-minded daughter of a homosexual father, who sought even fifty years after his death to know who he really was, and the last vanguard of patriarchal Edwardian propriety, who adamantly tried to refuse her access. After a visit to Charles Hagberg Wright at the London Library, she made furious notes about this pilgrimage. She learned that "[a]ll of Father's MS have been destroyed by [Brown's] executors . . . [He thought that] the M/S/ which were destroyed were of a nature that they thought it better to destroy."[4] Furse angrily concluded that manuscript copies of notes for *Sexual Inversion,* and also manuscripts of *A Problem in Greek Ethics* and *A Problem in Modern Ethics*—all the foundational documents of modern gay rights advocacy—"were most likely consigned to the flames."[5]

Furse didn't give up after this initial rebuff. Hagberg Wright sent her request up the bureaucratic chain but again told her that he believed she wouldn't wish to read the material. Again, she was denied access.

Furse looked outward for the missing pieces of her father's legacy. She advertised in the newspapers, asking readers to reply to her if they had memories of her father. A newspaper picked up the story and wrote an article about a daughter's efforts to solve the "family mystery" of her father's missing papers. Goaded into action at last, Hagberg Wright grudgingly conceded that he would get her in to read the memoirs. But he issued a warning: "personally I would like [the manuscript] destroyed."

Katharine Symonds Furse sent the librarian a copy of *Sexual Inversion,* which was, by the 1940s, widely respected and discussed. "Have you studied *Sexual Inversion* at all?" she challenged him. She was letting Hagberg Wright know that, as a modern woman, she preferred real knowledge of her father, whose conflicts she understood and whose orientation she accepted, to false concerns about her presumed modesty.

At last, Katharine was allowed to read her father's memoirs. Sadly, she too ultimately censored herself and did not write about her father's homosexuality in her own memoir, *Hearts and Pomegranates;* as to reading his, she wrote of being completely absorbed.[6]

Marks made on the manuscript detailing her father's secret life, however, remain from this reading of hers. They show his daughter defending his right, even in death, to express his truth. In a section on different forms of love, Symonds reflects on the distinction between "the human kindly friendly love which I had given liberally to my beloved wife and children, to my father and sister and my companions" and "the passionate sexual love of comrades."

Horatio Brown, next to the words about the first kind of love, wrote the softening word "affection"; against the second description of "love," he proposed the word "lust."

Katharine Symonds Furse, though, demurred at this softening. She took the risk of defacing a London Library manuscript. She added in pencil, on the same page, a firm rejection of the recommendations of the now-deceased Horatio Brown:

> Let JAS words stand.
> KF June 1949.[7]

In his memoirs, Symonds gave the editor of the future the keys to a code embedded in his work. Symonds instructed his readers of the future to find two of the secret poems from the locked black box, "Dead Love" and "The Tale of Theodore"—poems that he had included in his bequest to Brown, who gave the trove to Gosse, who embargoed the whole of it for fifty years. Symonds's preparation of the memoirs ensured that the future reader would be able to read the true story of this first love: "A privately printed series of poems, entitled 'Dead Love' and 'The Tale of Theodore' portray the state of mind at that epoch better than I can now describe it [. . .]"

We, after years of difficult access, are to take these poems, now available—if you go to the Morgan Library—and map them against chapter 6 of *The Memoirs.* Another secret poem, now sadly lost, the one titled "John Mordan," should, according to Symonds, be mapped against chapter 12 of *The Memoirs.* That would tell the story of his affair with "W."

Symonds also urged readers of *The Memoirs* to look afresh at more than fifty poems from his otherwise banal published books of poems: *Animi Figura* (1882)—you recall the coded notations on the copy in the Morgan Library—and *Vagabunduli Libellus* (1884). He had embedded within the ordering of the poems in both books the solution to a hidden puzzle of which readers of the 1880s would be unaware. But readers of his posthumous future, our present, can now, with his detailed instructions, finally grasp it. He outlined the order in which the selected poems should actually be read and explained that the material surrounding them was inconsequential padding, designed to misdirect most readers of the 1880s: "Taken in the order I have indicated, and detached from the artificial context framed to render publication possible, these sonnets faithfully describe the varying moods, perplexities and conflicts of my passion [for Fusato] before it settled into a comparatively wholesome comradeship."[8] In other words, if we now order the poems in this different way, the story of Symonds's great mature love would manifest its true shape. Thus he ensured that the two books of poems that readers of the 1880s had thought they understood would mean something else altogether to readers more than a century later.

Now that I knew from *The Memoirs* that Symonds embedded clues for the future in his self-published volumes, at the Morgan Library I took another look at *Fragilia Labilia*. The poem about his Italian lover—the one whose likely composition date he'd obscured—had been scored with the words, "Omit. Omit," as you recall.

But—the printers' instruction was fake. There *is* no version of *Fragilia Labilia* that actually omits these poems.

Symonds *didn't* omit these verses.

They waited dormantly for almost a hundred and forty years to tell the world that the poet loved a "sea-lover" connected with Venice, who was his "master," whose memory makes "DAVOS" feel like "this prison"—and whose kisses renew his sense of vitality and hope.

At the Morgan Library, to solve the puzzle Symonds left us, I asked again for *Vagabunduli Libellus*, and for *Animi Figura*, one of the two books with the code embedded in *The Memoirs*. The first volume is an oddity. It has impressive hard board covers and is faced in costly leather, with embossed print on the spine, as if to flaunt its status as "a book"; the catalog states, with a question mark, that it was published in London (1884? it speculates) by Kegan Paul Trench and Co.

But . . . the title pages have no publisher. No location. And indeed . . . nowhere in the volume or outside of it—nowhere at all—can you find an author. *Just* poems.

A second volume of *Vagabunduli Libellus* had a startling difference. In this one, Symonds had hand-drawn a title page, acknowledging himself as the author—even adding a quotation from Plato, in Greek. He had pasted a provenance sheet on the verso page. And he had used the first few blank pages to handwrite some of the secret poems. They were "in a book." They were "published."

And in this one were secret instructions to the future. On page 18, on the page titled "The Envoy to a Book," he had handwritten, "Print only i. vi. vii. viii."

In the first verse, he bids farewell to his "comrade"—"ten years of storm and sunshine shared with thee [. . .] I chose thee [. . .]" We skip "ii," about the value of work and renunciation. We skip "iii," about rebirth of the soul; skip "iv," about the weakness of spirit and the narrator beseeching the Lord to help him—skip "v," about the "calm scholar's undisturbed demesne" and its domestic peace. Go to "vi": the love story picks up.

Thou art a foundling of the world's highway
Waif of the open road, field, forest, fell;
Wheree'r my wandering feet were forced to stray
We communed. These thy printed pages tell
Mute to the world, to him who knows thee well
[. . .] where bland summer shines
On shores and towers Italian; thou hast been
Cradled and rocked to life on Nature's breasts [. . .]

In "vii" he is more daring, and nearly names his Italian lover:

[. . .] transparent Junes
And Autumn calms in Venice, nurtured thee [. . .]

And thou the long long months of cold hast known,
Here mid these mountains; months by comradeship,
Of thee made swift and sweet; hast taken tone
Sterner and firmer from the fellowship [. . .][9]

And on page 25, a sweet testimony to the patience of his beloved Italian gondolier in following him to the snowy Alps, Symonds writes a red "29" above the printed page number "25"; in this volume the true pagination includes the added poems of love written in by hand. This he continues through the printed volume, repaginating it—as a new cache of handwritten secret poems appear pasted in again, on pages 154–57.

And now that I know what I am looking for, stanza viii is a wink to the future:

> *Farewell! The men who greet thee, greet a book.*
> *For better or worse. Five volumes they*
> *Welcome; or wearily pursue their way [. . .]*
> *This new history, they say*
> *Claims some attention from us for a day;*
> *No Nile of learning this, a garrulous brook.*
> *Well, let them talk. There is an irony*
> *In the fate that waits for books. Thy face, O friend,*
> *Hath for my soul a story, which 'twere vain*
> *To ask the unkindly world to comprehend.*
> *Nay, have we not our secret? I would fain*
> *Veil from the sight of men, thy mystery.*[10]

There is some irony, indeed, "in the fate of books." Symonds interpolated banal false or cover stanzas in between the real, intended stanzas detailing the love he felt for the gondolier—and anticipated the boredom of his contemporary, uncomprehending readers. But he doesn't care: the world is "unkindly" and would repudiate the truth, so "let them talk" about the book's banality.

Because Symonds knows he has written, in code, between the distraction verses in this unsigned volume, a love poem on a minor epic scale for his beloved:

"Nay, have we not our secret?"

"Thy face," he tells the one reader who really matters, the one he truly loves—"hath for my soul a story." Even the title of the verse sequence now makes sense: "Envoy to a Book"—an "envoy" is a special messenger bearing a sealed message.

The poem, reread in only its selected coded stanzas, *is* the "Envoy to a Book."

And that love, which the coded stanzas reveal and conceal, is the real story whose "fate" is to be hidden for 140 years.

I then did more. Symonds instructed in *The Memoirs* that his future readers take a series of verses from *Animi Figura*, then jump over to pick up the series of verses from *Vagabunduli Libellus*, then return, hopscotching from verse to intended verse, back to *Animi Figura*:

> He outlines the exact order in which they should be re-read [. . .]
> "Taken in the order I have indicated, and detached from the artificial context framed to render publication possible, these sonnets faithfully describe the varying moods, perplexities, and conflicts of my passion [for Fusato] before it settled into a comparatively wholesome comradeship."[11]

The skipped verses involve an artificially invoked and placed female love object, who never was intended as part of the imagined future final reading. She is there for "cover."

But when you put both of the books together in the way Symonds instructed and read only the verses identified in the way he directed, you do have the entire story of a homosexual man "tormented by Chimaera," who then falls in love with the Venetian "sea-lover." Regis describes this meta-story as a "dual narrative." If you follow these precise, even obsessively coded instructions, by holding the two books side by side and reading back and forth between them, while following the directions of which heterosexually oriented verses to ignore, the great love story between these two men got told at last:

> "These [sonnets] are [. . .] *Animi Figura*, "L'Amour de L'Impossible,"
> I, ii, iii, iv, v, vi" [. . .]
>   *Vagabunduli Libellus* [. . .] I, ii, iii, xii, xiii, xviii, xix, xx, xi, xxii
> [, . . .] lxii [. . .]
>   *Animi Figura* [. . .] I–iv."

I got chills as I understood what I was reading. Symonds had played alchemically with both time and chronological order to do something I had never seen any other writer do—or even dream of. With a kind of mad brilliance he had created a time capsule/Rubik's Cube, making use of both the present and the future to ensure that future readers could solve the puzzle he had left for them, and thus unlock his truly intended love story. And he tasked the unlocking of the puzzle to a reader whom he had faith would someday exist: an editor who would care so much about his work, more than a century in the future, that she would not only follow his instructions but also explain them to the world. He didn't just have faith that there would be such a person to be his voice; he also believed that she in turn would have a publisher. And when present and future spoke to each other, a passionate and fully declared love story would click into place and emerge into life.

Part of the puzzle that Symonds prepared can never be fully decoded. The "John Mordan" poems were written between 1866 and 1875, during his affair with Norman Moor. This epic review of the love of men for men "in all periods of civilization" was broken up, scattered to various places; as we have seen, some pieces have been lost or destroyed altogether, after friends told Symonds that it should be suppressed. Symonds asks his future editor to print "John" as an appendix to his memoirs. But Dr. Regis regrets that "Symonds' request to have it printed as an appendix cannot be fulfilled" unless the work comes to light in the future.

This is spooky enough—a living editor is regretting being unable to fulfill a courtesy requested of her by a writer who is dead. The other poems, though, she points out, do exist and can be put together in the puzzle format that Symonds prescribed to the future.

Even spookier: Symonds left notes to his future editor across from the title page on one set of poems. Symonds explains that he knows he will be dead when he has this dialogue with the editor who is not yet alive: "This book is in a deep sense of the term a posthumous publication," Symonds wrote of his own future demise. "In spite of its imitative immaturity, the feelings that produced it were spontaneous and genuine, and the editor has reason to believe that they will find an echo in not a few young minds."

Dr. Regis writes, "Reading these words in the Special Collection at Bristol was an uncanny experience, for here was Symonds feeding me lines. He writes [to me] as his editor."[12] In 1889 or 1890, Symonds had put the copy of the poem away, annotated as it was with editorial directions he had written to someone who didn't yet exist: to the unborn Amber Regis, for her to fulfill in 2016–17.

Symonds's incredibly daring, long-shot bet on the human race had paid off. Amber Regis had indeed been born, and educated; a young professor, who is active on social media and is clearly adored by her students, she exists, as Symonds had prophetically wagered. She had sought a doctorate in literature, focusing on queer studies—something that, in the 1880s, was impossible even to imagine—but now her field, too, existed. Regis, now trained, had indeed, as Symonds had intended his future editor to do long ago, sat down in front of the long-sealed package, opened it, and read.

And she did indeed find, as Symonds had hoped long ago, that what she read would "find an echo in not a few young minds," and should be brought out into the world, and now she did indeed have a publisher to assist her: Palgrave Macmillan, which was no longer risking prosecution to do so, and which readily did the work of production and distribution to deliver Symonds's long-silent message into my hands, and into the hands of others. The author, long dead, and the young editor, vibrantly alive, were in a relationship that had been planned on by the former in 1881.

A man had made a bet on a better evolution of history; so now, having bet rightly, his ghost had a team of dedicated living helpers.

The director of operations may have been dead, but he was no less importunate. His directions about how to produce, distribute, and interpret his message leapt off the page. He had orchestrated this team from 140 years in the past. Now I too had joined it.

And now his message has reached your own hands, dear Reader.

How much of a long shot was Symonds's bet? The world could so plausibly have gone in another direction. The people who fought, over the past 150 years, for the civil rights of gay men and lesbians, transgender people, and people who are not gender binary and the people who fought to defend rights to freedom of speech and of the press might easily have gotten discouraged. The books might never have been written. The booksellers might have kept the banned books in their cartons, the seals untorn.

Or the publishers and booksellers might never have fought back in their many court proceedings. These writers and booksellers might have quietly agreed to feel guilt, make deals, withdraw publications, cancel print runs.

In this alternative history, people might have conceded and complied. Anti-sodomy and anti-homosexuality laws, laws against free speech and publication, might still be in place today everywhere as they still are in some parts of the world; indeed, these laws might have continued to worsen.

In the face of these fights and confrontations, the Western world might have decided to go the way of Moxon, Swinburne, and Comstock, rather than the way of the feminist reformer Josephine Butler, or the avant-garde writers Whitman, Symonds, and Wilde. In which case: No *Ulysses*. No "Howl." No Stonewall.

There would never have been a Dr. Amber Regis, with her thoughts and sense of what she is free to think and do. Or me, with mine.

Or you, Reader, with yours.

I continued my headlong racing into *The Memoirs*.

Symonds tells the truth, in clear and compelling prose, about his sexual development; he accounts for his earliest sexual fantasies; he describes the sexual cultures of Harrow and Oxford. He narrates his efforts to suppress "the wolf" through getting married, through labor, and through research. Excerpts from Catherine's journals, which he conscientiously included, acknowledge her unhappiness a year and a half after the two were wed. Symonds explains that the two had long talks in which she came to understand and even accept her husband's true nature. But in spite of the pain he knew he had to cause his wife, he still refuses to identify his desires as "depicting a psychological monster." *The Memoirs* declare this to the future.

And then, in the rushing, immediate prose, which is so different from his stilted public voice written for the Victorian present, Symonds relates his formative boyhood story:

> In the month of January 1858 Alfred Pretor wrote me a note in which he informed me that Vaughan had begun a love affair with him. I soon found that the boy was not lying, because he showed me a series of passionate letters written to him by our head master . . .
>
> On those occasions, my young brain underwent an indescribable fermentation. I remember once that, while we sat together reading Greek iambics, he began softly to stroke my right leg from the knee to the thigh [. . .]
>
> As it was, I began to coquette with vice. I fell in love with a handsome powerful boy, called Huyshe, and I remember stealing his seat in chapel; but I never spoke to him. I also fell in love with Elliot Yorke [. . .] At that moment I nearly gave way to sensuality. I was narcotized by the fellow's contact and the forecast of coming pleasure.

It so happened that I stumbled on the Phaedrus. I read on and on, till I reached the end. Then I began the Symposium and the sun was shining on the shrubs outside the ground floor room in which I slept, before I shut the book up [. . .] Here in the Phaedrus and the Symposium [. . .] I discovered the true Liber Amores at last, the revelation I had been waiting for [. . .] It was as though the voice of my own soul spoke to me through Plato [. . .] Harrow and Vaughan and Pretor vanished into unreality. I had touched solid ground. I had obtained the sanction of the love that had been ruling me since childhood. Here was the poetry, the philosophy of my own enthusiasm for male beauty, expressed with all the magic of unrivaled style [. . .] I perceived that masculine love had its virtue as well as its vice, and stood in this respect upon the same ground as normal sexual appetite. I understood, or thought I understood, the relation which those dreams of childhood and the brutalities of vulgar lust at Harrow bore to my higher aspiration after noble passion.[13]

He describes the first shared love, with W.—whom he now names outright, Willie Dyer: "I took Willie's slender hand in my own, and gazed into his large brown eyes fringed with heavy lashes. . . . A quite indescribable effluence of peace and satisfaction, blent with yearning, flowed from his physical presence [. . .] From that morning, I date the birth of my real self," he writes.

Thirty two years have elapsed since then, and I still can hardly hold my pen when I attempt to write about it. Much sentimental nonsense has been talked about first love. Yet I am speaking the bare truth when I say that my affection for this boy exhausted my instinctive faculty of loving. I have never felt the same unreason and unreasoning emotion for another human being.

I could not marry him, modern society provided no bond comradeship whereby we might have been united. So my first love flowed to waste.[14]

The Memoirs shows that after Dr. Symonds's blackmailing of Dr. Vaughan, Symonds disclosed his own love for Willie Dyer to Dr. Symonds.

When my father learned the truth about my romantic affection for Willie Dyer, he thought it right to recommend a cautious withdrawal from the intimacy. The arguments he used were conclusive. Considering the very delicate position in which I stood with regard to Vaughan, the possibility of Vaughan's story becoming public, and the doubtful nature of my own emotion, prudence pointed to a gradual diminution or cooling-off of friendship.[15]

The Memoirs reveals a story behind what we thought we knew of "W."—of Symonds's love affair with Willie Dyer, which "In Memoriam Arcadie" so mournfully renounced.

Symonds's father made the case to his son that the kind of blackmail and punishment he directed against the headmaster would enmesh his own son eventually, unless Symonds gave up Willie Dyer. Dr. Symonds pressed his son to see that "under the existing conditions of English manners" the relationship would injure Symonds's own reputation. Symonds writes that he was being instructed to see himself as "an aberrant being who was being tutored by my father's higher sense of what was right in conduct." He also realized that his "passion" was not dissimilar to the feelings that had driven Dr. Vaughan.

His conclusion is modern and still heartbreaking:

Under this pressure of arguments from without, a sense of weakness within, and of conventional traditions which had made me what I was, I yielded. I gave up Willie Dyer as my avowed heart's friend and comrade. I submitted to the desirability of not acknowledging the boy I loved in public. *But I was not strong enough to break the bonds which linked us, or to extirpate the living love I felt for him. I carried on our intimacy in clandestine ways, and fed my temperament in sweet emotions in secret.* [Italics mine][16]

This was shocking to read.

Symonds *hadn't* in fact put "his heart's friend and comrade" away, as he had *pretended* to do—for fifty handwritten pages of quatrains—in the copy of "In Memoriam Arcadie" that he had laboriously composed, and that I had transcribed at the Morgan Library. The "Set Apology" stated, indeed, that there had never even *been* a relationship. Symonds in fact had laid out all of these false clues, prepared all of these complex textual misrepresentations, for readers such as his father, so that he could keep his "heart's friend" secretly, but not become a social outcast. But. *The Memoirs* reveal that his relationship with Willie Dyer lasted for several years *after* he wrote the purported eulogy for the end of the relationship—the 1859–60 handwritten document, which he had probably shown to his father. It lasted *after* the "Set Apology" of 1862, which he had written into the flyleaf, that disavowed any factual basis behind the *description* of the purportedly renounced relationship. And the two young men's romantic relationship survived for several years after—until it faded, typically enough for first love, naturally away.

In spite of everything, love had won.

CHAPTER 30

"All Goes Onward and Outward, Nothing Collapses"

As I was concluding the writing of this book, I left my home in New York City to spend time doing final research in Oxford. I noticed that in both countries, in so many ways, Symonds, Whitman, Solomon, and Wilde are still alive.

In New York City's West Village, Whitman's influence is all around. His words are scattered even today throughout the urban landscape. There is a plaque outside the wall of the firehouse of Squad 18, on a street near my home. The firefighters lost several members of their team in the rescue efforts of September 11, 2001. The names of the dead, all young men who perished in the fires and devastation of that day, are engraved on that plaque.

I remember one of them: a tall, brown-eyed firefighter, Manuel Mojica, or "Manny." When my son was a small boy, Manny used to lift him up, which my son adored, to let him sit in the driver's seat of the parked fire truck. On one memorable day, Manny had even let my son sound the fire truck horn.

"We will never forget," the firefighters had written of their lost comrades. They chose to remember and honor Manny Mojica and their other comrades with a single line from "Song of Myself," from *Leaves of Grass*. The section of the poem is titled "Heroes." The entire passage, in the book, reads:

> *I am the mash'd fireman with breast-bone broken,*
> *Tumbling walls buried me in their debris,*
> *Heat and smoke I inspired, I heard the yelling shouts of my comrades,*
> *I heard the distant click of their picks and shovels;*
> *They have clear'd the beams away, they tenderly lift me forth.*[1]

The complete passage was probably too cruel for a memorial that the men of Squad 18, and the world, would see every day; instead, the last line of the passage was mounted on the exterior wall, cast in bronze, for always:

They have cleared the beams away, they tenderly lift me forth.

As I wrote at the beginning of this book, everyone who looks, finds his or her own Whitman. The firefighters on Tenth Street had found theirs.

As my friend the British poet Steven Matthews explains, when we suffer in deep distress, we need poetry; we reach for it when we suffer griefs too big for ordinary words.

A little farther north from the firehouse, there is a new AIDS memorial. That disease, of course, ravaged the gay male community in New York and decimated communities of friends, lovers, and whole groups of comrades in the neighborhood of the West Village, as in the country as a whole.

The new memorial is a lovely small triangular park, freshly planted with trees. Mothers and babies go there to sun; lovers of all kinds hold hands quietly and watch the water spill silently over the edge of a shimmering circular fountain. Whitman had written about an image of similar peace between lovers, in a very different New York City, 165 years earlier:

I walk or sit indifferent—I am satisfied,
He ahold of my hand has completely satisfied me.

The founders of the park had the lines below, from "Song of Myself," inscribed in the granite of the memorial. They form a spiral to walk while following the music and logic of the words. The lines that this community chose are about the indestructible nature of love and its survival beyond death:

What do you think has become of the young and old men?
And what do you think has become of the women and the children?
They are alive and well somewhere,
The smallest sprout shows there is really no death,
And if ever there was it led forward life, and does not wait at the end
*   to arrest it,*
And ceas'd the moment life appear'd.

All goes onward and outward, nothing collapses,
And to die is different from what any one supposed [. . .]²

This community too had reached for and found their Whitman.

Whitman had been prophetic about himself, just as Symonds had been prophetic about us.

Whitman is indeed deathless. If you are willing to notice, scattered throughout the landscape of New York City, he is alive everywhere you look.

I sat on a bench alone, having joined the neighborhood of lovers. I looked, along with them, at the shimmering surface of the fountain. I thought about how I had been surrounded intimately, during these years of writing, by the voices of these dead men. But were they indeed dead?

As Whitman had asked—what does it mean to be dead? John Addington Symonds, Walt Whitman, Oscar Wilde, Simeon Solomon—were they not around us everywhere?

I felt that their words and thoughts, once so hidden, so hunted down, so burned, so torn up, so marginal, hadn't been destroyed. As Rabbi Akiba ben Joseph wrote: "The paper burns, but the words fly away."³

The words hadn't been destroyed—they were indestructible. The fragments and dust of the thoughts that they had embodied had come drifting on high winds to the present from the past, floating, allowing roots for new growth, and materializing at last in new forms, as our vibrant modern world. But the words first of all had to be written, and read.

Whitman lines from *Leaves of Grass* carved into New York City's AIDS memorial, 2016.

Without the courage of these lonely souls long ago writing alone, without the courage of a handful of publishers, printers, and booksellers, without the courage of readers, and without these words' difficult escape from censorship, the good things I saw around me would never have been possible.

Who knows what words we lose even now to that silencing? What worlds? What does it mean, indeed, to be dead?

It seemed to me that censorship was the one true meaning of death.

Across the Atlantic, the dead men about whom I had been writing lived on as well.

I was back in Oxford.

As we walked up the muddy paths of Christ Church Meadow, my companion pointed upward. "Look!" A tattered rainbow flag, which for the past couple of decades had become the symbol throughout the West of the gay rights movement, lay over the stone ledge of an arched window above the park. The soft late-spring wind lifted it gently. It was June— Pride month.

The following day, walking alone toward New College, I turned a corner onto Holywell Street. Above the wide lawn of Mansfield College was a new tower, turreted and gleaming in the blue air. I noticed a rainbow flag again. Not draped over a student's bedroom window, this one had been hoisted up the tower by the college administration. It rippled in the breeze.

I looked to the left: on the crenellated crest of the medieval ramparts of New College—one of the university's oldest colleges—another rainbow flag flew.

I went to Broad Street and turned left, past the Bodleian; I glanced over to Brasenose—the college of Walter Pater, who had so bravely spoken out on behalf of *Bacchus* and whose own career was almost destroyed. A rainbow flag, high on a flagpole, was flying; it was visible from every window in the Bodleian Library.

I returned to Broad Street, the heart of the town and the university; majestic sixteenth-century limestone buildings faced brightly colored plaster-and-wood Tudor shopfronts. I looked down the unusually wide cobblestone street, which was flanked on one side by the august Sheldonian Theatre, encircled with the stone heads of distinguished classical figures, and on the other by the Weston Library. This was probably one of the views that had led Wilde to call Oxford "the loveliest thing in England."

There was the elaborate Victorian façade of Balliol College, Symonds's college, where he had fallen in love with Willie Dyer ("W.") as a teenager, and also where he had forsworn—or rather, not forsworn—that very first love, that "amour d'impossible." Where, most likely, Symonds had written his long, anguished love poem "In Memoriam Arcadie"—and where he had also written, with resentment, the "Set Apology."

I told the Balliol porter that I was studying Symonds, and he allowed me to pass inside.

I turned and walked inside the first of two pristine courtyards. Deep purple and saturated pink wallflowers spilled over window boxes above velvety lawns. I passed under an arch to the second courtyard, where Symonds may have embraced his young love, Willie Dyer—standing close together, perhaps at night, outside the arched Cotswold-stone dorm rooms, and looking together, as the poem describes, and as young lovers do, at the illuminated windows of the chapel. Maybe this was the courtyard where they must have had the terrible discussion in which they agreed—or Symonds tried to decide—that because of family and social pressure, even though they loved each other, they had to part.

Maybe this was where they secretly met, after all, in spite of all of the adults around them declaring that they must never see each other again.

It was daylight now, a new day. From the tower above Balliol College a rainbow flag was flying. I emerged onto Broad Street and turned left to walk to Long Wall. Just before the arched High Street bridge over the Cherwell was the entry gate to Magdalen College. Knights and dragons carved in stone defend its turret. Stone roses, mysteriously squared and symmetrically thorned, repeat in a pattern, softening the ramparts.

I asked at the Porters' Lodge about the rooms where Oscar Wilde had lived as an undergraduate, where he returned after "nipping up" his "viva" at which he had discussed Whitman, and where, perhaps, he had first read Symonds on Greek love. "Could I please see Wilde's rooms?" I asked.

"Oh," said the porter peremptorily, "those rooms are closed to the public."

I explained to him a bit more about my mission.

He then, rather surprisingly, took out a detailed college map and showed me exactly where Wilde's former rooms were located. They were up a staircase at the end of the medieval cloisters and were now tucked away behind kitchens and storage rooms.

"No one can go in there," he explained, smiling slightly. "If you go up *these* staircases," he said, pointing at the map, "and you push on *this* door, you will find it locked."

That was an odd thing to say, I thought. But I thanked him sincerely and took the map.

I entered the cloisters and, from the shadows, admired the smooth green grass. All cloisters in Oxford mix beauty and death, since notables, from medieval knights to Victorian dons, are buried in the very walls;

some, indeed, are interred underfoot. You have to be careful not to step on their headstones.

There is no escaping what the dead wish to say to living students. The messages that they left for future generations, inscribed on their walled tombstones, accompany you as you walk the cool arched passageways.

I came to one dark corner and emerged out of the cloister, as instructed. Before me now, as the map had indicated, was an ancient, uncared-for wooden staircase, so battered by centuries of young men's footsteps that the treads were slanting. Were the steps Victorian? Or from an even earlier period? I went up to a landing, turned, climbed up to another one, and went up again onto another flight of steps that were even more splintered and uneven.

Down a hallway off the final landing, I found a set of double doors. There was a simple plaque: WILDE ROOMS. I pushed on what, as the porter had mysteriously instructed me, should have been the locked doors.

They swung open.

There was a dusty, beautiful, oddly proportioned room: a rectangle that was far longer than it was wide. It was a storage room now, and used, it seemed, at times for meetings. Old laminate desks and outdated wooden chairs were piled haphazardly in its corners. I tried to muffle my steps as I walked in. The room was indeed not open to the public, and I did not want anyone to find and stop me.

At the far end, a single arched Gothic window extended nearly from the floor to the ceiling, overlooking the river. I walked over to it. I smiled; the Magdalen porter, who may have had his own reasons for breaking the rules a bit and helping me with my quest, had given me opaque instructions that, if I only followed them literally, allowed me to enter a space that was usually off limits.

I saw that Wilde had had his own magical world there. To the left of the window was a private territory of roof, a secretive terrace, onto which you could climb and read. A small set of steps went out to what must have been, in Wilde's time, a balcony, to the right; here one could sit with one's friends and a bottle of wine, and perhaps a textbook about Greek poets, or a stray book of poems, perhaps by an American poet.

The balcony looked across the river, at the secret meadows of Magdalen and away from the public ones. Across the rustic bridge, the tree-shaded meadows were lushly overgrown. You could sit in these rooms and terraces, alone or in community, and see nothing in any direction but beauty and privacy and a small kingdom made of gargoyles, river, arches, hidden iron-work ladders, lead casements, deer among ancient trees, and shifting light.

You could imagine anything here. You could imagine a world that was free.

Magdalen College had, after Wilde's 1895 trial and disgrace, erased his name from its public mentions honoring alumni. More recently, though, the college had put up a kind of shrine: a display showing the original covers of many of Wilde's major works. It now was showcasing Wilde's successes—the famous plays, *The Importance of Being Earnest*, *Lady Windermere's Fan*—and more. The college also honored the period of his life when he was a convicted felon, and had also mounted on the display wall the cover of *De Profundis*—Wilde's heartbroken and furious letter to Lord Alfred Douglas, written from his prison cell.

I turned back into the room. Three display cases were built into the thick medieval walls. Each case was lined, incongruously, with mirroring. And in each, an upright white artificial lily was poised.

If you push on the locked doors, they will swing open.

I walked back outside the college, then turned and glanced above the Porters' Lodge. I saw that there, too, from Magdalen's own famous tower, hoisted higher than any other as far as the eye could see, buffeted and released by the caressing wind, a rainbow flag flew, looping and soaring, above the city of spires.

Epilogue

P arliament at last reformed, but did not abolish, *Regina v. Hicklin* by passing the Obscene Publications Act of 1959.[1] This repealed the offense of
"obscene libel" and allowed defendants to justify obscenity on the basis of their
innocence of intention—and on the basis of the "defence of the public good."

In 1960, Penguin published *Lady Chatterley's Lover* and was prosecuted.
The chief prosecutor, Mervyn Griffith-Jones, echoed Lords Campbell and
Cockburn, asking if this was a book "you would even wish your wife or
servants to read?"[2]

But times had changed—this phrase was now roundly satirized. The
jury's verdict was "not guilty."

A second edition of the book, in 1961, included a publisher's dedication:
"For having published this book, Penguin Books was prosecuted under the
Obscene Publications Act, 1959 at the Old Bailey in London from 20
October to 2 November 1960. This edition is therefore dedicated to the
twelve jurors, three women and nine men, who returned a verdict of 'not
guilty' and thus made D. H. Lawrence's last novel available for the first time
to the public in the United Kingdom."

That decision ushered in decades of relative freedom of speech in Britain—freedom that, as in America, is only recently again imperiled.

"Bespectacled, intense, streetwise, Ginsberg showed me 'Howl' with some
hesitation," recalled the American poet and bookseller Lawrence Ferlinghetti,
describing his first encounter with the great anarchic mid-twentieth-century
poem, and with the young Beat poet from New Jersey, Allen Ginsberg.

Ferlinghetti, proprietor of the North Beach bookstore City Lights, in
San Francisco, which still stands, knew that "the world had been waiting
for this poem [. . .] the repressive, conformist, racist, homophobic world of
the 1950s cried out for it."[3]

Ginsberg explained, in a letter to his agent, that the section of "Howl"
called "America" was "a rather gay exposition of my own" and that the poem
says "I am thus and so I have a right to do so, and I'm saying it out loud for
all to hear." "Without self-acceptance," the young poet wrote, "there can be
no acceptance of other souls."[4]

On November 1, 1956, Ferlinghetti published a thousand copies of *Howl and Other Poems* in his City Lights Pocket Poet series.

In 1957, a bookseller, Samuel Roth, with a bookstore in Greenwich Village, New York City, was prosecuted for distributing such obscene material as *Photo* magazine (*Roth v. United States*). In the Supreme Court ruling, the court held that literature was protected by the First Amendment: the new test would be "whether to the average person, applying contemporary standards, the dominant theme of the material as a whole appeals to the prurient interest."[5]

On March 25, 1957, Chester MacPhee, the San Francisco collector of customs, impounded 520 copies of *Howl*, under the *Roth* decision. He did so on the basis that it was obscene: as he said, "You wouldn't want your children to come across it." The ACLU told the customs collector that it would contest the legality of the seizure.

In June of that year, a bookseller named Shigeyoshi Murao, son of a family that had been in an internment camp for Japanese citizens during World War II, was arrested for selling *Howl* at City Lights by two undercover inspectors; a warrant went out for the arrest of Ferlinghetti as well.

In October, after a much-followed trial, Judge Clayton W. Horn, using the *Roth* decision, found that *Howl* was not obscene—as it had "redeeming social importance."

In his decision, he wrote: "The freedoms of speech and press are inherent in a nation of free people. These freedoms must be protected if we are to remain free, both individually and as a nation [. . .] The people owe a duty to themselves and to each other to preserve and protect their Constitutional freedoms from any encroachment by government [. . .] the defendant is found not guilty."[6]

Just as Whitman had somehow walked beside Symonds still after Whitman's own death, holding Symonds's hand through the most difficult task of his life—his final release of his great manifesto—now Whitman somehow walked beside Ginsberg, into the young man's own fiery trial of words.

In "A Supermarket in California," a poem included in *Howl*, the young Beat poet is accompanied by this "lonely old courage-teacher" in the suburban dusk:

> *What thoughts I have of you tonight, Walt Whitman, for I walked*
> *down the sidestreets under the trees with a headache of self-conscious*
> *looking at the full moon [. . .]*

I saw you, Walt Whitman, childless, [. . .] dear father. Graybeard, lonely
   old courage-teacher [. . .]

After the trial, the volume sold by the tens of thousands—awakening a
generation from the conformity and slumber, the "racism and homophobia,"
as the publisher put it, of the postwar era.

Ginsberg, who as a lonely gay adolescent in Paterson, New Jersey,
had been astonished by Whitman, had written "Howl" to commemorate
the centennial of the publication of *Leaves of Grass*.[7] Now reviewers were
hearing echoes of Whitman in Ginsberg's poem.

It wasn't only reviewers who heard the voice of Whitman as a palimpsest
under the words of this bespectacled young renegade of the 1950s.

The day after Ferlinghetti had heard Ginsberg read "Howl" at the Six
Gallery on Fillmore Street, he'd sent Ginsberg a telegram, just as Emerson
had sent a missive to Whitman.

And it read, like Emerson's:

"I greet you at the start of a great career."

Acknowledgments

I benefited from the generosity of a number of extraordinary teachers, mentors, and guides, without whose wisdom this book could not have been written or revised.

Thank you, first and foremost, to my doctoral thesis adviser at the University of Oxford, Dr. Stefano-Maria Evangelista of Trinity College, Oxford, whose work *British Aestheticism and Ancient Greece: Hellenism, Reception, Gods in Exile* first opened up for me the engagement among Victorian gay men with the heritage of classical Greece. Dr. Evangelista advised me to read John Addington Symonds, and he read my doctoral thesis many times, giving detailed critiques. His patient, comprehensive pedagogy and his profound knowledge of both Victorian letters and queer studies provided vital illumination. The academic research I completed for my 2012–16 Oxford doctoral thesis undergirds the story, retold here in language for a general audience, of this group of "sexual dissidents" and of what they faced. I am sincerely grateful to the admissions office of the English Faculty at the University of Oxford for readmitting me to complete my graduate studies at midlife, and to the Rhodes—now Mandela Rhodes—Scholarship for its support.

Secondly, but as importantly, I owe a very great debt to Professor Paul Johnson, head of the Department of Sociology at the University of York, coauthor of *Religion, Law and Homosexuality*, and author of "Buggery and Parliament: 1533–2017," among other important texts, and to Professor H. G. Cocks, associate professor of the Department of History at the University of Nottingham and author of the landmark *Nameless Offences: Homosexual Desire in the 19th Century*, among other significant books and articles. These scholars are both pioneers in the field of the history of sodomy laws in Britain.

I had made several errors in interpretation of the legal record in the first edition of this book, which some readers may know. Not being a legal historian, I knew I needed expert guidance for an appropriate revision. I could not have had more distinguished mentors in this task.

Prof. Johnson and Prof. Cocks both gave professional scholars' reports to me to help me revise this edition and suggested very important changes. I am so grateful to these scholars, whose work is iconic in this field, for having made time in their schedules to share their insights with me, and for the many subsequent conversations they had with me that deepened my understanding of this challenging subject in this period. I was privileged to have what at times amounted to a digital seminar with two of the leading pioneers in queer legal history.

Thank you to the staffs of the Bodleian Library, the Oxford English Faculty Library, and the library at New College, all at the University of Oxford.

Dr. Elleke Boehmer of Wolfson College, Oxford, the distinguished novelist and scholar of postcolonial studies, carefully reviewed my thesis and gave many valuable critiques, as did the writer Rebecca Abrams.

The then-warden of New College, Sir Curtis Price, and to his wife, the composer Rhian Samuel, warmly welcomed me into the New College community and into their home. The New College staff also made me, and my children, very welcome. I am grateful to the fellows at New College who arranged for me to be part of the New College fellows' community by inviting me to be a Distinguished Visiting Fellow.

Sincere thanks to the Rothermere American Institute, at the University of Oxford, for granting me a research fellowship and office space at the Library of the Rothermere American Institute; thank you to Baroness Helena Kennedy, QC, formerly warden of Mansfield College, for inviting me to share my work on *Outrages* from Mansfield College's platform. Thank you so much to Dr. Michèle Mendelssohn, who oversaw the Rothermere American Institute Fellowship and hosted my lecture to present this material at the Rothermere, as well as reading and discussing my work with me in 2016. Dr. Anna Camilleri, then of Christ Church, Oxford, invited me to present my research to the university's undergraduates. Thank you to Balliol College, Oxford University, John Addington Symonds's home college, which hosted my presentation of this research to undergraduates. The Ashmolean Museum of the University of Oxford invited me to present this research in a lecture, as did Rodolfo Lara Torres of Rhodes House, who convened Rhodes House's first LGBTQ+ studies conference and its Humanities Forum, at both of which I presented Symonds's story.

The then-warden of Rhodes House, Charles Conn, and his wife, Camilla Borg, and the Rhodes House staff have often housed my family and me there so kindly. The novelist Rebecca Abrams and her family generously did the same; Abrams also shared insights from her own life of writing.

Barnard College granted me a research fellowship in the Barnard Center for Research on Women, and Barnard College's Athena Center for

Women and Leadership, also provided a position that helped to support this research with access to the Barnard and Columbia University libraries.

Heartfelt thanks to Dr. Kathleen Wilson, Professor of History and Cultural Studies at Stony Brook University and author of *A New Imperial History: Culture, Identity and Modernity in Britain and the Empire 1660–1840* (2004), and Director of the Humanities Institute, and to Dean Sacha Kopp, formerly Dean of Arts and Sciences at that university, for the 2016 visiting professorship during which I taught this material. I appreciate my wonderful students at Stony Brook University for showing how relevant to young people of any era are the struggles of the young people described here.

I am grateful to my longtime editor Lennie Goodings and to skilled copyeditor Zoe Gullen, both of Virago, who both did thoughtful work on many versions of the manuscript, and whose incisive suggestions always made the manuscript stronger. Zoe Hood worked her continual magic to get the word out about this book to readers. Thank you to Margo Baldwin, my publisher at Chelsea Green Publishing, for the US publication of this book; her support for my work goes back to her publication of my book *The End of America: Letter of Warning to a Young Patriot*, in 2008. I have appreciated her and Chelsea Green Publishing for over a decade as the champions of independent publishing that they are. I am indebted too to Chelsea Green's talented team, including editor Brianne Goodspeed, and Sean Maher and Christina Butt in publicity. Proofreader Nancy Ringer and indexer Shana Milkie addressed the manuscript with care; Patricia Stone oversaw the production of the Chelsea Green's edition with scrupulous attention and thoughtfulness. It's an honor to be published by both of these mission-driven publishers.

Jane Dystel is an agent extraordinaire; Amy Bishop, Lauren Abramo, and the team at Dystel, Goderich & Bourret also skillfully supported this book.

Helen Churko, Lucy LePage, and Carton Sedgely represented me as a lecturer during their years at Royce Carlton; they too believed in the importance of telling this story and supported it.

Profound thanks to Will Schwalbe, author of *The End of Your Life Book Club* and *Books for Living*, who since our freshman year in college has always been my best reader, for insights on nuances in debates among commentators on LGBTQ+ history, as well as for critical editorial recommendations. As his own work so powerfully shows, no one could better understand or help me to express the importance of protecting the act of reading. I owe a debt to a great playwright and novelist, the late Larry Kramer, whose courageous life and work combine to make him an icon for our era. A few times, since I was a young writer, Mr. Kramer has communicated with me about the activist's life—guidance that I took to heart. He took time from his own demanding work to read an early manuscript of *Outrages* and to give me precious feedback. It is difficult for me to express what his lifelong example as an activist, his work, and his occasional words of wisdom have meant to me.

Thank you, too, in a different context, to Will Schwalbe, along with David Cheng, Tom Molner, and Andrew Brimmer, for the many decades I have been lucky enough to have them as my extended family. Their love, and the lasting, beneficent influence they have shed on my children, helped inspire me to write this book.

I appreciate the professional, scholarly manuscript reading by legal scholar and LGBTQ+ rights advocate Scott Long. Thank you to Baroness Helena Kennedy, Queen's Counsel, as well, for her legally oriented reading, and to Sir Stephen Sedley, Queen's Counsel, of Mansfield College and of the Oxford University Faculty of Law, who shared his deep expertise in British jurisprudence. Dr. Ivan Crozier, Conjoint Professor at the University of Newcastle, Australia, read an earlier version of this book. Dr. Anne Hanley, Lecturer in History and Science and Medicine at Birkbeck, University of London, shared her expertise on the Contagious Diseases Acts and the treatment of women in "lock hospitals."

Professor Mary Poovey, the distinguished feminist historian, emerita of New York University, and author of the classic text *Uneven Developments: The Ideological Work of Gender in mid-Victorian England* (Chicago: University of Chicago Press) was also a scholarly reader, as was Professor Mary Shanley, the legal historian, former Margaret Stiles Halleck Professor of Political Science at Vassar College, and author of the equally important *Feminism, Marriage and the Law in Victorian England*. Prof. Shanley gave a scholarly reading of the revised version of this book and shared her deep expertise in British Victorian feminism and the law. Dr. Stuart Anderson, Professor of Law at the University of Otago, New Zealand, and one of the editors of the *Oxford History of the Laws of England: 1820–1914: Private law* (vol. XII) (Oxford University Press) gave a much-valued scholar's report as well. I thank these most distinguished scholars for their time and professional expertise and review.

My children, Rosa and Joe Shipley, tirelessly supported this book, and my husband, Brian O'Shea, offered his equally steady support.

Thank you to my mother, Dr. Deborah Wolf, and my grandmother, Dr. Fay Goleman, though she is not with us. My mother wrote a book on the lesbian community in San Francisco in the 1970s, *The Lesbian Community*, and has been a role model in every life circumstance for communicating the message that all love is equally precious. My grandmother's graduate research was on communities of gay men in Chicago in the 1930s. I am grateful for their heritage of celebrating LGBTQ+ lives. Warm thanks to my cousin Mira Weil, an educator in trans-positive curricula at the University of Massachusetts, for instructive conversations about the questions involved in writing about queer lives from the position of an ally.

It is difficult to express how much I appreciate the Morgan Library and Museum in New York City, notably the archivist Ms. Maria Molestina and her colleagues. My thanks, too, to the librarians at the Henry W. and Albert A. Berg Collection of English and American Literature in the New York Public Library, and to those in New York University's Elmer Holmes Bobst Library's Special Collections Center.

The story told in *Outrages* reminded me continually, as I researched it, of what a vanguard and often dangerous role printers, publishers, booksellers, and librarians always have had, and often have even today.

They are indeed the "sentinels" of a society, though not in the way that Flaubert's censors intended.

Their steadfast defense of writing and reading is just what this story seeks to honor.

Timeline

1855: Walt Whitman, *Leaves of Grass* (US)

1855: Introduction of penal servitude for sodomy and other crimes. (UK)

1857: *Madame Bovary* trial; author, editor, and printer prosecuted for "offending public mores" (France)

1857: Legal action against Charles Baudelaire's *Les Fleurs du Mal* (France)

1857: Obscene Publications Act criminalizes the author's intention (UK)

1857: Matrimonial Causes Act includes sodomy with "rape and bestiality" as grounds for allowing a woman to civilly divorce a man (UK)

1859–61: John Addington Symonds, "In Memoriam Arcadie" (unpublished)

1860: Unexpurgated "Calamus," *Leaves of Grass* (US)

1861: Offences Against the Person Act streamlines sodomy convictions (UK)

1864: Contagious Diseases Act legalizes incarceration with forced pelvic examinations and without trial (UK)

1865–66: Scandal of Algernon Charles Swinburne's *Poems and Ballads*; Edward Moxon withdraws publication contract

1866: Contagious Diseases Act reaffirms state power to incarcerate women with forced pelvic examination and without trial (UK)

1867: William Rossetti's bowdlerized edition of *Leaves of Grass* (UK)

1867–68: *Regina v. Hicklin* criminalizes the reader's reception of a book (UK)

1870: Married Women's Property Act (UK)

1871: Boulton and Park trial: the state forces rectal exams on men accused of same sex offenses (UK)

1871: Robert Buchanan (pseudonym Thomas Maitland) review, "The Fleshly School of Poetry," (UK)

1873: Arrests of Simeon Solomon for attempted sodomy (UK)

1873: Comstock Act criminalizes "obscene publications" sent through the mail (US)

1873: John Addington Symonds, *A Problem in Greek Ethics* (unpublished)

1873: Symonds's first letter to Whitman: what does "Calamus" mean?

1873: John Addington Symonds, *Studies of the Greek Poets*

1876: Revised Customs Consolidation Act legalizes state confiscation at sea of obscene materials (UK)

1876: Walt Whitman, *Democratic Vistas* (US)

1878: Trial of Annie Besant and Charles Bradlaugh for obscene publication (UK)

1878: Secret sodomy poems: John Addington Symonds's *Rhaetica* and *Eudiades and a Cretan Idyll* (privately published; UK)

1882: Revised Married Women's Property Act (UK)

1882: Massachusetts attorney general threatens Whitman with prosecution for *Leaves of Grass*; print run canceled (US)

1882: Walt Whitman retrieves plates, publishes *Leaves of Grass* (US)

1882: Oscar Wilde visits Walt Whitman in Camden, NJ (US)

1885: Criminal Law Amendment Act (Labouchere Amendment) caps punishment for gross indecency at two years' hard labor (UK)

1888: Publisher Henry Vizetelly sentenced to penal servitude for publishing a translation of the French novel *Nana* (UK)

1889: Revised Vagrancy Act legalizes public flogging for sodomy (UK)

1890: Whitman's rebuttal letter to Symonds (US)

1892: Death of Walt Whitman, Camden, NJ (US)

1893: Death of John Addington Symonds, Rome (Italy)

1895: Oscar Wilde trials: Wilde sentenced to two years' hard labor for gross indecency (UK)

1896: John Addington Symonds, *A Problem in Modern Ethics* (privately published; UK)

1897: Publication of Havelock Ellis and J. A. Symonds's *Sexual Inversion*

1927: Embargo on John Addington Symonds's unexpurgated memoirs

2017: Publication of John Addington Symonds's unexpurgated memoirs

Photo Credits

Notes

INTRODUCTION

1. Jonathan Dollimore coined this phrase in his 1991 book *Sexual Dissidence: Augustine to Wilde, Freud to Foucault* (Oxford: Oxford University Press, 1991).

CHAPTER 1: "IN MEMORIAM ARCADIE"

1. Graham Robb, *Strangers: Homosexual Love in the Nineteenth Century*, (London, UK; W. W. Norton & Co., 2003) 137; see also Rictor Norton, "The John Addington Symonds Pages," 1997, rictornorton.co.uk/symonds/memoirs.htm.
2. Christopher Ricks, *Tennyson* (Berkeley: University of California Press, 1972), 20–37.
3. Arthur E. Baker, *A Tennyson Dictionary* (New York: Haskell House Publishers, 1916), 57.
4. H. G. Cocks, email communication with the author and *New York Times*, October 22–25, 2019.
5. H. G. Cocks, email communication with the author, April 5, 2020. Prof. Cocks explains the frequent ambiguity in what was actually being prosecuted in the records, which he calls "fragments": "The question of 'attempts' to commit sodomy is a difficult one, as the law of attempts is a rather obscure business. In addition 'unnatural offences' were often not reported by legal writers. However, by the early 17th century the common law said that all attempts to commit a crime were crimes in themselves. And it seems clear from the cases that did come to court that gradually, from the late 17th century/early 18th century onwards, the courts regarded all homoerotic acts as 'attempts' to commit the felony even if the parties did not intend actual penetration. They therefore counted as 'misdemeanours.' If you look at bills of indictment for 'assault with intent' or indecent assault in the 18th/early 19th century the offence is usually described as 'putting and placing' the hands of the defendant on the complainant, 'with intent to commit the detestable (etc) crime of sodomy.' So that tells you how it was construed in the formal language of the indictment (which did not actually describe what had happened, but merely presented it in an acceptable legal form to the court). We can only know what the courts did, and how they construed certain acts as crimes." (Email communication with the author, July 2–November 25, 2019.)
6. Prof. H. G. Cocks, email communication with the author, July 2019.

7. Paul Johnson, email communication with the author, October 22, 2019. Prof. Johnson references his essay "Buggery and Parliament, 1533–2017," *Parliamentary History* 38, no. 3 (2019): 325–41.

8. Graham Robb, *Strangers: Homosexual Love in the Nineteenth Century*, 23 and appendix 1: Criminal Statistics, 272–3.

9. H. G. Cocks adds a caution: "However, the total number of 'unnatural offences' also included quite a few things like sexual assaults on children and bestiality (the latter being about 25% of the total in England and Wales) [. . .] However, it is right to say that more consenting acts than ever before were part of the rising total number of 'unnatural offences' because there were more offences of that kind coming to court." Email communications with the author, July 2–August 22, 2019.

10. "In the 1830s and earlier [. . .] nude bathing was common for men." "Splashing in the Serpentine," in *A Social History of Swimming in England: 1800–1918*, edited by Christopher Love (London: Routledge, 2008), 20.

CHAPTER 2: "A GENTLE ANGEL ENTER'D"

1. "Schools: Harrow School," in *A History of the County of Middlesex*, vol. 1, *Physique, Archaeology, Domesday, Ecclesiastical Organization, the Jews, Religious Houses, Education of Working Classes to 1870, Private Education from Sixteenth Century*, edited by J. S. Cockburn, H. P. F. King, and K. G. T. McDonnell (London, 1969), 299–302; British History Online, http://www.british-history .ac.uk/vch/middx/vol1/pp299-302, accessed May 31, 2020.

2. J. Strong, "The Thirteen Tribes of Long Island: The History of a Myth," *Hudson Valley Regional Review* #9, no. 2 (1992), http://www.hudsonrivervalley.org /review/pdfs/hvrr_9pt2_strong.pdf.

3. Walt Whitman, "Mannahatta" and "Starting from Paumanok," in *Leaves of Grass* (Boston: James R. Osgood and Co., 1881–82), https://whitmanarchive.org /published/LG/1881/index.html.

4. Walt Whitman, *Walt Whitman: The Correspondence*, vol. 1, *1842–1867*, edited by Edwin Haviland Miller (New York: New York University Press, 2007), 8–10.

5. Jonathan Ned Katz, *Love Stories: Sex between Men before Homosexuality* (Chicago: University of Chicago Press, 2003), 38.

6. Walt Whitman, "The Child's Champion," *The New World*, November 20, 1841, https://whitmanarchive.org/published/fiction/shortfiction/per.00319.html.

7. Katz, *Love Stories*, 39.

8. Ibid.

9. See George Painter, "The Sensibilities of Our Forefathers: The History of Sodomy Laws in the United States," https://www.glapn.org/sodomylaws /sensibilities/introduction.htm, accessed May 30, 2020.

10. Ibid. "The American colonies of England were created beginning more than four decades after the Elizabethan statute reestablishing 'buggery' as a temporal crime.

"English common and statute law were not necessarily in force in the colonies at the time of their establishment. Three of the original 13 colonies—Delaware, New Jersey, and New York—were not settled by the English and, of the ten that were, only in Maryland and, possibly, Virginia were English laws presumed to be in force from the beginning of colonization without local enactment. Death was the penalty of choice by statute and, in some cases, by usage."

See also Doron S Ben-Atar and Richard D Brown, *Taming Lust: Crimes against Nature in the Early Republic* (Philadelphia, PA: University of Pennsylvania Press, 2014): "To be sure, the old English penal code prescribed hanging for those convicted of sodomy or bestiality [. . .] [A]s recently as 1785 Pennsylvania had executed a man for 'buggery'; and though that state and several others had recently deleted sodomy from their slate of capital crimes, every New England state retained the death penalty for sodomy, which encompassed bestiality. Moreover Massachusetts and Connecticut were known to operate their gallows with some frequency, having executed some thirty-two people since the 1780s [. . .] In the 1790s these states executed fewer people than in the prior decade, but their penal scorecards remained deadly." Ben-Atar and Brown note that from the time of Saint Augustine and extending into the penal codes of the colonial period in America, the term "sodomy" included "its subcategory bestiality."

11. See Painter, "The Sensibilities of Our Forefathers."

12. As several courts have stated, "sodomy" is derived from the biblical reference to the destruction of the towns of Sodom and Gomorrah. Originally, sodomy referred only to two sexual acts: anal intercourse between two men or a man and a woman, or sexual intercourse between a human being and an animal of the opposite sex. "There were only four reported fellatio cases in the United States," writes George Painter, before 1900, and none involving cunnilingus. In two of those four fellatio cases, convictions were not permitted to stand because they did not conform to the historical definition of sodomy. In the other two, fellatio prosecutions were found allowable only because of broader statutory language. In each of these latter cases, the interpreting courts let it be known that, without the broader language, convictions could not be upheld. Ibid.

13. "Historical Report: Diversity of Sexual Orientation," Kinsey Institute, Indiana University, https://kinseyinstitute.org/research/ publications/historical-report -diversity-of-sexual-orientation.php.

14. Jennie Rothenberg Gritz, "But Were They Gay? The Mystery of Same-Sex Love in the 19th Century," *The Atlantic*, September 7, 2012, https://www .theatlantic.com/national/archive/2012/09/but-were-they-gay-the-mystery -of-same-sex-love-in-the-19th-century/262117/.

15. Katz, *Love Stories*, 5.

16. Ibid., 6.

17. Ibid., 10.

18. See George Chauncey, *Gay New York: Gender, Urban Culture, and the Making of the Gay Male World, 1890–1940* (New York: Basic Books, 1995).

19. "The heterosexual-homosexual binarism that governs our thinking about sexuality today, and that, as we shall see, was already becoming hegemonic in middle-class sexual ideology, did not yet constitute the common sense of working-class sexual ideology." Ibid., 48.

20. See, for instance, Sylvia Henneberg, "Neither Lesbian nor Straight: Multiple Eroticisms in Emily Dickinson's Love Poetry," *Emily Dickinson Journal* 4, no. 2 (Fall 1995): 1–19.

21. Lillian Faderman, "Emily Dickinson's Letters to Sue Gilbert," *Massachusetts Review* 18, no. 2 (Summer 1977): 197–225.

22. Daniel Engber, "Louisiana's Napoleon Complex: The French Influence on Pelican State Jurisprudence," *Slate*, September 12, 2005, https://slate.com /news-and-politics/2005/09/is-louisiana-under-napoleonic-law.html, accessed May 30, 2020.

23. Michael D. Sibalis, "Napoleonic Code," *GLBTQ Archive*, 2015, http://www .glbtqarchive.com/ssh/napoleonic_code_S.pdf.

24. Ibid.

25. Judith Kelleher Schafer, *Brothels, Depravity, and Abandoned Women: Illegal Sex in Antebellum New Orleans* (Baton Rouge: Louisiana State University Press, 2011), 52.

26. Elliott Ashkenazi, *The Business of Jews in Louisiana, 1840–1875* (Tuscaloosa: University of Alabama Press, 1988), 8.

27. Elizabeth Fussell, "Constructing New Orleans, Constructing Race: A Population History of New Orleans," in "Through the Eye of Katrina: The Past as Prologue?," special issue, *Journal of American History* 94, no. 3, (December 2007): 846–55.

28. Walt Whitman, "Song of Myself," section 5, *Leaves of Grass* (Brooklyn, NY: Rome Brothers, 1855). Cited in *Canadian Journal* 1 (November 1856): 541–51, https://whitmanarchive.org/criticism/reviews/lg1855/anc.00029.html.

29. Walt Whitman, Notebooks, "The HRC Manuscript," unpaginated, in "A Proto-version of the Poem That Would Eventually Become 'Song of Myself,'" Ed Folsom, ed., "Walt Whitman's Manuscript Drafts," University of Iowa, http://bailiwick.lib.uiowa.edu/whitman/specres04.html.

30. Walt Whitman, "The HRC Manuscript," notes for "Song of Myself," date uncertain, University of Iowa, http://bailiwick.lib.uiowa. edu/whitman /specres04.html; see also Ed Folsom, "Whitman's Manuscript Drafts of 'Song of Myself,'" *Leaves of Grass*, 1855, Library of Congress, http://bailiwick.lib .uiowa.edu/whitman/.

CHAPTER 3: 1855: *LEAVES OF GRASS*

1. Walt Whitman, "Poem of Walt Whitman, an American," in *Leaves of Grass* (Brooklyn, NY: Fowler & Wells, 1856), 5. https://whitmanarchive.org /published/LG/figures/ppp.00237.013.jpg.

2. See David Friedrich Strauss, *The Life of Jesus, Critically Examined*, Vol. 1, (Cambridge, UK: Cambridge University Press, 2010).

3. Walt Whitman, *Leaves of Grass: The Original 1855 Edition* (Mineola: Dover Publications, 2007), 22.

4. Ibid., 21, 39–40.

5. Ibid., 24.

6. Ibid., 39.

7. Ibid., 56–57.

8. Ibid.

9. Ibid.

10. For more on the invention of Whitman's and Wilde's personal iconography, see David M. Friedman, *Wilde in America: Oscar Wilde and the Invention of Modern Celebrity* (New York: W. W. Norton, 2014); and Michèle Mendelssohn, "Notes on Oscar Wilde's Transatlantic Gender Politics," *Journal of American Studies* 46, no. 1 (February 2012): 126. Michèle Mendelssohn's *Making Oscar Wilde* (Oxford: Oxford University Press, 2018) is a crucial resource regarding Wilde's persona in America, as well.

11. "Revising Himself: Walt Whitman and Leaves of Grass," Ralph Waldo Emerson (1803–1882) to Walt Whitman (1819–1892), no byline, Library of Congress, https://www.loc.gov/exhibits/whitman/.

CHAPTER 4: INVENTING THE MODERN CRIME OF OBSCENITY

1. Ian Hunter, David Saunders, and Dugald Williamson, *On Pornography: Literature, Sexuality, and Obscenity Law* (London: Macmillan Press, 1993), 87.

2. John Sutherland, *The Lives of the Novelists: A History of Fiction in 294 Lives* (London: Profile Books, 2011), 22.

3. Amanda Goodrich, "The Free Speech Battle That Forced Britain's Eighteenth-Century Radicals to Flee," *The Conversation*, December 18, 2015, https:// theconversation.com/the-free-speech-battle-that-forced-britains-18th-century -radicals-to-flee-50502.

4. Lynda Nead, *Victorian Babylon: People, Streets, and Images in Nineteenth-Century London* (New Haven, CT: Yale University Press, 2000), 195.

5. "What Was Chartism?" UK National Archives, https://nationalarchives.gov.uk /education/politics/g7/, accessed June 3, 2019.

6. Walter M. Kendrick, *The Secret Museum: Pornography in Modern Culture* (Berkeley: University of California Press, 1996), 71.

7. Herbert R. Lottman, *Flaubert: A Biography* (New York: Little, Brown, 1989), 136.

8. Ibid.

9. Ibid., 136–68.

10. Christine Haynes, "The Politics of Publishing during the Second Empire: The Trial of 'Madame Bovary' Revisited," *French Politics, Culture & Society* 23, no. 2 (Summer 2005): 1–27. See page 2: "It was not authorship but publication that was targeted by the law on the press."

11. See also Clara Tuite, "Not Guilty, Negative Capability, and the Trials of William Hone," in *Censorship and the Limits of the Literary: A Global View*, edited by Nicole Moore (London: Bloomsbury, 2015).

12. https://www.ldoceonline.com/dictionary/sedition.

13. Lottman, *Flaubert*, 141.

14. Ibid., 140.

15. The Obscene Publications Act of 1857, Hansard 1803–2005, UK Parliament, n.d., http://hansard.millbanksystems.com/acts/obscenepublications-act-1857, accessed January 22, 2013.

16. Kevin Birmingham, *The Most Dangerous Book: The Battle for James Joyce's Ulysses* (New York: Penguin Books, 2014), 168. See also Katherine Mullin, "Poison More Deadly Than Prussic Acid: Defining Obscenity after the 1857 Obscene Publications Act (1850–1885)," in *Prudes on the Prowl: Fiction and Obscenity in England, 1850 to the Present Day*, edited by David Bradshaw and Rachel Potter (Oxford: Oxford University Press, 2013), 11–29.

17. Katherine Mullin, ibid.

18. Ibid., 15–16.

CHAPTER 5: THE WAR AGAINST "FILTH"

1. See Edwin Chadwick, *Report on the Sanitary Conditions of the Labouring Population of Great Britain*, edited with an introduction by M. W. Flinn (Edinburgh: Edinburgh University Press, 1965; originally published in 1842).

2. Cynthia J. Davis, "Contagion as Metaphor," *American Literary History* 14, no. 4 (Winter 2002): 828.

3. Stephen Halliday, *The Great Filth: The War against Disease in Victorian England* (London: History Press, 2003), 134–35.

4. Peta Mitchell, *Contagious Metaphor* (London: Bloomsbury, 2013), 13.

5. Jenny Gilbert, "Dirt: The Filthy Reality of Everyday Life, The Wellcome Collection, London," *The Independent*, Sunday, April 3, 2011, https://www.independent.co.uk/arts-entertainment/art/reviews/dirtthe-filthy-reality-of-everyday-life-wellcome-collection-london-2260487.html.

6. Stephanie J. Snow, "Sutherland, Snow, and Water: The Transmission of Cholera in the Nineteenth Century," *International Journal of Epidemiology* 31, no. 5 (2002): 908–9.

7. Hansard 1803–2005, http://hansard.millbanksystems.com/acts/n#Nuisances %20Removal%20Act, accessed August 9, 2014.

8. W. N. Spong, "The Compulsory Vaccination Act," *Correspondence* 62, no. 1582 (December 24, 1853): 613.

9. Chris Godfey, "Section 28 Protesters Thirty Years On: 'We Were Arrested and Put in a Cell Up by Big Ben,'" *The Guardian*, March 27, 2018, https://www .theguardian.com/world/2018/mar/27/section-28-protesters-30-years-on-we -were-arrested-and-put-in-a-cell-up-by-big-ben; "Local Government Act 1988," http://www.legislation.gov.uk/ukpga/1988/9/section/28/enacted, accessed May 30, 2020.

CHAPTER 6: SODOMY AS PART OF THE 1857 REFORM OF DIVORCE LAW

1. Mary Lyndon Shanley, "'One Must Ride Behind': Married Women's Rights and the Divorce Act of 1857," *Victorian Studies* 25, no. 3 (Spring 1982): 357.

2. Prof. Stuart Anderson, correspondence with the author, April 21, 2020.

3. Shanley, "'One Must Ride Behind.'"

4. Mary Lyndon Shanley, *Feminism, Marriage, and the Law in Victorian England, 1850–1895* (Princeton: Princeton University Press, 1993), 9.

5. Barbara Leigh Smith Bodichon, *A Brief Summary in Plain Language of the Most Important Laws Concerning Women, Together with a Few Observations Thereon* (London: John Chapman, 1854), 3–11, in *Women, the Family, and Freedom: The Debate in Documents*, vol. 1, *1750–1880*, by Susan Groag Bell and Karen M. Offen (Palo Alto, CA: Stanford University Press, 1983), 300–305.

6. Ibid.

7. Shanley, *Feminism, Marriage, and the Law*, 22.

8. Ibid., 29.

9. See Mary Beth Combs, "'A Measure of Legal Independence': The 1870 Married Women's Property Act and the Portfolio Allocations of British Wives," *Journal of Economic History* 65, no. 4 (2005): 1028; Elizabeth M. Craik discusses the relationship of marriage to property law for Victorian women in *Marriage and Property* (Aberdeen, Scotland: Aberdeen University Press, 1984), 159–89.

10. Henry Miller, "100 Years Since British Women Got the Vote, Here's the Story of How It Happened," World Economic Forum, February 8, 2018, https:// www.weforum.org/agenda/2018/02/how-17-000-petitions-helped-deliver -votes-for-women.

11. See Combs, "'A Measure of Legal Independence,'" 1028.

12. See Craik, *Marriage and Property*, 159–89.

13. See Shanley, "'One Must Ride Behind,'" 350–59.

14. Shanley, *Feminism, Marriage, and the Law*, 33.

15. Shanley, "'One Must Ride Behind,'" 356.

16. Shanley, *Feminism, Marriage, and the Law*, 24.
17. Ibid.
18. Ibid., 25.
19. Ibid., 37.
20. Caroline Norton, *A Letter to the Queen on Lord Chancellor Cranworth's Marriage and Divorce Bill* (London: Longman, Brown Green and Longmans, 1855), https://digital.library.upenn.edu/women/norton/alttq/alttq.html.
21. Ibid., 39.
22. Ibid., 35.
23. Ibid., 16.
24. Ibid., 40.
25. Ibid., 41.
26. Kelly Hager, "Chipping Away at Coverture: The Matrimonial Causes Act of 1857," *Branch Collective*, November 2012, http://www.branchcollective.org/?ps_articles=kelly-hager-chipping-away-at-coverture-the-matrimonial-causes-act-of-1857.
27. Shanley, *Feminism, Marriage, and the Law*, 47–48.
28. Hansard, "Divorce and Matrimonial Causes Bill—Committee," HL Deb, May 25, 1857, https://api.parliament.uk/historic-hansard/lords/1857/may/25/divorce-and-matrimonial-causes-bill.
29. Joan Perkin, *Women and Marriage in Nineteenth-Century England* (London: Routledge, 2002), 303.
30. Cited in Johnson, "Buggery and Parliament, 1533–2017," 332.
31. Hansard; Henry Kha and Warren Swain, "The Enactment of the Matrimonial Causes Act 1857: The Campbell Commission and the Parliamentary Debates," *Journal of Legal History* 37, no. 3 (2016): 303–30, doi: 10.1080/01440365.2016.1235796.
32. Shanley, *Feminism, Marriage, and the Law*, 28.
33. Paul Johnson discusses the Matrimonial Causes Act in relation to sodomy in his article "Buggery and Parliament, 1533–2017."
34. Leviticus 18:22, *King James Bible*, https://www.biblegateway.com/passage/?search=Leviticus+18%3A22&version=KJV.
35. The Hon. Michael Kirby, "The Sodomy Offense: England's Least Lovely Criminal Export?" *Journal of Commonwealth Criminal Law*, inaugural issue (2011): 22–23.
36. Alok Gupta, *This Alien Legacy: The Origins of "Sodomy" Laws in British Colonialism*, (New York: Human Rights Watch, December 2008), http://www.hrw.org/node/77014/section/2. The British historian Prof. H. G. Cocks disagrees with this interpretation and argues that Fleta and Britton were unlikely to have been literal descriptions of the law. However, other scholars do believe it reflected medieval law, as he notes in *Visions of Sodom*:

"Both [Fleta and Britton] included sodomy in a catalogue of other crimes, and did not single it out for specific analysis. Neither source described the actual state of the law at the time of writing. Fleta (supposedly written by a lawyer imprisoned in the Fleet in the late thirteenth century) says that 'Those who have dealings with Jews or Jewesses, those who commit bestiality, and sodomists, are to be buried alive.' Fleta, *Seu Commentarius Juris Anglicani* (London: Fletcher Gyles, 1735), 37.3, 84. Britton may have been written by the judge Henry de Bracton (d. 1268), and groups sodomites with sorcerers, heretics, renegades and those burning another's corn. See Baker, *Introduction to English Legal History*, 183–85; Britton, 2 vols., ed. F. M. Nichols (Oxford: Oxford University Press, 1865) 1:41–42. Bailey suggests that Fleta's opinion that the punishment of sodomy was burial alive was taken from Tacitus's *Germania*. Bailey, *Homosexuality*, 145–51; Smith, *Homosexual Desire*, 42–44" (H. G. Cocks, *Visions of Sodom*, ch. 4, note 1, p. 268). For more on the view that Fleta and Britton did reflect medieval law, Cocks refers readers to Bruce R. Smith, *Homosexual Desire in Shakespeare's England: A Cultural Poetics* (Chicago: University of Chicago Press, 1991): 42.

37. Dr. John Boswell, *Christianity, Social Tolerance, and Homosexuality: Gay People in Western Europe from the Beginning of the Christian Era to the Fourteenth Century* (Chicago: University of Chicago Press, 2005), 333–34.

38. Ibid., xxiv.

39. H. G. Cocks, *Nameless Offences*, 21.

40. Upchurch, *Before Wilde*, 144.

41. For more on this issue, see also Johnson, "Buggery and Parliament 1533–2017," 330.

42. H. G. Cocks, email communication with the author, April 5, 2020.

43. Ibid.

44. "The Recorder's Report," *Morning Chronicle*, November 26, 1828.

45. "Compound Microscope," Permanent exhibit of microscopes, Museo Galileo, Florence, Italy. (https://www.museogalileo.it/it/)

46. Permanent exhibit of microscopes, Museo Galileo, Florence, Italy. (https://www.museogalileo.it/it/)

47. H. G. Cocks in *Nameless Offences* identified this case as being the last execution for sodomy in England, a conclusion that has been widely reproduced subsequently (Cocks, *Nameless Offences*, 38). See, for instance, this later table: Capital Punishment U.K., 1800–1827, Public Executions, http://www.capitalpunishmentuk.org/1800.html.

48. *Rex v. Reekspear* (9 Geo. IV c. 31), enacted June 27, 1828, 1 Mood. C. C. 342, 183. Cited in *Nineteenth-Century Writings on Homosexuality: A Sourcebook*, edited by Chris White (London: Routledge, 1999), 35.

49. This distinction between British and French sodomy penalties would be a central theme in Symonds's call to abolish the status of sodomy as a crime in *A Problem in Modern Ethics* (1891).

50. "Labour and the Poor," *Morning Chronicle*, May 2, 1850.

51. "Police, Prisons and Penal Reform," https://www.parliament.uk/about /living-heritage/transformingsociety/laworder/policeprisons/overview /metropolitanpolice/.

52. Conversation with Baroness Helena Kennedy, Mansfield College, June 19, 2016.

53. "General Intelligence," *Hull Packet and East Riding Times*, February 13, 1857.

54. Penal Servitude Act 1857 (20 and 21 Vict), http://www.legislation.gov.uk /ukpga/Vict/20-21/3, accessed June 12, 2020.

55. Penal Servitude Act 1857 (20 and 21 Vict. c. 3), legislation.gov.uk, National Archives, n.d., accessed February 5, 2013.

56. Ibid; Clare Anderson, "Transnational Histories of Penal Transportation: Punishment, Labour and Governance in the British Imperial World, 1788–1939," *Australian Historical Studies*, 47, no. 3, (August 31, 2016), https:// doi.org/10.1080/1031461X.2016.1203962.

57. "Punishments at the Old Bailey, Late 17th Century to the Early 20th Century," Proceedings of the Old Bailey, 1674 to 1913, http://www.oldbaileyonline.org /static/Punishment.jsp, accessed June 23, 2011.

58. "The Trial of Thomas Burns," Proceedings of the Old Bailey, 1674–1913, https://www.oldbaileyonline.org/browse.jsp?id=def1-862-18570817&div =t18570817-862#highlight, accessed June 23, 2011.

59. "Naval and Military Intelligence," *Reynold's Newspaper*, July 12, 1857, accessed October 15, 2013.

60. H. G. Cocks, *Nameless Offences*, 28.

61. See Upchurch, *Before Wilde*, 93.

62. Ibid.

63. H. G. Cocks, *Nameless Offences*, 23.

64. H. G. Cocks, email communication with the author, April 5, 2020. Charles Upchurch also discusses the class politics of arrest and extortion at length: *Before Wilde*, 93–96.

65. Graham Robb, *Strangers*, 23.

66. See the 1885 Labouchere Amendment and commentary at https://www .parliament.uk/about/living-heritage/transformingsociety/private-lives /relationships/collections1/sexual-offences-act-1967/1885 -labouchere-amendment/.

67. Randolph Trumbach, author of *Sex and the Gender Revolution*, vol. 1, *Heterosexuality and the Third Gender in Enlightenment London*, Chicago Series on Sexuality, History and Society (Chicago: University of Chicago Press, 1998), and Jeffery Weeks, author of *Coming Out: Homosexual Politics in Britain from the Nineteenth Century to the Present* (London: Quartet Books, 1977; 2nd revised edition, with new chapter and bibliography, 1990), are recognized by queer history scholars as having done some of the earliest pioneering work on this issue.

CHAPTER 7: FORMATIVE SCANDALS

1. Dictionary of Victorian Photography, http://www.19thcenturyphotos.com /Dr-Vaughan-122446.htm.

2. "Crimes Tried at the Old Bailey: Assault with Sodomitical Intent," https:// www.oldbaileyonline.org/static/Crimes.jsp#assaultwithsodomiticalintent.

3. "The fact that men who had sex with other men were placed in the same category as paedophiles, zoophiles and rapists can be interpreted as a sign of institutional homophobia." Robb, *Strangers*, 21.

4. "The Trial of Thomas John Davey and William Willman," Proceedings of the Old Bailey, 1674–1913, https://www.oldbaileyonline.org/browse.jsp?id =t18580104-197-offence-1&div=t18580104-197#, accessed August 8, 2013.

5. "The Trial of James Stevens," Proceedings of the Old Bailey, 1674–1913, http:// www.oldbaileyonline.org/browse.jsp?id=def1-770-18580816&div=t18580816 -770&terms=attempt#highlight, reference number t18580816-770, accessed August 8, 2013.

6. "The Trial of Daniel Patching," Proceedings of the Old Bailey, 1674–1913, http://www.oldbaileyonline.org/browse.jsp?id=def1-935-18581025&div =t18581025-935&terms=unlawfullymeeting#highlight, reference number t18581025-935, accessed August 7, 2013.

7. Plato, "Phaedrus," translated by Benjamin Jowett, http://www.gutenberg.org /ebooks/1636http://classics.mit.edu/Plato/phaedrus.html.

8. Phyllis Grosskurth, *The Woeful Victorian: A Biography of John Addington Symonds* (New York: Holt, Rinehart and Winston, 1964), 34.

9. See Linda Dowling, *Hellenism and Homosexuality in Victorian Oxford* (Ithaca, NY: Cornell University Press, 1995); and Stefano-Maria Evangelista, "Pater, 'Winckelmann,' and the Aesthetic Life," in *British Aestheticism and Ancient Greece: Hellenism, Reception, Gods in Exile* (London: Palgrave Macmillan, 2009), 23–54.

10. Grosskurth, *Woeful Victorian*, 58.

11. "The Trial of Thomas Silver," Proceedings of the Old Bailey, 1674–1913, https://www.oldbaileyonline.org/browse.jsp?id=t18591128-47-offence -1&div=t18591128-47#highlight, reference number t18591128-47, accessed July 16, 2020.

12. "The Trial of Richard Roche," Proceedings of the Old Bailey, 1674–1913, https://www.oldbaileyonline.org/browse.jsp?id=t18700228-300-offence -1&div=t18700228-300#highlight, reference number t18700228-300.

13. "The Trial of William Mepham," Proceedings of the Old Bailey, 1674–1913, http://www.oldbaileyonline.org/browse.jsp?id=def1-275-18600227 &div=t18600227-275&terms=attempt#highlight, reference number t18600227-275, accessed August 10, 2013.

14. "The Trial of William Dunlop," Proceedings of the Old Bailey, 1674–1913, http://www.oldbaileyonline.org/browse.jsp?id=def1-355-18600402&div

=t18600402-355&terms=attempt#highlight, reference number t18600402-355, accessed August 12, 2013.

15. "The Trial of John Spencer," Proceedings of the Old Bailey, 1674–1913, https://www.oldbaileyonline.org/browse.jsp?id=t18600709-612-offence -1&div=t18600709-612#highlight, reference number t18600709-612.

CHAPTER 8: CALAMUS: "PATHS UNTRODDEN"

1. Sara Oliver Gordus, "Walt Whitman's Watering Hole: Pfaff's Cellar, NYC," therumpus.net, July 2, 2010, https://therumpus.net/2010/07/walt-whitman's -watering-hole-pfaff's-cellar-nyc.

2. Gregory Eiselein, "'Leaves of Grass,' 1860 Edition," in *Walt Whitman: An Encyclopedia*, edited by J. R. LeMaster and Donald D. Kummings (New York: Garland Publishing, 1998), reproduced by permission in Walt Whitman Archives, https://whitmanarchive.org/criticism/current/encyclopedia/entry_23.html.

3. Walt Whitman, "Enfans d'Adam," in *Leaves of Grass* (Boston: Thayer and Eldridge, 1860–61), 287, https://whitmanarchive.org/published/LG/1860 /clusters/57.

4. James E. Miller, Jr., "Children of Adam," [1860], https://whitmanarchive.org /criticism/current/encyclopedia/entry_11.html.

5. Walt Whitman, "Calamus," in *Leaves of Grass* (Boston: Thayer and Eldridge, 1860–61), 341–42, https://whitmanarchive.org/published/LG/1860/clusters/76.

6. Ibid.

7. Kenneth M. Price and Ed Folsom, "Life and Letters: Biography," https:// whitmanarchive.org/biography/walt_whitman/index.html.

8. Walt Whitman, *Leaves of Grass* (Boston: Thayer and Eldridge, 1860–61), 292–93, https://whitmanarchive.org/published/LG/1860/poems/60.

9. Ibid., 288.

10. Ibid., 359–60.

11. Ibid.

12. Ibid., 364–65.

13. Ibid., 289–91, https://whitmanarchive.org/published/LG/1856/poems/26.

14. Customs Consolidation Act of 1853, https://api.parliament.uk/historic -hansard/acts/customs-consolidation-act-1853.

15. Unsigned review, "Walt Whitman and His Critics," *Leader and Saturday Analyst*, June 30, 1860, 614–15, https://whitmanarchive.org/archive1/works /leaves/1860/reviews/leader.html.

16. "Review of Leaves of Grass (1855)," *The Critic* 15 (April 1, 1856): 170–71, https://whitmanarchive.org/criticism/reviews/lg1855/anc.00024.html.

17. Ibid.

18. Walt Whitman, *Leaves of Grass* (Brooklyn, NY: 1855), 79–80, https:// whitmanarchive.org/published/LG/1855/whole.html.

19. "Leaves of Grass," *The Spectator*, July 1860, 669–70.
20. "Leaves of Grass," *Literary Gazette* 106 (July 1860): 798–99.
21. "Walt Whitman," *London Review and Weekly Journal of Politics, Society, Literature, and Art*, June 8, 1867, 641–43.
22. Ibid.
23. Ibid.
24. Ibid.
25. "Offences Against the Person Act 1861," 1861 c. 100 (Regnal. 24_and_25 _Vict), https://www.legislation.gov.uk/ukpga/Vict/24-25/100/contents.
26. "Offences Against the Person Act 1861," 1861 Chapter 100 24 and 25 Vict., https://srhr.org/abortion-policies/documents/countries/07-United-Kingdom -Offences-against-the-Person-Act-1861.pdf.
27. Offences Against the Person Act, Sections 61–63, http://www.legislation.gov .uk/ukpga/Vict/24-25/100/enacted.
28. Gupta, *This Alien Legacy*, 20.
29. "The Trial of Joseph Mead," Proceedings of the Old Bailey, 1674–1913, http:// www.oldbaileyonline.org/browse.jsp?id=def1-673-18610819&div=t18610819 -673&terms=attempt#highlight, reference number t18610819-673, accessed August 13, 2013.
30. "The Trial of John Griffiths," Proceedings of the Old Bailey, 1674–1913, https://www.oldbaileyonline.org/browse.jsp?id=def1-54-18611125&div =t18611125-54#highlight, accessed August 13, 2013.
31. Wathen Mark Wilks Call, "Review of *Leaves of Grass* (1860–61)," *Westminster Review*, October 1, 1860, 590.
32. Catalog entry, *Leaves of Grass*, 1855 Horsell, Fine Books and Manuscripts Auction, June 14, 2016, http://www.sothebys.com/fr/auctions/ecatalogue /2015/fine-books-and-manuscripts-n09516/lot.291.html.

CHAPTER 9: SYMONDS'S SECOND SCANDAL

1. Grosskurth, *Woeful Victorian*, 58.
2. Sean Brady, *Masculinity and Male Homosexuality in Britain, 1861–1913* (London: Palgrave Macmillan, 2005), 172.

CHAPTER 10: "GOBLIN MARKET": ATTRACTION AND AVERSION

1. William Michael Rossetti, *The Germ: Thoughts towards Nature in Poetry, Literature, and Art*, British Library, https://www.bl.uk/collection-items /pre-raphaelite-journal-the-germ.
2. Christina Rossetti et al., *The Rossetti-Macmillan Letters*, edited by Lona Mosk Packer (Berkeley: University of California Press, 1963), 31–32, 37, 38, 39, 40–41, 44.

3. Jan Marsh's *Christina Rossetti: A Writer's Life* (New York: Penguin, 1994) documents Christina Rossetti's reading of these publications. See pages 108, 149, 248, 282, and 284.

4. Ibid., 51.

5. Deborah Ann Thompson, "Anorexia as a Lived Trope: Christina Rossetti's 'Goblin Market,'" in "Diet and Discourse: Eating, Drinking, and Literature" special issue, *Mosaic: An Interdisciplinary Critical Journal* 24, no. 3/4 (Summer/Fall 1991): 89–106.

6. Whitman, *Leaves of Grass* (Brooklyn, NY: 1855), 47.

7. *Christina Rossetti: The Complete Poems*, edited by R. W. Crump (London: Penguin, 2001), 567.

8. Ibid., 563.

9. See Lucinda Hawksley, *Lizzie Siddal: The Tragedy of a Victorian Supermodel* (London: Andre Deutsch Ltd., 2017); Lucinda Hawksley "The Tragedy of Art's Greatest Supermodel," BBC, January 7, 2020, https://www.bbc.com/culture/article/20200103-the-tragedy-of-arts-greatest-supermodel.

10. Jan Marsh, "Did Rossetti Really Need to Exhume His Wife?" *Times Literary Supplement*, February 15, 2012, https://www.the-tls.co.uk/articles/public/did-rossetti-really-need-to-exhume-his-wife/.

11. See Christina Rossetti, *Goblin Market and Other Poems* (London: Macmillan, 1862), https://catalog.hathitrust.org/Record/100613555.

12. David Michael Reid Bentley, "The Meretricious and Meritorious in Goblin Market: A Conjecture and an Analysis," in *The Achievement of Christina Rossetti*, edited by David A. Kent (Ithaca, NY: Cornell University Press, 1987) 57–81; and Dianne D'Amico, *Christina Rossetti: Faith, Gender, and Time* (Baton Rouge: Louisiana State University Press, 1999), 108.

13. Rossetti, *Goblin Market and Other Poems*, 1–32, https://catalog.hathitrust.org/Record/100613555.

14. Ibid.

15. Ibid.

16. Ibid.

17. Ibid.

18. Judith Walkowitz, *Prostitution and Victorian Society: Women, Class, and the State* (Cambridge, UK: Cambridge University Press, 1982); see also Michael Mason, *The Making of Victorian Sexuality* (Oxford: Oxford University Press, 1994), 13–31.

19. Lona Mosk Parker, ed., *The Rossetti-Macmillan Letters* (Berkeley: University of California Press, 1963), 34–48.

20. Ibid., 48.

21. See Dante Gabriel Rossetti's 1874 painting *Proserpine*, now in the Tate Gallery in London, for an equally overtly erotic pomegranate: https://www.tate.org.uk/art/artworks/rossettiproserpine-n05064.

CHAPTER 11: THE STATE SEIZES THE FEMALE BODY

1. John Frith, "Syphilis—Its Early History and Treatment until Penicillin and the Debate on Its Origins," *History* 20, no. 4 (November 2012), https://jmvh.org /article/syphilis-its-early-history-and-treatment-until-penicillin-and-the -debate-on-its-origins/.

2. Walkowitz, *Prostitution and Victorian Society*, 16, 22; and Martha Vicinus, *Suffer and Be Still: Women in the Victorian Age* (London: Methuen, 1980), 81.

3. Philippa Levine, "Venereal Disease, Prostitution, and the Politics of Empire: The Case of British India," *Journal of the History of Sexuality* 4, no. 4 (1994): 579.

4. Margaret Hamilton, "Opposition to the Contagious Diseases Acts, 1864–1886," *Albion* 10, no. 1 (July 11, 2014), https://doi.org/10.2307/4048453.

5. Walkowitz, *Prostitution and Victorian Society*, 69.

6. Dr. Anne R. Hanley, *Medicine, Knowledge and Venereal Diseases in England, 1886–1916* (London: Palgrave Macmillan, 2017), 107–46.

7. Hamilton, "Opposition to the Contagious Diseases Acts."

8. Vicinus, *Suffer and Be Still*, 94–95.

9. Hamilton, "Opposition to the Contagious Diseases Acts."

10. Dr. Anne R. Hanley, interview, New College, Oxford, June 2016.

11. Hanley, *Medicine, Knowledge, and Venereal Diseases in England, 1886–1916*, 147–87.

12. Michel Foucault, *The History of Sexuality*, vol. 1, *An Introduction* (New York: Pantheon Books, 1978), 18.

CHAPTER 12: "I WILL GO WITH HIM I LOVE"

1. Whitman, *The Correspondence*, vol. 1, *1842–1867*, 12.

2. Ibid.

3. Ibid., 13.

4. "The Love of Comrades" in "My Dear Boy: Gay Love Letters through the Centuries," edited by Rictor Norton 1997–98, http://rictornorton.co.uk /whitman2.htm, accessed March 20, 2019 and June 12, 2020.

5. Whitman, *The Correspondence*, vol. 1, *1842–1867*, 14.

6. J. A. Symonds, *The Memoirs of John Addington Symonds*, edited by Phyllis Grosskurth (London: Hutchinson, 1984), 253.

7. Ibid., 212.

8. Ibid., 214–15.

9. Ibid.

10. Ibid., 215.

11. Ibid., 256.

12. *The Memoirs of John Addington Symonds: A Critical Edition*, edited by Amber K. Regis (London: Palgrave Macmillan, 2017). This is the source I use for all quotes from the memoirs from here forward.

13. Ibid., 217.

14. "Karl Ulrichs' Sexual Classification Scheme," unsigned article, LGBTdata.com, http://www.lgbtdata.com/karl-ulrichssexual-orientation-classification -scheme.html, accessed March 3, 2019 and June 12, 2020.

15. "A Darkness! you are gentler than my lover antiquity." Emily Rutherford, "Arthur Sidgwick's Greek Prose Composition: Gender, Affect, and Sociability in the Late-Victorian University," *Journal of British Studies* 56, no. 1 (January 2017), 91–116, https://doi.org/10.1017/jbr.2016.116.

16. Symonds, *Memoirs*, 238.

17. Ibid., 257.

18. Ibid., 259.

19. Ibid.

20. Ibid., 260–61.

21. Ibid., 261.

22. Ibid., 275.

23. Ibid., 277.

24. Whitman, *Leaves of Grass* (Brooklyn, NY: 1860), 354–55.

25. Norton, "Gay History & Literature: Essays by Rictor Norton."

26. Algernon Charles Swinburne, *Poems and Ballads and Atalanta in Calydon*, edited by Morse Peckham (New York: Bobbs Merrill, 1970), 82, 183. Clive Simmonds, "Publishing Swinburne: The Poet, His Publishers and Critics" (PhD thesis, University of Reading, UK, 2013), 34–45.

27. Algernon Charles Swinburne, "Anactoria," in *Swinburne's Poems*, vol. 1, *Poems and Ballads* (London: Chatto & Windus, 1904), 57, as reproduced by the Swinburne Archive at the University of Indiana, http://swinburnearchive .indiana.edu/swinburne/view#docId=swinburne/acs0000001-01-i010.xml ;query=;brand=swinburne.

28. Clyde Kenneth Hyder, *Swinburne: The Critical Heritage* (New York: Barnes and Noble, 1970), xiv. The review was originally published on April 8, 1865.

29. "Swinburne's Folly," *Pall Mall Gazette*, August 20, 1865.

30. *The Letters of Algernon Charles Swinburne*, vol. 1, edited by Edmund Gosse and Thomas James Wise (New York: John Lane Company, 1919), 49.

31. *Letters of Swinburne*, vol. 1, 42, 44.

32. *Algernon Charles Swinburne: Major Poems and Selected Prose*, edited by Jerome J. McGann and Charles L. Sligh (New Haven, CT: Yale University Press, 2004), xvii.

33. *The Uncollected Letters of Algernon Charles Swinburne*, vol. 1, edited by Terry L. Meyers (London: Pickering & Chatto, 2004), 265.

34. Algernon Charles Swinburne, *Poems and Ballads* (London: J. C. Hotten, 1866), 122.

35. See Richard Dellamora, *Masculine Desire: The Sexual Politics of Victorian Aestheticism* (Chapel Hill: University of North Carolina Press, 1990).

36. "The Trial of Samuel Ketch," Proceedings of the Old Bailey, 1674–1913, https://www.oldbaileyonline.org/browse.jsp?id=t18660813-714-offence -1&div=t18660813-714#highlight, accessed May 30, 2020.

CHAPTER 13: *REGINA V. HICKLIN*: "TO DEPRAVE AND CORRUPT"

1. *Regina v. Hicklin*, The Queen, on the Prosecution of Henry Scott; Appellant v. Benjamin Hicklin and Another, L.R. 3 Q.B. 360 (1868). Court of the Queen's Bench (20 and 21 Vict. c. 83, s. 1). Cited in J. E. Hall Williams, "Obscenity in Modern English Law," in *Law and Contemporary Problems* (Durham, UK: no publisher cited, 1955), http://scholarship.law.duke.edu/cgi/viewcontent.cgi ?article=2657&context=lcp632, accessed September 2, 2014.

2. Ibid., 62–66.

3. Ibid., 62–63.

4. Ben Yagoda, "Trial and Eros," *American Scholar* 79, no. 4 (2010): 93.

5. Colin Manchester, "A History of the Crime of Obscene Libel," *Journal of Legal History* 12, no. 1 (1991): 47–48, doi: 10.1080/01440369108531027.

6. Wayne Bartee and Alice Bartee, *Litigating Morality: America in Legal Thought and Its English Roots* (New York: Praeger, 1992), 67.

7. Manchester, "History of the Crime of Obscene Libel," 36–57.

8. Symonds, *Memoirs*, 329.

9. Ibid., 281; and Richard Giles, "Symonds' Annotations. In the 1860 Leaves of Grass," supplement, *Walt Whitman Review* (1980): 21–36.

10. *The Letters of John Addington Symonds*, vol. 1, edited by Herbert M. Schueller and Robert L. Peters (Detroit: Wayne State University Press, 1968), 701.

11. Symonds, *Memoirs*, 291.

12. Ibid., 298.

13. Ibid., 316.

14. Ibid., 318.

15. Ibid., 335.

16. Ibid., 341.

17. Symonds, *Letters*, vol. 1, 706.

18. "Walt Whitman," *London Review and Weekly Journal of Politics, Society, and Art*, June 8, 1867, http://www.whitmanarchive.org/criticism/reviews/leaves1867 /anc.00192.html, accessed August 10, 2012.

19. Walt Whitman, *Selected Letters of Walt Whitman*, edited by Edwin Haviland Miller (Iowa City: University of Iowa Press, 1990), 134.

20. Horace Traubel, *With Walt Whitman in Camden* (New York: Mitchell Kinnerley, 1914), 163, https://archive.org/details/withwaltwhitman00traugoog/page/n7.

21. William Michael Rossetti, *Some Reminiscences of William Michael Rossetti*, vol. 2 (New York: Charles Scribner's Sons, 1906), 398–408.

22. James E. Miller, "Sex and Sexuality," in *Walt Whitman: An Encyclopedia*, http://www.whitmanarchive.org/criticism/current/encyclopedia/entry_49.html, accessed November 12, 2013.

23. J. C. Hotten, "Poems by Walt Whitman, Selected and Edited by William Michael Rossetti," *The Examiner*, April 18, 1868.

24. William Michael Rossetti, *Some Reminiscences*, Cambridge Library Collection, Literary Studies (Cambridge, UK: Cambridge University Press, 2013), 398–408, doi: 10.1017/CBO9781139583671.007.

25. [Review of *Poems by Walt Whitman*] *The New Eclectic*, 1868, 371–75, https://whitmanarchive.org/criticism/reviews/poems/anc.00194.html.

26. Whitman, *The Correspondence*, vol. 2, *1868–1875*, 133.

27. Whitman, *The Correspondence*, vol. 1, *1842–1867*, 332–33.

28. "Pictures & Sound: Gallery of Images," http://whitmanarchive.org/multimedia/image003.html?sort=year&order=ascending&page=1, accessed August 16, 2012.

29. "The Trial of Stephen Alexander," Proceedings of the Old Bailey, 1674–1913, http://www.oldbaileyonline.org/browse.jsp?id=t18680608-524-offence-1&div=t18680608-524&terms=guilty#highlight, reference number t18680608-524, accessed March 12, 2013.

30. Symonds, *Memoirs*.

31. Ibid., 347–51.

32. "Phallus Impudicus," in Symonds, *Memoirs*, 347–51.

33. Symonds, *Memoirs*, 365.

34. Symonds, *Letters*, vol. 2, 836.

CHAPTER 14: DANGEROUS POEMS

1. Josephine Butler, in Vicinus, *Suffer and Be Still*, 95–96.

2. Margaret Hamilton, "Opposition to the Contagious Diseases Acts, 1864–1886," *Albion: A Quarterly Journal Concerned with British Studies* 10, no. 1 (Spring 1978): 14–27.

3. Symonds, *Letters*, vol. 2, 72.

4. Ibid., 72–73.

5. Ibid., 55.

6. Ibid., 56.

7. Ibid.

8. Ibid., 63.

9. John Addington Symonds to Henry Graham Dakyns, Saturday, October 2, 1869, ibid., 83–84.

10. Ibid., 102–4.

11. Ibid.

12. Ibid., 117.

13. Ibid., 119.

14. Oliver S. Buckton, *Secret Selves: Confession and Same-Sex Desire in Victorian Autobiography* (Chapel Hill: University of North Carolina Press, 1998), 97–98.

15. Symonds, *Letters*, vol. 2, 133.

16. Ibid., 143.

17. Ibid., 147.

18. Ibid., 148.

CHAPTER 15: SIX SIGNS: "THE ANUS AND THE STATE"

1. Auguste Ambroise Tardieu, *Étude Medico-Legale sur les Attentats aux Moeurs*, 3rd ed. (Paris: J. B. Bailliere, 1859), cited in Scott Long, "When Doctors Torture: The Anus and the State in Egypt and Beyond," *Health and Human Rights* 7, no. 2 (2004): 142–43, https://www.researchgate.net/publication/239597185 _When_Doctors_Torture_The_Anus_and_the_State_in_Egypt_and_Beyond.

2. Auguste Ambroise Tardieu, *Étude Medico-Legale sur les Attentats aux Moeurs*, 3rd ed. (Paris: J. B. Bailliere, 1859), 145–47, 153.

3. Long, "When Doctors Torture."

4. Alfred Swaine Taylor, *A Manual of Medical Jurisprudence* (Philadelphia: Hency C. Lea, 1866), 597.

5. Ibid., 558.

6. Ibid., 626.

7. Long, "When Doctors Torture," 114.

8. See Katherine Denise Watson, *Forensic Medicine in Western Society: A History* (London: Routledge, 2011).

9. Long, "When Doctors Torture," 114.

10. Ivan Crozier, "'All the Appearances Were Perfectly Natural': The Anus of the Sodomite in Nineteenth-Century Medical Discourse," in *Body Parts: Critical Explorations in Corporality*, edited by Christopher E. Forth and Ivan Crozier (Lanham, MD: Lexington Books, 2005), 65–84. H. G. Cocks, in contrast to the conclusions of Ivan Crozier, believes that such examinations were rare: "These are all difficult areas, and in the absence of detailed documentation we have to proceed carefully basing things on what we can know.

"On the question of medical testimony, it may have been used in some trials, for instance that of Boulton and Park and one or two others. And medical jurists like Alfred Swaine Taylor did discuss certain cases and the work of continental writers. However, in most run of the mill cases medical testimony was not used to the best of my recollection. As far as I recall most cases turned on the evidence of the people involved. It is difficult to tell, as in press reports and other sources this evidence is almost always passed over as too indecent to be described. However, when it is described the 'passive' partner usually simply talked about having been penetrated and then said something like 'I felt myself wet behind' or something like that. The standards of criminal evidence were very different and most trials in the early part of the century (it was only until 1828 that emission in the body had to be proved, R v Reekspear notwithstanding) were short and did not feature expert evidence which one of the protagonists would have had to pay for. These trials were more of a dialogue between accused and defendant who each gave their testimony. In the later part of the century it still seems to have been the case that medical evidence was used quite rarely in trials for 'unnatural offences.'" Email communication with the author, July 2019.

Graham Robb describes "examination of pederasts" via observation of the anus and introduction of the doctor's finger "into the orifice," as late as 1893. Robb, *Strangers*, 56.

11. Long, "When Doctors Torture," 114.
12. Edward Bristow, *Vice and Vigilance: Purity Movements in Britain since 1700* (New York: Gill and Macmillan, 1977), 75–79.
13. British Periodicals (ProQuest), https://onlinelibrary.london.ac.uk/resources /databases/british-periodicals-proquest.
14. Nikolai Endres, "Kertbeny, Károly Mária (1824–1882)," glbtq archive, 2015, http://www.glbtqarchive.com/ssh/kertbeny_km_S.pdf.
15. The Proceedings of the Old Bailey Online, 1674–1913, accessed January 2012–November 2015.
16. "The Trial of Richard Farmer and Alfred Biggs," Proceedings of the Old Bailey, 1674–1913, https://www.oldbaileyonline.org/browse.jsp?id=t18700110-168 -offence-1&div=t18700110-168#highlight, accessed July 16, 2020.
17. "The Trial of Alexander Campbell and Arthur Fisk," Proceedings of the Old Bailey, 1674–1913, https://www.oldbaileyonline.org/browse.jsp?id=t18700606 -524&div=t18700606-524&terms=Unnatural_Offence_Campbell#highlight, accessed March 17, 2013.
18. "The Trial of Isaac Church," Proceedings of the Old Bailey, 1674–1913, https://www.oldbaileyonline.org/browse.jsp?id=t18700711-597-offence -1&div=t18700711-597#highlight, accessed March 17, 2013.
19. Leviticus 18:22, King James Version, https://www.biblegateway.com/passage /?search=Leviticus+18%3A22&version=KJV.
20. Deuteronomy 22:21, King James Version: "Then they shall bring out the damsel to the door of her father's house, and the men of her city shall stone her with stones that she die." http://biblehub.com/deuteronomy/22-21.htm.
21. Robb, *Strangers*, 21.

CHAPTER 16: CRIMINALIZING "EFFEMINACY": THE ARRESTS OF FANNY AND STELLA

1. Robb, *Strangers*, 99.
2. Neil McKenna, *Fanny and Stella: The Young Men Who Shocked Victorian England* (London: Faber and Faber, 2013), 1–125 see chapter 1, "Leading Ladies."

3. C. Willett Cunningham, *English Women's Clothing in the Nineteenth Century* (New York: Dover Publications, 1990), 256.

4. Ibid.

5. Robb, *Strangers*, figure 2.

6. "My Dear Boy: Gay Love Letters through the Centuries," edited by Rictor Norton, 1997–98, http://rictornorton.co.uk/fanny.htm.

7. Robb, *Strangers*, 105–14.

8. Symonds, *Memoirs*, 103.

9. Sir Walter Morgan and Arthur George MacPherson, "The Indian Penal Code (Act XLV of 1860)," 2 Crescent Place, Blackfriars, London, January 1, 1863: 326.

10. Central Government Act, Section 377, in the Indian Penal Code, Indian Kanoon, https://indiankanoon.org/doc/1836974/.

11. M. D. Kirby, "The Sodomy Offense," *Journal of Commonwealth Criminal Law* 22 (2011): 26–27; see also M. L. Freeland and R. S. Wright, "Model Criminal Code: A Forgotten Chapter in the History of the Criminal Law," *Oxford Journal of Legal Studies* 1 (2011): 307.

12. Morgan and MacPherson, "The Indian Penal Code, (Act XLV of 1860)," 324.

13. Act 027 of 1871: Criminal Tribes Act of 1871, https://www.casemine.com/act/in/5a979daf4a93263ca60b7266.

14. Laurence W. Preston, "A Right to Exist: Eunuchs and the State in Nineteenth-Century India," *Modern Asian Studies* 1, no. 2 (1987): 371–87, https://www.jstor.org/stable/312652?seq=1#page_scan_tab_contents.

15. Vagrancy Act 1838 (1 & 2 Vict. c. 38), cited in "Vagrancy," *Police Journal: Theory, Practice and Principles* 27, no. 3 (July 1, 1954), 232–37.

16. "Aeropagitica: A Speech of Mr John Milton for the Liberty of Unlicenc'd Printing, to the Parlament of England," 1644, from the John Milton Reading Room, Dartmouth College, https://www.dartmouth.edu/~milton/reading_room/areopagitica/text.html. Also, see Amanda Foreman, *Georgiana: Duchess of Devonshire* (New York: Random House, 1999), and P. Douglass, *Lady Caroline Lamb: A Biography* (London: Springer, 2004).

17. Algernon Charles Swinburne, *The Dark Blue*, edited by John Christian Freund (London: Sampson Low, Son, and Martson, 1871).

18. Robert Buchanan, "The Fleshly School of Poetry," *The Contemporary Review*, August–November, 1871, from the Rossetti Archive, http://www.rossettiarchive.org/docs/ap4.c7.18.rad.html#buchanan003.

CHAPTER 17: "MY CONSTANT COMPANION"

1. Symonds, *Letters*, vol. 2, 167.

2. Ibid., 166–67.

3. Ibid., 174.

4. Ibid., 184.

5. Ibid., 188.

6. Marion Walker Alcaro, "Gilchrist, Anne Burrows," https://whitmanarchive
.org/criticism.

7. Whitman, *Selected Letters of Walt Whitman*, 158–59.

8. Symonds, *Letters*, vol. 2, 201–2.

9. Ibid., 201–3.

10. Ibid.

11. Ibid.

12. Ibid.

13. Traubel, *With Walt Whitman in Camden*, 203–4.

14. Symonds, *Letters*, vol. 2, 205.

15. John Addington Symonds, *A Problem in Greek Ethics: Being an Inquiry into the
Phenomenon of Sexual Inversion, Addressed Especially to Medical Psychologists and
Jurists*. Self-published. No date. Morgan Library and Museum, New York.

16. Ibid.

17. Ibid., 228.

18. Ibid., 252.

19. "The Trial of Andrew Sobolski," Proceedings of the Old Bailey, 1674–1913,
https://www.oldbaileyonline.org/browse.jsp?id=t18730203-179-offence
-1&div=t18730203-179#highlight, reference number t18730203-179,
accessed September 5, 2012.

20. "The Trial of Charles Casebow," Proceedings of the Old Bailey, 1674–1913,
http://www.oldbaileyonline.org/browse.jsp?id=t18730707-467-offence-1&div
=t18730707-467&terms=guilty#highlight, reference number t18730707-467,
accessed September 5, 2012.

CHAPTER 18: COMSTOCK: CENSORSHIP CROSSES THE ATLANTIC

1. "Society for the Suppression of Vice," http://www.victorianlondon.org/crime
/suppression.htm. See also M. J. D. Roberts, "Making Victorian Morals? The
Society for the Suppression of Vice and Its Early Critics, 1802–1882," *Journal
of Historical Studies* 21, no. 83 (1984).

2. David J. Pivar, *Purity Crusade* (New York: ABC-CLIO, 1974), 78–85.

3. "The Comstock Act of (1873)," in *Controlling Reproduction: An American History*,
edited by Andrea Tone (Lanham, MD: SR Books, 1997), 140–42. See also
Anthony Comstock, O. B. Frothingham, and J. M. Buckley, "The Suppression
of Vice," *North American Review* 135, no. 312 (November 1882): 484–501.

4. Pivar, *Purity Crusade*, 237.

5. M. McGarry, "Spectral Sexualities: Nineteenth-Century Spiritualism, Moral
Panics, and the Making of United States Obscenity Law," *Journal of Women's
History* 12, no. 2 (2000): 8–29.

6. "Anthony Comstock Dies in His Crusade," *New York Times*, September 22, 1915.

7. Kenneth M. Price, "Whitman, Walt, Clerk," *Prologue magazine* 43, no. 4 (Winter 2011), https://www.archives.gov/publications/prologue/2011/winter /whitman.html.

8. R. Darby, "Pathologizing Male Sexuality: Lallemand, Spermatorrhoea, and the Rise of Circumcision," *Journal of the History of Medicine* 60 (2005): 283–319.

9. A. W. Bates, "Dr. Kahn's Museum: Obscene Anatomy in Victorian London," *Journal of Research in Society and Medicine* 99, no. 12 (2006): 618–24.

10. "Exposed: The Victorian Nude," 2001–2002, the Tate Gallery, https://www .tate.org.uk/whats-on/tate-britain/exhibition/exposed-victorian-nude /exposed-victorian-nude-room-guide.

11. See John Addington Symonds, *Studies of the Greek Poets* (London: Smith, Elder & Co., 1876).

12. Symonds, *Letters*, vol. 2, 281–82.

13. Ibid.

CHAPTER 19: THE ARRESTS OF SIMEON SOLOMON

1. Dante Gabriel Rossetti, *Blanzifiore (Snowdrops)*, 1873, http://www.rossetti archive.org/docs/s227.rap.html.

2. William A. Peniston, "Pederasts and Others: Urban Culture and Sexual Identity in Nineteenth-Century Paris," *Haworth Gay & Lesbian Studies* (Abingdon, UK: Routledge, 2004), 77–78.

3. "Simeon Solomon Two-Part Biography," https://www.simeonsolomon.com /simeon-solomon-biography.html.

4. H. W. Percival, *The Word*, vol. 10 (New York: Theosophical Publishing Company, 1910), 290.

5. This copy of John Addington Symonds's *Studies of the Greek Poets* from the library of Oscar Wilde is now in the Morgan Library and Museum, New York.

6. John Addington Symonds, *Studies of the Greek Poets* (London: Smith, Elder, 1873), https://babel.hathitrust.org/cgi/pt?id=hvd.hw3q7o;view=1up;seq=1.

7. Ibid.

8. Symonds, *Letters*, vol. 2, 388.

9. Ibid., 205.

10. Walt Whitman, "A Passage to India," https://www.poets.org/poetsorg/poem /passage-india.

11. Oscar Wilde, *The Complete Letters of Oscar Wilde*, edited by Rupert Hart-Davis and Merlin Holland (New York: Henry Holt, 2000), 15, 20.

12. Elizabeth Prettejohn, *After the Pre-Raphaelites: Art and Aestheticism in Victorian England* (Manchester, UK: Manchester University Press), 39.

13. Simeon Solomon, *The Bride, the Bridegroom, and the Friend of the Bridegroom*, 1868, from the Birmingham Museum, http://www.birminghammuseums.org

.uk/explore-art/items/1981P91/the-bride-thebridegroom-and-the-friend-of
-the-bridegroom?

14. Walter Pater, "A Study of Dionysus, 1: The Spiritual Form of Fire and Dew,"
Fortnightly Review 20 (December 1876): 752–72.

15. Ibid.

16. Ibid.

CHAPTER 20: ANNIE BESANT AND CHARLES BRADLAUGH

1. Customs Consolidation Act of 1876, 1876 C. 36. https://www.legislation.gov
.uk/ukpga/Vict/39-40/36/contents/enacted.

2. Customs Consolidation Act of 1876, legislation.gov.uk, the National Archives,
n.d., accessed June 22, 2013.

3. Roger Manvell, *The Trial of Annie Besant and Charles Bradlaugh* (New York: Elek
Paul, 1976), 9.

4. Ibid., 10.

5. Charles Knowlton, *The Fruits of Philosophy*, cited in Caroline Meek and Claudia
Nunez-Eddy, "The Fruits of Philosophy (1832) By Charles Knowlton," in *The
Embryo Project Encyclopedia*, https://embryo.asu.edu/pages/fruits-philosophy
-1832-charles-knowlton#:~:text=In%20The%20Fruits%20of%20Philosophy,the
%20pamphlet%20in%20London%2C%20England, accessed May 30, 2020.

6. Ibid.

7. Ibid., 77.

8. See Anne Taylor, *Annie Besant: A Biography* (Oxford: Oxford University
Press, 1992).

9. Manvell, *Trial of Annie Besant and Charles Bradlaugh* (New York: Elek Paul, 1976).

10. Ibid., 160–61.

CHAPTER 21: "THE GREEK SPIRIT"

1. Rev. Richard St. John Tyrwhitt, "The Greek Spirit in Modern Literature,"
Contemporary Review 29 (December 1876–May 1877), 552–66.

2. Ibid., 552.

3. Ibid.

4. Symonds, *Letters*, vol. 2, 161–63.

5. Phyllis Grosskurth, *John Addington Symonds: A Biography* (London: Longmans,
1964), 143.

6. "The Trial of George Wright," Proceedings of the Old Bailey, 1674–1913,
https://www.oldbaileyonline.org/browse.jsp?id=t18770409-367-offence
-1&div=t18770409-367#highlight, accessed September 6, 2012.

7. "The Trial of John Sweeting," Proceedings of the Old Bailey, 1674–1913,
https://www.oldbaileyonline.org/browse.jsp?id=t18771022-810-offence
-1&div=t18771022-810#highlight.

8. "The Trial of Jules Mannett," Proceedings of the Old Bailey, 1674–1913, https://www.oldbaileyonline.org/browse.jsp?id=t18771119-65&div=t18771119-65&terms=Mannett#highlight, accessed September 6, 2012.

9. "Deekes," Proceedings of the Old Baily, 1674–1913, https://www.oldbailey online.org/browse.jsp?id=t18771119-65&div=t18771119-65&terms =Francis_Deekes#highlight.

10. Symonds, *Letters*, vol. 2, 446–47.

CHAPTER 22: "WERE I AS FREE": THE SECRET SODOMY POEMS

1. Symonds, *Letters*, vol. 2, 581.

2. See John Addington Symonds, "Rhaetica," unpublished, 1878, Morgan Library and Museum, New York.

3. Grosskurth, *John Addington Symonds: A Biography*, 4.

4. John Addington Symonds, *Many Moods: A Volume of Verse* (London: Smith, Elder, 1878), 165.

5. John Addington Symonds, "Dead Love," self-published, 1870s, Arrowsmith, Bristol, Morgan Library and Museum, New York.

6. John Addington Symonds, *Eudiades and a Cretan Idyll*, self-published, 1870s, no location, Morgan Library and Museum, New York.

7. Ibid., 22–30.

8. Ibid., 24.

9. Ibid.

10. Ibid.

11. Ibid.

12. Ibid., 28.

13. Ibid.

14. Ibid.

15. Ibid.

16. Ibid., 37.

17. Ibid., 30.

18. Ibid.

19. Ibid.

20. Graham Robb points out in *Strangers: Homosexual Love in the Nineteenth Century* that this historical categorizing of consensual sex along with violent crime, bestiality, and child molestation is one of the core tenets of "institutional homophobia."

21. "The Trial of John Clayton," Proceedings of the Old Bailey, 1674–1913, http://www.oldbaileyonline.org/browse.jsp?id=t18810523-576-offence-1&div =t18810523-576&terms=guilty#highlight, reference number t18810523-576, accessed September 6, 2012.

22. John Addington Symonds, *Sketches and Studies in Italy and Greece* (London: Smith, Elder & Co., 1879).

CHAPTER 23: "LOVE AT FIRST SIGHT"

1. Symonds, *Memoirs*, 513.
2. Ibid., 515.
3. Ibid., 518.
4. "Walt Whitman at the Lilly," Indiana University Bloomington, https://collections.libraries.indiana.edu/lilly/exhibitions/exhibits/show/whitmanlilly.
5. Matthew Fellion and Katherine Inglis, *Censored: A Literary History of Subversion and Control* (Montreal: McGill-Queen's University Press, 2017), 109.
6. Walt Whitman, in Richard Maurice Bucke, *Walt Whitman* (New York: Wilson & McCormick, 1884) 149.
7. Walt Whitman, "Introduction," in *Leaves of Grass* (1882), Henry W. and Albert A. Berg Collection of English and American Literature (unpaginated).
8. Ibid.
9. Ibid.
10. Ibid.
11. "A Rare Bit of Whitman: Leaves of Grass, 1882, the Author's Edition," Special Collections at Virginia Tech, December 6, 2013, https://vtspecialcollections.wordpress.com/2013/12/06/a-rare-bit-ofwhitman/#jp-carousel-1313.
12. "Walt Whitman at the Lilly," http://www.indiana.edu/~liblilly/digital/exhibitions/exhibits/show/whitmanlilly.

CHAPTER 24: PILGRIMAGE TO CAMDEN

1. Walter Pater: *The Renaissance: Studies in Art and Poetry, the 1893 Text*, edited by Donald Hill (Berkeley: University of California Press, 1980).
2. "Photographs by Napoleon Sarony; New York City 1882. Oscar Wilde in America," http://www.oscarwildeinamerica.org/sarony/sarony-photographs.html, accessed September 3, 2013.
3. Matther Hofer and Gary Scharnhorst, eds., *Oscar Wilde in America: The Interviews* (Urbana and Chicago: University of Illinois Press, 2010), 111.
4. Ibid., 29.
5. Ibid., 193.
6. Ibid., 29.
7. Wilde, *Complete Letters of Oscar Wilde*, 127.
8. Account of Wilde's visit to Whitman in David M. Friedman, *Wilde in America: Oscar Wilde and the Invention of Modern Celebrity* (New York: W. W. Norton, 2014), 108–15.
9. Ibid., 144–45.

10. Algernon Charles Swinburne, "To Walt Whitman in America," in *The Poems of Algernon Charles Swinburne*, vol. 2 (London: Chatto & Windus, 1904), 120–25.

11. Terry L. Myers, "Swinburne and Whitman: Further Evidence," *Walt Whitman Quarterly Review* 14, no. 1 (1996): 1–11, https://ir.uiowa.edu/cgi/viewcontent .cgi?article=1490&context=wwqr.

12. Algernon Charles Swinburne, in Joann P. Krieg, *Whitman and the Irish* (Iowa City: University of Iowa Press, 2000), 177.

13. Ibid., 177–78.

14. Wilde, *Complete Letters of Oscar Wilde*, 100.

15. Symonds, *Letters*, vol. 2, 730–31.

16. "Amends," in John Addington Symonds, *Animi Figura* (London: Smith Elder, 1882), Morgan Library and Museum, New York.

17. John Addington Symonds, *Fragilia Labilia*, self-published (1884), Morgan Library and Museum, New York.

18. Symonds, *Letters*, vol. 2, 973.

19. Ibid., 974.

CHAPTER 25: THE LABOUCHERE AMENDMENT: "GROSS INDECENCY"

1. W. T. Stead, "The Maiden Tribute of Modern Babylon: The Report of Our Secret Commission," *Pall Mall Gazette*, 1885, in "Undercover Reporting: Deception for Journalism's Sake: A Database," New York University Libraries, http://dlib.nyu.edu/undercover/ii-maidentribute-modern-babylon-w-t-stead -pall-mall-gazette.

2. Ibid.

3. *Criminal Law Amendment Act, 1885, with Introduction Notes & Index* (London: Shaw & Sons, 1885), 68–69.

4. There is disagreement; as noted above, among scholars about the effect of the Labouchere Amendment. Prof. Paul Johnson and Robert M. Vanderbeck, in *Law, Religion and Homosexuality*, p.37, footnote 10, argue that it expanded the law by capturing sex acts other than sodomy (Paul Johnson and Robert M. Vanderbeck, *Law, Religion and Homosexuality* [Abingdon: Routledge, 2014]). Prof. H. G. Cocks argues rather that it enshrined existing penalties (email communications with the author, July 2019, November 2019). See also "1885 Labouchere Amendment," Parliament.gov.uk, https://www.parliament .uk/about/living-heritage/transformingsociety/private-lives/relationships /collections1/sexual-offences-act-1967/1885-labouchere-amendment/.

5. Joseph Bristow, *Effeminate England: Homoerotic Writing after 1885* (London: Open University Press, 1995).

6. "Text of Criminal Law Amendment Act 1885, 48 & 49 Vict. C 69, s. 11," *Criminal Law Amendment Act, 1885, with Introduction Notes & Index*, 68–69.

7. Trudy Ring, "The Briggs Initiative: Remembering a Crucial Moment in Gay History," *The Advocate*, August 31 2018, https://www.advocate.com/politics /2018/8/31/briggs-initiative-remembering-crucial-moment-gay-history.

8. H. G. Cocks, in *Nameless Offences: Homosexual Desire in the Nineteenth Century* (New York: I. B. Tauris, 1993), 50.

9. Terry L. Meyers, "Swinburne and Whitman: Further Evidence," *Walt Whitman Quarterly Review* 14 (1996): 1–11.

10. Algernon Charles Swinburne, "Whitmania," as quoted in *Walt Whitman: The Critical Heritage*, edited by Milton Hindus (London: Routledge, 2014), 199–200.

11. Krieg, *Whitman and the Irish*, 178.

12. Ibid., 179–80.

13. John Addington Symonds, "A Note on Whitmania," *Fortnightly Review* vol. 42, no. 249 (September 1887): 459–60.

CHAPTER 26: PROPHETS OF MODERNITY

1. Walt Whitman, "A Backward Glance O'er My Own Road," 1888, held in the Berg Collection, New York Public Library (unpaginated); and Pratt, "A Backward Glance O'er Travel'd Roads," 1891, in the Walt Whitman Archive, https://whitmanarchive.org/published/LG/1891/poems/399.

2. Krieg, *Whitman and the Irish*, 180.

3. "Indecent Advertisements Act 1889," https://api.parliament.uk/historic -hansard/acts/indecent-advertisements-act-1889.

4. Even these biographies were scrutinized by authorities and libraries for necessary expurgations. See *Christopher Marlowe*, edited by Havelock Ellis (London: Vizetelly & Co., 1887), with an introduction by John Addington Symonds. The volume is catalogued in the Morgan Library and Museum in New York City as the "unexpurgated ed."

5. See the "complete and unabridged" edition of Zola's *Nana*, published by Wilco Publishing House, Kala Ghoda, Mumbai, India, 2009.

6. "Translations from M. Zola. A Heavy Penalty," *Chinese Times*, December 29, 1888.

7. Wilco unabridged edition of Zola's *Nana*, 31.

8. Frederick Brown, *Zola: A Life* (New York: Farrar, Straus & Giroux, 1995), 431.

9. Ibid., 432.

10. Symonds, *Memoirs*, 518.

CHAPTER 27: "THE LIFE-LONG LOVE OF COMRADES"

1. Sir Richard Francis Burton, *The Book of a Thousand and One Nights and a Night*, vol. 10 (London: Kama Shastra Society, 1885).

2. Whitman, *Selected Letters of Walt Whitman*, 63–64.

3. Horace Traubel, *Intimate with Walt: Selections from Whitman's Conversations with Horace Traubel, 1888–1892*, edited by Gary Schmidgall (Iowa City: University of Iowa Press, 2001), xiv.

4. Ibid.; and Andrew C. Higgins, "Symonds, John Addington," Walt Whitman Archive, https://whitmanarchive.org/criticism/current/encyclopedia /entry_56.html.

5. Traubel, *With Walt Whitman in Camden*, https://whitmanarchive.org/criticism /disciples/traubel/WWWiC/2/whole.html; and Schueller and Peters, *The Letters of John Addington Symonds*, vol. 3, 484–85.

6. "Note" by Herbert M. Schueller and Robert L. Peters, in *The Letters of John Addington Symonds*, vol. 3, 649–50.

7. Walt Whitman, *Walt Whitman: The Correspondence*, vol. 5, *1890–1892*, edited by Edwin Haviland Miller (New York: New York University Press, 1969), 351.

CHAPTER 28: *A PROBLEM IN MODERN ETHICS*

1. Symonds, *Letters*, vol. 3, 829.

2. Grosskurth, *Woeful Victorian*, 281.

3. Ibid.

4. Ibid., 282.

5. See Edward Carpenter, *Homogenic Love, and Its Place in a Free Society* (Manchester, UK: Labour Press Society, 1894).

6. As cited in John Addington Symonds, *Walt Whitman: A Study* (London: John C. Nimmo, 1893), 81.

7. C. P. Cavafy, *Collected Poems*, translated by Edmund Keeley and Phillip Sherrard and edited by George Savidis (Princeton, NJ: Princeton University Press, 1992), http://www.cavafy.com/poems/content.asp?id=74.

8. Ed Cohen, "Typing Wilde: Construing the 'Desire to Appear to be a Person Inclined to the Commission of the Gravest of All Offenses,'" *Yale Journal of Law and Humanities* 5, no. 1 (1993), https://digitalcommons.law.yale.edu /yjlh/vol5/iss1/2.

9. "This Day in History: May 25, 1895," www.history.com/thisday-in-history /oscar-wilde-is-sent-to-prison-for-indecency.

10. Angela Buckley, "Oscar Wilde Comes to Reading Gaol—120 Years On," Getreading.com, November 22, 2015, https://www.getreading.co.uk/news /berkshire-history/oscar-wilde-comes-readinggaol-10472787.

11. Oscar Wilde, *The Ballad of Reading Gaol*, by C. 3.3. [Oscar Wilde] (London: Leonard Smithers, 1898), 26.

12. Symonds, *A Problem in Modern Ethics*, 44, from Project Gutenberg, www .gutenberg.org/ebooks/32588.

13. Ibid., 117.

14. Ibid., 69.

15. Ibid., 53.
16. Ibid.
17. Ibid., 183.
18. Ibid., 192.
19. Dalya Alberge, "Letters Unravel Mystery of the Death of Oscar Wilde's Wife," *Guardian*, January 1, 2015, https://www.theguardian.com/culture/2015/jan/02 /death-oscar-wilde-wife-solved, accessed May 30, 2020.
20. Vyvyan Holland, *Son of Oscar Wilde* (London: Carroll & Graf, 1999), 137.
21. Grosskurth, *Woeful Victorian*, 293.
22. Sexual Offences Act 1967, Ch. 60: Section 1, http://www.legislation.gov.uk /ukpga/1967/60/pdfs/ukpga_19670060_en.pdf.
23. Ibid.

CHAPTER 29: "AS WRITTEN BY HIMSELF"

1. Horatio F. Brown, *John Addington Symonds: A Biography* (London: John C Nimmo, 1895).
2. Grosskurth, *John Addington Symonds: A Biography*.
3. Phyllis Grosskurth issued an expurgated version in 1984.
4. Symonds, *Memoirs*, 26.
5. Ibid.
6. See Dame Katharine Furse, *Hearts and Pomegranates: The Story of Forty-Five Years, 1875 to 1920* (London: Peter Davies Ltd., 1940).
7. Symonds, *Memoirs*, 36.
8. Ibid., 13.
9. Symonds, *Vagabunduli Libellus* (Davos: unpublished, 1884), 25, from the Morgan Library and Museum, http://dspace.wbpublibnet.gov.in:8080/jspui /bitstream/10689/14908/10/Index.pdf.
10. Ibid., 25, 29.
11. Amber Regis, in Symonds, *Memoirs*, 13.
12. Ibid., 14.
13. Ibid., 152
14. Ibid., 157.
15. Ibid., 177.
16. Ibid.

CHAPTER 30: "ALL GOES ONWARD AND OUTWARD, NOTHING COLLAPSES"

1. *The Collected Writings of Walt Whitman. Leaves of Grass: A Textual Variorum of the Printed Poems.* Vol. *Poems, 1855–1856*, edited by Sculley Bradley, Harold W. Blodgett, Arthur Golden, and William White (New York: New York University Press, 1980), 52.

2. Ibid., 7–8.

3. Epigraph page, unpaginated, *Howl on Trial: The Battle for Free Expression*, edited by Bill Morgan and Nancy J. Peters (San Francisco: City Lights Books, 2006).

EPILOGUE

1. Obscene Publications Act 1959, UK Public General Acts 1959 c. 66 (Regnal. 7 and Eliz 2), http://www.legislation.gov.uk/ukpga/Eliz2/7-8/66/contents.

2. The Queen vs Penguin Books: 'Lady Chatterley's Lover' by D H Lawrence, prosecution for obscenity. National Archives (May 5, 2007), 1960–61, LO/2/148.

3. Morgan and Peters, *Howl on Trial*, xii.

4. Ibid., 41.

5. Leo Hamalian, "Nobody Knows My Names: Samuel Roth and the Underside of Modern Letters," *Journal of Modern Literature* 3 (1974): 889–921.

6. "The Decision," by Judge Clayton W. Horn, in *Howl on Trial*, 197–99.

7. Martin Torgoff, *Bop Apocalypse: Jazz, Race, the Beats, and Drugs* (New York: Da Capo Press, 2016), 138.

Selected Bibliography

PRIMARY SOURCES

Alcott, Bronson A. *Conversations with Children on the Gospel*, vol. 2. Boston: James Munroe, 1837.

"Asher Yatzar," Torah.org. http://www.torah.org/learning/tefila/one/asheryatzar .html. Accessed August 21, 2014.

Auden, Wystan Hugh. *W. H. Auden: Collected Poems*. Edited by Edward Mendelson. London: Faber and Faber, 1976.

Bell, Mackenzie. *Christina Rossetti: A Biographical and Critical Study*. New York: Haskell House, 1898.

Blasphemous Libel Bill of 1819. Hansard 1803–2005, http://hansard.millbank systems.com/commons/1819/dec/15/blasphemous-libel-bill-petition-of-the.

Bodichon, Barbara Leigh Smith. *A Brief Summary in Plain Language of the Most Important Laws Concerning Women; Together with a Few Observations Thereon*. London: John Chapman, 1854.

Braddon, Mary Elizabeth. *Lady Audley's Secret*. London: Penguin, 2010. Originally published in 1862.

Brady, Sean. *John Addington Symonds (1840–1893) and Homosexuality: A Critical Edition of Sources*. London: Palgrave Macmillan, 2012.

Brontë, Charlotte. *Villette*. London: Vintage, 2003. Originally published in 1853.

Brown, Horatio. *John Addington Symonds: A Biography, Compiled from His Papers and Correspondence*. London: Nimmo, 1895.

Browning, Elizabeth Barrett. *Elizabeth Barrett Browning: Selected Poems*. Baltimore: Johns Hopkins University Press, 1988.

Buchanan, Robert, writing as Thomas Maitland. "The Fleshly School of Poetry." *Contemporary Review* 18 (November 1871).

———. "Poems. By Dante Gabriel Rossetti. Fifth Edition. London: F. S. Ellis." *Contemporary Review* 18 (November 1871).

Butler, Josephine R. E. "The Voice of One Crying in the Wilderness." In *Josephine Butler and the Prostitution Campaigns: Diseases of the Body Politic*, edited by Jane Jordan and Ingrid Sharp. London: Routledge, 2003.

Cady Stanton, Elizabeth. "On Marriage and Divorce." Speech, August 18, 1871, San Francisco. http://gos.sbc.edu/s/stantoncady3.html.

Caird, Mona. *A Romance of the Moors*. New York: Henry Holt, 1891.

———. *The Wing of Azrael*. Montreal: John Lovell & Son, 1889.

Carpenter, Edward. *Homogenic Love and Its Place in a Free Society*. Manchester, UK: Manchester Labour Society, 1894.

Cavafy, Constantine. "Ithaka." In *Collected Poems*, edited by George Savidis. Princeton, NJ: Princeton University Press, 1992.

Channing, Rev. William Ellery. *A Discourse Delivered at the Ordination of the Rev. Frederick A. Farley as Pastor of the Westminster Congregational Society in Providence, Rhode Island, Sept. 10, 1828*. Boston: Bowles and Dearborn, 1828.

Clark, William, William Lawrence Marshall, and Herschel Bouton Lazell. *A Treatise on the Law of Crimes*. London: Wm. S. Hein, 1996.

Cocks, H. G. *Nameless Offences: Homosexual Desire in the 19th Century*. London: I. B. Tauris, 2009.

Collins, Wilkie. *Armadale*. Oxford: Oxford University Press, 1989. Originally published in 1866.

———. *The Law and the Lady*. Oxford: Oxford World Classics, 2008. Originally published in 1875.

———. *The Woman in White*. New York: Barnes & Noble Classics, 2005. Originally published in 1860.

"Comstock Law of (1873)." America Law and Legal Information. http://law .jrank.org/pages/5508/Comstock-Law-1873.html.

Criminal Law Amendment Act, 1885, with Introduction Notes & Index. London: Shaw & Sons, 1885.

Customs Consolidation Act of 1876. http://www.legislation.gov.uk/ukpga/Vict /39-40/36/contents/enacted.

Daily News. "Law Intelligence." November 18, 1853.

———. "The Officers of St. Clement Danes and Mr. Serjeant Adams." September 5, 1851.

Dickinson, Emily. *Emily Dickinson: The Complete Poems*. Edited by Thomas H. Johnson. London, UK: Faber and Faber, 1975.

Douglas, Alfred Bruce. "Two Loves." *Chameleon*, 1892. http://law2.umkc.edu /faculty/projects/ftrials/wilde/poemsofdouglas.htmnd.

———. *Two Loves & Other Poems: A Selection*. East Lansing, MI: Bennet & Kitchel, 1990. Originally published in 1892.

Egerton, George. *Keynotes*. Cambridge, UK: John Wilson & Son, 1893.

Ellis, Havelock. *The New Spirit*. London: Walter Scott, 1892.

Ellis, Havelock, and John Addington Symonds. *Sexual Inversion*. London: Macmillan, 1897.

———. *Sexual Inversion: A Critical Edition*. Basingstoke, UK: Palgrave Macmillan, 1988.

———. *Studies in the Psychology of Sex: Sexual Inversion*. Philadelphia: F. A. Davis & Co., 1901. https://archive.org/details/sexualinversion00elligoog.

Ellman, Richard, et al. *Wilde and the Nineties: An Exhibition and an Essay*. Princeton, NJ: Princeton University Press, 1966.

Era. "Answers to Correspondents." April 1850.

Faderman, Lillian, ed., *Chloe Plus Olivia: An Anthology of Lesbian Literature from the 17th Century to the Present*. New York: Penguin Books, 1995.

Fern, Fanny. "Leaves of Grass." *New York Ledger,* May 10, 1856.

Gaskell, Elizabeth Cleghorn. *Ruth.* Oxford: Oxford University Press, 2008. Originally published in 1853.

Hares-Stryker, Carolyn, ed. *An Anthology of Pre-Raphaelite Writings.* New York: New York University Press, 1997.

Holland, Merlin, ed. *The Wilde Album: Public and Private Images of Oscar.* New York: Henry Holt & Co., 1998.

Holmes, Anne Summer. "The Double Standard in the English Divorce Laws, 1857–1923." *Law and Social Inquiry* 20, no. 2 (1995).

Holy Bible, Conteyning the Old Testament and the New (King James Version). "Printed at London by Robert Barker, Printer to the Kings Most Excellent Maiestie. Anno Dom. 1611."

Hotten, J. C. "Poems by Walt Whitman, Selected and Edited by William Michael Rossetti." *Examiner,* April 18, 1868. Author name misspelled in the original as "Hotton."

King, Andrew, and John Plunkett. *Victorian Print Media: A Reader.* Oxford: Oxford University Press, 2005.

Krafft-Ebing, Richard von. *Psychopathia Sexualis.* New York: Arcade Publishing, 1998. Originally published in 1886.

Lang, Cecil Y. *The Swinburne Letters,* vols. 1–4. New Haven, CT: Yale University Press, 1960.

Ledger, Sally, and Roger Lockhurst, eds. *The Fin de Siecle: A Reader in Cultural History c. 1880–1900.* Oxford: Oxford University Press, 2000.

Lewes, George Henry, or George Eliot. "Transatlantic Latter-Day Poetry." *Leader* (London). June 7, 1856. Unsigned. https://whitmanarchive.org/archive1/works/leaves/1855/reviews/leader.html.

Macaulay, G. C. "Walt Whitman." *Nineteenth Century,* December 1882.

Mahaffy, John Pentland. *Social Life in Greece, from Homer to Menander.* London: Macmillan and Co., 1877.

Mansel, H. L. "Sensation Novels." *Quarterly Review* 113 (April 1862).

Mill, J. S. *The Subjection of Women.* London: Longmans, Green, Reader & Dyer, 1869.

Morris, William. *News from Nowhere: Or, an Epoch of Rest: Being Some Chapters from a Utopian Romance.* London: Longmans, Green and Co., 1908.

Mosk Parker, Lona, ed. *The Rossetti-Macmillan Letters.* Berkeley: University of California Press, 1963.

New York Times. "Why Is Walt Whitman Unappreciated?" November 11, 1901.

Nietzsche, Friedrich. *Beyond Good and Evil: Prelude to a Philosophy of the Future.* Translated by Helen Zimmern. London: T. N. Foulis, 1909.

Noel, Roden. *Mr. Swinburne on Walt Whitman.* London: Time, December 1879.

"Parliamentary Debates," Hansard 1803–2005. http://hansard.millbanksystems
.com/commons/1851/jul/23/administration-of-criminal-justice#S3V0118P0
_18510723_HOC_30.

Pater, Walter. *Greek Studies*. London: Macmillan, 1910. Originally published in 1894.

———. "A Study of Dionysis." *Fortnightly Review* 26 (December 1876).

Percival, H. W. *The Word*, vol. 10. New York: Theosophical Publishing
Company, 1910.

Price, Kenneth, ed. *Walt Whitman: The Contemporary Reviews*. Cambridge, UK:
Cambridge University Press, 1996.

Proceedings of the Old Bailey, 1674–1913. The Old Bailey Online. https://
www.oldbaileyonline.org/.

Pusey, Edward Bouverie. "The Dangers of Riches: Seek God First and Ye Shall
Have All." In *Two Sermons Preached in the Parish Church of St. James Bristol*.
Oxford: Parker, 1850.

Queen-Empress v. Khairati. 1884 Indian Law Report, vol. 6, Allahabad High
Court, 1884.

Regina v. Hicklin. The Queen, on the Prosecution of Henry Scott, Appellant v.
Benjamin Hicklin and Another, L.R. 3 Q.B. 360 (1868). Court of the Queen's
Bench. By 20 & 21 Vict. c. 83, s. 1.

Rex v. Reekspear. 9 Geo. IV c. 31. Enacted June 27, 1828. 1 Mood. C.C. 342, 183.
Cited in *Nineteenth-Century Writings on Homosexuality: A Sourcebook*, edited
by Chris White. London: Routledge, 1999.

Rossetti, Christina. *Christina Rossetti: Poems and Prose*. Edited by Simon Hum-
phries. Oxford: Oxford University Press, 2008.

———. *The Complete Poems of Christina Rossetti*. Edited by R. W. Crump.
London: Penguin, 2001.

———. *Goblin Market and Other Poems*. London: Macmillan, 1862, 1865.

———. *Letter and Spirit*. London: Society for Promoting Christian
Knowledge, 1883.

———. *The Letters of Christina Rossetti*, vol. 1, *1843–1873*. Edited by Antony H.
Harrison. New York: University of Virginia Press, 2004.

———. *The Letters of Christina Rossetti*, vol. 2, *1874–1881*. Edited by Antony H.
Harrison. New York: University of Virginia Press, 2004.

———. *"Maude" by Christina Rossetti*. Edited by Elaine Showalter and Penny
Mahon. London: Pickering Women's Classics, 1993.

———. *Verses: Dedicated to Her Mother*. London: G. Polidori, 1847. Privately printed.

Rossetti, Dante Gabriel. *Dante Gabriel Rossetti: His Family-Letters, with a Memoir
by W. M. Rossetti*. Edited by William Michael Rossetti. London: Ellis, 1895.

Rossetti, William Michael, ed. "Memoir and Notes." In *The Poetical Works of
Christina Rossetti, with Memoir and Notes by William Rossetti*. London:
Macmillan, 1904.

———. *Some Reminiscences of William Michael Rossetti*, vol. 2. London: Brown Langham & Co., 1906.

Saintsbury, George. "Leaves of Grass." *The Walt Whitman Archive*, 10 October 1874. Edited by Matt Cohen, Ed Folsom, and Kenneth M. Price. https://whitmanarchive.org/criticism/reviews/tei/anc.00076.html.

Saturday Review. "Walt Whitman's Poems." May 2, 1868.

Shelley, Percy Bysshe. *The Major Works*. Edited by Zachary Leader and Michael O'Neill. Oxford: Oxford University Press, 2003.

Stephen, James F. *A History of the Criminal Law of England*. London: Macmillan, 1883.

Swinburne, Algernon Charles. *The Complete Works of Algernon Charles Swinburne*, vol. 1. Edited by Edmund Gosse and Thomas James Wise. London: William Heinemann, 1925.

———. *The Complete Works of Algernon Charles Swinburne*, vol. 2. Edited by Edmund Gosse and Thomas James Wise. London: William Heinemann, 1925.

———. *The Dark Blue*. Edited by John Christian Freund. London: Sampson Low, Son, and Martson, 1871.

———. *The Letters of Algernon Charles Swinburne*, vol. 1. Edited by Edmund Gosse and Thomas James Wise. New York: John Lane Company, 1919.

———. *Poems and Ballads*. London: Edward Moxon, 1866.

———. *Poems and Ballads*. London: J. M. Hotten, 1866.

———. *Poems and Ballads, Atalanta in Calydon*. Edited by Morse Peckham. New York: Bobbs Merrill, 1970.

———. *The Swinburne Letters*, vols. 1–4. Edited by Cecil Y. Lang. New Haven, CT: Yale University Press, 1960.

———. *Swinburne Replies: Notes on Poems and Reviews, Under the Microscope*. Syracuse: Syracuse University, 1996.

———. *The Uncollected Letters of Algernon Charles Swinburne*, vol. 1. Edited by Terry L. Meyers. London: Pickering & Chatto, 2004.

———. "Whitmania." In *The Literary World: Choice Readings from the Best New Books, with Critical Reviews*, vol. 36, July–December 1887. London: James Clark & Co., 1887.

Symonds, John Addington, trans. *The Autobiography of Benvenuto Cellini*. New York: P. F. Collier & Son, Harvard Classics, 1909–14.

———. *The Autobiography of Michelangelo Buonarroti; Based on Studies in the Archives of the Buonarroti Family at Florence*. New York: Read Books, 2009. Originally published in 1893.

———. *Christopher Marlowe*. Edited by Havelock Ellis. London: Vizetelly & Co., 1887.

———. *Christopher Marlowe*. London: E. Benn, 1951.

———. *Fragilia Labilia*. 1894. Held at the Morgan Library and Museum, New York.

———. *Fragilia Labilia*. London: Thomas B. Mosher, 1902.

———. "In Memoriam Arcadie." Held in the Morgan Library and Museum, New York. 1859–61. Manuscript.

———. *The Letters of John Addington Symonds*, vols. 1–3. Edited by Herbert M. Schueller and Robert L. Peters. Detroit: Wayne State University Press, 1968.

———. *Many Moods: A Volume of Verse*. London: Smith, Elder, and Co., 1878.

———. *The Memoirs of John Addington Symonds*. Edited by Phyllis Grosskurth. London: Hutchinson, 1984.

———. "A Note on Whitmania." *Fortnightly Review*, vol. 42. London: Chapman & Hall, 1887, 459–60.

———. *A Problem in Greek Ethics: Being an Inquiry into the Phenomenon of Sexual Inversion, Addressed Especially to Medical Psychologists and Jurists*. Aeropagitica Society, 1901, 1908 (privately printed in Holland for the society). https://www.gutenberg.org/files/32022/32022-h/32022-h.htm.

———. *A Problem in Modern Ethics: Being an Inquiry into the Phenomenon of Sexual Inversion, Addressed Especially to Medical Psychologists and Jurists*. London: 1896. https://archive.org/details/aprobleminmoder00symogoog/page/n6.

———. *Rhaetica*. Privately printed, 1878. Held in the Morgan Library and Museum, New York.

———. *Shakespeare's Predecessors in the English Drama*. London: Smith, Elder, and Co., 1884.

———. *Sketches and Studies in Italy and Greece*. London: John Murray, 1917.

———. *Studies of the Greek Poets*. London: Adam and Charles Black, 1877.

———. *Studies of the Greek Poets*, vol. 2. London: Smith, Elder, 1879.

———. *Tales of Ancient Greece: Eudiades and a Cretan Idyll*. Privately printed, 1878.

———. *Tales of Ancient Greece: Eudiades and a Cretan Idyll*. London: Arrowsmith, 1878.

———. *Walt Whitman: A Study*. London: John C. Nimmo, 1893.

Theresa of Avila. *Interior Castle*. Translated by E. Alison Peers. New York: Image Publishing, 1972.

Tyrwhitt, Richard St. John. "The Greek Spirit in Modern Literature." *Contemporary Review*, May 1877.

Vagrants' Bill—Whipping. Hansard Parliamentary Debates. Hansard 1803–2005. June 3, 1824. http://hansard.millbanksystems.com/commons/1824/jun/03/vagrants-bill-whipping#S2V0011P0_18240603_HOC_30.

Wathen, Mark Wilks Call. "Review of Leaves of Grass (1860–61)." *Westminster Review*, October 1, 1860.

White, Chris, ed. *Nineteenth-Century Writings on Homosexuality: A Sourcebook*. New York: Taylor & Francis, 2002.

Whitman, Walt. "A Backward Glance O'er My Own Road." 1882. Manuscript. Held in the Berg Collection, New York Public Library.

———. "A Backward Glance O'er Travell'd Roads." *Leaves of Grass*. Philadelphia: David McKay, Publisher, 1891–92. The Walt Whitman Archive. http:// whitmanarchive.org/published/LG/1891/poems/399.

———. "Commentary." Walt Whitman Archive, http://www.whitmanarchive .org/criticism/reviews/leaves1855/index.html.

———. *Democratic Vistas and a Passage to India*. New York: "Electroplated by Smith McDougal," 1871.

———. *Faint Clews and Indirections: Manuscripts of Walt Whitman and His Family* [c. 1850–80]. Edited by Clarence Gohdes and Rollo G. Silver. New York: AMS Press, 1971.

———. *Leaves of Grass: The Original 1855 Edition*. Mineola, NY: Dover Publications, 2007.

———. *Leaves of Grass*. 1856. Held in the University of Virginia Library, Lynchburg. Image available at http://etext.lib.virginia.edu/etcbin/toccernew2 ?id=Whi56LG.sgm&images=images/modeng&data=/texts/english/modeng /parsed&tag=public&part=front.

———. *Leaves of Grass*. Boston: Thayer and Eldridge, 1860.

———. *Leaves of Grass*. Edited by William Michael Rossetti. London: Hotten and Pickering, 1867.

———. *Leaves of Grass*. Pirated edition. No location: no publisher, 1872.

———. *Leaves of Grass*. London: Trubner, 1876.

———. *Leaves of Grass*. Thayer and Eldridge, 1882.

———. *Poems by Walt Whitman, Selected and Edited by William Michael Rossetti*. London: John Camden Hotten, 1868.

———. *Selected Letters of Walt Whitman*. Edited by Edwin Haviland Miller. Iowa City: University of Iowa Press, 1990.

———. "Tale of a Shirt: A Very Pathetic Ballad," *Sunday Times & Noah's Weekly Messenger*, March 31, 1844. Walt Whitman Archive, http://www .whitmanarchive.org/published/periodical/periodical_titles/per.00182.

———. *The Uncollected Poetry and Prose of Walt Whitman, Much of Which Has Been But Recently Discovered*. Edited by Emory Holloway. Garden City, NY: Doubleday Page & Co., 1921.

———. *The Walt Whitman Archive II: A Facsimile of the Poet's Manuscripts*. Edited by Joel Myerson. New York: Garland, 1993.

———. *The Walt Whitman Archive III: Whitman Manuscripts at the University of Virginia, Part I*. Edited by Joel Myerson. New York: Garland, 1993.

———. *Walt Whitman: The Correspondence*, vol. 1, *1842–1867*. Edited by Gay Wilson Allen and E. Sculley Bradley. New York: New York University Press, 1961.

———. *Walt Whitman: The Correspondence*, vol. 2, *1868–1875*. Edited by Edwin Haviland Miller. New York: New York University Press, 1985.

———. *Walt Whitman: The Journalism*, vol. 2. New York: Peter Lang, 1969.

———. *Walt Whitman's Autograph Revision of the Analysis of Leaves of Grass.* Edited by Richard Maurice Bucke. New York: New York University Press, 1974.

———. *Walt Whitman's Song of Myself: A Sourcebook and Critical Edition.* Edited by Ezra Greenspan. New York: Routledge, 1990.

———. *Whitman Manuscripts at the University of Virginia.* Edited by Joel Myerson and Walker Clifton. New York: Garland, 1993.

———. *Whitman's Manuscripts: Leaves of Grass (1860), A Parallel Text.* Edited by Fredson Bonner. Chicago: University of Chicago Press, 1955.

Whitman, Walt, and Anne Gilchrist. *The Letters of Anne Gilchrist and Walt Whitman.* Edited by Thomas Harned. Garden City, NY: Doubleday, 1918.

Wilde, Lady [Jane]. "Speranza." In *Poems by Speranza.* Dublin: M. H. Gill & Son, Ltd., 1907.

Wilde, Oscar. "Un Amant de Nos Jours." *Daily Chronicle,* July 2, 1890.

———. "Collection of Original Manuscripts, Printed Books [. . .]" Collected by H. Hyde. Held in the Fales Collection, Bobst Library, New York University.

———. *The Complete Fairy Tales of Oscar Wilde.* London: Duckworth, 1908.

———. *The Complete Letters of Oscar Wilde.* Edited by Merlin Holland and Rupert Hart-Davis. New York: Henry Holt, 2000.

———. *The Complete Works of Oscar Wilde: Stories, Plays, Poems, and Essays.* Edited by J. B. Foreman. New York: HarperPerennial, 2008.

———. *The Complete Works of Oscar Wilde,* vol. VI: *Journalism I,* and vol. VII, *Journalism II.* Edited by John Stokes and Mark W. Turner. Oxford: Oxford University Press, 2013.

———. "Leaves of Grass." *Spectator,* July 14, 1860.

———. *The Leisure Hour,* Paternoster Row. London, 1872.

———. Manuscript of *The Picture of Dorian Gray* (1890). Held in Morgan Library and Museum, New York.

———. *The Oscar Wilde File.* Edited by Jonathan Goodman. London: W. H. Allen & Co., 1988.

———. *Oscar Wilde in America: The Interviews.* Edited by Matthew Hofer and Gary Scharnhorst. Urbana: University of Illinois Press, 2010.

———. "Oscar Wilde: Manuscripts Autograph Letters, First Editions, A Collection of Original Manuscripts, Letters and Books of Oscar Wilde Including His Letters Written to Robert Ross from Reading Gaol and Unpublished Letters Poems & Plays Formerly in the Possession of Robert Ross, C. S. Millard (Stuart Mason) and the Younger Son of Oscar Wilde." Catalogue 161. London, Dulau & Co. Held in Fales Collection, Bobst Library, New York University.

———. "Walt Whitman." *London Review and Weekly Journal of Politics, Society, Literature, and Art,* June 8, 1867.

———. "Walt Whitman." *Saturday Review* (London), March 18, 1876. https://whitmanarchive.org/criticism/reviews/poems/anc.02005.html.

———. "Walt Whitman: Selections from His Prose and Verse: What Whitman Stands For." *New York Times*, June 18, 1898. Unsigned review. https://www .nytimes.com/1898/06/18/archives/walt-whitman-selections-from-hisprose -and-verse-what-whitman.html?mtrref=www.google.com&gwh =1BB934763A15975FE80B2001CD5B9F9B&gwt=pay.

———. "Walt Whitman and His Critics." *Leader and Saturday Analyst* (London), June 30, 1860. https://whitmanarchive.org/criticism/reviews/lg1860/anc.00041.html.

———. "Walt Whitman's Poems." *Saturday Review*. London. May 2, 1868.

SECONDARY SOURCES

Adams, James Eli. *Dandies and Desert Saints: Styles of Victorian Masculinity*. Ithaca, NY: Cornell University Press, 1995.

Amigoni, David. "Translating the Self: Sexuality, Religion, and Sanctuary in John Addington Symonds's Cellini and Other Acts of Life Writing." *Biography* 32, no. 1 (Winter 2009).

Andrews, Jorella. *Showing Off: A Philosophy of Image*. London: Bloomsbury, 2014.

Armstrong, Isobel. *Victorian Poetry: Poetry, Poetics, and Politics*. London: Routledge, 1993.

Arseneau, Mary. *Recovering Christina Rossetti: Female Community and Incarnational Poetics*. London: Palgrave Macmillan, 2004.

Arsenau, Mary, Antony H. Harrison, and Lorraine Janzen Kooistra, eds. *The Culture of Christina Rossetti: Female Poetics and Victorian Contexts*. New York: Ohio University Press, 1999.

Ashkenazi, Elliott. *The Business of Jews in Louisiana, 1840–1875*. Tuscaloosa: University of Alabama Press, 1988.

Austin, J. L. *How to Do Things with Words*. Cambridge, MA: Harvard University Press, 1962.

Austin, J. L., and Ed Folsom. *Whitman and the World*. Iowa City: University of Iowa Press, 1995.

Babington, Percy L. *Bibliography of the Writings of John Addington Symonds*. London: John Castle, 1925.

Ballaster, Ros. *Seductive Forms: Women's Amatory Fiction from 1684 to 1740*. Oxford: Clarendon, 1992.

Barrett, Michele. *Women's Oppression Today: The Marxist/Feminist Encounter*. London: Verso, 1989.

Bartee, Wayne, and Alice Fleetwood Bartee. *Litigating Morality: America in Legal Thought and Its English Roots*. New York: Praeger, 1992.

Bates, A. W. "Dr. Kahn's Museum: Obscene Anatomy in Victorian London." *Journal of Research in Society and Medicine* 99, no. 12 (December 2006).

Beckson, Karl, ed. *Oscar Wilde: The Critical Heritage*. London: Routledge, 1974.

Behrendt, Patricia Flanagan. *Oscar Wilde: Eros and Aesthetics*. London: Macmillan, 1991.

Bekken, Jon. "These Great and Dangerous Powers: Postal Censorship of the Press." *Journal of Communication Inquiry* 15 (Winter 1991).

Bentley, David Michel Reid. *English Criminal Justice in the Nineteenth Century*. London: Continuum, 1998.

———. "The Meretricious and Meritorious in Goblin Market: A Conjecture and an Analysis." In *The Achievement of Christina Rossetti*, edited by David A. Kent. Ithaca, NY: Cornell University Press, 1987.

Berlin, Isaiah, et al., eds. *Essays on J. L. Austin*. Oxford: Clarendon Press, 1973.

Blanch, Leslie. *The Wilder Shores of Love*. New York: Da Capo Press, 2002.

Booth, Wayne C. "Censorship and the Values of Fiction." *English Journal* 53, no. 3 (March 1964).

Borg, Marcus J. *Meeting Jesus Again for the First Time: The Historical Jesus and the Heart of Contemporary Faith*. New York: HarperOne, 1995.

———. *Jesus: Uncovering the Life, Teachings, and Relevance of a Religious Revolutionary*. New York: HarperOne, 1989.

Boswell, John. *Christianity, Social Tolerance and Homosexuality: Gay People in Western Europe from the Beginning of the Christian Era to the Fourteenth Century*. Chicago: University of Chicago Press, 1980.

Bowley, Marton. "Radical Review of Sex Offense Law." *London Times*, August 11, 2000, p. 8.

Boyer, Paul S. *Purity in Print: The Vice-Society Movement and Book Censorship in America*. New York: Scribner's, 1968.

Brady, Sean. *Masculinity and Male Homosexuality in Britain, 1861–1913*. New York: Palgrave Macmillan, 2005.

Brendon, Piers. *The Decline and Fall of the British Empire, 1781–1997*. London: Vintage, 2010.

Bristow, Edward. *Vice and Vigilance: Purity Movements in Britain Since 1700*. New York: Gill and Macmillan, 1977.

Bristow, Joseph. *Effeminate England: Homoerotic Writing after 1885*. London: Open University Press, 1995.

Bristow, Joseph. *Effeminate England: Homoerotic Writing after 1885*. New York: Columbia University Press, 1995.

Bristow, Joseph, ed. *Oscar Wilde and Modern Culture: The Making of a Legend*. New York: Ohio University Press, 2009.

Bronski, Michael. *A Queer History of the United States*. New York: Beacon Press, 2012.

Butler, Judith. *Bodies That Matter: On the Discursive Limits of "Sex."* London: Routledge, 1993.

Calder-Marshall, Arthur. *Lewd, Blasphemous & Obscene: Being the Trials and Tribulations of Sundry Founding Fathers of Today's Alternative Societies*. London: Hutchinson, 1972.

Carlton, David, Anne Etienne, and David Thomas. *Theatre Censorship: From Walpole to Wilson*. Oxford: Oxford University Press, 2008.

Casey, Ellen Miller. "'Highly Flavoured Dishes' and 'Highly Seasoned Garbage': Sensation in the Athenaeum." In *Victorian Sensations: Essays on a Scandalous Genre*, edited by Kimberley Harrison and Richard Fantina. Columbus: Ohio State University Press, 2006.

Cavitch, Max. "Audience Terminable and Interminable: Anne Gilchrist, Walt Whitman, and the Achievement of Disinhibited Reading." *Victorian Poetry* 43, no. 2 (Summer 2005).

Chandrasekhar, S. *Reproductive Physiology and Birth Control: The Writings of Charles Knowlton and Annie Besant*. Piscataway, NJ: Transaction Publishers, 2002.

Chauncey, George. *Gender, Urban Culture and the Making of the Gay Male World, 1890–1940*. New York: Basic Books, 1995.

Clifford, David, and Laurence Roussillon, eds. *Outsiders Looking In: The Rossettis Then and Now*. New York: Anthem Press, 2004.

Cocks, H. G. "Making the Sodomite Speak: Voices of the Accused in English Sodomy Trials, c. 1800–98." *Gender and History* 18, no. 1 (April 2006).

———. *Nameless Offences: Homosexual Desire in the Nineteenth Century*. New York: I. B. Tauris, 1993.

———. "Safeguarding Civility: Sodomy, Class, and Moral Reform in Early Nineteenth-Century England." *Past and Present* 190, no. 1 (2006).

———. "Trials of Character: The Use of Character Evidence in Victorian Sodomy Trials." In *Domestic and International Trials, 1700–2000: The Trial in History*, vol. 2, edited by R. A. Melikan. Manchester, UK: Manchester University Press, 2003.

———. *Visions of Sodom: Religion, Homoerotic Desire, and the End of the World in England, c. 1550–1850*. Chicago: University of Chicago Press, 2017.

Cohen, Ed. *Talk on the Wilde Side*. London: Routledge, 1990.

Cohen, William. *Sex Scandal: The Private Parts of Victorian Fiction*. Raleigh–Durham, NC: Duke University Press, 1996.

Colligan, Collette. *The Traffic in Obscenity from Byron to Beardsley: Sexuality and Exoticism in Nineteenth-Century Print Culture*. Palgrave Studies in Nineteenth-Century Writing and Culture, no. 13. London: Palgrave Macmillan, 2007.

Combs, Mary Beth. "'A Measure of Legal Independence': The 1870 Married Women's Property Act and the Portfolio Allocations of British Wives." *Journal of Economic History* 65, no. 4 (2005).

Conley, Carolyn. *The Unwritten Law: Criminal Justice in Victorian Kent*. Oxford: Oxford University Press, 1991.

Craik, Elizabeth M., ed. *Marriage and Property*. Aberdeen: Aberdeen University Press, 1984.

Cromton, Lewis. *Homosexuality and Civilization.* Cambridge, MA: Harvard University Press, 2006.

Cronin, Richard, Alison Chapman, and Antony H. Harrison, eds. *A Companion to Victorian Poetry.* Oxford: Blackwell, 2002.

Crozier, Ivan. "'All the Appearances Were Perfectly Natural': The Anus of the Sodomite in Nineteenth-Century Medical Discourse." In *Body Parts: Critical Explorations in Corporeality,* edited by Christopher E. Forth and Ivan Crozier. Oxford: Lexington Books, 2005.

———. "The Medical Construction of Homosexuality and Its Relation to the Law in Nineteenth-Century England." *Medical History* 45 (2001).

———. "Striking at Sodom and Gomorrah: The Medicalization of Homosexuality and Its Relation to the Law." In *Criminal Conversations: Victorian Crimes, Social Panic, and Moral Outrage,* edited by Judith Rowbotham and Kim Stevenson. Columbus: Ohio State University Press, 2005.

Crozier, Ivan, and Gethin Rees. "Making a Space for Medical Expertise: Medical Knowledge of Sexual Assault and the Construction of Boundaries between Forensic Medicine and the Law in Late Nineteenth-Century England." *Law, Culture, and the Humanities* 8, no. 2 (June 2012).

Cruise, Colin. "'Lovely Devils': Simeon Solomon and Pre-Raphaelite Masculinity." In *Re-Framing the Pre-Raphaelites: Historical and Theoretical Essays,* Edited by Ellen Harding. Aldershot, UK: Scolar Press, 1996.

Daly, Mary. *Beyond God the Father: Toward a Philosophy of Women's Liberation.* New York: Beacon Press, 1998.

D'Amico, Diane. *Christina Rossetti: Faith, Gender, and Time.* Baton Rouge: Louisiana State University Press, 1999.

D'Amico, Diane, and David A. Kent. "Rossetti and the Tractarians." *Victorian Poetry* 44, no. 1 (Spring 2006).

Darby, R. "Pathologizing Male Sexuality: Lallemand, Spermatorrhoea, and the Rise of Circumcision." *Journal of the History of Medicine and Allied Sciences* 60, no. 3 (2005): 283–319.

Davidson, Roger, and Lesley A. Hall. *Sex, Sin, and Suffering: Venereal Diseases and European Society since 1870.* London: Routledge, 2001.

Davis, Cynthia J. "Contagion as Metaphor." *American Literary History* 14, no. 4 (Winter 2002).

Dececco, John, and William Peniston. *Pederasts and Others: Urban Culture and Sexual Identity in Nineteenth-Century Paris.* New York: Routledge, 2011.

De Grazia, Edward. *Censorship Landmarks.* New York: R. R. Bowker Company, 1969.

———. *Girls Lean Back Everywhere: The Law of Obscenity and the Assault on Genius.* New York: Random House, 1992.

Dellamora, Richard. *Masculine Desires: The Sexual Politics of Victorian Aestheticism.* Chapel Hill: University of North Carolina Press, 1990.

Delphy, Christine, and Diana Leonard. *Close to Home: A Materialist Analysis of Women's Oppression.* Amherst: University of Massachusetts Press, 1984.

Denisoff, Dennis. *Aestheticism and Sexual Parody, 1840–1940.* Cambridge, UK: Cambridge University Press, 2006.

Dennis, Donna. *Licentious Gotham: Erotic Publishing and Its Prosecution in Nine-teenth-Century New York.* Cambridge, MA: Harvard University Press, 2009.

———. "Obscenity Law and Its Consequences in Mid-Nineteenth-Century America." *Columbia Journal of Gender and Law* 16, no. 1 (2007).

De Riencourt, Amaury. *Sex and Power in History.* New York: Delta, 1974.

Dollimore, Jonathan. *Sexual Dissidence: Augustine to Wilde, Freud to Foucault.* Oxford: Oxford University Press, 1991.

Donoghue, Denis. *Walter Pater: Lover of Strange Souls.* New York: Knopf, 1995.

Douglas-Fairhurst, Robert. *Becoming Dickens: The Invention of a Novelist.* Cambridge, MA: Harvard University Press, 2011.

Dowling, Linda. *Hellenism and Homosexuality in Victorian Oxford.* Ithaca, NY: Cornell University Press, 1994.

Eagleton, Terry. *Literary Theory: An Introduction.* Oxford: Blackwell, 2006.

Easley, Alexis. "Gender and the Politics of Literary Fame: Christina Rossetti and 'The Germ.'" *Critical Survey* 13, no. 2 (2001).

Ellman, Richard. *Oscar Wilde.* New York: Penguin, 1988.

Eltis, Sos. *Revising Wilde: Society and Subversion in the Plays of Oscar Wilde.* Oxford: Clarendon Press, 2006.

Emsley, Clive. *Crime and Society in England, 1750–1900.* London: Longman, 1987.

Ernst, Morris L., and Alan U. Schwartz. *Censorship: The Search for the Obscene.* New York: Macmillan, 1964.

Evangelista, Stefano-Maria. *British Aestheticism and Ancient Greece: Hellenism, Reception, Gods in Exile.* London: Palgrave Macmillan, 2009.

———. "'Life in the Whole': Goethe and English Aestheticism." *Publications of the English Goethe Society* 82 (2013): 180–92.

———. *The Reception of Oscar Wilde in Europe.* London: Continuum, 2010.

Faderman, Lillian. *Surpassing the Love of Men: Romantic Friendship and Love Between Women from the Renaissance to the Present.* New York: Harper Paperbacks, 1998.

Fiske, Shanyn. *Heretical Hellenism: Women Writers, Ancient Greece, and the Victorian Popular Imagination.* Athens: Ohio University Press, 2008.

Flanders, Judith. *The Victorian City.* New York: St. Martin's Press, 2012.

Flint, Kate. *The Woman Reader: 1837–1914.* Oxford: Oxford University Press, 1995.

Foldy, Michael S. *The Trials of Oscar Wilde: Deviance, Morality, and Late-Victorian Society.* New Haven, CT: Yale University Press, 1997.

Foucault, Michel. *The History of Sexuality,* vol. 1, *An Introduction.* New York: Vintage, 1990.

Frawley, Maria. "Feminism, Format, and Emily Faithfull's Victoria Press Publications." *Nineteenth-Century Feminisms* 1 (Fall/Winter 1999).

Freeland, M. L. "R. S. Wright's Model Criminal Code: A Forgotten Chapter in the History of the Criminal Law." *Oxford Journal of Legal Studies* 1 (1981).

Garrison, Laurie. *Science, Sexuality, and Sensation Novels: Pleasures of the Senses.* Basingstoke, UK: Palgrave Macmillan, 2011.

Gatrell, V. A. C. *The Hanging Tree: Execution and the English People, 1770–1868.* Oxford: Oxford University Press, 1994.

Gibson, Ian. *The Erotomaniac: The Secret Life of Henry Spencer Ashbee.* London: Faber and Faber, 2002.

Gilbert, Sandra M., and Susan Gubar. *The Madwoman in the Attic: The Woman Writer and the Nineteenth-Century Literary Imagination.* New Haven, CT: Yale University Press, 1979.

Gordon, Linda. *Women's Body, Women's Right.* New York: Viking, 1976.

Gorham, Deborah. *The Victorian Girl and the Feminine Ideal.* London: Croon Hill, 1982.

Gorra, Michael. *Portrait of a Novel: Henry James and the Making of an American Masterpiece.* London: Liveright, 2012.

Gougeon, Len. "Emerson, Whitman, and Eros." *Walt Whitman Quarterly Review* 23 (2006).

Grosskurth, Phyllis. *The Woeful Victorian: A Biography of John Addington Symonds.* New York: Holt, Rinehart and Winston, 1964.

Gupta, Alok, with Scott Long. "This Alien Legacy: The Origins of 'Sodomy' Laws in British Colonialism." In *Human Rights, Sexual Orientation and Gender Identity in The Commonwealth*, edited by Corinne Lennox and Matthew Waites, London: University of London Press, 2013. 83–124. doi:10.2307/j.ctv512st2. Accessed 20 July 2020.

Hager, Kelly. "Chipping Away at Coverture: The Matrimonial Causes Act of 1857." In *BRANCH: Britain, Representation, and Nineteenth-Century History*, edited by Franco Felluga. Extension of Romanticism and Victorianism on the Net. http://www.branchcollective.org/?ps_articles=kelly-hager-chipping -awayat-coverture-the-matrimonial-causes-act-of-1857/.

Haight, Anne Lyon, and Chandler B. Grannis. *Banned Books: 387 B.C. to 1978 A.D.* New York: R. R. Bowker, 1978.

Hall, Lesley. *Sex, Gender, and Social Change in Britain.* London: Macmillan, 2000.

Hamburger, Lotte, and Joseph Hamburger. *Contemplating Adultery: The Secret Life of a Victorian Woman.* New York: Fawcett Columbine, 1991.

Hannoush, Michele. "Reading the Trial of the Fleurs du Mal." *Modern Language Review* 106, no. 2 (April 2011): 374–87. http://www.jstor.org/stable/10.5699 /modelangrevi.106.2.0374.

Harris, W. C. "Whitman's Leaves of Grass: The Writing of a New American Bible." *Walt Whitman Quarterly Review* 16 (1988).

Harrison, Antony H. "Christina Rossetti: Illness and Ideology." *Victorian Poetry* 45, no. 4 (Winter 2007): 415–28.

———. *Christina Rossetti in Context.* Chapel Hill: University of North Carolina Press, 1988.

———. "Swinburne's Losses: The Poetics of Passion." *ELH* 49, no. 3 (Autumn 1982): 689–706.

———. *Victorian Poets and Romantic Poems: Intertextuality and Ideology.* Charlottesville: University of Virginia Press, 1990.

Harrison, Antony H., and Beverly Taylor, eds. *Victorian Literature and Art.* DeKalb: Northern Illinois University Press, 1992.

Haskins, Susan. *Mary Magdalen: Myth and Metaphor.* New York: Riverhead Books, 1993.

Heath, Deana. "Commodities of Empire: Obscenity, Empire, and Global Networks." *Commodities of Empire Working Paper* 7 (April 2008). http://www.open.ac.uk/Arts/ferguson-centre/commodities-of-empire/working-papers/WP07.pdf.

———. *Purifying Empire: Obscenity and the Politics of Moral Regulation in Britain, India, and Australia.* Cambridge, UK: Cambridge University Press, 2014.

Heidt, Sarah J. "Let JAS Stand: Publishing John Addington Symonds' Desires." *Victorian Studies* 46, no. 1 (Autumn 2003).

Hilliard, Christopher. "'Is It a Book That You Would Ever Wish Your Wife or Your Servants to Read?': Obscenity Law and the Politics of Reading in Modern England." *American Historical Review* 118, no. 3 (2013): 653.

Hofer, Matthew, and Gary Scharnhorst, eds. *Oscar Wilde in America.* Urbana: University of Illinois Press, 2010.

Holland, Merlin. *Irish Peacock and Scarlet Marquess.* London: Fourth Estate, 2003.

Holland, Vyvyan. *Oscar Wilde and His World.* London: Thames and Hudson, 1966.

Holmes, Ann Summer. "The Double Standard in the English Divorce Laws, 1857–1923." *Law and Social Inquiry* 20, no. 2 (1995).

Hsu, Esther T. "Christina Rossetti, John Keble, and the Divine Gaze." *Victorian Poetry* 46, no. 2 (Summer 2008).

Hyam, Ronald. *Empire and Sexuality: The British Experience.* Manchester, UK: Manchester University Press, 1990.

Hyde, H. Montgomery, ed. *The Trials of Oscar Wilde.* New York: Dover, 1962.

Hyder, Clyde Kenneth. *Swinburne: The Critical Heritage.* New York: Barnes and Noble, 1970.

Irigaray, Luce. *This Sex Which Is Not One.* Translated by Catherine Porter. Ithaca, NY: Cornell University Press, 1985.

Jackson, Charles Kains. *John Addington Symonds—A Portrait.* New York: Bruno, 1915.

Jantzen, Grace. *Power, Gender, and Christian Mysticism.* Cambridge, UK: Cambridge University Press, 1995.

Jenkins, Ruth Y. *Reclaiming Myths of Power: Women Writers and the Victorian Spiritual Crisis.* Cranbury, NJ: Bucknell University Press, 1995.

Johnson, Elizabeth. *She Who Is: The Mystery of God in Feminist Theological Discourse.* New York: Crossroad Press, 1996.

Johnson, Paul. "Buggery and Parliament, 1533–2017." *Parliamentary History* 38, no. 3, 325–341. https://doi.org/10.1111/1750-0206.12463.

Johnson, Paul and Robert M Vanderbeck. *Law, Religion and Homosexuality.* Abingdon: Routledge, 2015.

Jones, Kathleen. *Learning Not to Be First: The Life of Christina Rossetti.* Gloucestershire, UK: Windrush Press, 1991.

Kaplan, Cora. *Victoriana: Histories, Fictions, Criticism.* Edinburgh: Edinburgh University Press, 2007.

Kaplan, Justin. *Walt Whitman: A Life.* New York: HarperCollins, 2003.

Kaplan, Morris, B. *Sodom on the Thames: Sex, Love, and Scandal in Wilde Times.* Ithaca, NY: Cornell University Press, 2005.

Karl, Frederick R. *George Eliot: The Voice of a Century, A Biography.* New York: W. W. Norton, 1996.

Kelly, Patrick, J. *Imperilled Innocents: Arthur Comstock and Family Reproduction in Victorian America.* Princeton, NJ: Princeton University Press, 2007.

———. "Victorian Vice." *Reviews in American History* 26, no. 4 (1998).

Kendrick, Walter M. *The Secret Museum: Pornography in Modern Culture.* Berkeley: University of California Press, 1996.

King, Andrew, and John Plunkett. *Victorian Print Media: A Reader.* Oxford: Oxford University Press, 2005.

Kirby, M. D. "The Sodomy Offense." *Journal of Commonwealth Criminal Law* 22 (2011).

Knapp, Ronald. *Of Life Immense: The Prophetic Vision of Walt Whitman.* New York: Outskirts Press, 2007.

Kooistra, Lorraine Jantzen. *Christina Rossetti and Illustration: A Publishing History.* Athens: Ohio University Press, 2002.

Ladenson, Elizabeth. *Dirt for Art's Sake: Books on Trial from "Madame Bovary" to "Lolita."* Ithaca, NY: Cornell University Press, 2007.

Leach, William. *True Love and Perfect Union: The Feminist Reform of Sex and Society.* Middletown, CT: Wesleyan University Press, 1989.

Leckie, Barbara. *Culture and Adultery: The Novel, the Newspaper, and the Law, 1857–1914.* Philadelphia: University of Pennsylvania Press, 1999.

Ledger, Sally. "The New Woman and Feminist Fictions." In *The Cambridge Companion to the Fin de Siecle,* edited by Gail Marshall. Cambridge, UK: Cambridge University Press, 2007.

Levine, Herbert J. *Minor Prophecy: Walt Whitman's New American Religion.* Bloomington: Indiana University Press, 1989.

Levine, Phillipa. "Venereal Disease, Prostitution, and the Politics of Empire: The Case of British India." *Journal of the History of Sexuality* 4, no. 4 (1994).

Long, Scott. "When Doctors Torture: The Anus and the State in Egypt and Beyond." *Health and Human Rights* 7, no. 2 (2017). https://www.researchgate .net/publication/239597185_When_Doctors_Torture_The_Anus_and_the _State_in_Egypt_and_Beyond.

Lottman, Herbert. *Flaubert*. New York: Little, Brown, 1989.

Louis, Margot K. *Persephone Rises, 1860–1927: Mythography, Gender, and the Creation of a New Spirituality*. Wellington, New Zealand: University of Victoria Press, 2009.

Lycett, Andrew. *Wilkie Collins: A Life of Sensation*. New York: Hutchinson, 2013.

MacCalman, Ian. *Radical Underworld: Prophets, Revolutionaries, and Pornographers in London, 1795–1840*. Oxford: Oxford University Press, 1988.

MacKey, Thomas C. *Pornography on Trial: A Reference Handbook*. Goleta, CA: ABC-CLIO, 2002.

Manchester, Colin. "A History of the Crime of Obscene Libel." *Journal of Legal History* 12, no. 1 (1991).

Mangham, Andrew. "'What Could I Do?': Nineteenth-Century Psychology and the Horrors of Masculinity in *The Woman in White*." In *Victorian Sensations: Essays on a Scandalous Genre*, edited by Kimberly Harrison and Richard Fantina. Columbus: Ohio State University Press, 2006.

Manvell, Roger. *The Trial of Annie Besant and Charles Bradlaugh*. New York: Elek Paul, 1976.

Marcus, Stephen. *The Other Victorians: A Study of Sexuality and Pornography in Mid-Nineteenth-Century England*. New York: Transaction Press, 2008.

Marsh, Jan. *Christina Rossetti: A Literary Biography*. London: Jonathan Cape, 1994.

Marshall, Megan. *Margaret Fuller: A New American Life*. Boston: Houghton Mifflin Harcourt, 2013.

Marshik, Celia. *British Modernism and Censorship*. Cambridge, UK: Cambridge University Press, 2009.

Mason, Stuart, ed. *Bibliography of Oscar Wilde*. Oxford: T. W. Laurie, Ltd., 1906.

Masson, Jeffrey Moussaieff. *A Dark Science: Women, Sexuality, and Psychiatry in the Nineteenth Century*. New York: Farrar, Straus and Giroux, 1986.

Maxwell, Catherine. "Tasting the 'Fruit Forbidden': Gender, Intertextuality, and Christina Rossetti's 'Goblin Market.'" In *The Culture of Christina Rossetti: Female Poetics and Victorian Contexts*, edited by Mary Arseneau, Antony H. Harrison, and Lorraine Janzen Kooistra. Athens: Ohio University Press, 1999.

McElroy, John Harmon, ed. *The Sacrificial Years: A Chronicle of Walt Whitman's Experience in the Civil War*. Boston: David R. Godine, 1999.

McGarry, M. "Spectral Sexualities: Nineteenth-Century Spiritualism, Moral Panics, and the Making of United States Obscenity Law." *Journal of Women's History* 12, no. 2 (2000): 10.1353/jowh.2000.0042.

McLaren, Angus. *The Trials of Masculinity: Policing Sexual Boundaries, 1870–1930*. Chicago: University of Chicago Press, 1997.

Mendelssohn, Michele. *Henry James, Oscar Wilde, and Aesthetic Culture*. Edinburgh: Edinburgh University Press, 2007.

Merkle, Denise. "Vizetelly & Company as (Ex)change Agent: Towards the Modernization of the British Publishing Industry." In *Agents of Translation*, edited by John Milton and Paul Padio Bandia. New York: Benjamins Translation Library, 2009.

Meyers, Terry L. "Swinburne and Whitman: Further Evidence." *Walt Whitman Quarterly Review* 14 (Summer 1996).

Michie, Elsie B. *Outside the Pale: Cultural Exclusion, Gender Difference, and the Victorian Woman Writer*. Ithaca, NY: Cornell University Press, 1993.

Millet, Kate. *Sexual Politics*. Chicago: University of Illinois Press, 2000.

Morgan, Thais E. "Perverse Male Bodies: Simeon Solomon and Algernon Charles Swinburne." In *Outlooks: Lesbian and Gay Sexualities and Visual Cultures*, edited by Peter Horne and Reina Lewis. London: Routledge, 1996.

Nead, Lynda. *Victorian Babylon: People, Streets, and Images in Nineteenth-Century London*. New Haven, CT: Yale University Press, 2008.

Norton, Rictor. "Gay History & Literature: Essays by Rictor Norton." http://rictornorton.co.uk.

Orrells, Daniel. *Classical Culture and Modern Masculinity*. Oxford: Oxford University Press, 2011.

Pagels, Elaine. *Beyond Belief: The Secret Gospel of Thomas*. New York: Random House, 2003.

——. *The Origin of Satan*. New York: Vintage, 1995.

Palazzo, Lynda. *Christina Rossetti's Feminist Theology*. London: Palgrave Macmillan, 2002.

Paul, James C. N., and Murray L. Schwartz. *Federal Censorship: Obscenity in the Mail*. New York: Free Press, 1961.

Phegley, Jennifer. "Motherhood, Authorship, and Rivalry: Sons' Memoirs of the Lives of Ellen Price and Mary Elizabeth Braddon." In *Women Writers and the Artifacts of Celebrity in the Long Nineteenth Century*, edited by Ann R. Hawkins and Maura C. Ives. Farnham, UK: Ashgate Publishing Ltd., 2012.

Pivar, David. *Purity Crusade*. New York: ABC-CLIO, 1974.

Pollock, Sir Frederick, and Frederic William Maitland. *The History of English Law before the Time of Edward I*. Indianapolis: Liberty Fund, 2010.

Poovey, Mary. "Covered but Not Bound: Caroline Norton and the 1857 Matrimonial Causes Act." *Feminist Studies* 14, no. 3 (Autumn 1988).

Powell, Kerry. *Acting Wilde: Victorian Sexuality, Theatre, and Oscar Wilde*. Cambridge, UK: Cambridge University Press, 2009.

Prins, Yopi. "Elizabeth Barrett, Robert Browning, and the Difference of Translation." *Victorian Poetry* 29 (1991).

Psomiades, Kathy Alexis, and Talia Schaffer, eds. *Women and British Aestheticism.* Lynchburg: University of Virginia Press, 1999.

Pyckett, Lyn. *The "Improper" Feminine: The Women's Sensation Novel and the New Woman Writing.* New York: Psychology Press, 1992.

Reade, Brian. *Sexual Heretics: Male Homosexuals in English Literature from 1850 to 1900.* London: Routledge & Kegan Paul, 1970.

Rembar, Charles. *The End of Obscenity: The Trials of Lady Chatterley's Lover, Tropic of Cancer, and Fanny Hill by the Lawyer Who Defended Them.* New York: Random House, 1968.

Reynolds, David. *Walt Whitman's America: A Cultural Biography.* New York: Vintage, 1996.

Richardson, Angelique, and Chris Willis, eds. *New Women in Fiction and Fact: Fin de Siecle Feminisms.* London: Palgrave Macmillan, 2001.

Robb, Graham. *Strangers: Homosexual Love in the Nineteenth Century.* New York: W. W. Norton & Co., 2003.

Roberts, Elizabeth. *A Woman's Place: An Oral History of Working-Class Women.* London: Wiley Blackwell, 1995.

Roberts, M. J. D. *Making English Morals: Voluntary Association and Moral Reform in England, 1787–1886.* Cambridge, UK: Cambridge University Press, 2004.

———. "Morals, Art, and the Passing of the Obscene Publications Act, 1857." *Victorian Studies* 28, no. 4 (Summer 1985).

Robertson, Michael. *Worshipping Walt: The Whitman Disciples.* Princeton, NJ: Princeton University Press, 2009.

Robinson, Paul R. *Gay Lives: Homosexual Autobiography from John Addington Symonds to Paul Monette.* Chicago: University of Chicago Press, 1999.

Roe, Dinah. "'Good Satan': The Unlikely Poetic Affinity of Swinburne and Christina Rossetti." In *Algernon Charles Swinburne: Unofficial Laureate*, edited by Stefano-Maria Evangelista and Catherine Maxwell. Manchester, UK: Manchester University Press, 2013.

Rosenblum, Dolores. *Christina Rossetti: The Poetry of Endurance.* Carbondale: Southern Illinois University Press, 1986.

———. "Christina Rossetti's Religious Poetry: Watching, Looking, and Keeping Vigil." In *Victorian Woman Poets: A Critical Reader*, edited by Angela Leighton. Oxford: Blackwell Publishing, 1996.

Rousseau, George. *Children and Sexuality: From the Greeks to the Great War.* Oxford: Palgrave Macmillan, 2008.

Rowbotham, Sheila. *Edward Carpenter: A Life of Liberty and Love.* London: Verso, 2009.

Ruiz, Mario M. "Virginity Violated: Sexual Assault and Respectability in Mid- to Late-Nineteenth-Century Egypt." *Comparative Studies of South Asia, Africa, and the Middle East* 25, no. 1 (2005).

Russett, Cynthia E. *Sexual Science: The Victorian Construction of Womanhood.* Cambridge, MA: Harvard University Press, 1989.

Ryder, Sean. "Son and Parents: Speranza and Sir William Wilde." In *Oscar Wilde in Context*, edited by Kerry Powell and Peter Raby. Cambridge, UK: Cambridge University Press, 2014.

Salmon, Daniel A., Stephen P. Teret, C. Raina MacIntyre, David Salisbury, Margaret A. Burgess, and Neal A Halsey. "Compulsory Vaccination and Conscientious or Philosophical Exemptions: Past, Present, and Future." *Lancet* 367 (1996).

Savage, Gail. "The Operation of the 1857 Divorce Act, 1860–1910: A Research Note." *Journal of Social History* 16, no. 4 (Summer 1983).

Schachter-Shalomi, Zalman. *Jewish with Feeling.* New York: Riverhead Books, 2005.

Schafer, Judith Kelleher. *Brothels, Depravity, and Abandoned Women: Illegal Sex in Antebellum New Orleans.* Baton Rouge: Louisiana State University Press, 2011.

Schmidgall, Gary. *The Stranger Wilde: Interpreting Oscar.* London: Abacus, 1994.

Scott Smith, Daniel. "Family Limitation, Sexual Control, and Domestic Feminism in Victorian America." In *Clio's Consciousness Raised*, edited by Lois Banner and Mary Hartman. New York: Harper & Row, 1974.

Seidman, Steven. *Romantic Longings: Love in America, 1830–1980.* New York: Routledge, 1991.

Senior, F. B. "Labouchere's Amendment to the Criminal Law Amendment Bill." *Historical Studies* 17, no. 67 (1976).

Sharpe, J. A. *Judicial Punishment in England.* London: Faber and Faber 1990.

Showalter, Elaine. "Desperate Remedies: Sensation Novels of the 1860s." *Victorian Newsletter* 49 (Spring 1976).

Sinfield, Alan. *The Wilde Century: Effeminacy, Oscar Wilde, and the Queer Moment.* New York: Columbia University Press, 1994.

Skinner, S. A. *Tractarians and "the Condition of England": The Social and Political Thought of the Oxford Movement.* New York: New York University Press, 2004.

Snow, Stephanie J. "Sutherland, Snow, and Water: The Transmission of Cholera in the Nineteenth Century." *International Journal of Epidemiology* 31, no. 5 (2002): 908–9.

Sova, Dawn B. *Literature Suppressed on Sexual Grounds.* New York: Banned Books/ Facts on File, 2006.

Stephen, James F. *A History of the Criminal Law of England.* London: Macmillan, 1883.

Stern, Chaim, ed. *Gates of Prayer for Shabbat and Weekdays.* New York: Central Conference of American Rabbis, 1994.

St. John-Stevas, Norman. *Obscenity and the Law.* London: Secker & Warburg, 1956.

Taylor, Ann. *Annie Besant: A Biography.* Oxford: Oxford University Press, 1992.

Thomas, Donald. *A Long Time Burning: The History of Literary Censorship in England.* London: Routledge & Kegan Paul, 1969.

Thomas, Tracy A. "The Feminist Origins of Family Law: Elizabeth Cady Stanton's Contributions to the Field." University of Akron Legal Studies Paper 4.1., 1987.

Traubel, Howard. *With Walt Whitman in Camden.* Oregon City: Oregon House, 1996.

Travis, Alan. *Bound and Gagged: A Secret History of Obscenity in Britain.* London: Profile Books, 2001.

Trumbach, Randolph. "Renaissance Sodomy, 1500–1700" and "Modern Sodomy: The Origins of Homosexuality, 1700–1800." In *A Gay History of Britain: Love and Sex Between Men Since the Middle Ages.* Oxford: Greenwood World Publishing, 2007.

Turner, Mark W. "Journalism." In *Oscar Wilde in Context*, edited by Kerry Powell and Peter Raby. Cambridge, UK: Cambridge University Press, 2013.

Upchurch, Charles. *Before Wilde: Sex Between Men in Britain's Age of Reform.* Berkeley, CA: University of California Press, 2013.

Vicinus, Martha. *Suffer and Be Still: Women in the Victorian Age.* London: Methuen, 1980.

———. *A Widening Sphere: Changing Roles of Victorian Women.* Bloomington: University of Indiana Press, 1977.

Walkowitz, J. *Prostitution and Victorian Society.* Cambridge, UK: Cambridge University Press, 1980.

Warren, Earl, Jr. "Obscenity Laws: A Shift to Reality?" *Santa Clara Lawyer* 11 (1970). http://digitalcommons.law.scu.edu/lawreview/vol11iss1/1.

Watt, Ian. *The Rise of the Novel: Studies in Defoe, Richardson, and Fielding.* Middlesex, UK: Penguin, 1959.

Weeks, Jeffery. *Sex, Politics and Society: The Regulation of Sexuality Since 1800.* Abingdon: Routledge, 2012.

Williams, J. E. Hall. "Obscenity in Modern English Law." *Law and Contemporary Problems* 20 (Fall 1955).

Wing-Cheong Chan, Barry Wright, and Stanley Yeo, eds. *Codification, Macaulay, and the Indian Penal Code: The Legacies and Modern Challenges of Criminal Law Reform.* Farnham, UK: Ashgate, 1988.

Wise, Julia M. "From Langham Place to Lancashire: Poetry, Community, and the Victoria Press's 'Offering to Lancashire.'" *Victorian Poetry* 47, no. 3 (Fall 2009).

Wolfram, Sybil. "Divorce in England: 1700–1857." *Oxford Journal of Legal Studies* 5, no. 2 (Summer 1985): 155–86.

Wood, Janice Ruth. "Foote Work for Free Speech: The Contributions of Doctors Edward Bliss Foote and Edward Bond Foote to Anti-Comstock Operations, 1872–1915." PhD diss. Southern Illinois University, 2004.

Wright, Danaya C. "Untying the Knot: An Analysis of the English Divorce and Matrimonial Causes Court Records, 1858–1866." 38 U. Rich. L. Rev. p. 903 (2004), available at http://scholarship.law.ufl.edu/facultypub/205. Accessed June 12, 2013.

Yagoda, Ben. "Trial and Eros." *The American Scholar* 79, no. 4 (Autumn 2010).

Zacks, Richard. *Island of Vice: Theodore Roosevelt's Doomed Quest to Clean Up a Sin-Loving City*. New York: Doubleday, 2012.

Index

Note: Page numbers in *italics* refer to photographs and illustrations. "JAS" refers to John Addington Symonds.

About the Author

BRIAN O'SHEA

Naomi Wolf's most recent books include the *New York Times* bestsellers *Vagina*, *The End of America*, and *Give Me Liberty*, in addition to the landmark bestseller *The Beauty Myth*. A former Rhodes Scholar, she completed a doctorate in English language and literature from the University of Oxford in 2015, was a research fellow at Barnard College and the University of Oxford, and taught rhetoric at the George Washington University and Victorian studies at Stony Brook University. Wolf lives in the Hudson River Valley.

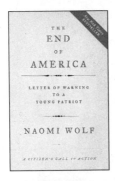